CHICANOS AND FILM

CHICANOS AND FILM

REPRESENTATION AND RESISTANCE

edited by CHON A. NORIEGA

University of Minnesota Press
Minneapolis   London

Originally published as *Chicanos and Film: Essays on Chicano Representation and Resistance* by Garland Publishing, Inc., New York, 1992.

Published by the University of Minnesota Press
2037 University Avenue Southeast, Minneapolis, MN 55414
Printed in the United States of America on acid-free paper.

Library of Congress Cataloging-in-Publication Data

Noriega, Chon A., 1961-

Chicanos and film: representation and resistance / edited by Chon A. Noriega.
   p. cm.
   Originally published: New York : Garland Pub., 1992
   Includes bibliographical references and index
   ISBN 0-8166-2218-3
   1. Mexican Americans in motion pictures. 2. Motion pictures—United States. 3. Motion pictures—Mexico. 4. Film criticism.
   I. Noriega, Chon A., 1961–
PN1995.9.M49C49   1992
791.43′652036872—dc20
                                              92-21976
                                                 CIP

The University of Minnesota is an
equal-opportunity educator and employer.

Contents

The Mexican Film Industry

Part Two: Critical Issues in Chicano Cinema

Acknowledgments

I am grateful to numerous people for their support of this collection. Initial research into the subject was done as part of a bibliographic project for Roberto Trujillo, Curator of Mexican American Collections, Stanford University Libraries. I am indebted to Roberto for his encouragement and advice in conceptualizing the collection. Tomás Ybarra-Frausto and Kathleen Newman were of immeasurable help at strategic points throughout the project. In addition, I have benefited from numerous and lengthy conversations with Lillian Jiménez, Charles Ramírez Berg, Rosa Linda Fregoso, Yvette Nieves-Cruz, and David Maciel. A special thanks to my wife, Gabrielle James Forman, for her insight, humor, and, above all, patience.

In all respects, this book could not have been undertaken without the considerable encouragement and support of the Chicano and Latino filmmakers, video artists, and media professionals. In particular, I am grateful to Lourdes Portillo and José Luis Ruiz, who have served as spiritual advisors and have freely shared their numerous contacts, documents, films, and other resources. Thank you all. Without your creative vision and *movidas* we would be left with someone else's mere "images."

Finally, I would like to thank my father, Saturnino Noriega, who introduced me to *comedias rancheras*, kung fu flicks, spaghetti westerns, and other "American" films, and whose generosity is matched only by its timeliness.

I wish to thank the following sources for permission to reprint articles:

"Stereotyping and Chicano Resistance: An Historical Dimension" originally appeared in *Aztlán* 4, no. 2 (1973): 257–70. It is reprinted by permission of José E. Limón.

"Legislating Languages: *The Ballad of Gregorio Cortez* and the English Language Amendment" originally appeared in *Americas Review* 17, no. 2 (Summer 1989): 61–71. It is reprinted by permission of Carl Gutiérrez-Jones and *Americas Review*.

"Ya Basta con Yankee Imperialist Documentaries!" was published in *Cine-Aztlán Film Bibliography* (Santa Barbara, Calif.: Cine-Aztlán, 1974), 20–25. Mimeographed chapbook. No copyright. Authors' identity and location unknown.

"Towards the Development of a Raza Cinema" originally appeared in *Perspectives on Chicano Education,* ed. Tobias and Sandra Gonzales (Stanford, Calif.: Chicano Fellows/Stanford University, 1975), 155–73. It was later excerpted in *Tin Tan* 2, no. 5 (1977): 5–7. It is reprinted by permission of Francisco X. Camplis.

"Notes on Chicano Cinema" originally appeared in *Chicano Cinema Newsletter* 1, no. 4 (1979): 6–8. It was later reprinted in *Jump Cut* 23 (October 1980): 9–10; and *La Opinión* (November 16, 1980): cultural supplement, 3–4. It is reprinted by permission of Luis Torres, former editor of *Chicano Cinema Newsletter.*

"Filming a Chicana Documentary" originally appeared in *Somos* 2, no. 5 (June 1979): 42–45. It is reprinted by permission of Sylvia Morales.

"Eso me está pasando" originally appeared in *Tonantzin* 7, no. 1 (January/February 1990): 17. It is reprinted by permission of Ray Navarro.

Introduction

Chon A. Noriega

This book is an attempt to respond to recent developments in three related areas: the representation of Chicanos and Chicanas in Hollywood and the Mexican cinema; the continued growth and diversification of a Chicano countercinema; and the emergence of Chicano film criticism as a distinct subfield within both Chicano and film studies.[1]

Since Gary D. Keller's ground-breaking collection, *Chicano Cinema: Research, Reviews, and Resources,* published in 1985, Chicano cinema has entered a third phase, one that brings it into direct negotiation with Hollywood and, to a lesser extent, Mexico. In the earlier phases, Chicano cinema expressed the cultural nationalism of the Chicano civil rights movement, and, after 1979, an international perspective due to encounters with both New Latin American Cinema and the "world market" of television and studio distribution. In 1987, Chicano cinema entered into the so-called mainstream with the commercial success of Luis Valdez's *La Bamba* and three other Chicano-themed and Chicano-produced features also released by major Hollywood studios: *Born in East L.A.* (1987), *Stand and Deliver* (1988), and *The Milagro Beanfield War* (1988). Meanwhile, Chicano filmmakers and video artists continued to work in and diversify the shorter formats: documentaries, short dramas, *telenovelas* (soap operas on social issues), experimental videos, multimedia installations, and music videos.

Concurrent with these developments, Chicano scholars have likewise entered into a *renacimiento* that has ushered in new archival materials and research as well as diverse critical approaches. Chicano film criticism, as with earlier studies on female, homosexual, and other ethnic or racial representations, emerged in the mid-1970s with "image" analyses of Hollywood films. Shortly thereafter, however, "image" analysis began to be criticized for its failure to engage the "specifically cinematic dimensions" of film: narrative structure, camera movements, montage, mise-en-scène, and so on.[2] But the strategic importance of those practices labeled as "image" analysis cannot be overstated, because other film scholars are not likely to consider the issue of "Chicanos and film" until the Chicano "image" has been extracted from and shown to exist within the "specifically cinematic dimensions" that are the object of current scholarship. In this respect, Chicano film criticism can find common cause and potential direction from the development of black, feminist, gay, and lesbian film criticisms. This is not to imply that Chicano film criticism either begins or ends with "image" analysis, but rather to recuperate "image" analysis as a vital cultural reclamation project that researches, documents, and evaluates our cinematic representation. Without it we remain invisible to ourselves and to the dominant culture.

But what *is* "image" analysis? This is not an easy question to answer, since "image" analysis often stands in as a catch phrase for all those things that a proposed textual analysis or, more recently, critical theory will avoid, such as demands for "authenticity," "realism," and "positive images." But recent attempts to bifurcate ethnic film studies into neat, bipolar categories of "image" analysis versus critical theory reinscribe these same assumptions within their poststructuralist discourse.[3] Thus, while the current critical theories say one thing at the level of content, older assumptions resurface within the form and context of their articulation. After all, do the diverse critical practices subsumed under the label of "image" analyses somehow lack theory? Does a Bakhtinian analysis somehow escape the polyphony or clash of discourses that it imputes to cinematic texts? What often goes unnoticed is that the "image" analyses and alternative media institutions and practices of racial minorities were direct components of the various civil rights movements. To that extent, both must be seen as theoretical as well as political expressions. Interestingly, proponents of a new approach of "critical theory" in ethnic film studies often focus on Hollywood.

This discussion is meant to open up other, more constructive ways of seeing the development of ethnic film criticism. An alternative periodization of Chicano film criticism would start with interpretive studies of social resistance to stereotypes,[4] the institutional basis for racist stereotypes,[5] and, since the early 1980s, interdisciplinary examinations of Chicano social history and the social sciences, including such established historians as Carlos Cortés, David Maciel, and Alex Saragoza. In their emphasis on the political aspects of representation, their scholarship established the parameters for subsequent Chicano film criticism.

In the past decade, Chicano scholars such as Rosa Linda Fregoso, Carl Gutiérrez-Jones, and Charles Ramírez Berg have applied critical and film theory to Chicano, Mexican, and Hollywood films. Their collective work will, in a sense, define the relationship between the critical theories that now dominate film studies and the historical and cultural approaches that underpin Chicano studies. As these scholars are well aware, there remains a strong potential that "theory" will colonize Chicano film texts, that is, be applied to Chicano cinema with no other goal than to prove itself, albeit in a new context.[6]

There is an added paradox for Chicanos inherent in critical discourse, as Rosaura Sánchez points out in "Postmodernism and Chicano Literature": "The questioning and subsequent denial of the subject comes precisely at a moment in history when women and marginalized ethnic minorities are trying to assume their subject status to create a voice for themselves."[7] Chicano scholars, then, must situate their critique in the uncharted spaces between cultural affirmation and the decentered subject of poststructuralist and postmodern theories. The result has often been a complex, strategic sense of place and identity in which the Chicano critical and artistic text shifts between cultural nationalism, postnationalism, and postmodernism. For the Chicano film theorist, the critical text operates within the domain outlined by Chicana lesbian poet-critics Cherríe Moraga and Gloria Anzaldúa, engaging in "acts of translation" or an inclusive, nonrational "divergent thinking."[8] The essays by Carmen Huaco-Nuzum and Víctor Fuentes in this volume represent "acts of translation" in a literal sense—both were written in Spanish, then translated—but also in a figurative one, insofar as their discursive style remains that of

Latin American letters. Rosa Linda Fregoso and Victor Valle, on the other hand, offer a more bicultural articulation of Latin American narrative forms and Chicano humor into the structure and substance of their critiques. Fregoso tells the history of Chicana-produced film and video in a circular, nonlinear fashion reminiscent of the *testimonio* (and feminist writings), and Valle both describes and exemplifies the *crónica* in his personal meditation on the press and Chicano cinema.

First and foremost, this collection represents an attempt to bring together the most recent scholarship of the diverse group of academics, critics, and artists who research and write about "Chicanos and film." Part One, "Representation and Resistance," examines Chicano representation in the American and Mexican cinema in terms of stereotypes, resistance, and participation, as well as historical developments in film narrative and ethnic discourse. Part Two, "Critical Issues in Chicano Cinema," examines Chicano-produced film and video in terms of production, distribution, signification, and reception. Part Three, "Manifestos and Testimonials," reprints the seminal Chicano film manifestos of the 1970s, in which Chicano cinema was envisioned as both an extension of the Chicano civil rights movement and New Latin American Cinema. In the past decade, the Chicano film and art manifesto seems to have given way to the testimonial or artist statement, which challenges the hegemony of the manifesto as collective expression. More important, the testimonial (as with experimental genre) allows for the expression of gay, lesbian, and female voices within Chicano art, culture, and politics. In this manner, for example, Ray Navarro is able to resituate AIDS in the *barrio* around cultural nationalist concepts ("the Conquest of Aztlán"), and his testimonial on Latino AIDS media reveals the most recent and urgent direction undertaken by Chicano cinema and its professional infrastructure. Sylvia Morales's account of the making of *Chicana* (1979), like the earlier Latin American *testimonio*, represents a transcribed and mediated oral history. Morales's account, however, is also transpersonal, including other voices from the all-Chicana production team.[9]

Representation and Resistance

To date, U.S. film scholarship has seldom, if ever, considered the issue of Chicano and Latino representation and participation in the

American film industry. Genre criticism in particular has been all but blind to the presence of Chicanos in genres that have, at times, been constructed around a Chicano or Chicana "Other"—Westerns, social problem films, and the more recent urban violence films. Too often, for example, scholarship on the Western limits the critical paradigm to the dialectic—or, if we read recent revisionist historical accounts of the Old West, the red herring—of the Individual and Society. Perhaps because theorists identify the "absent cause" in these films in the ethnocentric terms of class conflict or psychoanalysis, the resultant criticism, like Manifest Destiny itself, remains an internal dialogue even as it expands into new territory. This becomes doubly problematic insofar as film scholarship on the Western in many respects initiated or revived genre criticism.

The repressed history of the "classic" Western operates on two levels: textual and contextual. The period represented in the "classic" Western text is, of course, the Border Conflict era, or the eighty years following the Mexican-American War in which Anglo Americans violated the Treaty of Guadalupe Hidalgo, solidifying legal and economic control over the Southwest. In a paradigmatic strategy within film scholarship, Jim Kitses identifies the period as the "brief span" in which the "frontier" both opened and closed, designating westward expansion into an ostensible void as "the raw material of the western."[10]

The period of "classic" Western film production occurred at a time in which state and federal agencies initiated programs that deported nearly four million "Mexicans," half of whom either had been born in the United States or had legal immigrant status. At the same time, some 500,000 Mexican American men served in the Second World War, earning a disproportionate number of medals, and the United States—having deported or drafted Mexican Americans, and interned 120,000 Japanese Americans—initiated the Bracero Program in response to the sudden labor shortage, importing unskilled Mexican agricultural labor on a short-term basis. It is also within this period (1930–60) that Mexican-Americanism replaced the *mexicano* cultural and political identity of the Border Conflict era (1848–1929) with its liberal reformist, assimilationist politics and social institutions poised against the dominant culture's nativism and deportation policies.[11]

I want to suggest, then, that the subtext or repressed history that drives many "classic" Westerns (as well as concurrent social problem films) is that of the ephemeral status of Mexican American citizenship in American society. Taken as a whole, these films register contradictory attitudes about the Mexican American's "place" in society, with the "borders" set at various points between miscegenation, segregation, deportation, and death. In fact, since the Western's origin in the silent "greaser" films, its political unconscious would appear to be resolved through the emplacement of ethnic Americans within a prescribed class/racial/gender nexus.

In "Stereotyping and Chicano Resistance: An Historical Dimension" (1973), anthropologist José E. Limón reveals organized *mexicano* resistance in the Spanish-language press of South Texas to the silent "greaser" films. Limón's essay, perhaps the first scholarship on Chicanos and film, appeared at a time when the Chicano Movement was still in progress and serves as a forceful reminder that Chicano resistance has a historical dimension.[12]

Despite the phenomenal popularity of the so-called Latin Lovers, many of them Mexican-born actors, social histories on Hollywood have not documented the Latino presence. In "Latino Participation in the Hollywood Film Industry, 1911–1945," social scientist Antonio Ríos-Bustamante presents initial archival information on Latino technicians, actors, and filmmakers and also describes the urgent need for immediate efforts to document, collect, and preserve early Latino film materials. His research reveals behind-the-scenes negotiations between Latino actors and studios over Latino representation, information that provides the basis for a more sophisticated analysis of stereotypes.

Between the 1930s and 1950s, concurrent with the Mexican American Generation, Hollywood studios produced at least nine social problem films "about" Mexican Americans, a significant departure from the numerous Westerns "with" Mexican characters. In *"Bordertown,* the Assimilation Narrative, and the Chicano Social Problem Film," film scholar Charles Ramírez Berg presents the first in-depth analysis of these films, delineating the narrative and ideological structures that tie them to what he calls a pangeneric (and panethnic) assimilation narrative. In his strategic coalition of feminist, gay, and black film theories, Ramírez Berg exemplifies the "critical pluralism" his article calls for in future scholarship on ethnic representation.

These first three essays in the collection work toward the incorporation of Latino resistance, participation, and representation into the social and aesthetic history of Hollywood. In "Of Mestizos and Half-Breeds: Orson Welles's *Touch of Evil*," English and comparative literature scholar William Anthony Nericcio examines the critical reception of *Touch of Evil* (1958), from film reviews to auteur biographies to Stephen Heath's influential "Film and System: Terms of Analysis" (1975). In all cases, Nericcio argues, the critics invoke a stereotypical or "predictable" conception of the "Mexican," even though the film itself works against these assumptions.

In the 1980s, the so-called Decade of the Hispanic, Chicano representation appeared to undergo a dramatic change, at least in terms of the relative increase of roles and recognition for Latino actors. In "Latino Sacrifice in the Discourse of Citizenship: Acting against the 'Mainstream,' 1985–1988," film scholar Kathleen Newman examines the career of Chicano actor/star Edward James Olmos. Newman, like Ramírez Berg, identifies the ideological function of commercial film and television as a "discursive renegotiation" of Chicano citizenship, a renegotiation that requires a "Latino sacrifice" in order to maintain the "mainstream." It is of note that in the periods Ramírez Berg and Newman examine the discourse of citizenship often coincided and overlapped with a postwar crisis in national self-definition.

Implicit in discussions of Chicano and ethnic representation is the question of methodology, especially insofar as interpretive studies tend toward quantitative assessments of stereotypes, narrative structures, and ideological formations. In "Who is Maria? What is Juan? Dilemmas of Analyzing the Chicano Image in U.S. Feature Films," historian Carlos E. Cortés examines the difficulties inherent in a longitudinal analysis of Chicano representation: the sheer number of films produced, the deterioration of numerous films, and the limited resources available to determine social impact. Cortés's nine guidelines provide a broad context for the analysis of Chicano representation, one that stresses, among other things, the interrelationship between various ethnic depictions (for example, Puerto Rican and Chicano): within a text, across texts, and across media. Overall, Cortés's work provides a semiological and sociological counterpart (if not antecedent) to Ella Shohat's concept of "ethnicities-in-relation" and other recent theoretical discussions within cinema studies.[13]

The Mexican cinema also has a considerable history of Chicano representation, one whose stereotypes—the *pocho* and *bracero*—rival the greaser, bandido, and gang member of Hollywood. In both instances, the Chicano characters are constructed as the "Other" within narratives of national character or citizenship. In "Pochos and Other Extremes in Mexican Cinema; or, El Cine Mexicano se va de Bracero, 1922–1963," historian David R. Maciel continues his earlier archival research and genre analysis on Chicano representation since the 1960s.[14] In particular, he brings to light a group of films on the Chicano social bandits, or avengers, who emerged in response to the oppression of Mexicans (now U.S. citizens) in the Southwest following the Mexican-American War.

In the United States, Mexican cinema has had a continued and significant impact on the Latino community, first in Spanish-language theaters and more recently on Spanish-language television. In "Cinematic Orphans: Mexican Immigrants in the United States since the 1950s," historian Alex M. Saragoza extends his earlier study on the role of Mexican cinema in the United States between 1940 and 1952.[15] Saragoza's essays are an important contribution to a more complex analysis of Mexican (and Chicano) cinema and its reception within a diverse Mexican-origin community that includes *recién llegados* (recent immigrants), *mexicanos*, Mexican Americans, and Chicanos.

The critical attention to the class, cultural, and political stratifications within the Mexican-origin community returns us to the ideological struggle over "naming" or self-designation that first gave rise to the wide use of "Chicano" in the 1960s. In *"Ni de aquí, ni de allá*: Indigenous Female Representation in the Films of María Elena Velasco," film scholar Carmen Huaco-Nuzum postulates an *indígena* (female indigenous) subject whose experience of cultural displacement in some respects "deconstructs" the geopolitical boundaries between Mexico and the United States. In particular, she examines the popular Mexican comedies of actor-director María Elena Velasco, whose persona of the India María—like those of Cantinflas and Chaplin—is able to disrupt social hierarchies for popular audiences in Mexico and the United States. In their attention to class, race, and gender relations *within* the Mexican-origin population, Saragoza and Huaco-Nuzum—like many of the contributors in this book—push at the boundaries of "Chicanos and film," pointing toward the broader power relations, multiple identities, and discourses that circulate between Mexico and the United States.

Critical Issues in Chicano Cinema

Since the late 1960s, Chicano filmmakers and video artists have struggled to create an alternative to what they identified as "six decades of abusive stereotypes." As with the issue of representation and participation within the American film industry, the nature and impact of Chicano cinema has yet to be considered within film studies. Indeed, Chicano cinema, which emerges as a direct component of the Chicano civil rights movement (1965–75) and which continues to draw and build upon these origins, is rarely, if ever, mentioned in historical accounts of political cinema, let alone the cinema of the 1960s and 1970s.

Although what constitutes a "Chicano" film continues to be the subject of debate, we can start with the definition offered by the filmmakers: a film (or video) by and about Chicanos. The word "by" is taken to mean that the writer, producer, or director is Chicano. The filmmakers tend to apply a third criterion when only the producer is Chicano: that he or she had significant involvement in the creative process. At times, however, Chicano film scholars have identified Herbert Biberman's *Salt of the Earth*, Robert M. Young's *Alambrista! The Illegal*, and the documentaries of Les Blank as Chicano films. In these instances, the criterion had to do with the fact that the texts' cultural sensibility was thought to be *chicanesca*, or Chicano-like.[16] Given the paucity of films identified as *chicanesca*, I have decided to rely upon the Chicano filmmakers' definition, since it grounds the debate in questions of production (or participation) as well as of signification. Such a move is admittedly more "strategic" than definitive, especially since it implies certain essential markers of biology, culture, and politics, and may therefore serve to silence some even as it seeks a voice for others. Nonetheless, a need remains to consider the domain of discourse for Chicano filmmakers and video artists.

For the most part, Chicano cinema has been defined by its engagement of an identity politics. In its thematics, Chicano cinema engages the "documentary impulse" of the Chicano Movement in its effort to reclaim the past and place it in direct relationship with the present.[17] Critical writings and course titles often describe that process in terms of a "Chicano experience" on film, a phrase that positions history and politics within the framework of cultural identity. In the Movement period, Chicano-produced films and television shows documented the concurrent social protests: antiwar marches in *Requiem-29* (1971); the creation of a Latino political party in *La Raza Unida* (1972) and *Cristal* (1975); the farmworkers' strikes in *Sí Se Puede* (1973); and protests for education reform in *Guadalupe* (1976). Films also documented other, quotidian modes of resistance: *Cinco Vidas* (1972), *Carnalitos* (1973), *Agueda Martínez: Our People, Our Country* (1976), and *Después del Terremoto/After the Earthquake* (1979). Later, filmmakers turned to the history of the Chicano experience before the Movement. These films, most often dramas or docudramas, identified individual and group resistance to social and political oppression: *Incident at Donnyville* (1979), *Zoot Suit* (1981), *The Ballad of Gregorio Cortez* (1983), *The Lemon Grove Incident* (1985), *Break of Dawn* (1988), *Distant Water* (1990). Since the late 1970s, Chicano cinema also began to document or draw upon those social practices that remained after the social protest movement ended: Chicano art, literature, and music. Cultural production, which had been integral to the Movement as well as to the mise-en-scène of earlier films, now became the lens through which to envision resistance since the Reagan era: *Chicano Park* (1988), *Mi Otro Yo* (1988), *La Ofrenda: The Days of the Dead* (1989), and *Una Lucha por Mi Pueblo* (1990).[18]

Since the mid-1960s, Chicano experimental filmmakers have parodied the essential identity of much Chicano cultural production. For example, Juan Salazar's *Entelequía* (1978) decenters the all-inclusiveness of Chicano identity in *I Am Joaquin*, the "epic" poem (1967) and film (1969) of the Chicano Movement, by mispronouncing the title as the English phonetic *I Am Joking*. Identity politics, however, remains central. But if *I Am Joaquin* appeals to five hundred years of *mestizo* resistance in order to collapse the binary oppositions of Spanish and Indian, conqueror and exploited, past and present, *Entelequía* insists on an ironic stance that allows for contradictory expressions of *Chicanismo*. More recently, Chicana video artists such as Frances Salomé España and Sandi M. Peña have explored the gender as well as cultural construction of the Chicano and Chicana subject.

Not all Chicano-produced films, however, foreground or make explicit reference to issues of representation and cultural identity, even if the filmmakers identify themselves as "Chicano" or their work as the product of (at least in part) a de facto "Chicano" perspective. Super-8 filmmaker Willie Varela, for example, situates his work within the tradition of New American Cinema. Nino Rodríguez, like many others, finds his work pegged as "political" and "racial" not on the basis of its form and content, but because he is Chicano, or a person of color. In this respect, contextual factors lead critics and curators to attribute an identity politics (or the expectation of one) to all Chicano-produced media. Given the continued presence of the color line, this tendency will no doubt persist, whether argued as a politics or problem of representation. What such examples point out, I hope, is that "identity" cannot be equated with the text or its producers, but rather occupies provisional, multiple, and contradictory spaces within discourse.

In "Between a Weapon and a Formula: Chicano Cinema and Its Contexts," I provide an initial social history of Chicano cinema and outline a conceptual framework for the analysis of Chicano-produced film and video. In particular, I attempt to identify the cultural or bicultural elements that inform Chicano cinema across production, distribution, signification, and reception.

From the start, Chicana filmmakers have contributed to the development of a Chicano countercinema, and, since the mid-1970s, Chicana-produced films and videos have been influential in the reorientation of the dominant cultural paradigms of that practice. In "Chicana Film Practices: Confronting the 'Many-Headed Demon of Oppression,' " film scholar Rosa Linda Fregoso provides the first extended analysis of seminal Chicana-produced films, identifying a Chicana counteraesthetic that confronts both cultural and sexual discourses that act to silence the Chicana voice and erase or distort the Chicana image.

On another level, the popular comedies of Richard "Cheech" Marin, the Chicano half of "Cheech and Chong," tend to fall outside the "canon" of both Chicano and Hollywood cinemas, even though Marin is perhaps the only Chicano to be identified with the popular culture of both the Chicano Movement and "The Sixties."[19] In "Self-Directed Stereotyping in the Films of Cheech Marin," film scholar Christine List rereads the Cheech and Chong films in light of Marin's solo effort *Born in East L.A.* and revisionist scholarship on ethnic humor. She identifies Marin's self-derogatory Chicano characters as an "ingroup-created stereotype" that uses humor in order to critique ethnocentrism. Thus, she is able to resituate Marin's "doper" persona within the Chicano Movement as a critical counterpart to Luis Valdez's *pachuco* character.

In "Legislating Languages: *The Ballad of Gregorio Cortez* and the English Language Amendment" (1989), English literature scholar Carl Gutiérrez-Jones examines the Moctesuma Esparza and Robert M. Young adaptation of Américo Paredes's now-classic study, *"With His Pistol in His Hand": A Border Ballad and Its Hero* (1958). Like Cherríe Moraga, mentioned previously, Gutiérrez-Jones identifies as central "the question of who should bear the responsibility for translation."[20] Gutiérrez-Jones then frames the issue within both the legal discourse on Chicanos and the critical discourse on translation.

The commercial success of *La Bamba* resulted in an initial critical backlash within Latino intellectual and academic circles, one focused on what appeared to be a "Latino Boom" within the commercial film and television industry. In "Chicano Cinema: A Dialectic between Voices and Images of the Autonomous Discourse Versus Those of the Dominant," Spanish literature scholar Víctor Fuentes identifies a cultural subtext beneath the conventional surfaces of recent Chicano feature films.[21] In some instances, the subtext derives from the mythopoetics and politics of the Chicano Movement and contests or belies the proassimilation tendencies of the manifest narrative.

Given their bicultural thematics and aesthetics, Chicano feature films have often been dismissed in the mainstream press for a lack of story structure or narrative coherence. In "Story Structure in Latino Feature Films," political scientist Mario Barrera, who coproduced the documentary *Chicano Park* (1988), draws upon his recent experiences writing a feature-film screenplay. He applies the practitioner-oriented concepts on story structure—as opposed to the theoretical discussions on film narrative—to pivotal Chicano-themed and Chicano-produced feature films, revealing significant structural variation, especially given the limited number of such films. Barrera's article lays the foundation for a critical practice—whether it be historical, aesthetic, ideological, or theoretical—that takes as its start a "close reading" of the formal properties of the Chicano film text.

Such a critical practice, however, must also be aware of the specific conditions of production and distribution that Chicano filmmakers encounter. In "Crossover: Hispanic Specialty Films in the U.S. Movie Marketplace," David Rosen, a former television producer (currently an international marketing executive with Commodore), presents a production history and market analysis of *The Ballad of Gregorio Cortez*, *El Norte*, and *Stand and Deliver*.[22] Rosen reveals the financial innovations and resourceful production strategies (*movidas*) that made the films possible and that in some measure provided useful models for future American independent feature films. His case studies also highlight the personal commitment of the Chicano actors and filmmakers who went into production as well as the grass-roots or community outreach—at times in opposition to the saturation promotion of the studio distributors.

Finally, a crucial element in the ability of Chicano-produced films to reach broader audiences and thereby have an impact, has been the reportage and reviews in the "mainstream" press. In "A Chicano Reporter in 'Hispanic Hollywood': Editorial Agendas and the Culture of Professional Journalism," former *Los Angeles Times* reporter Victor Valle provides an insider's account of the power relations and frames of reference that determine if and how Chicano and other ethnic cultural productions are written about.

This book examines "Chicanos and film" with an eye toward the larger categories within which that field exists. In the final analysis, "Chicanos and film" falls within the domain of two national cultures: American and Americas. In the former, we exist within the United States, as Chicano, Latino (or Hispanic), ethnic (or minority), and—not without struggle—American. In the latter, our social emplacement again begins within the United States, then opens up to Mexico, Latin America, and the Americas. Our representation for the most part has been limited to the commercial film and television industries of Hollywood and Mexico. Chicano cinema, however, functions within the two domains—across Hollywood, independent American, Mexican (itself divided into state, independent, and commercial productions), and New Latin American cinemas.

In the spirit of these diverse and overlapping categories and the potential for dynamic and fruitful connections, we offer this book as another step in what should be a critical dialogue within film scholarship. It is hoped that the materials presented will be useful not just with respect to Chicano film studies but also in scholarship and courses on American cinema, popular culture, and social history, as well as other, more specific areas of investigation: the documentary, film, and video genres; the avant-garde; auteurs; independent cinema; New Latin American Cinema; novel and play adaptations; feminist and women-centered cinema; music videos; and such themes/issues as immigration, education reform, religion, the family, the arts, youth culture, labor, social protests, and AIDS. The relationship of Chicano cinema to other film practices must be explored in greater detail. Filmmakers and scholars have examined the historical and aesthetic relationship to New Latin American Cinema. There have also been comparative studies of Chicano representation within Mexican, Hollywood, and Chicano feature films from the perspective of feminism, language, and border issues. Additional scholarship must continue to examine Chicano cinema within the context of national and transnational issues and practices, so that theoretical formulations develop from the widest possible material base. The goal is twofold: to delineate the contours of an alternative film practice, and to redefine the notion of an "American" cinema so that it includes, as a matter of course, Chicano cinema and other alternatives.

In making these connections, film scholars must detour from the paved road of good intentions and enter the rough terrain where we must of historical necessity stumble, collide, and step on each other's feet before we reach a deeper, more honest understanding of where we have been and where we should go. As Puerto Rican film curator and scholar Lillian Jiménez once put the matter, "Get in there and dirty your hands."[23] Some things, after all, cannot be done in the abstract.

Notes

1. In Spanish, nouns are gender-identified through an "o" or "a" suffix, with a distinction between *Chicano* (male) and *Chicana* (female). When used alone, the male form, *Chicano*, denotes both male and female. The use of *Chicano* in a general context, however, tends to present the same problems as the word or suffix "man" does in English: it provides convenient cover for an essentially male discourse. Various alternatives have been proposed, the most popular being Chicano/a. Like many Chicana feminist critics, however, I use *Chicano* as a cultural and political self-designation vis-à-vis the dominant culture, but (I hope) avoid the implicit male emphasis usually given the term. Also, at times I make a clear distinction between *Chicano* and *Chicana* critical and cinematic practices.

2. See, for example, Robert Stam and Louise Spence, "Colonialism, Racism, and Representation: An Introduction," *Screen* 24, no. 2 (1983). Rpt. in *Movie and Methods: Vol. 2*, ed. Bill Nichols (Berkeley: University of California Press, 1985), 632–49.

3. This seemed to be a recurrent strategy during the 1991 Conference of the Society for Cinema Studies, where the theme was "Multi-Culturalism." If, as Manthia Diawara argued, the conference "moved the study of Black film, Chicano film, and Asian film from the margins to the center," perhaps the strategy spoke to some of the underlying anxieties over the incorporation of "multi-culturalism" into the field; see Manthia Diawara, "Cinema Studies, the Strong Thought and Black Film: Guest Editor's

Introduction," *Wide Angle* 13, nos. 3 and 4 (1991): 4. For a recent example of the "image" analysis versus critical theory argument, see Lester D. Friedman's preface to his edited collection, *Unspeakable Images: Ethnicity and the American Cinema* (Urbana: University of Illinois Press, 1991), 1–9.

4. Perhaps the first scholarship on Chicano cinematic representation and resistance is José E. Limón, "Stereotyping and Chicano Resistance: An Historical Dimension," *Aztlán: A Journal of Chicano Studies* 4, no. 2 (1973): 257–70. Limón's article is reprinted in this volume.

5. Thomas M. Martínez, "Advertising and Racism: The Case of the Mexican-American," *El Grito: A Journal of Contemporary Mexican-American Thought* 2, no. 4 (Summer 1969): 3–13; Blaine P. Lamb, "The Convenient Villain: The Early Cinema Views the Mexican-American," *Journal of the West* 14, no. 4 (October 1975): 75–81; and Francisco J. Lewels, "Racism in the Media—Perpetuating the Stereotype," *Agenda: A Journal of Hispanic Issues* (1978): 4–6.

6. The development of a critical discourse in Chicano studies, and in literary studies in particular, has been the subject of intense debate. See Angie Chabram, "Chicano Critical Discourse: An Emerging Cultural Practice," *Aztlán: A Journal of Chicano Studies* 18, no. 2 (Fall 1987): 45–90. For a provocative application of critical theory to Chicano literature, see Ramón Saldívar, *Chicano Narrative: The Dialects of Difference* (Madison: University of Wisconsin Press, 1990).

7. Rosaura Sánchez, "Postmodernism and Chicano Literature," *Aztlán: A Journal of Chicano Studies* 18, no. 2 (Fall 1987): 6.

8. Cherríe Moraga, *Loving in the War Years: lo que nunca pasó por sus labios* (Boston: South End Press, 1983), 126; Gloria Anzaldúa, *Borderlands/La Frontera: The New Mestiza* (San Francisco: Spinsters/Aunt Lute, 1987), 79.

9. Recent testimonials by media artist Frances Salomé España and filmmaker Lourdes Portillo will be published by Third Women Press (Berkeley) as part of the proceedings of the "Chicana Writes! On Word and Film" conference, University of California-Irvine, April 1990.

10. Jim Kitses, *Horizons West* (London: Secker and Warburg/BFI, 1969), 8.

11. See Mario T. García, *Mexican Americans: Leadership, Ideology and Identity, 1930–1960* (New Haven: Yale University Press, 1989); Carlos Muñoz, Jr., *Youth, Identity, Power: The Chicano Movement* (London: Verso, 1989), chapters 1 and 5; and John R. Chávez, *The Lost Land: The Chicano Image of the Southwest* (Albuquerque: University of New Mexico Press, 1984). For an account of the politics of Mexican American citizenship in the concurrent Hollywood social problem film, see Chon A. Noriega, "Citizen Chicano: The Trials and Titillations of Ethnicity in the American Cinema, 1935–1962," *Social Research: An International Quarterly on the Social Sciences* 58, no. 2 (Summer 1991): 413–38.

12. Subsequent research on the resistance to the "Mexican" stereotypes of American cinema, however, has focused on the protests and studio bans undertaken by Mexico and other Latin American countries.

13. Ella Shohat, "Ethnicities-in-Relation: Toward a Multicultural Reading of American Cinema," in Friedman, ed., *Unspeakable Images*, 215–50.

14. David R. Maciel, "Visions of the Other Mexico: Chicanos and Undocumented Workers in Mexican Cinema, 1954–1982," in *Chicano Cinema: Research, Reviews, and Resources*, ed. Gary D. Keller (Binghamton, N.Y.: Bilingual Review/Press, 1985), 71–88.

15. Alex Saragoza, "Mexican Cinema in the United States, 1940–1952," *History, Culture, and Society: Chicano Studies in the 1980s*, National Association of Chicano Studies (Ypsilanti, Mich.: Bilingual Press/Editorial Bilingüe, 1983), 107–24.

16. Francisco A. Lomelí and Donaldo W. Urioste's concept of *literatura chicanesca* has not been applied to film, but I think that it does describe the predominant approach to exemplary Anglo-produced films. Although intended to differentiate between texts on the basis of cultural perspective, *literatura chicanesca*—as with the initial concepts for black literature—carries a strong potential for biological essentialism. See Lomelí and Urioste, *Chicano Perspectives in Literature* (Albuquerque: Pajarito Publications, 1976), 12.

17. I am grateful to Tomás Ybarra-Frausto for the concept of a "documentary impulse" within the Chicano Movement.

18. The films listed here do not constitute a comprehensive list for each category. In addition, I have not mentioned the numerous documentaries on immigration, *pintos* (Chicano inmates), and other social issues.

19. This in itself is an important issue, given the recent and numerous books, documentaries, and feature films on "The Sixties" or counterculture that do not even mention the concurrent Chicano civil rights movement.

20. Other Latino scholars have made similar arguments, based upon the social and legal history of Latinos in the United States: "Language, then, is the necessary terrain on which Latinos negotiate value and attempt to reshape the institutions through which it is distributed," Juan Flores and George Yúdice, "Living Borders/Buscando América: The Languages of Latino Self-Formation," *Social Text: Theory/Culture/Ideology* 24 (1990): 57–84.

21. The literal translation of the original Spanish-language title of this essay would produce the phrase, "the autochthonous discourse" ("*el discurso autóctono*"). In English, Fuentes uses "autonomous" in order to stress the tactical nature of a Chicano discourse within Hollywood cinema.

22. Rosen's article is based upon his book-length report on "specialty films" in the 1980s, *Off-Hollywood: The Making and Marketing of Independent Films* (1990), commissioned by the Sundance Institute and the Independent Feature Project, and published by Grove Weidenfeld.

23. Lillian Jiménez, "First Steps to Latino Alternatives," *The Independent* 6 (July/August 1983): 19. For the first overview of Puerto Rican cinema, see Lillian Jiménez, "From the Margin to the Center: Puerto Rican Cinema in the United States," *Centro Bulletin* 2, no. 8 (Spring 1990): 28–43.

Part One
Representation and Resistance

Stereotyping and Chicano Resistance
An Historical Dimension (1973)

José E. Limón

In the past ten years activist sectors within the Chicano community have attacked the various forms of social subordination faced by Chicanos in the United States. One such critical reaction to the Chicano condition has manifested itself in organizational activity dedicated to the political and economic liberation of the community—activity such as that of the Raza Unida Party and the United Farmworkers. Complementing this work, other Chicano activists have undertaken an intellectual and cultural criticism of the social conditions afflicting their native community. Their writings have appeared in a variety of forums, but perhaps most notably in the pages of *Aztlán* and *El Grito*.[1]

One particular target of both public protest and academic criticism is the purveyance of denigrating Mexican stereotypes in Anglo-American cultural and academic expression, particularly in the mass media. Like similar unflattering stereotypes of other subordinate groups, those of the Chicano depict him as dirty, violent, hypersexual, treacherous, and thieving, although he also often appears as cowardly, apathetic, and dormant. According to contemporary Chicano critics, the social sciences disguise these gross notions in terms and concepts such as "present time oriented," "immediate gratification," "machismo," and "nonachiever" when studying the Chicano. Only rarely does the Chicano appear in positive imagery in Anglo-American social expression. In these few instances he is transmuted into a colorful, romantic figure full of rich, mysterious life forces.[2] In all cases reality is carefully avoided.

The Chicano counterattack has come from several quarters. In the public domain several social action groups have pressured major national corporations to drop their advertisements depicting Mexicans as slovenly bandits with an insatiable lust for Fritos and Elgin watches.[3] Local groups have also participated in this kind of public protest. During 1969-71 the Mexican American Youth Organization at the University of Texas at Austin protested a campus dramatization of Texas Independence Day that featured drunken cowardly "Mexicans" put to flight by the heroic white forces of Texas. The dramatization was finally canceled.[4]

On the academic front several scholars have taken up arms, none more effectively than Professor Américo Paredes and Nick Vaca. In an early work Professor Paredes executes a flanking attack on one set of stereotypes by demonstrating that machismo is a rather universal, historically determined trait to be found as much in Anglo-American culture as among Mexicans. Nick Vaca exposes the academically cloaked versions of stereotypes in his exhaustive review of social science literature dealing with Chicanos. In a less exhaustive work Octavio Romano-V. also takes a critical look at the social sciences. In this same vein Miguel Montiel attacks the social sciences for their uncritical use of machismo as a culture-specific trait, and Miguel Tirado questions the notion of Chicano apathy in his survey of Chicano political groups. Deluvina Hernández focuses on the effects of stereotypes on educational research, and Raúl Fernández offers a provocative, if all too brief, analysis of the relationship between stereotypes and economic roles. The socioeconomic effects of stereotyping also concern Thomas Martínez in his landmark analysis of stereotypes in U.S. advertising. In another academic area Francisco Ríos surveys a number of stereotypes in U.S. literature noting their deleterious effects on Chicano children. Raymund Paredes relates the negative Mexican imagery in Stephen Crane's work to Anglo-American socioeconomic expansion at the turn of the century. Finally, in a recent article, Philip D. Ortego continues this line of literary criticism by questioning the validity of John Steinbeck's Chicano characterization in *Tortilla Flat*.[5]

This sort of critical response to stereotypes is part of the general reaction to social subordination and is not merely a matter of injured cultural pride. Stereotypes are seen as a mechanism employed by the dominant society to rationalize its behavior toward subordinate groups. This rationalizing function is inherent in the nature of all stereotypes.[6] Recently Guillermo Flores has defined the relationship between stereotyping and social subordination in a more precise and innovative fashion. According to Flores, stereotyping is one of the mechanisms through which colonizers achieve a racial-cultural domination of colonized populations—a process that parallels and reinforces the political and economic forms of domination. Extending the traditional Marxist notion of economic surplus value, Flores develops the concept of racial-cultural surplus value to account for the "status differences and psychological gratifications which the colonizer enjoys because of his objective social and class superordinate position." Racial-cultural surplus value supplements the economic and political benefits that accrue to the colonizer. As mechanisms for reducing the validity of native cultures, stereotypes are necessary for the psychological gratification and social prestige that constitute this second kind of surplus value. And, of course, they also justify the mistreatment of subordinate societies.[7]

Intellectual and public criticism of stereotyping is, of course, not unique to Chicanos. We can find parallel reactions within the Black and Jewish communities, for example. The contemporary Chicano appraisal of stereotypes is not unique in still another sense. Chicano protest on this question is not confined to the post-1965 contemporary period; it has an historical dimension. The purpose of this study is to demonstrate that at least fifty years before the present wave of activity, Texas Mexicans were casting a critical eye on Mexican stereotypes as they appeared in political writings, films, drama, and poetry.

With Friends like These . . .

The publication of John Kenneth Turner's series of articles— "Barbarous Mexico"—from October 1909 to the end of 1910 aroused much controversy in Mexico and the United States. Appearing in the *American Magazine* and later in other journals, the articles attacked the Porfirio Díaz regime and the inhumane socioeconomic conditions of Mexico. In the best U.S. muckraking style, Turner wrote vivid descriptions of Mexico's poor under the Díaz dictatorship.

> Like half-starved wolves the ragged workers ringed about the simple kitchen; grimy hands went out to receive their meed of supper. . . . The meal consisted of . . . tortillas, the bread of Mexico's poor . . .

boiled beans, and a bowl of fish—putrid, stinking fish, fish that reeked
with an odor that stuck in my system for days.[8]

Agricultural workers were periodically beaten for the smallest error or
"any other little shortcoming that any of the bosses may imagine that
he detects in [a worker's] makeup."[9] We also learn of several army
massacres of Yaqui Indians. The conditions of agricultural workers
were more than matched by Mexico City's "ragged, ill nourished
wretches" who, for three pennies, could purchase

a bare spot to lie down in, a grass mat, company with the vermin that
squalor breeds, rest in a sickening room with hundreds of others—
snoring, tossing, groaning brothers and sisters in woe.[10]

As an ideological ally of Mexican left-wing revolutionary groups,
Turner hoped to rally U.S. sympathy for the incipient revolution in
Mexico through such depictions. On the whole the articles were well
received by the U.S. Anglo public with its eyes well sensitized to the
muckraking style and to the image of total Mexican cruelty and
degeneracy fostered by nineteenth-century popular literature.[11] As
one would expect, the series did not meet opposition from official
Mexican circles and their Anglo-American associates.

The supporters of Díaz, however, were not the only ones who
reacted negatively to Turner's work. In his zeal for social change
Turner and his muckraking prose aroused the indignation and deep
concern of the Idar family of Laredo, Texas, publishers of *La Crónica*, a
weekly newspaper. In large part Nicasio Idar and his family shared
Turner's opposition to Díaz. They were also committed editorially "al
beneficio de la raza méxico-texana."[12] While generally agreeing that
Mexico was in the grips of an inhuman dictatorship, the Idars were
extremely concerned about the stereotypic thrust of Turner's writing.
They felt that Anglo-Americans, particularly Anglo-Texans, would
convert these descriptions into stereotypes of all Mexicans and use
this skewed vision as a further justification for continuing a system of
racial oppression including discrimination, segregated schools, economic and legal inequality, and periodic official and unofficial violence against Texas Chicanos.[13]

Such is the argument of a November 1910 article in *La Crónica*
reviewing Turner's articles and their effect on Texas Mexicans. The
author criticizes Turner and his Mexican cohorts even as he comments

negatively on the political situation in Mexico. He does both from a distinctly Texas-Mexican perspective. He is concerned about the social conditions forcing people to leave Mexico:

> En México son pocos los privilegios de que goza el mexicano. Es tan dura la vida de los mexicanos allá . . . que se tienen que expatriar . . . allá la empleomania se ha convertido en nobleza hereditaria y el pueblo soberano en vasallo de propios y extraños.[14]

Nevertheless the social conditions of Mexicans do not excuse Turner's descriptions, nor do these descriptions help in the Texas-Mexican struggle for a better life.

> De nada sirve el afán infatigable de los mexicanos pensadores de Texas que trabajan constantemente por la instrucción de la raza; su insistencia no es apreciada y sus esfuerzos resultan poco menos que inútiles. Los artículos escritos por el autor de "México Bárbaro" han producido su efecto, así como los artículos escritos por plumas de malos mexicanos que solo destilan odio y que pintan á la mexicana como una nación de bárbaros cuya única ambición es el licor, el juego, y los toros.[15]

The effect referred to is the violence visited upon Mexicans in Texas.

> Aquí en esta tierra de la democracia acaba de darse un caso que desdice mucho de la civilización que se proclama; pero que es el efecto natural de los artículos publicados por esos depurtadores de su patria. Un mexicano fue quemado vivo por una horda de salvajes enfurecidos que no respetaron ni la ley ni el derecho.[16]

The writer is referring to the case of Antonio Rodríguez, a Mexican national arrested for the murder of an Anglo-American woman near Rocksprings, Texas, on November 2, 1910. We shall never know of his guilt or innocence, for he was taken from the authorities by a mob of Anglo-Americans who tied him to a tree and burned him to death. His assailants were never taken into custody.[17] In this same article *La Crónica* denounces the authorities for failing to take appropriate action. Turner and his associates, however, are directly blamed for helping to create the social climate that caused Anglo-Americans to have such little regard for Mexican life.

Yet Turner was aware of these possible negative effects. In the preface to the final book version of his articles he takes account of the possible misinterpretation of his prose and seems to be aware of reactions such as that of *La Crónica* when he comments, "the term 'bar-barous' which I use in my title is intended to apply only to Mexico's form of government rather than to its people."[18] In the final chapter entitled "The Mexican People" Turner himself criticizes Mexican stereotypes and their social implications.

> Incurable laziness, childish superstition, wanton improvidence . . . uncontrollable propensity for theft, drunkenness, and cowardice are some of the vices attributed to the Mexican people.[19]

He strongly disagrees: "The truth of the whole malignment of Mexicans as a people seems very plain. It is a defense against indefensible conditions . . . and excuse for hideous cruelty."[20]

Unfortunately it seems the *La Crónica* reviewer never read the comments or, if he did, they did not move him sufficiently to write another review reevaluating his attitude toward John Kenneth Turner. As it turned out Turner's writings offended Texas-Mexican sensibilities and, in *La Crónica*'s estimation, contributed to Texas-Mexican social subordination. As our reviewer notes, Turner was not the only culprit in this case. He also mentions certain *malos mexicanos* who were also writing denigrating articles about Mexicans. Although they are not identified in any way, it is likely that our reviewer was reading anti-Díaz publications such as those of Carlos de Fornaro or the Flores Magón group.[21] Whatever their identity, their work is intimately associated with Turner's and all are held responsible for perpetuating stereotypes whose net social effect is to make " . . . despreciable nuestra raza en este país y hacer más dura su existencia."[22]

American Culture Comes to South Texas

La Crónica's strong sensitivity to Turner's writings can perhaps be explained by the climate that encouraged such negative images of the Mexican, particularly in U.S. popular culture. It is clear, for example, that readers of *La Crónica* were subjected to a steady offensive dose of melodrama and early films of the Wild West featuring Mexicans as dark, cruel, cowardly "Heavies"—a tradition well established by the sensationalized dime novel accounts of the West. These early moving pictures were constructed on the simple prejudiced formula of stout-hearted, morally righteous white cowboys locked in mortal combat with the dark villainy of Mexican bandits, red savages, or fallen

Anglos dressed in black.[23] Billy Anderson was the earliest "star" of these films followed closely by Tom Mix and William S. Hart. Literally hundreds of such films were made during the period from 1906 through the 1920s. Indeed, during several years of the period Anderson was making a picture every week.[24] Lewis Jacobs has summarized the prevalent attitude toward the Mexican in these films:

> A flood of Western pictures began soon after a few companies moved West. . . . Typical of the current style was the story of *The Pony Express* (1907) relating the capture of a rider by "greasers." The rider's horse runs away and "tells" a group of cowboys who gallop to the scene and put the "greasers" to flight. [25]

In 1911, *La Crónica* launched a series of attacks on these films, which were being shown throughout Texas. Interestingly enough, the first article does not precisely focus on the Mexican stereotype but is instead written in support of the Native American Indian community. The writer notes that several prominent Native Americans have lodged a protest with the Bureau of Indian Affairs in Washington, D.C., concerning the Native American image in Anglo-American films. They complain

> . . . que se les asigna el papel de villanos y cobardes en casi todos los asuntos que desarrollan las películas, y dicen que tales actos no están en armonia con el verdadero modo de ser de los indios.[26]

The writer then makes a crucial comparative statement:

> No nos sorprende la queja de los indios norteamericanos . . . porque igual queja tendrían que hacer los mexicanos . . . y otras razas latinas, que generalmente son las únicas y más difamadas en dichas sensacionales películas americanas (como se ven en la frontera de Texas) . . . tan solo para demostrar el grado de cultura de los sabios fabricantes de películas, que no tienen más ingenio que el concebir escenas con muchos balazos, caballos, "cowboys" y se acabó.[27]

At least two outstanding features of this critical statement should be noted: first, the sense of alliance between Native Americans and Latino peoples, and second, the pointed remark that these culturally demeaning films are being exhibited in the Texas-Mexican border country.

Other articles appearing in October and November of 1911 continue the attack on the film industry. On October 12, *La Crónica* asked for the support of the Texas-Mexican press in putting an end to these degrading films. Texas-Mexican theater owners were also urged to follow the example of Sr. Francisco E. Solórzano, owner of Teatro Solórzano, who refused to receive these films.[28] In November, Solórzano and another theater owner named Sr. Alarcón announced their joint decision to write a letter to the filmmakers refusing further shipments of these films.[29]

In an earlier piece, *La Crónica* noted the pernicious social effects of these motion pictures.

> Juzgamos muy indigna y condenamos con toda la energía . . . toda exhibición en que se ponga en ridículo al mexicano . . . porque la exhibición de esos hechos se graban indeleblemente en el cerebro de los niños y está contribuyendo mucho á desarrollar el desprecio con que las otras razas ven a la raza mexicana que la empresa de películas ha escogido para burlarse de ella.[30]

Further, *La Crónica* pointed to a community reaction to these stereotyping films.

> Con frecuencia familias y hombres cultos abandonan los salones . . . cuando ven que se exhiben películas en que se hace representar al mexicano como asesino, cobarde, ó infame, papel que en verdad no nos corresponde. Con gusto publicaremos los nombres de las empresas cinematográficas que rehusen las películas denigrantes para los mexicanos.[31]

The popular melodramas of the time also came under fire in the pages of *La Crónica*. A December 1911 article criticizes current plays whose chief intent is to place "en ridículo a los mexicanos, haciéndoles figurar en papeles denigrantes, abjectos, cobardes ó ridículos." According to the writer, these melodramas were totally lacking in style, plot, and serious thematic content, and he strongly protested "esos descardos insultos . . . seguros que los hombres de honor y delicadeza sacionarán nuestra protesta." Finally, in a personal refutation of the Mexican-as-illiterate-peon image, he urged his readers to attend good dramas in English because there they could learn " . . . la buena pronunciación del idioma de Shakespeare."[32]

Time brought little relief to the Idars and the Texas-Mexican community. In 1917, Eduardo Idar, Don Nicasio's son, editorialized against stereotypes in the pages of *Evolución*, a newspaper that he continued to publish in Laredo after his father's death in 1914. Idar attacked the continuing use of the Mexican bandit image in U.S. films. Mexico, he argued, is recognized as a great nation everywhere except in the United States, whose film industry continued to portray it as a culturally and morally inferior country. Such is the theme of those films "en que los personajes de ladrones, traidores y pícaros son mexicanos." He demanded to know why the industry always represented North American Anglos

> como completos caballeros y miembros cultísimos de un gran pueblo, mientras que nos presenta a los mexicanos como seres amorales y repugnantes, como miembros miserables de un pueblo despreciable y bárbaro.[33]

The Texas-Mexican position was not entirely without sympathy within the Anglo-American community. According to Idar, a Mr. Frank A. Barton of Caléxico, California, had protested the showing of the film *Liberty* on the grounds that it inspired racial hatred for Mexicans and was particularly offensive to Mexican women. Idar, of course, agreed completely, and urged Texas Mexicans to lodge similar protests against the exhibition of such films.[34]

A New Generation and Stereotypes

These products of Anglo-American popular culture continued to plague Texas Mexicans as they entered a new era of political and social activity in the twenties—an era marked by what has been called "the politics of accommodation" to the U.S. Anglo way of political and cultural life.[35] One of the principal leaders in this trend was Alonso S. Perales, a native of Alice, Texas, and a lawyer, diplomat, and central figure in the formation of the League of United Latin American Citizens (LULAC).[36] His reaction to the Mexican stereotype reflects this new desire to adapt and accommodate the Chicano to U.S. Anglo life. Perales perceived the presence of stereotypes as a major obstacle in the development of better relations between Anglos and Chicanos at a local level, and between the United States and Latin America at the international level.

When a law student in Washington, D.C., Perales wrote a letter to the *Washington Post* protesting the Washington presentation of the satirical comedy *The Bad Man* starring Frank Conroy. We can best appreciate Perales's protest if we read excerpts from *Washington Post* reviews of the play:

> Arriving at the theatre . . . before his performance as Pancho Lopez, the Mexican bandit in *The Bad Man*, Mr. Conroy is a rather well groomed personage; he suggests "good condition" and baths . . . but when he walks on the stage a little later as the "greaser" he has become violently different . . . he is now greasy and dust covered, his hair is inky black and his skin shows the *mestizo* mixed breed.[37]

In addition, according to our reviewer, a "Spanish American" was hired to teach Conroy "un-American pronunciations and surprise endings for all his words."[38] Another reviewer tells us that Pancho López "slays without bitterness and without compunction; he takes no prisoners, because they are too much trouble. . . . He prides himself in his butcheries. . . . "[39]

Perales objected to the entire presentation " . . . as an American citizen who is proud of his racial origin and on behalf of every worthy Mexican living in and outside the City of Washington." The play "is an injustice to the Mexican people in general and an outright insult to the official representation of the Mexican government and to all the other Spanish-American diplomatic officials . . . " because it tends to "create the erroneous impression that all Mexicans are bandits."[40] Perales argued that every nation, including the United States, had its share of bandits, and that such presentations did nothing to further racial relations.

> It is to be deplored, indeed, that while worthy American institutions and organizations are sparing no effort to foster a better understanding between the Spanish and Anglo-American peoples, and at this very moment a mixed Mexican-American commission is conferring in Mexico City for the purpose of bettering the relations between the two countries, that American theatrical interests should see fit to thwart their work by selecting for presentation before the American public the lowest type of individual to be found among the Mexican people.[41]

This same desire to promote interracial and international harmony reappeared again in a 1936 Perales letter to the president of the School Board for the San Antonio Independent School District. Perales protested the forthcoming publication of a volume of poetry written by students at a San Antonio high school because it included two poems—"Tortilla Makers" and "Peons"—that Perales found offensive.

I will examine only "Tortilla Makers" since it more clearly illustrates the cause of his irritation.

The author of this short poem actually seems to have a pro-Mexican attitude, but, like John Kenneth Turner, his efforts to evoke sympathy for poor San Antonio Mexicans are based on a descriptive style with stereotyping tendencies. We are presented with images of " . . . dirty hands of dirty women / making tortillas" and "Sounds of Mejicanos gurgling cheap wines." The air smells of "peons and horses and peons / who work for fifty cents a day / to feed dirty children / with dirty tortillas."[42]

Perales did not appreciate the imagery whatever its social intention. He wrote to the San Antonio School Board on behalf of LULAC council #16 to "energetically protest" the publication of the poems.

> I would like to say that these poems do not do justice to the Mexican people and do much damage to the cause of inter-racial cooperation and goodwill. We would appreciate you order to suppress these poems before the book goes into circulation.[43]

And, indeed, a heavy cover was pasted over "Tortilla Makers" before the book went into circulation.[44]

Conclusions

The well-intentioned efforts of the young poet and those of John Kenneth Turner may be understood as special cases in this narrative of stereotype resistance. In both, descriptive overzealousness touched upon nerves made raw by a not-so-well-intentioned, indeed, a pernicious perpetuation of Mexican stereotypes in other forms of U.S. Anglo popular culture. The presence of Mexican stereotypes in U.S. cultural expression from 1910 to 1936 should come as no surprise, reflecting as it did the prevalence of a popular and "scientific" racism in the country.[45] As new waves of Anglo-Americans established their control over southern Texas during this period, it is only natural to expect the importation of the popular psychic mechanisms that would rationalize the social oppression created by these new forces.

What may be surprising to some is the historical presence of native Texas-Mexican resistance to the inherent racism of these stereotypes. The strong, intelligent counterattack of those supposedly apathetic, degenerate, illiterate Texas Mexicans is, perhaps, the ultimate refutation of those stereotypes and constitutes one more chapter in the narrative that Professor Carlos Cortés has called a "Chicano history of resistance and revolution."[46]

Like other phenomena in contemporary Chicano life such as creative writing, political activity, and labor organizing, the struggle against stereotypes is not confined to the post-1965 period but should be understood as a historical activity—an activity taking at least two forms. The writers of *La Crónica* and *Evolución* protested in defense of their cultural pride, but more important they pointed to the pernicious linkage between stereotypes and the treatment of Mexicans in Texas much in the manner of contemporary protest. Perales, on the other hand, did not stress this socially oppressive relationship but preferred to frame his objections in terms of the harmful effects the stereotypes would have on cooperation and goodwill between Anglos and Mexicans at the local and international levels.

Whether or not Perales's moderate attitude on this one issue verifies the currently prevalent notion of a post-1921 tradition of Texas-Mexican individuals and groups "oriented primarily by middle class values and interests, precarious and insecure in their position," awaits a full-scale study of Perales and this entire tradition.[47] On the other hand, a thoroughgoing study of the more militant tradition exemplified by *La Crónica* and *Evolución* will probably reveal individuals and groups solidly in command of their native cultural resources, regionally oriented to a geographical area largely theirs before the appearance of the Anglo-American, and politically aware of a need for concerted social action predicated upon the unity of *la raza*.

While noting these general tendencies in Chicano stereotype resistance, the present study is not intended as a full account of this activity. More remains to be done on this issue in terms of other time periods, geographical areas, and cultures. At this time my chief intent has been to introduce a diachronic dimension into the study of this question and to add new information and analysis to the gradually developing Chicano historical narrative.

Notes

1. For a general summary of this activity, see Rodolfo Acuña, *Occupied America: The Chicano's Struggle toward Liberation* (San Francisco: Canfield Press, 1972), 222-45.
2. See Cecil Robinson, *With the Ears of Strangers: The Mexican in American Literature*

(Tucson: University of Arizona Press, 1963) for a now-classic discussion of Mexican stereotypes in U.S. popular literature.

3. Armando Rendón, *Chicano Manifesto* (New York: Macmillan, 1971), 55-56.

4. Author's personal notes.

5. Américo Paredes, "Estados Unidos, México y el machismo," *Journal of InterAmerican Studies* 9 (1967): 65-84. Translated into English as "The United States, Mexico and Machismo," trans. Marcy Stein, *Journal of the Folklore Institute* 8 (1971): 17-37; Nick C. Vaca, "The Mexican American in the Social Sciences, 1912-1970. Part 1: 1912-1935," *El Grito: A Journal of Contemporary Mexican American Thought* 3, no. 3 (1970): 3-24, and Part 2, *El Grito* 4, no. 1 (1970): 17-51; Octavio Romano-V., "The Anthropology and Sociology of the Mexican American: The Distortion of Mexican American History," *El Grito* 2, no. 1 (1968): 13-26; Miguel Montiel, "The Social Science Myth of the Mexican American Family," *El Grito* 3, no. 4 (1970): 56-76; Deluvina Hernández, "The Political Economy of Stereotypes," *Aztlán* 1, no. 2 (1970): 39-45; Thomas Martínez, "Advertising and Racism: The Case of the Mexican American," *El Grito* 2, no. 4 (1969): 3-13; Francisco Armando Ríos, "The Mexican in Fact, Fiction and Folklore," *El Grito* 2, no. 4 (1969): 14-28; Raymund A. Paredes, "Stephen Crane and the Mexican," *Western American Literature* 6, no. 1 (1971): 31-38; Philip D. Ortego, "Fables of Identity: Stereotype and Caricature of Chicanos in Steinbeck's *Tortilla Flat*," *Journal of Ethnic Studies* 1, no. 1 (1973): 39-43.

6. Gordon W. Allport, *The Nature of Prejudice* (New York: Doubleday, 1958), 184-200.

7. Guillermo V. Flores, "Race and Culture in the Internal Colony: Keeping the Chicano in His Place," in *Structures of Dependency*, ed. Frank Bonilla and Robert Girling (Palo Alto, Calif.: Stanford University, 1973), 189-223.

8. John Kenneth Turner, *Barbarous Mexico*, ed. Sinclair Snow (Austin: University of Texas Press, 1969), 22.

9. Ibid., 25.

10. Ibid., 97-98.

11. Ibid., xix. For an account of the Mexican image in U.S. popular literature see Cecil Robinson, *With the Ears of Strangers*, particularly chapter 3, "A Discourse on Race, on Sex, on Death," and chapter 6, "Mexican Traits, a Latin Look." See also James Lewry Evans, "The Indian Savage, the Mexican Bandit, the Chinese Heathen," Ph.D. dissertation (University of Texas at Austin), 1967. Alfred Kazin, *On Native Grounds: An Interpretation of Modern American Prose Literature* (New York: Harcourt, Brace, 1970) offers a thorough discussion of muckraking in chapter 4, "Progressivism: The Superman and the Muckrake."

12. See any masthead of *La Crónica*, Texas Newspaper Collection, Eugene C. Barker Library at the University of Texas at Austin.

13. See my "El Primer Congreso Mexicanista de 1911: A Precursor to Contemporary Chicanismo," *Aztlán* 5, no. 1 & 2 (special double issue on "Politics and the Chicano").

14. "Barbarismos," *La Crónica* (Laredo, Texas) (November 12, 1910), 1.

15. Ibid.

16. Ibid.

17. "Mexican Who Killed Burned by Mob," *San Antonio Light and Gazette* (November 4, 1910), 1. See also "All Quiet in Edward County—Lynching at Rock Springs Done by Americans, Says Ranger Captain," *San Antonio Daily Express* (November 22, 1910), 10. For a brief discussion of the incident's impact on the Mexican political situation see Stanley R. Ross, *Francisco I. Madero, Apostle of Mexican Democracy* (New York: Columbia University Press, 1955), 137. An obviously anti-Díaz and anti-

American account is Ricardo Flores Magón's "La repercusión de un linchamiento," in *Semilla Libertaria I* (México, D.F.: Grupo Cultural "Ricardo Flores Magón," 1923), 67-72, which originally appeared in *Regeneración* (Los Angeles), November 12, 1910. A brief but intriguing discussion of the Chicano legendry spawned by the incident may be found in Américo Paredes's "Mexican Legendry and the Rise of the Mestizo" in *American Folk Legend: A Symposium*, ed. Wayland Hand (Berkeley and Los Angeles: University of California Press, 1971), 97-107.

18. Turner, *Barbarous Mexico*.

19. Ibid., 282.

20. Ibid., 286.

21. After the usual bibliographic checks and consultations with leading experts in Mexican history, I am unable to determine the identity of the *"malos mexicanos."* For very general examples of this kind of anti-Díaz writing see Carlos de Fornaro, *México tal cual es* (Philadelphia: International Publishing Co., 1909); and Ricardo Flores Magón, "El pueblo y la tiranía," *Semilla Libertaria I* (México, D.F.: Grupo Cultural "Ricardo Flores Magón," 1923), 58-59, a reprint of the original article in *Regeneración*, November 5, 1910. This article is particularly critical of the cowardly, slothful, illiterate Mexican masses that refuse to rise up against Díaz.

22. "Barbarismos," *La Crónica* (Laredo, Texas) (November 12, 1910), 1. I should note that *La Crónica* actually published three earlier articles criticizing Turner: Aaron Johnson, "México bárbaro" (January 5, 1910), 1; "Bárbaro Yankee" (unsigned) (July 9, 1910), 4; and Alfred Henry Lewis, "Los depuatadores de México" (September 3, 1910), 4. The latter is an edited translation of "The Maligners of Mexico," *Cosmopolitan* 47, no. 4 (March 1910): 432b-432e. None of these, however, addresses the stereotype issue directly; instead, they reply to Turner by simply denying the existence of such conditions in Mexico and pointing to deficiencies in U.S. society.

23. Lewis Jacobs, *The Rise of the American Film* (New York: Columbia University Teachers College Press, 1968), 74-75. For a fine illustration of this imagistic opposition see the photograph in Richard Griffith and Arthur Mayers, *The Movies* (New York: Simon and Schuster, 1970), 94-95.

24. Jacobs, 144.

25. Ibid., 75.

26. "Los indios norteamericanos protestan malos efectos del cinematógrafo," *La Crónica* (March 2, 1911), 5.

27. Ibid.

28. "Las vistas cinematográficas y los mexicanos," *La Crónica* (October 12, 1911), 1.

29. "La Cuestión Cinematográfica," *La Crónica* (November 2, 1911), 1.

30. Nicasio Idar, "El Cinematógrafo," *La Crónica* (October 19, 1911), 3.

31. Ibid.

32. "Las compañías dramáticas americanas," *La Crónica* (December 14, 1911), 1.

33. Eduardo Idar, "Por El Honor de Mexico," *Evolución* (March 2, 1917), 2.

34. Ibid.

35. Alfredo Cuéllar, "Perspective on Politics" in Joan Moore, *Mexican Americans* (Englewood Cliffs, N.J.: Prentice-Hall, 1970), 137-56.

36. Alonso S. Perales, *En defensa de mi raza I* (San Antonio: Artes Gráficas, 1936), ii-iii.

37. "Conroy Is Real 'Mexican' in His 'Bad Man' Role," *Washington Post* (May 14, 1923), Amusements section, 5.

38. Ibid.

39. " 'The Bad Man' Scores a Hit at the Belasco," *Washington Post* (May 14, 1923), Amusements section, 5.

40. Alonso S. Perales, "Protest Against the 'Bad Man,' " *Washington Post* (May 17, 1923), 6. Reprinted in Spanish as "Una presentación teatral que no hace justicia al pueblo mexicano," in *En defensa de mi raza I*, 8-9.

41. Ibid.

42. "Tortilla Makers," in *If Crickets Hear* (San Antonio: Thomas Jefferson High School, 1936), 66.

43. Alonso S. Perales, "Protesta contra unos versos ofensivos para el pueblo mexicano," *En defensa de mi raza I*, 82-83.

44. I have a copy of *If Crickets Hear* in my possession.

45. John Higham, *Strangers in the Land: Patterns of American Nativism, 1860-1925* (New Brunswick, N.J.: Rutgers University Press, 1955), especially chapter 6, "Toward Racism: The History of an Idea."

46. Carlos Cortés, "A Chicano History of Resistance and Revolution," public lecture at the University of Texas at Austin (April 23, 1971).

47. Juan Gómez-Quiñones, "Research Notes on the Twentieth Century," *Aztlán* 1, no. 1 (Spring 1970): 116.

Latino Participation in the Hollywood Film Industry, 1911–1945

Antonio Ríos-Bustamante

The electronic media—film, radio, and television—have exercised a profound and steadily growing influence upon society and how we have viewed ourselves since the beginning of the twentieth century. Nowhere has this influence been more apparent than in the case of the Hollywood film industry. The Mexican and Latino communities in the United States not only were influenced by the film industry, but some Latinos were major participants from the beginning.

The early period of silent film production from about 1911 to 1919 was a time of relative opportunity for many non-Anglo Americans—including some talented Latinos—to enter the new industry. The uncertain popular and financial success of film production offered a chance to those willing and gifted enough to become producers, directors, players, and technicians. Other key factors included the subtle but universal cross-cultural communication qualities characteristic of the silent film, which "spoke" through images to all nations. Non-Anglo ethnic groups were able to play a major role in early filmmaking, since racial and cultural barriers had not yet hardened into the later ethnic stereotyping, typecasting, and racial exclusion of some groups from film production. The relatively lower cost of production also permitted some Latinos, African Americans, and other non-Anglos to enter the business and technical aspects of early filmmaking.

Latino participation in the film industry took several forms. Latinos worked as stars, supporting actors and actresses, bit players, directors, assistant directors, and several types of studio employees. Actresses Beatriz Michelena[1] and Myrtle Gonzalez[2] were among the first "leading ladies" of the silent screen. Frank Padilla[3] and Eustacio Montoya[4] were among the first cinematographers.

Myrtle Gonzalez was the early film industry's first Latina star. A native Mexican Californian, she was the daughter of a Los Angeles grocer, Manuel G. Gonzalez. As a child, Gonzalez showed a talent for singing and by the turn of the century was a member of the Los Angeles Belesco Theatre Company. In 1911, she appeared in the film *Ghosts*, produced by Vitagraph. Between 1911 and her untimely death from influenza in 1917, she received star billing as "leading lady" in more than forty Vitagraph and Universal Pictures films. In marked contrast to the experience of later Latinas who used their own names, Gonzalez portrayed vigorous outdoor heroines.

Beatriz Michelena was the daughter of a tenor in the San Francisco Opera. By 1900, she was a star on the San Francisco musical stage, and in 1914 she appeared in her first film, *Salomy Jane,* produced by the California Motion Picture Corporation. In January 1915, the major film trade paper *Motion Picture World* featured her picture on its cover with the caption, "Beatriz Michelena, Greatest and Most Beautiful Artist Now Appearing in Motion Pictures." Between 1914 and 1919, she starred in sixteen feature films; many of these romanticized the Gold Rush and the Spanish Mexican period, and others depicted European or international themes.

The experiences of Gonzalez, Michelena, and other Latino actors of the period before 1920, such as Antonio Moreno and Pedro de Cordova, suggest several explanations for their success and rise to stardom. First, these actors all had achieved significant success in the theater or musical stage by the time feature films first appeared. The new industry's need for experienced and popular players created an opportunity for talented actors, including Latinos.

Second, most of these Latino players were light-skinned. It should be stressed, however, that unlike later Latino players, these early players were able to star with Spanish surnames, even prior to the Latin Lover craze that made Latinos temporarily fashionable. This is an important point when we realize that in the next six decades, light-skinned Latino actors would be routinely advised to anglicize their surnames and hide their identity. The reason the early Latino actors did not have to change their names was due, in part, to the fact that they attained recognition prior to the full development of the star system and the public relations reconstruction of star personas.

It must be strongly emphasized, however, that opportunities for early Latino participation in filmmaking were never unlimited, and discriminatory barriers existed from the start, but had not yet had time to crystallize, harden, and become systematic. Filmmaking was a new and still uncertain endeavor, with yet undefined spaces and structures within which some Latinos could find opportunities.

Racial stereotyping and distortions of Latino, Latin American, and Spanish history and culture were present from the earliest days. An Anglo American racial system in which racial purity was the desired norm could neither comprehend nor condone Latino racial mixture and multiracialism. From this perspective, all Spanish-surnamed persons—even near-blonds like Cuban René Cardona, who even portrayed the Prince of Wales in one film—were viewed with some degree of racial suspicion. For that reason, the Latino superstars of the 1920s seldom if ever portrayed Latino characters. At the same time, many talented Latino and Latina actors since the silent era have found themselves either trapped in stereotypical "greaser" roles or denied work. These actors included Julian Rivero, Leo Carillo, Lupe Velez, and Margo. Stereotyping and exclusion were especially acute for Latinos and Latinas of mestizo and mulatto appearance who were relegated to the greaser, bandido, and "Native" bit or extra roles.

Although such racial attitudes were reflected in films since the silent era, systematic discrimination took time to develop. It took several decades for the largely European immigrant leaders of the film industry to Americanize themselves completely and internalize the contemporary American value system on race. In effect, the Western, Central, and Eastern Europeans had to learn or acquire a racial bias against Mexicans, Cubans, Puerto Ricans, and other Latin Americans. As the film industry and its financial and artistic elite adopted and elaborated an idealized American dream culture, racial hierarchy and exclusion of nonwhites from significant and profitable participation in film production became an "All American" norm of Hollywood.[5]

The 1920s witnessed the successful rise of filmmaking as a business and its recognition as a new and influential industry. Success was not for all, however. Barriers to the participation of non-Anglo/Europeans increased sharply during the 1920s. While Latinos, especially Mexicans, were virtually barred from the financial and technical side of film production, the temporary but phenomenal popularity of the Latin Lover and Vamp allowed a few Latino performers to rise to star status. Ramon Novarro and Dolores Del Rio, for example, were among the greatest superstars of the 1920s and early 1930s. Positively, the romantic and erotic Latin image implied recognition that Latin Americans and Romance peoples produced persons of great beauty and attractiveness, as do all human beings. Negatively, however, the image of the Latin Lover was transformed through conscious and unconscious stereotyping into the image of the Latino gigolo and Latina vamp.[6] Negative stereotyping both reconfirmed and catered to existing subliminal and conscious prejudice against Latinos and other ethnic, racial groups by Anglo Americans and Europeans as well as by elitist Latin Americans and Spaniards.

Always just beneath the surface of the romantic Latin image were the older, more negative nineteenth-century stereotypes of the vicious "greaser with a knife" and the "greaser girl of easy virtue," which the early silent films had incorporated from the dime western and western novel.[7] After the decline of the romantic Latin image in the early 1930s, these older stereotypes would be even more fully revived in the form of the "Mexican bandit" and the "cantina girl who falls for the Gringo." These stereotypes have continued into the 1970s and 1980s in gang and drug films.

Contrary to false images of the passive Latino community, Latinos in the United States and Latin America did not meekly accept these dangerous film stereotypes. United States Spanish-language newspapers were filled with articles criticizing negative images of Mexicans and other Latin Americans in Hollywood films. Mexican-born superstars Dolores Del Rio and Ramon Novarro also protested and refused to accept roles that insulted their ethnic identity and heritage. In May 1931, for example, the Los Angeles Spanish-language newspaper La Opinión reported that Dolores Del Rio had turned down a part in The Broken Wing because she found the role denigrating to Mexican identity.[8] The role she refused depicted a "cantina girl" who jilts a "Mexican bandit" for an American airplane pilot. The role was played by a lesser-known actress, Lupe Velez, who either was not as proud as Dolores Del Rio or who had little choice but to accept the part. Velez continued to be typecast in such parts until her tragic suicide in 1944.

Ramon Novarro and Dolores Del Rio also rejected studio press publicity that falsely identified them as "Spanish" and insisted that they be identified as Mexicans.[9] The anger of the Mexican Americans and other Latino communities was further reinforced by protests in Mexico and other Latin American nations against the derogatory depiction of Latin Americans in Hollywood films.[10] In 1930, the National Autonomous University of Mexico created a special commission to study the cultural effects of stereotyping as well as the impact of English-language films on Mexican audiences.[11] The findings regarding the U.S. film industry were critical. Hollywood was primarily concerned about the possibility of being denied access to the Latin American film import market. In effect, the studios could understand Spanish when it came to the profitable export of films to Latin America, but they ignored the concerns of Latinos living in the United States as voiced in *La Opinión* and other Spanish-language newspapers.

The most significant result of Latin American protests, and the simultaneous development of competitive Mexican and Argentine film production, was that large Hollywood studios—such as Paramount, Fox, RKO, and Warner Brothers—established Spanish-language film production departments. Between 1928 and 1939, these studios produced over one hundred Spanish-language versions of films produced in English, using separate casts composed of Latin American and Spanish actors. Mexican-born actor Gilbert Roland starred in both the English and Spanish versions of these type of films. Some original Spanish-language films were also produced. Since sound film was both a new and primitive process, it was believed that separate language versions—mostly in Spanish, French, and German—would sell better than dubbed or subtitled prints. The studios also believed that stars who spoke the language of the foreign film markets would be more popular, and hence more profitable.[12]

The Hollywood Spanish-language films created an additional market for the Latino actors who were already well known, such as Ramon Novarro, Gilbert Roland, and Antonio Moreno. It also created a studio demand for additional talent from Mexico and other Latin American countries and Spain.[13] Other important actors of the Hollywood Spanish-language films included Argentine singer Carlos Gardel (*El Tango en Broadway*, 1934; *El Día Que Me Quieras*, 1935), Mexican comedienne Delia Magana (*Así Es la Vida*, 1930), Mexican actresses Lupita Tovar and Lupe Velez, and Argentine-born actor Vincent Padula.[14]

Latino actors also continued to appear in significant roles in Hollywood English-language films. Lupita Tovar appeared in over a dozen films, including *Joy Street* (1929) and *The Yankee Don* (1931).[15] Dolores Del Rio and Ramon Novarro continued in leading roles in numerous films throughout the 1930s. Among the most versatile stars who continued working from the silent into the sound era was Antonio Moreno. A Spaniard, Moreno was to be known as the first "Latin Lover" of the silver screen, preceding the Italian idol Rudolph Valentino. After starring as a leading man into the late 1930s, Moreno continued to work as a supporting and character actor into the 1950s, sometimes appearing with Ramon Novarro and/or Gilbert Roland, as in *The Crisis* (1950). Moreno also directed *Santa* (1930), the Mexican film industry's first sound film, which starred Lupita Tovar.[16]

Other significant stars of the 1930s and 1940s included the fine Mexican actor Arturo de Cordova, who appeared in numerous films, including *For Whom the Bell Tolls* (1943) and *Frenchman's Creek* (1944).[17] René Cardona appeared in major supporting roles in well over thirty films, including *Prince of Wales* (1934) and *Gentlemen Prefer Blondes* (1935).[18] Mona Maris, born in the Dominican Republic, appeared in *That Night in Rio* (1941) and *Ali Baba and the Forty Thieves* (1944).[19] Don Alvarado (José Paige), from Albuquerque, New Mexico, and Leo Carillo, from Los Angeles, appeared in numerous supporting roles from the 1930s to 1950s.[20] Despite discrimination, individual Latinos managed to become directors, assistant directors, writers, and technicians. One of these individuals was Chico Day, assistant director to Cecil B. deMille on such classic films as *The Plainsman* (1936) and *The Ten Commandments* (1956).[21]

Los Angeles in the 1930s was the most important distribution center in the United States for Mexican, Argentine, and other Spanish-language film industries, since it had the second largest population of Latinos in the world after Mexico City. Los Angeles was then, and continues to be, a critically important market for Mexican films. During the Golden Age of Mexican cinema in the 1930s and 1940s, the Los Angeles Mexican community's enthusiastic patronage of Mexican films contributed to the industry's financial success. The importance of the region was underscored by the frequent live appearances in the United States made by Mexican film stars.

In the same period, there was also a significant crossover of actors, film technicians, and other studio employees between the Mexican, Latin American, and U.S. film industries. Renowned director-writer-actor Emilio "El Indio" Fernández and cinematographer Gabriel Figueroa, both Mexicanos, worked on occasion in Hollywood. Meanwhile, some North Americans worked in Mexico and Latin America.[22] Most notably, such stars as Dolores Del Rio, Lupita Tovar, and Antonio Moreno were major figures in both Hollywood and Latin American films at various points in their careers.

Because of the size and sophistication of its population, Los Angeles was already a major market for Mexican and Latin American popular culture—including film, music, and dance—by the 1920s. The Latino community possessed scores of Spanish-language live entertainment and movie theaters. With the rapid diffusion of radio, Spanish-language electronic media soon developed and could reach every home with a radio receiver. As a result of these developments, the Los Angeles Spanish-speaking media exercised a significant, if unacknowledged, cultural influence in the city and nearby areas. The Latino Hollywood/Hollywood Latino of the 1920s through 1950s— the stars, supporting actors, bit players, and studio employees—was an interconnected part of this larger Latino cultural community, with its linkages to Mexico and the rest of the Spanish-speaking world.

An examination of the film careers of successful Latino actors and actresses, pioneer independent producers, and studio directors and technicians provides support for the view that opportunities for participation in the film industry were in some respects greater in the period before the mid-1930s and the consolidation of the studio system. Although they are unknown today, Myrtle Gonzalez and Beatriz Michelena's experiences reveal the opportunities available to Latino players before 1919. Likewise, the fragmentary evidence on Eustacio Montoya and Frank Padilla suggests an early, but brief, Latino presence on the business and technical side of production. Despite the longevity of Antonio Moreno's career, the experiences of actors Ramon Novarro, Dolores Del Rio, Gilbert Roland, and Lupe Velez reveal rising barriers toward the end of the 1930s. With the demise of the Latin Lover and Spanish-language production, Latino actors and stars had fewer options. They could attempt to hide their ethnic or cultural identity, or accept stereotypical greaser, vamp, and Indian walk-on roles.

Film scholars must devote increasing attention to the research and documentation of the early history of Latinos in the U. S. film industry. The most difficult task facing Latino and Latina film historians is the reconstruction of the earliest phase of Latino participation in film. With the exception of the Latino and Latina superstars of the 1920s, there has been almost no recognition or documentation of this history by film historians.[23] Only through rare efforts by individual film scholars, such as Geoffrey Bell, do we have any information on the early Latino players and technicians. Location and preservation of sources is a critical problem in documenting this period. No conscious attempt has ever been made by film archives, libraries, and museums to document, collect, and preserve materials concerning early Latino participation in the U. S. film industry.

This neglect is especially the case with early films, photographs, papers, and other documentation. A classic example is the case of the over 40,000 feet of film shot, produced, and exhibited by independent filmmaker Eustacio Montoya in the 1910s and 1920s. Montoya's efforts to present his collection to archives for preservation were ignored. When a Mexican institution rescued the nitrate prints in the 1970s, they had deteriorated to the point that only a few still frames could be restored through advance digital computer methods. There is a fundamental need for a census of surviving early Latino-produced and Latino-themed films, similar to the effort currently under way to document early African American film production. Unless a systematic, institutionally sponsored and funded project is established soon, the remaining primary sources for Latino film participation before the 1930s will disappear forever.

There is an additional need for a systematic effort to identify and acquire for archives any remaining private Latino film materials or collections, such as those of early players, filmmakers, theater owners, and journalists. Such materials still exist, but are in severe danger of destruction or loss.

Because collection, preservation, and bibliographic projects have yet to be initiated, sources for the study of Latinos in the U. S. film industry before 1945 are widely scattered, poorly identified, and—until recently—generally ignored. Most recent scholarship on Latinos in film has focused on the post-1935 period, or upon stereotypical portrayals of Latinos by Anglo American actors such as Paul Muni. Only

in 1991 did the first histories of Latinos in the Hollywood film industry appear.[24]

The most accessible sources for the study of early Latino film participation prior to 1945 are located in major film archives, libraries,
and museums. For the most part, these sources are referenced by
name and title only. Biographical material for Latino players is either
limited in quantity or of a promotional nature, including studio press
materials. Published sources—such as film trade publications, year-
books, serials, and newspaper reviews and obituaries—are important
and more plentiful, but not always indexed. There appears to have
been almost no effort by archives to acquire and preserve the personal
papers, albums, and clippings of Latino players. The files and personal papers of Latino and Spanish-language journalists—primarily in
family hands—represent a potential, untapped treasure trove of primary information. Poster, still, script, and musical score collections
need to be systematically mined by researchers. Above all, serious
recognition and high priority must be given to the collection and
preservation of early Latino film materials if the Latino film heritage is
to be documented, understood, and incorporated into the history of
American cinema.

Notes

1. Geoffrey Bell, *The Golden Gate and the Silver Screen: San Francisco in the History of
the Cinema* (New York: Cornwall Books, 1984), 67–98. Film historian and documentary
film producer Geoffrey Bell has rediscovered and documented the contributions of
Beatriz Michelena, Frank Padilla, and other early San Francisco Bay Area Latino film
pioneers. Bell has deposited copies of stills from some of Michelena's films at the
Margaret Herrick Library of the Academy of Motion Picture Arts and Sciences.

2. "Myrtle Gonzalez Dead," *Los Angeles Times* (October 23, 1918): part 2, p. 1;
Daniel Blum, *A Pictorial History of the Silent Screen* (New York: Grosset and Dunlap,
1963), 101, 138; Evelyn Mack Truitt, *Who Was Who on Screen*, 3d ed. (New York: R. R.
Bowker, 1983); *Studio Directory*, 1916; A. H. Giebler, "News of Los Angeles and
Vicinity," *The Moving Picture World* (December 1917): 727.

3. Bell 74, 96.

4. Fernando Del Moral-González, "The Discovery of a Pioneer Film in Mexico,"
unpublished manuscript (no date). The contributions of Eustacio Montoya, a Tejano
filmmaker and cameraman who shot over 45,000 feet of film regarding the period of the
Mexican Revolution, 1914–21, have been rediscovered and documented by Mexican
documentary film producer Fernando Del Moral-González. Del Moral-González has
also produced a 27-minute documentary film about the pioneer Mexican American
filmmaker.

5. Neal Gabler, *An Empire of Their Own: How the Jews Invented Hollywood* (New

York: Crown Publishers, Inc., 1988); Craig W. Campbell, *Real America and World War I* (New York: McFarland & Co., 1985); Mbye B. Cham and Claire Andrade-Watkins, eds., *Blackframes: Critical Perspectives on Black Independent Cinema* (Cambridge: MIT Press, 1988); Anthony Slide, *Aspects of American Film History Prior to 1920* (Metuchen, N.J.: Scarecrow Press, 1978).

6. Allen L. Woll, *The Latin Image in American Film* (Los Angeles: UCLA Latin American Center Publications, 1977; rpt. 1980); Arthur G. Pettit, *Images of the Mexican American in Fiction and Film* (College Station: Texas A&M University Press, 1980); George H. Roeder, Jr., "Mexicans in the Movies: The Image of Mexicans in American Films, 1894–1947," Ph.D. dissertation, University of Wisconsin, Madison, 1971.

7. Cecil Robinson, *With the Ears of Strangers: The Mexican in American Literature* (Tucson: University of Arizona Press, 1963); Cecil Robinson, *Mexico and the Hispanic Southwest in American Literature* (Tucson: University of Arizona Press, 1977); David J. Weber, "Scarce More Than Apes: Historical Roots of Anglo American Stereotypes of Mexicans," *New Spain's Far Northern Frontier* (Albuquerque: University of New Mexico Press, 1979), 293–308.

8. Fidel Murillo, "Dolores Del Rio se ha negado a filmar una cinta denigrante," *La Opinión* (May 24, 1931).

9. Ibid.

10. Gaizka S. de Usabel, *The High Noon of American Films in Latin America* (Ann Arbor, Mich.: UNI Research Press, 1982); Helen Delpar, "Goodbye to the 'Greaser': Mexico, the MPPDA, and Derogatory Films, 1922–1926," *Journal of Popular Film & Television* 12, no. 1 (1984): 34–41.

11. Julio Jimenez-Rueda, "El Cine Sonoro: Otra Opinión sobre la Cuestión del Lenguaje Español y las Películas Habladas—El Problema Fundamental," *La Opinión* (January 14, 1930): 14.

12. de Usabel, *The High Noon of American Films in Latin America*; Alfonso Pinto, "Hollywood's Spanish Language Films," *Films in Review* 24, no. 8 (October 1973): 474–83; Antonio Ríos-Bustamante, "Latinos and the Hollywood Film Industry, 1920s to 1950s," *Americas 2001* 1, no. 4 (January 1988): 18–21.

13. Jimenez-Rueda, "El Cine Sonoro."

14. Ríos-Bustamante, "Latinos and the Hollywood Film Industry."

15. *International Motion Picture Almanac, 1928–1945* (New York: Quigley Publishing Company, 1928–45).

16. Dewitt Bodeen, *More from Hollywood: The Careers of 15 Great American Stars* (New York: A. S. Barnes and Company, 1977), 147–66.

17. *International Motion Picture Almanac, 1928–1945*; Studio Biography, MS, Biography Files, Margaret Herrick Library, Academy of Motion Picture Arts and Sciences.

18. Ibid.

19. Alfonso Pinto, "Mona Maris," *Films in Review* 31, no. 3 (November 1977): 146–59.

20. *International Motion Picture Almanac, 1928–1945*.

21. Bob Thomas, "Chico Day," *Action* (January–February 1971): 19–21.

22. Adela Fernandez, *El Indio Fernández: Vida y Mito* (Mexico City: Panorama Editorial, 1986), 55–56; Gregg Barrios, "El Indio's Golden Era of Movies," *Los Angeles Times* (August 28, 1983): Calendar section, 20; Beatriz Reyes Nevares, *The Mexican Cinema: Interviews with Thirteen Directors* (Albuquerque: University of New Mexico Press, 1976), 11–20.

23. A continuing example of the lack of awareness of the early participation of

Latinos in filmmaking is provided in a new book by film writer George (Hadad) Hadley-García, *Hispanic Hollywood: The Latins in Motion Pictures* (New York: Citadel Press, 1990). The book fails to mention the Latino participants in the early cinema as well as the existent research and documentation.

24. These new books are Antonio Ríos-Bustamante, *Latino Hollywood: A Pictorial History of Latinos in the Film Industry, 1911–1945* (Encino, Calif.: Floricanto Press, forthcoming); and George (Hadad) Hadley-García, *Hispanic Hollywood*.

Bordertown, the Assimilation Narrative, and the Chicano Social Problem Film

Charles Ramírez Berg

One of the key tenets of genre criticism is that genre films embed social concerns within their repetition of familiar narrative patterns, stock characters, genre-specific locales, and iconography. But as authors Roffman and Purdy argue in their book-length study, *The Hollywood Social Problem Film: Madness, Despair, and Politics from the Depression to the Fifties*, the Hollywood social melodrama or "social problem" film is the exception. A genre that flourished from the 1930s to the early 1960s, the social melodrama's project was to expose topical issues rather than to conceal them. "The problem film," Roffman and Purdy say, combined "social analysis and dramatic conflict within a coherent narrative structure," the genre's distinguishing feature being its didacticism.[1]

Among the myriad issues these films addressed were prejudice (for example, anti-Semitism in *Crossfire* and *Gentleman's Agreement*, both 1947; racial hatred in *Pinky, Intruder in the Dust, Home of the Brave*, all 1949, and *The Defiant Ones*, 1958; the neglect of the Native American in *Jim Thorpe—All American*, 1951, and *The Outsider*, 1961); alcoholism (*The Lost Weekend*, 1945); drug addiction (*The Man with the Golden Arm*, 1955); the reintegration of World War II soldiers into peacetime society (*The Best Years of Our Lives*, 1946); problems of soldiers crippled in combat (*The Men*, 1950); corruption in politics (*All the King's Men*, 1949); labor unions (*On the Waterfront*, 1954); and the media (*A Face in the Crowd*, 1957).

Roffman and Purdy's book is without a doubt the most thorough study of these films. But its attention to movies that focus on the intolerance experienced by Hispanics is slight and incomplete. In a chapter entitled "The Minorities," they devote only three and a half pages to Hispanics, who share space with Native Americans under the heading "Chicanos and Others." A couple of paragraphs in another chapter on postwar labor problems compare *On the Waterfront* with *Salt of the Earth* (1954, d. Herbert Biberman). *Bordertown* (1935, d. Archie Mayo) is mentioned briefly in a discussion of ethnic/racial films of the 1930s.[2]

In all, the authors look at five social melodramas that deal with Hispanics—all concerning Chicanos: *Bordertown, Salt of the Earth, Right Cross* (1950, d. John Sturges), *My Man and I* (1952, d. William Wellman), and *The Lawless* (1954, d. Joseph Losey). Since there were more social melodramas than these dealing with Hispanics in American society, a closer and more detailed analysis is called for. Fortunately, that work has already begun with Richie Pérez's discussion of some of the social melodramas that focused on Puerto Ricans—a Hispanic group completely ignored by Roffman and Purdy's study.[3]

In this essay I want to begin to fill the gap left by Roffman and Purdy by examining as a group those social melodramas that dealt with the problems of Mexican Americans in the United States. In my mind there are nine such films that together comprise the Chicano social problem film. To the five mentioned by Roffman and Purdy, I would add *A Medal for Benny* (1945, d. Irving Pichel), *The Ring* (1952, d. Kurt Neumann), *Trial* (1955, d. Mark Robson), and *Giant* (1956, d. George Stevens).[4] Although one or another of these has been dealt with on occasion, they have generally been approached individually and from a different critical vantage point.[5]

Leaving aside for the moment the question of whether or not social problem films as a whole truly constitute a genre, looking at them collectively allows us to note the overall trajectory of their approach to the issue of Chicano assimilation. More often than not they endorse the very system they set out to criticize. Their obligatory happy ending metaphorically or actually sends the Chicano (the films' Mexican American lead characters, except for *Salt of the Earth*, are all male) back to the *barrio* where he began, leaving him to cope with the negligible opportunity that exists for him there. In an alternative ending, the Chicano overcomes the barriers to assimilation and mainstream success only after he purges himself of the (from the patriarchal WASP point of view) more "problematic" aspects of his character. Regardless of resolution, however, these films clearly raise more questions about the station of Chicanos in U.S. society—and about the cherished melting-pot myth—than they answer.

I will frame my investigation by discussing the Chicano social problem film as part of a more encompassing narrative pattern: the pangeneric group of films I will call the "assimilation narrative."[6] A close analysis of the earliest of these films, *Bordertown*, will reveal its debt to the assimilation narrative as well as uncover the major ideological characteristics of the Chicano social melodrama. As I go I will refer, necessarily briefly, to the remaining films, postponing a more detailed reading of them for another time. For now I hope this introductory survey furnishes the reader with an overall sense of the ambivalent attitudes of these social melodramas toward Chicanos.

Bordertown and the Assimilation Narrative

> It's like the judge said: this is the land of opportunity. In America a man can lift himself up by his bootstraps. All he needs is strength—and a pair of boots. And I got 'em!
>
> —Johnny Ramírez (Paul Muni) after graduating from law school

Bordertown, the first Hollywood sound film to deal with a Mexican American's attempt to enter the mainstream and participate in the American Dream, is the prototypical Chicano social problem film. It foreshadows the Chicano social melodramas in the same way that *Little Caesar* (1930) forecasts the main themes of the gangster genre and *42nd St.* (1932) anticipates the backstage musical. *Bordertown* is (to use Robin Wood's words in a slightly different context) that "early major work in which all the tensions and contradictions that structure the later films are articulated, manifesting themselves as uncontainable within a coherent traditional value system or a 'satisfying' resolution."[7] Containing all the major elements of Chicano social melodramas, *Bordertown* also demonstrates Hollywood's contradictory attitudes about Chicano assimilation in particular and out-group assimilation to the patriarchal WASP mainstream in general.

Moreover, its story of Johnny Ramírez's quest for success and his subsequent realization of the vacuity of the American Dream constitutes the rough outline of the "assimilation narrative." This familiar formula dramatizes the trade-offs involved when first- or second-generation immigrant protagonists (or sometimes class, race, or gender Others) set out to better themselves in the American system. In this formula, success is defined in upwardly mobile, professional, and socioeconomic terms and goes hand in hand with mainstream assimilation. (There is no success outside the dominant.)

The general pattern assimilation narrative movies follow is that the protagonists realize that American success is incompatible with "the best human values," namely those espoused by their root culture. Since mainstream success in these films requires compromise and the loss of identity—giving up who you are for what you want to become—few protagonists from the margin ever really achieve success *and* assimilation. Trying to have it both ways exacts a high price, resulting in a tragedy of some kind, often involving the protagonist's death—as in the case of gangster movies, or Midge Kelly in *Champion* (1949)—or the death or misfortune of others. Jack Robin (born Jakie Rabinowitz), the cantor and music-hall performer played by Al Jolson in *The Jazz Singer* (1927), loses his father—first emotionally, then physically—on his rise to Broadway stardom. Johnny Ramírez's rise to wealth and power in *Bordertown* results in the death of two people and the madness of another.

This two-way split is the same predicament women characters face in the movies, and it is true, I think, for all Other characters seeking mainstream approbation. Just as women characters find themselves unable "to achieve a stable sexual identity, torn between the deep blue sea of passive femininity and the devil of regressive masculinity,"[8] so are Others from the margin caught between the socially constructed marginal roles they are assigned and the self-actuating ones they would like to adopt. In fact, Julia Kristeva has equated the marginality of women as defined under patriarchy with other fringe groups so positioned. "Call it 'woman,' " she writes, "or 'oppressed classes of society,' it is the same struggle, and never the one without the other."[9]

The best course of action is for ethnic/immigrant/class/gender Others to go home to their old ethnic neighborhood, the locus of all that is good and true. Abandoning their aspirations of mainstream integration and success, these characters can remain content in the knowledge that they have gained morality, a prize far greater than fame or fortune.

These films want to say that cultural pluralism—diverse peoples bringing the best human traits to the melting pot—renews national ideals and makes America great. They seemingly celebrate ethnic Americans by showing that their traditions, practices, and core beliefs contribute to—and in fact are identical with—established American values. But the assimilation narrative allows marginalized groups only *some,* not all, of the vaunted American traits. Among those sanctioned for minority group use are respect for truth and honesty, hard work, devotion to family, and loyalty to community (and, by extension, to the dominant ideology). It should be noted that these are passive, cooperative values that can be subscribed to by ethnic and minority citizens without their entering the mainstream and threatening the dominant. According to the assimilation narrative, these are most accessible to ethnic Americans who have succumbed to the de facto segregation that restricts them to the Other side of the tracks.

Paradoxically, then, those at the margin can best practice these "all-American" traits by remaining in the ghetto or the *barrio.* Others venturing into the Anglo mainstream looking for success betray both their cultural heritage and their national values. Accordingly, the best way for them to become good Americans is to stay where they are, the best way for them to assimilate is not to try, the best way for them to share in the American Dream is to select from the menu of passive values the dominant hands them.

At the same time these stories demonstrate that more active and aggressive traits—ambition, competitiveness, shrewdness, goal directedness coupled with delayed gratification, business acumen, thrift, organizational and managerial expertise, all qualities highly regarded by the dominant culture and characteristic of Anglo success in and out of the movies—are dangerous when practiced by ethnics/minorities. They are dangerous to the dominant, of course, but in these films the threat to the system is transformed into personal dissipation—adoption of these traits by the ethnic protagonist brings moral decay, not success. This being the case, the only recourse for ethnic protagonists is to save their souls: eschew such self-empowering characteristics, retreat from the corrosive mainstream, and return—geographically and socioeconomically—to the east side of town where they can survive in moral bliss, if in material and creative poverty.

Attempting to portray the unlimited range of upscale opportunities available to ethnics in America, these films instead preach class and economic stasis. Bucking the system is perilous. Ethnics who do

so lose cultural identity and moral purity, and become cultural criminals twice over: traitors to their ethnic heritage and to the "American
way of life." "The successful man is the outlaw," Robert Warshaw
wrote in his famous essay on the gangster genre, referring to
Hollywood's—and America's—ambivalence about success.[10] As
regards the master assimilation narrative (of which the gangster genre
is an substantial subset), we can say, "The successful Other is the outlaw." The message—racial/ethnic/female/working-class protagonists
"succeed" in the American system by staying on the fringe—may be
confounding for marginal groups, yet it remains an ideologically consistent maintenance myth for the dominant.

The assimilation narrative takes many forms in many genres and,
as I've suggested, may apply to all sorts of Others. I will cite just a few
examples to illustrate how prevalent the assimilation narrative has
been in Hollywood sound cinema: the successful but guilt-ridden
Jewish doctor in *Symphony for Six Million* (1932); the rise and fall of the
ethnic gangster in any number of gangster movies; and the temptation
and ensuing corruption of the working-class or ethnic/racial minority
fighter in the boxing genre. In the female variation of the assimilation
narrative, a woman's success demands her forsaking her femininity to
become, in act and in fact, a male: from Ingrid Bergman's coolly rational psychiatrist in *Spellbound* (1948), who is subsequently "corrected"
into a warm, "feeling" woman, to the twisted, cartoon villainy of
Sigourney Weaver's gruff, butch business executive in *Working Girl*
(1989).

All these cases describe a narrative process that Teresa L. Ebert
calls "ideological recuperation." Speaking about the heroines of
romance fiction, Ebert notes that the woman protagonist's main problem is that she "is not sufficiently a woman; she has not yet fully realized her sexuality, which in patriarchal ideology can only be her het-
erosexuality and which is synonymous with her gender."[11] Narrative
closure occurs when her "lack" or "deficiency" is "remedied" and she
becomes the "right" kind of woman. Similarly, in movie assimilation
narratives subjects from the margin are also "deficient" (that is, outside the mainstream). What they are supposed to learn is not how to
assimilate, but rather how to become the "right" kind of marginalized
subjects. Johnny Ramírez, the Mexican American lawyer in
Bordertown, learns his lesson well.

From Assimilation Narrative to Social "Problem": *Bordertown* as Conflicted Prototype

Not only is *Bordertown* an excellent illustration of the way the assimilation narrative overlaps with the Chicano social melodrama, it is also a paradigmatic example of the entire class of Chicano social problem films. Here, Robin Wood's delineation of the horror genre's normality-Monster conflict as symbolic of the tension between the dominant and the Other will prove useful.[12] Wood gives the formula for the basic horror film as "normality threatened by the Monster."[13] Similarly, the basic formula for the minority social melodrama is the mainstream threatened by the margin. Indeed, the "problem" of the ethnic/racial problem films is the perceived threat the margin's very existence poses to the dominant. The dilemma ethnic/racial Others raise for the American mainstream is how to combine two essentially incompatible ideas: the dominant's desire to preserve and protect its identity as a superior, racially pure in-group by exclusionary practices, and the implementation of the democratic ideal that guarantees freedom, equality, and opportunity for all American citizens. *Bordertown* follows the standard rags-to-riches-to-rags assimilation narrative. Johnny Ramírez, a tough kid from East Los Angeles, matures into a responsible adult and acquires ambition and dedication when, as the judge who delivers his law school's commencement address puts it, "he realized his opportunities and duties as an American citizen." Johnny dreams of being on the Supreme Court, but his first court appearance reveals him to be a miserable lawyer. He loses an easy case to rich socialite Dale Elwell (Margaret Lindsay) who is defended by an upper-crust lawyer friend. When he is called a "shyster" by the defense attorney, Johnny throws him to the ground, a violent outburst that has him disbarred.

Rejecting the entreaties of the parish *padre* to content himself with humble work in the Mexican Quarter, Johnny leaves Mamá and the *barrio* to obtain what he now understands to be the only things that matter in America: power and money. "A guy's entitled to anything he can grab," he tells his uncomprehending mother just before he goes. "I found that out. And I'm for grabbing from now on." Before long he is managing a casino for a bumbling but well-meaning Anglo proprietor, Charlie Roark (Eugene Pallette), in a Mexican bordertown. Though he rebuffs the amorous advances of Charlie's wife (Bette

Davis), she falls so deeply in love with him that she secretly murders
her husband to free herself for Johnny. When he still shows no interest
in her, Marie frames him for Charlie's murder, jeopardizing his ongoing courtship of Dale. Marie's crack-up on the witness stand (in one of
the most memorable scenes of Davis's career) frees Johnny to return to
Dale. But on a deserted highway one night, she rejects his proposal.
"Marriage isn't for us," she tells him. "You belong to a different tribe,
Savage." Pulling free from his grasp, she accidentally runs into a passing car and is killed. Johnny sells the casino, uses the money to endow
a law school in the *barrio*, and returns, in his words, "back where I
belong . . . with my own people."

Let me now single out some of the narrative and ideological features of *Bordertown* that are common to the Chicano social problem
films that followed.

1. *Stereotypical inversion.* Hollywood films that try to boost ethnics
often begin by denigrating Anglos (think, for example, what a band of
oafish louts the Anglos in *Dances with Wolves* are). *Bordertown* is no
exception, peopled as it is by frustrated, oversexed blondes (Marie);
flighty, materialistic socialites (Dale and her "fast" crowd of idle rich
thrill-seekers); harsh and inflexible authority figures who operate
from a strict brown-and-white moral code that justifies their intolerance of others ("If you knew any law," the judge tells Johnny after his
fight in the courtroom, "you'd still be mentally unfit to practice");
crude simpletons (like Johnny's boss, Charlie Roark); and gangsters
(the group that eventually buys the casino from Johnny). Naturally
the Chicano protagonist makes the sound ethical choice when he
recoils from such a thoroughly venal Anglo universe and retires to the
moral haven of the *barrio*.

This pattern is the basis for the conflict in the Anglo-centered social
problem narratives—the stories about an Anglo protagonist fighting
for social justice. In these films the white hero mediates between an
oppressed Chicano and a monolithically hostile Anglo citizenry: Leslie
Benedict (Elizabeth Taylor) versus the intolerant Texans in *Giant*; the
idealistic law professor (Glenn Ford) pitted against a politically ambitious lawyer and an angry mob in *Trial*; and the cynical-but-coura-
geous newspaper editor (Macdonald Carey) opposed to the racist
townsfolk in *The Lawless*. In a couple of Chicano-centered films (those
with a Mexican American protagonist) the stereotypical inversion is
even more pointed. Except for a sympathetic sheriff, the Anglos in *My*

Man and I are a band of chiseling lowlifes, and those in *A Medal for Benny* a community of hypocrites.

2. *The undiminished stereotyping of other marginal groups.* In Hollywood films dealing with a particular ethnic or racial group, the three key elements are the Anglo mainstream, the minority group, and the relationship between them. Busily building that specific ethnic group up and knocking the Anglo down, these films generally partake in a strange kind of Other tunnelvision, losing sight in the process of their insensitive stereotyping of any but the focused-upon ethnic or racial group. (An extreme recent example is the positive portrayal of the Sioux in *Dances with Wolves* existing alongside the film's vicious, cardboard depiction of the Pawnees.) In *Bordertown,* though Marie's Chinese servant appears in only a handful of scenes, he is the stereotypical hopping, misarticulating (substituting *l*'s for *r*'s) Chinese presence. Marie herself is a variation on the stereotypical "easy" blonde. Another example: Johnny may be a bad lawyer, but he is a lot better than his Mexican defense attorney. Johnny has to prompt him to move for a dismissal of charges after Marie's breakdown on the witness stand.

This practice in effect maps Others' relation to the mainstream. In *Bordertown,* for instance, Mexican Americans are marginal, Mexican nationals more so, and Chinese Americans even more so. Interestingly, both *Giant* and *My Man and I* place their poor white characters—Jett Rink (James Dean) in *Giant,* and Mr. and Mrs. Ames (Wendell Corey and Claire Trevor) in *My Man and I*—further from the center than Mexican Americans.

3. *The male Chicano protagonist.* Hollywood follows the path of least resistance in constructing its heroes. In the rare instance of a film hero being an ethnic character, Hollywood is careful to make him as palatable to mainstream audiences as possible. This is done mainly in three ways: (1) by making the protagonist male, (2) by casting Anglos in ethnic and racial roles (Douglas Fairbanks in *The Mark of Zorro,* 1920, and Tyrone Power in the 1940 remake), and (3) by giving the Other protagonist upper-class status (Zorro is a member of the landed gentry; his rebellion is in essence the struggle of New World elites to wrest California from Spanish aristocrats). It should not be surprising, therefore, that only one of the protagonists of these social problem films (Esperanza in the progressive *Salt of the Earth*) is female. Since in Hollywood films an ethnic woman can only be an overprotective

matriarch, the "other woman," or a harlot, this practice automatically relegates Chicanas to stereotypical roles.

4. *The overprotective mamá.* The naive, good-natured, long-suffering mother, like Johnny's, is the norm in these films, and the typical way ethnic mothers are portrayed in Hollywood movies in general, from *The Jazz Singer* to *I Remember Mama* (1948), from *Scarface* (1932) to *The Godfather* (1972). In the assimilation narrative, the mother figure serves as the font of genuine ethnic values and is the protagonist's (and the narrative's) cultural conscience. When the hero listens to the voice of "his people" he is listening to his mother. (In *A Medal for Benny*, the one case where this is reversed and the father is present but the mother is absent, Benny's simple, ineffectual father simply takes the mother's place as the resigned but authentic voice of goodness.) The Chicano protagonist's coming home to mamá in the end (having failed to establish a relationship with any other woman) confirms her castrating power. From the patriarchal point of view, she makes him a weak hero with an unresolved Oedipal complex, incapable of straying far from her apron strings.

Usually she stunts his growth by her smothering solicitude. But Johnny Monterez's mother in *Right Cross* reveals a darker, racially biased side to this (s)mothering. "There's no gringo alive," she tells her son's friend, Rick, "who don't think he's better than ten *mexicanos.*" Later, behind Rick's back, she indicates her distrust of him and all gringos. "That Rick," she tells Johnny, "born a gringo, die a gringo." The Mexican mother can't win in these films. Passive, obsequious ones raise weak Chicano males, active ones teach their sons to hate Anglos.

5. *The absent father.* Anglo families are complete and ideal, ethnic families fragmented and dysfunctional. The father's absence, from *Bordertown* to *La Bamba* (1987), is seldom explained. Once again, from the male-dominant point of view, the lack of an organizing paternal sensibility makes for an abnormal, structurally unstable family unit, subtly establishing the psycho-social reasons why ethnics are different from—and inferior to—the mainstream.

From the patriarchal perspective, the missing father is indicative of abnormal Oedipal development. Never able to identify fully with the father, the Chicano male cannot symbolically become like him, nor can he take his productive, "masculine" place in society. This interrupted transition from pleasure principle to reality principle, from the familial order to the social one, helps explain his antisocial behavior: Johnny Ramírez's sudden flash of violence in *Bordertown*, Johnny Monterez's short temper and Anglo paranoia in *Right Cross*, Angel's "murder" of the white girl in *Trial*. Instead of repressing his desire for his mother, the Chicano protagonist's mother love exists right on the surface. No wonder he is plagued by unfulfilled sexual and social relations and returns to her. Because of his arrested psychological development, the realm of (mainstream) language and culture is forever closed to him. From the phallocentric standpoint, he is relegated to "the half-light of the imaginary"[14] along with his mother.

This defective development results in two kinds of fatherless protagonists in Chicano social problem films: (1) the psychologically flawed ones, like Johnny Ramírez, who cannot succeed no matter how hard they try; and (2) the "salvageable" ones, less severe cases like Johnny Monterez in *Right Cross* and Chuchu Ramírez in *My Man and I*, who, evidently to compensate for the absence of the father, find an Anglo father surrogate to help them make the transition into the mainstream. For Johnny Monterez, it is his Anglo friend, Rick (Dick Powell), a happy-go-lucky sportswriter ("Help me!" Johnny pleads with Rick at one point). For Chuchu Ramírez it is none other than the president of the United States: wherever he goes, he carries a cherished letter from the chief executive with him that specifies Chuchu's place in American society. "The measure of your new country's greatness," the letter reads, "lies in its guarantee of justice and equality for all, and it counts on you to do your part to further that principle." For Chuchu, being a good American means being a patriotic "son"; his unquestioned ideological allegiance confers manhood.

Not coincidentally, the three Chicano male characters who are most well adjusted—Angel Obregón (Sal Mineo) in *Giant*, Tommy Cantanios (Lalo Rios) in *The Ring*, and Ramón Quintero (Juan Chacón) in *Salt of the Earth*—live in well-functioning (nonstereotypically portrayed) households. These films' break with Hollywood conventions (and the corresponding ideological baggage that goes with them) is indicative of the ways they operate to expose gaps in the dominant ideology rather than paper over them.

6. *The absent Chicana*. Except for the protagonist's mother, Chicanas do not exist, and certainly not as someone our Chicano hero would be romantically interested in. The implied message: Chicanas are so inferior to Anglo women they may be omitted from consideration alto-

gether. Here the progressiveness of the exceptions only proves the rigidity of the rule. The most notable is Rosaura Revueltas's Esperanza in the independently produced *Salt of the Earth*. Sonny Garcia (Gail Russell) in *The Lawless* is an independent woman committed to helping her people, but her character deteriorates as she takes on the narrative function of guide/love interest for the Anglo editor.[15]

Besides *Salt of the Earth*, only two films depict an all-Chicano romance. To its credit, the entire narrative in *A Medal for Benny* is propelled by Joe's (Arturo de Cordova) attempts to capture Lolita's (Dorothy Lamour) heart. But the film's conclusion frames their union in dominant terms: Joe is most worthy of Lolita's attention when he becomes a proper American and joins the army to fight the "japs" in the war. In contrast, for Tommy and his girl (Rita Moreno) in *The Ring*, the system is the problem, not the solution. They overcome numerous obstacles and gain a more mature relationship *despite* the system, not because of it. Finally, there is the interesting case of Juana (Elsa Cárdenas) in *Giant*, who marries into the Benedict family and becomes the only Chicana character in all these movies whose romantic involvement with an Anglo man goes unimpeded. (Johnny's sister has an Anglo boyfriend in *Right Cross*, but Johnny strongly disapproves of the relationship, and its outcome remains unclear at the film's end.)

7. *The alluring but flawed gringa.* In light of the above, the protagonist's only option for romantic involvement is with an Anglo woman. But given the pattern of stereotypical inversion and Hollywood's trepidation about portraying interracial love stories, she is bestowed with severe emotional and psychological problems (Dale Elwell is a materialistic snob and a bigot, and Marie's sexual starvation drives her to lust and murder). As a result, the romance is sabotaged from the onset. By the use of an insidiously contorted self-preserving logic, Anglo patriarchy maintains its genetic "purity" in part by negatively stereotyping Anglo women as childish miscreants. Thus Chuchu's fascination with the troubled Marie (Shelley Winters) in *My Man and I* is both inexplicable (what could she possibly have to offer him?) and ideologically nonthreatening (as a marginal barfly, her mingling with and marrying a Mexican is of little consequence to the dominant).

The other impediment to cross-cultural romance is the male ethnic character's considerable psychological defects, already alluded to. In *Trial*, the most reactionary of the Chicano social melodramas, Angel Chavez (Rafael Campos) is convicted of killing a white girl. Though the movie never proves that he is guilty of homicide, the prosecution's case (and, ultimately, the movie's) is that he tried to rape her and she died of a weak heart. This reiterates the powerful patriarchal fear of Other male's violation of white womanhood. The male Other (re)presents two kinds of threats: (a) biological (his tainting of the dominant gene pool) and (b) sexual (always framed as his inevitable defilement of white women, never as his presenting the Anglo male with romantic competition for the Anglo woman). With a psychologically defective Chicano male, the impossibility of legitimate sexual union is rationalized and the dual threat is safely contained. As these convoluted narrative-ideological dynamics disclose, the real violation to white women comes not from the male Other but from patriarchy's degradation of them.

8. *The reductive definition of success.* Even given the fact that in the American system the range of opportunities available to its minority members has been severely restricted throughout history, the options presented to the Chicano protagonist—succeed and die (morally or actually), or fail and live (in squalor though in moral equanimity)—are simplified in the extreme. This sort of absolutism is standard given Hollywood's wish-fulfillment narratives that define success—the quest to become the boxing champ of the world, or a Supreme Court justice—as an all-or-nothing proposition. Posed in such totalizing terms, however, the number of "successes" the American system allows in the movies is minuscule (one per protagonist per film) and these films reveal that both in and out of the movies achieving success is all but impossible for most people.

Hollywood has been expounding, explaining, and defending the exclusionist logic of this fable for decades, selling audiences the illusion of success even as they swallow the bitter pill of (preferred, safe) failure. Nevertheless, Anglo audiences can at least obtain pleasure from their identification with the Anglo hero's success. Mexican American audiences, on the other hand, must learn to identify with the Anglo hero in order to enjoy "the freedom of action and control over the diegetic world that identification with a [white] hero provides."[16] To the extent that such marginal viewer identification works, it justifies, celebrates, and naturalizes the WASP norm, and becomes a means for Other viewers to approach the mainstream and internalize its values. But spectators from the margin are divided subjects, and at some point they must realize that they are different from the Anglo hero, producing alienation and estrangement in them and serving to exacerbate their marginality. And Hollywood's providing Mexican American protagonists in the Chicano-centered social problem films (save for *Salt of the Earth*) does not really improve the situation. A principal reason is that the heroes in these movies do not enjoy the sort of unbridled success available to Anglo protagonists. They get a greatly scaled-down version of Anglo success or they get failure. Johnny Ramírez cashes in and returns to East L.A. ("To do what?" we may well wonder as the film ends.) In *Right Cross,* Johnny Monterez injures his right hand swinging at his Anglo "friend." This ends his fighting career, but domesticates him (somehow ridding him of his bad temper, his inferiority complex, and his "paranoia" about the WASP system). In the conclusion of *My Man and I,* Chuchu is freed from jail and wins the heart of his beloved: a troubled, alcoholic blonde. Giving up his dream of a boxing career, Tommy in *The Ring* burns his cape and gloves in an oil drum in his backyard. With Lucy's help, he learns to be satisfied with life in the *barrio.* In the Hollywood cinema, Anglo protagonists succeed by succeeding; in the Chicano social problem films, Mexican American protagonists succeed by failing.

Finally, again except for *Salt of the Earth,* this either/or-ism denies Chicano characters the possibility of redefining success in less grandiose—and more personal and local—terms. Working in their neighborhoods or otherwise contributing to the incremental betterment of their people is seldom a "successful" option. Sonny Garcia's local activism in *The Lawless* is an important exception. But by and large there is no instance of Chicano characters redefining success in the positive, personal, and regional way that the protagonist in *Pinky* (1949, d. Elia Kazan) did when she decides to stay in her hometown and teach Black students at a nearby nursing school. Since there is no middle ground, no possibility for regional success, there is no mistaking the fact that from the dominant's point of view (given Hollywood cinema's definition of success), the Chicano's return to the *barrio* represents a Big Failure.

When an Anglo hero, from Will Kane (Gary Cooper) in *High Noon* to Deckard (Harrison Ford) in *Blade Runner,* turns his back on the system and retreats from it, it signifies the ultimate heroism—the rugged individual rejecting a contemptible system. But when a Chicano makes the same rejection, he doesn't ride into the sunset with Grace

Kelly or discover a new Eden with Sean Young: he returns to the *barrio*, often alone. The Chicano couldn't make it in the big time, not so much rejecting the system as rejected by it. Clearly, WASP heroes have what it takes to succeed and have the added luxury of electing to accept or deny the system that allowed them that success. Other heroes only have what it takes to fail.

Given the constraints of the ideological patterns just described, it is obvious that the deck is stacked in significant ways against Chicanos in these films. Add to this the strictures of the Hollywood formula, which demands that an accessible hero find a happy resolution to the conflicts animated by the narrative, and we can appreciate why many of these social problem films deprecate the group they mean to celebrate. That *any* Hollywood film would ever attempt to tackle the Chicano "problem" is in a way amazing. That a few (*The Lawless, Giant,* and *The Ring* within the studio system; *Salt of the Earth* outside it) treated Chicanos humanely and contributed meaningfully to the discourse on American prejudice is astounding.

To be sure, much more work remains to be done with these films. Individual close readings are needed to investigate more fully the Anglo-centered films (Good Samaritan narratives,[17] more interested in their WASP heroes' redemption than in the fate of the Chicano characters) and the Chicano-centered ones (variations cut from the *Bordertown* template or about how Chicanos need to become "naturalized" to enter the mainstream).

It's also time for a full-blown appreciation of *Giant,* one of the most enlightened of all of Hollywood's wide-screen epics. Its female protagonist allows it to question some of the key principles of the dominant ideology: patriarchy, the imperialistic bent of America's westward expansion ["We really stole Texas, didn't we?" Leslie tells Bick (Rock Hudson) the day after she meets him. "I mean away from Mexico"], racism, the class system, and the social construction of manhood. Most impressively, it argues that the betterment of *Tejanos* will come not by simply adjusting an existing system, but by intermarriage and the raising of Anglo consciousness. Dramatically, Leslie's aiding the impoverished Mexican American ranch workers is important, but ideologically it is secondary to the fact that Bick's son married Juana, that Bick now has a *mestizo* grandson, and that (even if it's only at a familial level) Bick rejected racism. *Giant* is a fascinating anomaly—a long, sprawling, big-budget movie made in the regressive 1950s that follows through on its liberal program *and* was a critical and box-office success.

Beyond critical appreciations of well-intentioned films like *The Lawless* and *The Ring*, we need more social-historical research (along the lines of what has been done to explicate *Salt of the Earth*'s social and production history) to understand how these politically progressive productions came to be made at all. Finally, an area that urgently needs attention is the question of the spectatorship of ethnic and minority viewers, which could build profitably on the work of feminist, gay, and African American film theorists. If "in-built patterns of pleasure and identification impose masculinity as 'point-of-view,' " as Mulvey has argued,[18] then it follows that those same patterns impose a white, patriarchal, heterosexual, capitalistic, upper-middle-class, monogamous, English-speaking point of view as well. What do viewers from outside this perspective *do* when they watch a Hollywood movie? Dyer's discussion of the relationship between gay men and Judy Garland is an excellent starting point for such an investigation.[19] An associated issue is the mirrored relationship between the ethnic characters' success double-bind and the ethnic spectators' oscillation between Anglo identification and alienation.[20]

Finally, as this critical project unfolds, it is important that film scholarship itself not imitate the assimilation narrative. Commentators studying these films or dealing with issues related to people of color in the movies should not be shunted to the critical margin for doing so. Nor should these critics be asked to adopt current theoretical methodologies (criticism's dominant ideology) unquestioningly. Rather, it is hoped that their research will contribute to a true theoretical and critical pluralism, paving the way for film studies to become a richer, more complex field.

Notes

1. Peter Roffman and Jim Purdy, *The Hollywood Social Problem Film: Madness, Despair, and Politics from the Depression to the Fifties* (Bloomington: Indiana University Press, 1981), viii.

2. Roffman and Purdy, 252–56 and 264–67, and 158–62.

3. Richie Pérez, "From Assimilation to Annihilation: Puerto Rican Images in U.S. Films," *Centro Bulletin* 2, no. 8 (Spring 1990): 8–27.

4. In deciding which films to include, my sole criterion was that the film's narrative had to focus on the prejudicial treatment of Mexican Americans in the United

States. On that basis, several other films—all fascinating for their portrayal of Mexican Americans—were considered but finally excluded. The films I omitted were *Border Incident* (1949, d. Anthony Mann), *Ace in the Hole* (1951, d. Billy Wilder), *Touch of Evil* (1958, d. Orson Welles), and *Requiem for a Heavyweight* (1962, d. Ralph Nelson).

5. *Salt of the Earth* is probably the one film of this group most written about; see Michael Wilson and Deborah Silverton Rosenfelt, *Salt of the Earth* (Old Westbury, N.Y.: The Feminist Press, 1978) for the screenplay, a detailed commentary, a critique of the film, memoirs of some of the principals, and other documents. Also see director Herbert Biberman's *Salt of the Earth: The Story of a Film* (Boston: Beacon, 1965), as well as Ruth McCormick, "Salt of the Earth," *Cineaste* 5 (Fall 1972): 53–55, and Tom Miller, "*Salt of the Earth* Revisited," *Cineaste* 13, no. 13 (1984): 30–36.

On other of these films, see, for example, Gary D. Keller, "The Images of the Chicano in Mexican, United States, and Chicano Cinema: An Overview," in Gary D. Keller, ed., *Chicano Cinema: Research, Reviews, and Resources* (Binghamton, N.Y.: Bilingual Review/Press, 1985), 13–58. In the same collection see Linda Williams, "Type and Stereotype: Chicano Images in Film," 59–63, and Carlos E. Cortés, "Chicanas in Film: History of an Image," 94–108.

Also see Allen L. Woll's works on Hispanics in film: "Bandits and Lovers: Hispanic Images in American Film," in Randall M. Miller, ed., *The Kaleidoscopic Lens: How Hollywood Views Ethnic Groups* (Englewood, N. J.: Jerome S. Ozer, Publisher, 1980); *The Latin Image in American Film* (Los Angeles: UCLA Latin American Center Publications, 1980); and Woll and Miller, *Ethnic and Racial Images in American Film and Television: Historical Essays and Bibliography* (New York: Garland Publishing, 1987). Also, Arthur G. Pettit, *Images of the Mexican American in Fiction and Film* (College Station: Texas A&M University Press, 1980).

Additionally, a couple of these films are mentioned briefly and from a different perspective in two of my previous articles: "Immigrants, Aliens and Extraterrestrials: Science Fiction's Alien 'Other' as (Among *Other* Things) New Hispanic Imagery," *CineACTION!* 18 (Fall 1989): 3–17, and "Stereotyping in Films in General and of the Hispanic in Particular," *The Howard Journal of Communications* 2, no. 3 (Summer 1990): 286–300.

6. I am indebted to Steve Carr for coining the term "assimilation narrative."

7. Robin Wood, "Symmetry, Closure, Disruption: The Ambiguity of Blackmail," in *Hitchcock's Films Revisited* (New York: Columbia University Press, 1989), 243.

8. Laura Mulvey, "Afterthoughts on 'Visual Pleasure and Narrative Cinema' inspired by *Duel in the Sun*," in Constance Penley, ed., *Feminism and Film Theory* (New York: Routledge, 1988), 69–79.

9. Julia Kristeva, "La femme, ce n'est jamais ça," *Tel Quel* 59 (Fall 1974): 24, quoted in Toril Moi, *Sexual/Textual Politics: Feminist Literary Theory* (New York: Methuen & Co., 1985), 164. Translated by Moi.

10. Robert Warshaw, "The Gangster as Tragic Hero," in *The Immediate Experience* (1948; rpt. New York: Athenaeum, 1971), 133.

11. Teresa L. Ebert, "The Romance of Patriarchy: Ideology, Subjectivity, and Postmodern Feminist Cultural Theory," *Cultural Critique* 10 (Fall 1988): 39.

12. Robin Wood, "The American Nightmare: Horror in the 70s" and "Normality and Monsters: The Films of Larry Cohen and George Romero," chapters 5 and 6 in *Hollywood from Vietnam to Reagan* (New York: Columbia University Press, 1986).

13. Wood, *Hollywood from Vietnam to Reagan*, 78.

14. Laura Mulvey, "Visual Pleasure and Narrative Cinema," in Gerald Mast and

Marshall Cohen, eds., *Film Theory and Criticism* (New York: Oxford University Press, 1985), 804.

15. It is worth noting that both of these films were made by blacklisted filmmakers, and that their departures from the norm should not be taken as either accidental or coincidental.

16. Mulvey, "Afterthoughts," 70.

17. See Arthur G. Pettit, *Images of the Mexican American in Fiction and Film,* chapter 7.

18. Mulvey, "Afterthoughts," 70.

19. Richard Dyer, "Judy Garland and Gay Men," in *Heavenly Bodies: Film Stars and Society* (New York: St. Martin's Press, 1986), 141–94. See also Robin Wood, "Star and Auteur: Hitchcock's Films with Bergman," in *Hitchcock's Films Revisited,* 303–35.

20. Mulvey, "Afterthoughts," 70. Recent work on early Black spectatorship provides a useful culture-based model for Chicano and ethnic film reception. See Jane Gaines, "*The Scare of Shame*: Skin Color and Caste in Black Silent Melodrama," *Cinema Journal* 26, no. 4 (Summer 1987): 3–21; and Adrienne Lanier-Seward, "A Film Portrait of Black Ritual Expression: *The Blood of Jesus*," in *Expressively Black: The Cultural Basis of Ethnic Identity,* ed. Geneva Gay and Willie L. Baber (New York: Praeger, 1987), 195–212. Carlos Muñoz, Jr., reveals how Chicano scholarship itself has oscillated between assimilation and separatism since the 1930s. See "The Quest for Paradigm: The Struggle for Chicano Studies," in *Youth, Identity, Power: The Chicano Movement* (London: Verso, 1989), 127–69.

Of Mestizos and Half-Breeds
Orson Welles's *Touch of Evil*

William Anthony Nericcio

It is now almost impossible . . . to remember a time when people were not talking about a crisis in representation. And the more the crisis is analyzed and discussed, the earlier its origins seem to be.

Edward Said

When Detective Hank Quinlan first lays eyes on Mexican narcotics agent Ramon Miguel "Mike" Vargas in the 1958 thriller *Touch of Evil*, the first words out of his mouth are, "He don't look like a real Mexican." Later, in the midst of interrogating Manolo Sanchez shortly before framing him with the murder of bordertown industrialist Rudy Linneker, the same Quinlan cautions his harassed prey not to speak Spanish in front of him, concluding, "I don't speak Mexican." The status of the term Mexican in a Hollywood version of a Mexican American community would seem to require further thought. After all, what can "speak[ing] Mexican" mean in the unnamed Mexican bordertown, which, if we are to believe the comforting words of Vargas (Charlton Heston in brown face) "isn't the real Mexico . . . [as] all bordertowns bring out the worst in a country." The question of the Mexican, of what one could call Mexicanicity, in the corporate culture industry of Hollywood is anything but an abstract question, especially if one considers reviews, biographies, and theoretical commentaries where the designation Mexican in *Touch of Evil* is either ignored or glossed. A closer look at Welles's film—its production, distribution, and reception—yields curious findings for students of film history as well as those concerned with Ethnic American discourse.

In "Film and System: Terms of Analysis," Stephen Heath offers a brief plot summary of *Touch of Evil*: "During a murder investigation in a border town, Quinlan, the American detective in charge, is discovered by Vargas, a Mexican official, to have planted evidence framing the chief suspect. Despite attacks on his wife culminating in Quinlan's attempt to frame her for a murder he himself commits, Vargas manages to expose the crooked policeman" (12).

As Heath's synopsis only begins to suggest, *Touch of Evil* represents a veritable Rosetta stone for analysts of Mexican American culture and for those interested more broadly in border discourse.[1] Think of the space depicted in Welles's film: the bordertown and the half-breed, *la frontera y el mestizo*: a space and a subject whose identities are not fractured but *fracture* itself, where hyphens, bridges, border stations, and schizophrenia are the rule rather than the exception (Nericcio 169–70). It is Welles as Quinlan who names the unseen murderer of his wife, "half-breed." Only a culture with some radically essential category of the pristine Subject, could collectively support and sustain the derogatory valence of the half-breed. In this respect the following may be considered an initial meditation on the half-breed.

Contemporary analysts of Welles's film provided later commentators with *colorful* guidelines. Howard Thompson's wit in the *New York Times* is typical: "[Janet Leigh's] siege by some young punks in an isolated motel—should make any viewer leery of border accommodations for a long time to come. . . . And why, Mr. Heston, pick the toughest little town in North America for a honeymoon with a nice morsel like Miss Leigh" (25). Recent commentators pick up and develop the conceit of border-space as something other than desirable. Naremore speaks of the "hellish Mexican bordertown of Los Robles" (1978, 178), and William Johnson notes that the film is set in a "nightmare world behind everyday reality" (247). Of course, it is not just the bordertown but its inhabitants who are something less than desirable, as we see with Joseph McBride's clever description of " . . . the Grande [*sic*] family, the scurviest group of misfits this side of [Buñuel's] *Los Olvidados*" (137). Or, André Bazin's implicit ethnocentrism: "[Hank Quinlan] is, at least in certain respects, above the honest, just, intelligent [Miguel] Vargas, who will always lack that sense of life which I call Shakespearean" (124). How about Cervantean? It is as if our commentators have taken Vargas's apology to his annoyed wife Susan at face value, inculcating his shame, his outrage into their work, without his simultaneous disavowal: "This isn't the *real* Mexico. . . . "

But Vargas is not the commentators' only guide. Anglo American critics seem enchanted, almost hypnotized by Detective Hank

Quinlan's "enlightened" view of bordertown citizens. Note McBride's tone as he assesses Mexican shoe clerk Manolo Sanchez (Victor Millan): "the Mexican is silly, smug, absurd . . . Quinlan is brutal, unreasoning . . . but the Mexican offends us by being a fool, and Quinlan makes us admire his godlike insouciance . . . If we are to agree with the Mexican that he is being persecuted, we must do this not through facile sympathy with a noble figure of defiance; we must sympathize with a clown" (135). Amazing rhetoric, worthy of Hank Quinlan—film criticism becomes a means to an antiseptic slur, refined, but a slur nonetheless.

When film commentators tackle the problem of race in *Touch of Evil*, the results are mixed. James Naremore's recent reading serves as a good example of what happens when commonplace attitudes remain unquestioned in essays that are otherwise quite sensitive to issues of race. After a passage itemizing "the sexual psychology of race hatred" in *Touch of Evil*, Naremore hastily concludes: "Los Robles . . . *is quite true to the essence of bordertowns*[:] . . . strip joints and prostitution, a few ragged Mexican poor, and a couple of men trundling fantastic pushcarts . . . the town . . . exists by selling vice to the Yankees, functioning as a kind of subconscious for northerners just outside their own boundaries where they can enjoy themselves even while they imagine the Mexicans are less civilized" (1978, 188; emphasis added). Perhaps he should have written, *true to the essence of bordertowns as represented in Hollywood movies*. For all its useful moments, Naremore's critique devolves into a catalog of bordertown stereotypes.

Other critics lack Naremore's *feel* for the border. Terry Comito writes: "to our discomfort, Welles engineers our complicity in violent fantasies, sexual and racial, of the most devious sort, at the same time he appeases the liberal in us with safe homilies on the evils of prejudice. But the crucial border, in spite of the swarthy rapists with whom Welles teases us, is not the one between Mexico and the United States. . . . It is the boundary between the apparent solidity of our rational daylight world and the dark labyrinth in which, if we yield to its solicitations, we will lose our way. Welles's 'Mexico' is a place of the soul, a nightmare from which a lost Hollywood sweater girl begs mostly in vain to be awakened" (11). What Comito forgets, seduced perhaps by the neatness of his polarization (not United States/Mexico, but rational daylight world/dark labyrinth of the soul), is how it is not one *or* the other but one *and* the other; in essence, the ease with which abstract existential order is informed, indeed shaped by, the exclusions and misrepresentations we necessarily assign to the Other. How clichéd and commonplace to assign Mexico this "darkened" status. And so the interpreter reads away, forgetting something Welles at least had the foresight to suspect: the sweater girl suffers not in Mexico but in the United States, at the hands of Americans, albeit of Mexican-Italian-American ethnicity.

The commentators attribute to Welles an unproblematized positive humanism even as they do the opposite in their readings. So John Stubbs argues, in a passage "loaded" with humanistic doublespeak: "According to the odd double standard of Anglo-Saxon racism, the venturing forth of the Anglo-Saxon male into the more 'primitive' or 'libidinous' Latin race may be seen as a sexual proving grounds of sorts, but the encroachment by the male of the 'primitive' race into the Anglo-Saxon world for a partner is usually taken as a move threatening to Anglo-Saxon virility. In this case, Vargas is a challenging figure despite the 'social acceptableness' of his government position" (Stubbs 1985, 183). Even the quotation marks around "primitive" and "libidinous" do not prevent this commentator from perpetuating the stereotypes (albeit nuanced, sanitized, and academified) in the preceding lines. Who, after all, is uncomfortable with Vargas's marrying and having sex with a white woman? The border guards at the outset of the film? Perhaps. Quinlan? Surely. Vargas? Most certainly. In fact, Welles is at pains to reveal the Mexican's uncomfortableness (and his wife's frustration) with his sexual self. A second selection from Stubbs's essay shows a similar implicit reading that oddly fuses nationality and sexuality: "The . . . menace comes when a Grandi boy, probably 'Pancho,' shines his flashlight on Susan through her window . . . the act has sexual undercurrents, for the male invading the privacy of the Anglo-Saxon woman is a Mexican" (186). Would the act not have "sexual undercurrents" if the "male invading the privacy of the Anglo-Saxon woman" were Anglo? The *simile-zation* of Mexican for the sexual is worthy of future scrutiny because of the way Welles's characterizations both explode and reinforce this all-too-familiar stereotype.

In "Film and System: Terms of Analysis," Heath reconceptualizes film theory through a dense 90-page study of *Touch of Evil*, Welles's vision of that space where Mexicans, Americans, and Mexican

Americans interact. To the degree that Heath's work has impacted on that discipline called film theory, we might also say that border issues or obsessions are at its origin. Heath's findings on "Mexicans," then, become an issue in the interpretive disciplines that have attached themselves to the film since its appearance—especially insofar as we are dealing with characters who either "don't look Mexican" or "don't speak Mexican," in a space that "isn't the real Mexico."

The following passages from Heath's theoretical tour de force are significant in this regard. First, "Character: Introduction of Pancho, marked with 'Mexican-ness' and a certain foreboding of sensuality (pose, manner, expression, leather jacket, insouciance, Susan's reaction)" (38–39). What is this 'Mexican-ness,' and does Heath's use of inverted commas in any way clarify the difference between his and previous critics' usage of the word? Later, Heath writes, "Grandi speaks Spanish with Pancho [and is] endowed with 'Mexican-ness' in his appearance" (41). Again, what exactly does the sign "Mexican" signify? It is as if we had happened upon the only item that goes unquestioned in Heath's otherwise painfully scrupulous essay.

Unfortunately, Heath's conception of the "Mexican" has some rather predictable elements. At the end of his piece, discussing the relationship between clean and dirty, family and incest, chastity and sexuality, the subtext of his own narration becomes apparent: "Vargas can be played as Mexican or American (*or* rather than *and*: Vargas is outside the sense of confusion), one way in respect of Susan, another in the conflict with Quinlan (in fact, the latter—good Mexican versus rotten American—serves as a cover for the disengagement of Vargas-*Charlton Heston as pure, hence non-Mexican*, in the face of the *dirty sexuality* by which Susan is *contaminated*)" (95; emphasis added). Here even in passages that self-consciously question its usage of *Mexican*, *pure*, and *sexuality*, Heath's analysis reintroduces the terms in ways consistent with popular perceptions: the Mexican as impure (the greaser; the rapist), miscegenation as *dirty*. The subjectivity of the Mexican and the Chicano, their linkage in the film with the orgiastic, with the sexual, with the dark, is worthy of question, especially since in the film itself Welles works constantly to challenge patented Hollywood stereotypes. For if "Pancho" embodies sexuality, it is not that of the sort usually attributed to Mexicans, Mexican Americans, or Latinos in general. Let us turn to the first meeting between the young "Pancho" Grandi and Susan in the first minutes of *Touch of Evil*.

Rushing back to her hotel room on the Mexican side of the border, Susan is stopped/saved by a handsome, leather-jacketed young man (an unnamed Grandi played by Valentin de Vargas). Both characters pass under a neon sign reading "paradise":

> GRANDI: *Tengo un mensaje por usted.* . . . [pause as Janet Leigh struggles to understand his meaning] *No me entiende* [directed at a passing stranger].
>
> STRANGER: [translating for Grandi] Lady, he say you don't know what he wants.
>
> SUSAN VARGAS: I know very well what he wants.
>
> STRANGER: He saved your life, lady.
>
> SUSAN VARGAS: Tell him I'm a married woman.
>
> [Leigh discovers that the young man wants her to follow him back across the border to see Uncle Joe Grandi.]
>
> SUSAN VARGAS: [deciding to follow him] What have I got to lose. . . . [she directs her answer to her own question at interested stranger whose face she reads] . . . Don't answer that. . . . [to the young man] Lead on, Pancho!

In this scene, it is Susan who "reads" Pancho's advances into the text at hand: a large degree of the sexual tension that derives between the two is not so easily assigned to the "sexual" Mexican American. In Welles's film, at least, "Mexicanicity" is not equal to sexuality; and if there is an equation between the two, it is one that questions the identity of each item.

The film, then, represents what we can call *la quiebra* (from the Spanish verb *quebrar*): a break in the order of things; also, significantly, the moment when prior understandings of the order of things lose value, and are subject to bankruptcy.[2] Even as *Touch of Evil* presents images and events seemingly in synch with prior representations of the borderlands, of Mexicans, of Chicanos in word and image, it also plays upon (preys upon) these expectations, taking spectators to another place.

Consider the following *quiebra*. "Pancho" Grandi is no simple leering, dangerous greaser. Pancho (we never hear his name, only the one Susan ascribes to him) represents both a problematized Chicano subjectivity (he is a Mexican-Italian American) and a problematized sexual subjectivity (particularly in his relationship with Susan). In the scene transcribed above, it is Susan who reads desire between the lines of a simple attempt at communication: "I know very well what he wants." In addition, all their future "sexual" (Mexican?) encounters are mediated, and multivalent. The picture they take together is sweet, with both parties smiling at a baby no less; Pancho's note accompanying the picture ("a souvenir with a million kisses, Pancho") is written in a florid, almost feminine script.

But where does one situate Welles within this *quiebra*, especially considering the auteur emphasis given to Welles and his work? If one limits one's sources to biographies and homages it is easy to characterize Welles as a champion of the oppressed. Stubbs's view here is typical: "of course, abhorrence of any form of bigotry had long been a part of Welles's social and political liberalism" (183). Later we read that the multifaceted actor/radioman/director's social consciousness was part of what made him attractive to women, including Rita Hayworth (Leaming 341). Welles himself states his position in a political journal named *Free World*, writing, "this is our proposition: that the sin of race hate be solemnly declared a crime" (quoted in Leaming 346). He was even investigated by the FBI because of his commitment to humanitarian efforts and his leftist "subversive" productions (Naremore 1991, 24). It appears that Welles is unimpeachable when it comes to his progressive commitment to the oppressed souls on the planet.

Or is he? Let us return to *Touch of Evil*, to the scene that allows us to deepen our meditation on the half-breed. We begin with a drunk, defeated Hank Quinlan drowning his sorrows at the "Grandi Rancho Grande Cantina" on the American side of the border, and reflecting on the moment that changed his life forever:

QUINLAN: I don't usually talk about my wife.

PETE: Never when you're sober.

QUINLAN: She was strangled, Pete.

PETE: I know, I know . . .

QUINLAN: Binding cord. She was working up at the packing plant, so the killer had it right to hand. Smart . . . you don't leave fingerprints on a piece of string. . . . That half-breed done it, of course. We all knew that. . . .

PETE: [to the bartender] *La cuenta, la cuenta.*

QUINLAN: But I was just a rookie cop . . . I followed around after him eating my heart out trying to catch him . . . but I never did. . . . Pete, that was the last killer that ever got out of my hands.

It is the "mixed population" or Chicano community that arouses Quinlan's hatred, particularly the Grandis whose own undecidable lineage somehow recalls for Quinlan "the one that got out of his hands." Ultimately, *Touch of Evil* is a movie crafted between two strangulations: one seen, and one that occurs seventeen years before the action starts. Few commentators in fact remember that an unseen, unnamed half-breed (*el mestizo*) is at the heart of *Touch of Evil*. Both murders involve individuals of mixed cultural and national origins, what Welles as Detective Quinlan calls a "half-breed."

But this is Quinlan. How do we approach Welles's position on the question of race, on the question of the half-breed to which he here refers? The place to begin is with what Welles and his cinematic alter ego have in common: obsessions/interests/desires either with "Subjects" from South of the Border or with subjects who carry that border within them, in particular *mestiza* subjects. Naremore contends that "Welles may be the only German Expressionist who is authentically attracted to Latin cultures, and who is able to appropriate their 'feel' to his style" (1978, 205).

Much of Welles's work on film had a distinct Latin flavor. In February 1944, for example, Welles started preproduction on *Mexican Melodrama*, a film about Nazi spies in Mexico. The star, Dolores Del Rio, "interceded on his behalf with the Mexican government when they got edgy about the plot" (Leaming 267). Welles's various affairs with the leading ladies and chorus girls of Hollywood are now commonplace in tinsel-town folklore. Two of his longer-lasting relationships are pertinent here: a long affair with Dolores Del Rio and his marriage to Rita Hayworth (née Margarita Carmen Cansino). Hayworth worked in Tijuana and Aguascalientes in a Dancing Cansinos act with her father, an alleged Spaniard. Welles with predictable candor corrects this pretense: "She's half Gypsy, not half Spanish" (Leaming 322). This sensitivity to half-lineages is also revealed in another passage from Leaming's biography:

> At 6:30 in the morning [Welles] had arranged in advance to have someone drive him to Lake Mercer. He was very glad he had changed his plans when at Woodruff he found a drunk "cross-eyed half-breed" waiting for him in a Model-T. His new destination, Lake Falambeau, was in the midst of the Ojibway Indian Reservation, where Orson promptly hired several "squaws and a few antiques in the neuter gen-

der," as he wrote . . . to build a birchbark and deerskin wigwam on a parcel of land . . . his hosts had offered for this purpose. (64)

Here Welles's description of the Native American takes on added significance when we remember Quinlan's description of his wife's alleged murder by a half-breed—Welles and Quinlan come together, if only for an instant. One begins to piece together a hierarchy in the Wellesian order of things, engendering the suspicion that individuals of mixed inferior stock do not rate highly on that list. Welles gives further evidence of his attitude for those of suspect or divided stock when he assesses the lineage of his renamed wife Rita Hayworth: "I wasn't smart enough to know [Rita's jealousy] was neurotic. I just thought it was Gypsy, and I said, this is that Gypsy kick and I've got to cure her of that" (Leaming 325). The half-Gypsy, the half-breed, then becomes a point of departure for reexamining the work of this heralded director.

In 1942, Welles became involved in the Sleepy Lagoon case or the Zoot Suit trials. In Leaming's version of the series of events (known well to anyone even vaguely familiar with Mexican American history or Luis Valdez's play and film *Zoot Suit*) we hear about the murder of José Díaz on August 2, 1942: "The police harassment of the Mexican American community in Los Angeles that followed the discovery of Díaz's body (he had been run over by an automobile) was symptomatic of the intense wartime racism in the United States. The next night as they left local dance halls, young Chicanos were confronted by police who tore into their zoot suits with razor-tipped pokers" (334). These events led to what came to be called the Sleepy Lagoon murder case, the largest mass trial in American history, "constructed by the press in Los Angeles, anxious to invent a Mexican American crime wave . . . among the so-called zoot suiters" (Leaming 333–34). Eventually, Welles, as well as Rita Hayworth and Anthony Quinn, joined efforts to defend the seventeen Mexican American youths on trial. According to Leaming, "Welles's association with Roosevelt's Good Neighbor Policy as well as his inherent hatred of racists and Hearstian yellow journalism, caused him to become intensely interested in the case, and he agreed to pen the foreword to a political pamphlet about the trial and its international implications, which was published in June of 1943 with his name displayed prominently on the cover" (335). Welles, the boy wonder of Hollywood, the genius of

American cinema, the Fellini of the Americas, must now also be reck-
oned a champion of Chicano advocacy.

Before we get carried away at the irony of Welles the Chicano
champion portraying Quinlan the Chicanophobic/murderer, we
might look deeper into the events of that period. Leaming writes, "[In
1945] a singular plan was to put forth as a candidate for the Secretary
General of the United Nations the name of Orson Welles" (372).
Welles's memory of this speculation seems noteworthy: "I wasn't very
keen about it. . . . I was in on the founding of the thing, and at the
founding it was apparent to me that all the limitations we know now
were inherent in it, and that we were eventually going to be impris-
oned by what is now called the Third World. So I had a dim view of
its future" (372). With or without knowing it, we have returned once
again to the domain of the problematized subject, with
Welles/Quinlan himself at issue.

Orson Welles's *Touch of Evil* is as much about the contamination of
the United States by Mexico as it is about the contamination of Mexico
by the United States. What is obvious in previous commentaries is
that that "Mexican" contribution has remained unproblematized, has
in fact remained with almost predictable regularity synonymous with
the exotic, the dark, the sordid, the sexual, the decayed. Renato
Rosaldo's reminder of the conflict along one part of that border is relevant here: "military conquest transformed the Rio Grande from a fertile place of gathering together into a barbed line of demarcation"
(152), a space Gloria Anzaldúa aptly describes as "una herida abierta"
(3). The internalization of this fracture, of this *quiebra*, has often colored the development of narratives and strategies of reading that call
themselves Chicano. Edward Said's recent conclusion speaks to this
confluence: "exile, immigration, and the crossing of boundaries are
experiences that can therefore provide us with new narrative forms or,
in John Berger's phrase, with other ways of telling" (225). In this
respect, *Touch of Evil*—when filtered through the obsessions of its
director and critics—becomes a precursor to Chicano border narratives.

Welles's film is one that questions previous stereotypes, recalling
that "the celluloid Mexican stereotype is almost as old as the film
industry itself" (Lamb 75). One Mexicano (Vargas) does not lie, does
not steal, does not rape, does not even appear to desire his new wife,
does not use a knife, does not wear a sombrero; in fact, does not even

look or sound like a Mexican ("Mexican"?). One can find and document how Welles's *Touch of Evil* reinforces predictable stereotypes of the Mexicano subjectivity and of the Anglo subjectivity. Closer scrutiny reveals, however, that these expressionistic archetypes are mined with nuances of difference that self-consciously derail previous Hollywood stereotypes. Welles's characters accomplish this on the silver screen even as their commentators reveal the American critical community's apparent need (evident in much of the criticism surveyed here) for the reassuring logic stereotyped Mexicans and Mexican Americans provide. Welles's work is a true border text; it does not hide the wounds evident at the border.

I will close with an anecdote lifted from Leaming about what happened when the time came for the final editing of *Touch of Evil*: "over Orson's strenuous objections, [postproduction head Ernest] Nims and [production head Ed] Muhl decided that it was time to inspect the picture. Whereupon Welles left for Mexico . . . to work on his 'home movie' of *Don Quixote*" (523). Welles leaves *Touch of Evil* to work on *Don Quixote*—Cervantes's meditation on narration and representation—a project Welles never finished, a *quixotic* gesture if there ever was one. The result of these events, these Borges-like annoying details, is that commentators are left with a text in dispute, a mestizo-like halfbreed of a finished product whose lineage will be subject to endless debate. Leave it to the old gringo Welles to have produced a Chicano masterwork, to have *figured* the border out, to have represented it, and then to have parodied that representation in the material work of realizing and distributing the film.

Notes

1. Even a cursory summary of Heath's "Film and System" reveals his sensitivity to the problematic status of synopses in film theory, what he calls "the confusion of synopsis and interpretation" (12). In fact, Heath provides four synopses.

2. I will provide an expanded treatment of this concept, as well as of the status of Chicanos and Chicanas in U.S. mass culture, in a book-length study in progress, *Cinematext: Twentieth-Century Representations of Mexican Americans in Word and Image*.

References

A special thank you to my assistants Mark Schwartz and Laura Rossi for their diligence and dedication on this project.

Anzaldúa, Gloria. *Borderlands/La Frontera: The New Mestiza* (San Francisco: Spinsters/Aunt Lute, 1987).

Bazin, André. *Orson Welles: A Critical View* (New York: Harper and Row, 1978).

Comito, Terry. "A Biographical Sketch" and "Welles's Labyrinths: An Introduction to *Touch of Evil*" in *Touch of Evil: Orson Welles, Director,* ed. Terry Comito (New Brunswick: Rutgers University Press, 1985), 3–33, 35–42.

Heath, Stephen. "Film and System: Terms of Analysis, Part I." *Screen* 16, no. 1 (1975): 7–77.

———. "Film and System: Terms of Analysis, Part II." *Screen* 16, no. 2 (1975): 91–113.

Johnson, William. "Orson Welles: Of Time and Loss" in *Touch of Evil: Orson Welles, Director,* ed. Terry Comito, 235–47.

Lamb, Blaine T. "The Convenient Villain: The Early Cinema Views the Mexican-American." *Journal of the West* 14 (1975): 75–81.

Leaming, Barbara. *Orson Welles: A Biography* (New York: Penguin, 1985).

McBride, Joseph. *Orson Welles* (New York: Viking Press, 1972).

Naremore, James. *The Magic World of Orson Welles* (New York: Oxford University Press, 1978).

———. "The Trial: The FBI vs. Orson Welles." *Film Comment* 27, no. 1 (1991): 22–27.

Nericcio, William Anthony. "Autobiographies at la Frontera: The Quest for Mexican-American Narrative." *The Americas Review* 16, nos. 3–4 (1988): 165–87.

Rosaldo, Renato. *Culture and Truth: The Remaking of Social Analysis* (Boston: Beacon Press, 1989).

Said, Edward. "Representing the Colonized: Anthropology's Interlocutors." *Critical Inquiry* (Winter 1989): 205–25.

Stubbs, John C. "The Evolution of Orson Welles's *Touch of Evil* from Novel to Film." *Cinema Journal* 24, no. 2 (1985): 19–39; rpt. in *Touch of Evil: Orson Welles, Director,* ed. Terry Comito, 175–93.

Thompson, Howard. *New York Times* (May 22, 1958): 25; rpt. in *Touch of Evil: Orson Welles, Director,* ed. Terry Comito, 227–28.

Latino Sacrifice in the Discourse of Citizenship: Acting against the "Mainstream," 1985–1988

Kathleen Newman

In his recent book on contemporary Latin American culture, *Culturas híbridas: Estrategías para entrar y salir de la modernidad*, Néstor García Canclini devotes a section to the border culture of Tijuana/San Diego and writes of the "dynamic cultural production" specific to "hybrid cultures":

> If in the United States there are more than 250 Spanish-language radio and television stations, more than 1,500 publications in our language, and a great interest in Latin American literature and music, it is not just because there is a market of some 20 million "hispanics," that is, 8 percent of the national population. . . . It is also because the (so named) latino culture produces films like *Zoot Suit* and *La Bamba*, songs by Rubén Blades and Los Lobos, theater groups with sophisticated aesthetics like Luis Valdez's [Teatro Campesino], paintings and sculptures whose quality and whose capacity to make popular culture interact with modernist and postmodernist representation incorporates them into the North American mainstream.[1]

In this section of *Culturas híbridas*, in the description of the multicultural Americas—not just the "hybridity" of the border, but the multicultural, multiracial, multilingual history of the nations north and south of the U.S.-Mexico border—García Canclini draws upon the work in the 1980s of Guillermo Gómez-Peña, Emily Hicks, Tomás Ybarra-Frausto, Shifra Goldman, and Renato Rosaldo, among others, in which U.S. latino cultural production was asserted as central— rather than marginal or tangential—to U.S. cultural history. It is interesting to note, however, that in spite of a commitment to describing the culture of the Americas as multiple or hybrid, García Canclini cannot escape the word "mainstream" (which appears in English in the original text) or the recognition that, intertwined with a dynamic multiculturalism, there is a dynamic of cultural production in the United States that, in reproducing racism, produces a "mainstream." Thus, while García Canclini is correct to state that "latino culture produces films like *Zoot Suit* and *La Bamba*" because these and other Chicano films were the results of the unflagging efforts of Chicano filmmakers from the 1960s onward to change the anglocentric U.S. film industry (i.e., to give latinos creative control of their material), his phrasing deemphasizes the history of struggle involved in bringing multicultural representations into circulation in the national culture.

Though we should not conflate the various electronic media with the national culture (there are numerous experiences shared serially by all U.S. citizens that have nothing to do with these forms of communication), feature films and entertainment television do for the most part reach a national audience and usually do exceed the limits of regional or local cultures. Thus, the number of feature films and dramas for television made in the eighties with some level of creative control by Chicanos (*Zoot Suit, Seguín, The Ballad of Gregorio Cortez, El Norte, La Bamba, Born in East L.A., The Milagro Beanfield War, Stand and Deliver, Break of Dawn*) and the continuation of the latino documentary tradition (for example, *La Ofrenda: The Days of the Dead, In the Shadow of the Law, Vaya con Dios, Chicano Park*) indeed can be considered evidence of the impact of the Chicano and other latino political and cultural movements of the past twenty-some years on a national redefinition of citizenship as citizenship in a multicultural society, one that has been so for a very long time. Yet, not surprisingly, it is still easy to find in the national media, particularly in the realm of entertainment, counterexamples of the devalorization of latinos as citizens. In recent years it was still possible for a short-lived dramatic series for television, "Nasty Boys," to air an episode in which, combining various standard narrative formulas, the character of the latino policeman, undercover as a Colombian druglord, consigned his pregnant wife into the care of his anglo (white/English monolingual) police captain, into whose hands (rather than her midwife's) she safely delivered her baby in the middle of the Las Vegas strip. The particular deployment of the formal elements of sound and image of this episode served to suggest that the mediation of "mainstream" governmental authorities is necessary in order that the (allegedly generalizable) latino family, endangered by drugs and decadence, be stabilized into a (normative) nuclear family. In fact, it was the representation of the positive relation between the euro-descent captain and his latino officer that enabled and constructed the underlying racist and paternalist message.

Though the race relations instantiated by this episode still permeate the national electronic and print media, there have been some changes in the politics of casting, and these have had consequences in terms of meaning production at the level of the national culture. One of the less obvious is a specific change that took place between 1985 and 1988 in the representation of latinos on both the large and small screens. The change involved the casting of latino (male) actors as warrior-citizens, specifically as Vietnam veterans. On the lesser scale of the history of U.S. film and television industries, it is the moment in which a new narrative formula specifically involving latinos emerged from twists of older war-story formulae: in this newer formula a latino sacrifices himself for the specific good of his anglo military comrades, even if he and his comrades are part of a multiracial group. On the scale of the history of the Americas, this change might well be related to a disparate "disciplining of the populace," in the Foucauldian sense, with respect to the ongoing, allegedly clandestine intervention of the U.S. government in the wars of Central America in the early eighties (and the later revelations of Iran-Contra) and the noticeable national diversity of latino immigrants and undocumented workers arriving in the United States in the same period. In this sense, the new formula might be understood as the industries' anxiety about explicit political discussions and a concomitant narrative distraction in dramatic formulae, an insistence on the possibilities of latino-anglo solidarity and an erasure, to the extent possible, of representations of solidarity among latinos. Although this topic deserves further documentation and analysis, the concern of this article is both a larger and smaller scale of events: on the one hand, the constant discursive renegotiations of citizenship by which we are constituted as citizens of a specific nation, and, on the other, the minute audiovisual details that serve as evidence of these renegotiations. This essay examines how this specific change in the representation of latinos is related not merely to the political-economic constitution of citizenship but also to its *cultural* determinants. This change in the formula of the representation of war heroes and the introduction of the trope of latino sacrifice had contradictory results: on the positive side, *lo latino* was portrayed as central to U.S. national identity, and, on the negative, the very portrayal once again served to reinvent the "mainstream" and to continue to exclude latinos, even to this day, from full citizenship and all the attendant rights of equality.

The Exemplary Citizen: Castillo, 1985

Large-scale cultural transformations are never determined by one factor in isolation, much less by one televisual image, but, for the sake of periodization of the representation of U.S. latinos on film and television, it can be said that the trope of latino sacrifice is fully operative by November 22, 1985, the air date of the *Miami Vice* episode "Bushido," directed by Edward James Olmos. The supporting character of Lieutenant Castillo, which brought Olmos as an actor a greater level of national recognition than had his previous, much-praised roles in *Zoot Suit* and *The Ballad of Gregorio Cortez*, was the focus of this episode. Whereas in the first season, the regular viewer learned of Castillo's past as a DEA agent in Thailand and of government betrayals that lost him his wife, in this second season "Bushido" revealed a prior job with a national security agency such as the CIA (later seasons would reveal more information about the character's CIA or "special forces" activities in Vietnam). In the pivotal scene in terms of the plot, after some years of absence Castillo confronts his closest friend, Jack Gretsky (played by Dean Stockwell), an intelligence agent now supposedly renegade. Gretsky asks Castillo to take care of his Soviet wife and son and then maneuvers Castillo into killing him—a favor in actuality, as the viewer subsequently learns, because Gretsky was in great pain and near death with cancer. The two key visuals in this sequence will be analyzed at length here. The first is the embrace between Castillo and Gretsky, when Gretsky has passed the responsibility for the care of his family over to Castillo, and the second, after the killing, involves the movement into frame of the lead characters of Crockett and Tubbs (European American and African American, respectively) and the dialogue and blocking of the subsequent scene, which shifts the focus of the narrative from Castillo, just recently centrally framed, to anglo anxieties about authority and political action.

The embrace between Castillo and Gretsky locates this episode within the narrative formulas, emergent in the mideighties, that adjusted the World War II, Korean War, and Cold War war-story formulas and those of the buddy films of the seventies to the entertainment industry's long-anticipated recuperation of the Vietnam War as a historically distant storyline.[2] This period of the conservative recuperation of Vietnam as the "war that could have been won" manifested itself in episodic television in post-Rambo, "honorably-above-the-law" vigilante storylines and shows (*The A-Team, Airwolf*, and, at times, *Magnum, P.I.*). The liberal recuperation of the war would begin shortly with *Platoon* (1986) and *Full Metal Jacket* (1987). The embrace between Castillo and Gretsky is an example of "the death embrace" in which, near the end of a narrative, two men, at least one of whom has to be a Vietnam veteran, embrace before they kill or are killed. This updates formulae of earlier buddy films in which the intimacy of the friendship would be in some way noted (but not necessarily demonstrated by an embrace) before portraying a violent death. By 1987, this embrace has been explicitly and parodically sexualized: in Richard Donner's *Lethal Weapon*, gleefully exceeding every buddy film formula, the plot culminates in a final embrace between characters Riggs (Mel Gibson) and Murtaugh (Danny Glover), both Vietnam veterans; the two policemen turn in their exhausted embrace to fire their guns (near simultaneously) and kill one of the villains.[3]

In "Bushido" the embrace is explicitly the embrace between two warriors, two samurai. While it is an expression of their affection or love for one another, it is foregrounded as the realization of their bond as defenders of their country, even against their government, which is portrayed as corrupt. In the conversation before the embrace, which partially sexualizes the relationship, Gretsky reminds Castillo of a battle against "Hmong assassins" in a temple resembling one in which they now find themselves (a portion of dialogue that only Stockwell's acting skills could save as viable drama):

> . . . we lay there waiting in the dark and the air was so thick and ancient you couldn't breathe it. And when they came we stood in the middle of the floor, leaning with our backs to each other. It was our swords against their swords. We should have died then.

The event to which the character's nostalgia for a shared, seemingly timeless warrior code is linked is historically located in the Vietnam

War. The linkage alone transforms the routine telerealism of the narrative into political allegory. Furthermore, the evocation of two warrior-
citizens alone encircled by a foreign enemy (with, of course, no other
citizens or populace to sully the image) is to suggest a past lost but
still desired. This "desire" is reinforced by the subsequent dialogue of
the two "Company" agents over Gretsky's corpse:

> Two peas in a pod, Castillo, you and Gretsky. The last of the dino-
> saurs. I've got to hand it to you, you're a real problem solver. That guy
> was totally out of control. We either had to kill him or give him a
> medal.

The agent's remarks raise the stakes: Gretsky's desire for a purity of
war is not only individual but also governmental. It is a desire for a
period in which the U.S. government "was in control."

In terms of the status of the two characters, the affirmation that
Gretsky and Castillo are the last to have fought for the highest of
national values (values for which medals are awarded) locates the two
as citizens above the limits of their fallible nation, i.e., they are not
bound by the limits of nationhood. Though on the surface of the matter, the United States is portrayed in the dialogue as a morally bank-
rupt nation in which such honor and service are no longer useful to
the state, let alone tolerated, the allegorization of the two characters
links discursively to the now infamous "Vietnam syndrome" (which,
six years later, President Bush announced had ended with the Persian
Gulf War). The consequences of U.S. actions in Vietnam are interpreted as a failure to allow military men to carry out their highest duties
as citizens. This temporal displacement, however, this retro-morality,
terminates the allegory as quickly as it had begun. The allegory only
functions when both characters are alive, when the two in their
embrace are the definition of a level of moral, political action that
exceeds yet binds all nations. It is an allegory that erases the historical
record of the ruthless political interests of nations. Significantly,
Castillo's "solving the problem" of Gretsky collapses the warrior-
bond upon which the allegory is constructed. Without Gretsky,
Castillo alone is left to bear the burden of political honor, but this kind
of honor only exists if it is a *collective* honor. These meanings created at
the surface level of plot and dialogue are not the final deployment of
the terms of citizenship in this sequence of shots, however. The composition of the subsequent shots reveals that the ideological concerns

of this episode have more to do with how the discourse of citizenship is related to the race and class systems *interior* to the nation-state.

The partial sexualization of the warrior-bond, mentioned previously, is one of the mechanisms by which the characters are made to *embody* morality and the legitimate exercise of power. This embodiment subsequently is made literal when Castillo, who is seeking Gretsky for the murder of a drug dealer, tells Gretsky: "I can't let you walk. It's my duty. It's what I am." Castillo now embodies the law. These statements are made just before Gretsky, seeming to choose to resist arrest, pulls an automatic weapon and fires a spray of bullets that miss Castillo but trap him into killing Gretsky with one shot of a revolver. Afterward, Castillo is centrally framed in a medium closeup reaction shot that fades momentarily to black. When the image returns to the screen the camera pulls back from Castillo just enough to allow Crockett and Tubbs, entering screen-left, to form a diagonal with Castillo, which places the white Crockett in center frame between the latino and black characters. The next patterns in the blocking, in terms of race, become crucial to the range of meanings generated in the episode as a whole.[4] When the two anglo intelligence agents enter and all five characters are in a shot, the sequence left to right is agent, Castillo, Crockett, agent, Tubbs, with Tubbs standing slightly to the side. Crockett and Tubbs are in the background, but Crockett's face, framed between Castillo's and the agent's, is still the center of the image. When the agents leave, Crockett moves forward to stand next to Castillo and the camera moves in, framing the two, as Tubbs moves to the center back, his face now the one in the middle. Crockett turns to face Castillo, which places Crockett's face in profile and creates an alignment on a diagonal between the faces of Castillo and Tubbs. After a pause filled by the dolorous music sustaining the sequence from the death embrace onward, Crockett asks Castillo, "What do you want me to do?" At the reply "nothing," Crockett turns to gaze after the agents, and Castillo looks at Crockett gazing after the agents. First, the shift in central framing from Castillo to Crockett in these two scenes foregrounds at this point in the narrative the reactions of the anglo character. Both in the first blocking of the five characters, and in the second of the three regular cast members, Crockett moves and speaks in complicity with the other anglo characters. Second, the emotions of empathy or solidarity for the character of Castillo that the three regular cast members might have wished to communicate in their acting is ambiguous (given the small screen and the medium shots) and does not counteract the fact that the scene ends with an emphasis not only on the anglo lead character's inability to think of what to do but on his conceptualization of his responsibility as involving going after the anglo agents, not as taking care of his latino comrade. Third, the alignment on diagonal of the faces of Castillo and Tubbs in the final shot suggests greater solidarity between them than between Castillo and Crockett. In all, the formal elements of this sequence place another burden of responsibility on the latino character. Not only is Castillo responsible for the politics of nation and gender transferred to him by Gretsky in the previous scene, now he must compensate for Crockett's shortcomings, that is, the anglo's inability to deal with the systems of oppression, of which the anglo is a part.

Most of the popular press dealing with Olmos during the run of *Miami Vice* emphasized exactly the exemplarity of the character of Castillo and an audience fascination with morality in what seemed to be politically immoral times. Pete Hamill's early article "Soul on 'Vice' " in *New York* (September 29, 1986) had the subtitle, "As Lieutenant Castillo, Edward James Olmos is the moral center for Crockett and Tubbs." Hamill went on to say in the article:

> I know people who continue to watch *Miami Vice* because of the coiled, tense, centered performance of Olmos as Martin Castillo. The lieutenant lives and acts according to a moral code; he can *only* do what is right. In his controlled, oddly grieving way, Castillo accepts the world as it is, but insists on a code of conduct. There are some lines, he implies, that you do not cross. In a time of blurred values, Castillo embodies true courage. He has evolved into something we have not seen for a very long time: an adult hero. (54)

The character of Castillo, like El Pachuco and Gregorio Cortez, is one of the most important of the decade, not only for the excellence of Olmos's performances and the significance of the role in each specific drama, but also for these affirmations in the national, regional, and local media of a warrior-citizen, a "hero," who is Chicano. What is troubling in the press on *Miami Vice* and in the show itself, is that, while representing the United States as a multicultural society, in neither does the responsibility for morality and courage fall equally on the anglo characters. In the case of *Miami Vice*, the anglo characters are not equally responsible for undoing racism and other injustices. Although I would not claim this is the case in all films or television programs invoking questions of the responsibilities of citizenship specifically via the element of characters who are Vietnam veterans, in *Miami Vice*, at least, when the latino character has the role of formulaic warrior-citizen, a greater sacrifice for the nation seems to be required of his character. Castillo must be "centered," "grieving," but yet "controlled."

An example of what is perhaps the logical extreme of this trope of latino sacrifice occurred four years later on a nationally syndicated science fiction drama, *War of the Worlds*. In the opening episode of the second season, when both the Native American and African American characters were killed in order to introduce a new European American warrior-citizen, and to reconstitute the normative nuclear family as a single mother with teenage daughter and two surrogate bachelor fathers, all euro-descent, the sacrifice of life foregrounded in the narrative was marked as latino. The Vietnam veteran character of Colonel Ironhorse, played by Spanish/Portuguese-surnamed actor Richard Chaves, commits suicide to save the reconstituted anglo family, the ultimate defenders of democracy against "alien invasion."[5] The suicide is a particularly interesting twist on the death embrace. Chaves had once before played the death embrace, when in the feature film *Predator* (1987) his character, a latino in the special forces, was killed while being held in a side-embrace by star Arnold Schwarzenegger. The latino and Native American soldiers were the last two of the multiracial squad to die and, in delaying the alien predator, allowed the anglo lead character to survive and ultimately triumph. In *War of the Worlds*, the character of Ironhorse is a combination of these two characters from *Predator*, and Chaves's work in *Predator* clearly determined his casting in *War of the Worlds*, which would be intended to play to much the same audience. In the final scenes of the first episode of the second season, the exhausted Colonel, having been cloned by the aliens, must confront himself as enemy. The clone is holding a gun to the head of the teenage daughter while the anglo adults puzzle out some version of the question, "What do you want me to do?" The Colonel puts his gun under his chin and blows his brains out, knowing this will kill the alien clone, thus saving the reconstituted anglo family and the series.

Responsibility for this trope of latino sacrifice cannot be laid solely at the door of scriptwriters, story editors, and other members of the film and television industry. It is part of the discourse of citizenship in which the national populace as a whole participates. This discourse is most obvious in fiction feature films and episodic entertainment television dealing with any war in which the United States has involved itself, but it is also highly visible in discussions in the popular press about anything to which the label "mainstream" might be applied. By 1988, the year after the release of *La Bamba*, the trope of latino sacrifice had extended into the popular press in ways that were to be detrimental for the future casting of latino actors, both men and women. Another form of the death embrace emerged: it seems one strategy for denying the multiculturalism of the United States, to kill it off, is to embrace it.

The Exemplary Citizen: Olmos, 1988

Edward James Olmos was nominated for an Academy Award for his performance as East Los Angeles calculus teacher Jaime Escalante in *Stand and Deliver* (1988). The role is a far cry from the warrior figure of Castillo, and the fictional Escalante cannot possibly be imagined as having to bear the responsibility of a mythic national honor. *Stand and Deliver* recounts a case of "institutional racism" in which it is made very clear how the students and the teacher fought back and corrected the injustices done to them by the national educational system. The trope of latino sacrifice did not disappear, however; rather, it was transferred, as we shall see, from the characters that latino actors played on screen to the actors themselves.

In partial response to *Stand and Deliver, Time* magazine published a special issue on July 11, 1988 (vol. 132, no. 2), with the unforgettable banner "¡Magnífico! Hispanic culture breaks out of the barrio" in which tourist Spanish meets a verb with negative connotations. To add insult to injury, the table of contents had the following promotion of the articles on U.S. latino culture:

A Latin Wave Hits the Mainstream

Ever ready to borrow from other cultures, America is celebrating the spirited sounds and shapes, the flavors and flirtations of Hispanic style. The new influence is changing the way the country eats, dresses, dances, plays and learns—the way it lives. Look around. See the special lightning, the distinctive gravity, the portable wit, the personal spin. In theater and films, Latin playwrights and directors supply a fresh vision and voice. The names on the marquee have a Spanish ring:

Andy Garcia, Maria Conchita Alonso, the inspirational actor Edward James Olmos. In fashion and design, painting and architecture, critics laud the Latino artists whose work owes its strength to aesthetic merit, not simply to ethnic novelty. And as they cross over into the American imagination, Hispanics are sending one irresistible message: we come bearing gifts. (3)

So, in 1988 *Time* magazine believed it permissible to state that (a) latino culture is not U.S. culture, (b) it is new, and (c) it principally involves entertainment and aesthetics but not the political-economic structures of the nation. Did the Latin wave, as it hit, knock the editor on his or her head? How interesting that Spanish surnames have a Spanish ring. How comforting to the "imaginary" homogeneous, monolingual mainstream that it need not fear a multicultural Trojan horse.

The cover of this issue is a photo of a mural of "the inspirational actor" Edward James Olmos. In the lower left is a girl, smiling, leaning on her bicycle. If one were just to glance at this cover on a newsstand, given the style of the painting and its size with respect to the girl, one would assume it was a detail of a larger mural, one face among the many faces usually included in Chicano murals. In fact, it suggests that Olmos himself is now an icon in the mural movement, like Zapata or the Virgen de Guadalupe. This is not the case, as the regular box "A Letter from the Publisher" reveals:

> For our special issue on Hispanic-American culture, *Time*'s art department came up with an ingenious way of portraying Olmos on the cover. In predominantly Hispanic East Los Angeles, artist Joe Gonzalez has promoted a renaissance by painting uplifting murals on the sides of buildings. "So we asked ourselves," says executive art director Nigel Holmes, " 'Why not have Gonzalez paint us a mural that depicted Olmos?' " (4)[6]

Although both Joe Gonzalez and staff writer Guy D. Garcia are quoted in the piece as finding Olmos to be an example . . . a symbol . . . an inspiration, the publisher finds no irony in having commissioned the mural. It does not seem to occur to him that "an ingenious way of portraying Olmos on the cover" could be considered an attempt to manipulate the latino arts to answer *Time*'s need, rather than the community's, for inspirational image.

Olmos's long-time activism is exemplary, both at the community and national levels, and the record of his support of and his work on behalf of the latino arts is extensive. In fact, nearly every article on Olmos notes his personal commitment to the national distribution and community exhibition of *The Ballad of Gregorio Cortez,* his struggle with the producer and director of *Stand and Deliver* to keep the film accurate in its portrayal of Escalante and the students of Garfield High, and numerous other examples of his refusal to compromise his standards. Yet, nearly every article also tries in some way to make Olmos an icon—not for multicultural America, but for "the mainstream." In the *Time* special issue the writers used the common strategy in articles on film stars of comparing Olmos to the characters he plays. The suggestion in the following sentences is that Olmos's success requires of him a sacrifice.

> The actor's tendency to put himself on the line—both on the set and on the street—is motivated by a feeling that he has to maintain his personal code of honor in a corrupt world. . . . Moreover, the echoes of *Miami Vice* keep recurring in his personal and professional life. Like Lieut. Castillo, Olmos has always wrestled with the ninja in himself, walking the thin line between dedication and self-denial, success and prideful penury. (59–60)

But the comparison of actors with warriors has wider consequences. Consider the comments on and by actors Virginia Paris, Rosana DeSoto, and Olmos in an article on Olmos at the time of release of *Stand and Deliver.*

> Like Rosana DeSoto, another determined survivor, Virginia Paris knows not only about optimism but also about the entrenched barriers to keeping it alive. "You're not an actor," DeSoto says. "You're a warrior, a warrior for enlightenment."
> . . . It makes Edward James Olmos a warrior for a style that breaks the mold of expectation, a style true to the actor's conception of the role of ethnicity in American life. (46) [7]

Given that the racism still entrenched in the national culture and that the various enduring racial hierarchies in each region of the nation are central mechanisms of the U.S. political-economic structures, DeSoto's observation that she and her fellow latino actors are warriors is generalizable for all actors of color across the anglocentric (and emphatically monolingual) film and television industry. Unfortunately, at least since 1988, the heroism of this struggle is being recuperated in the national media dealing with entertainment as part of the discourse on citizenship, with the consequence that latino actors are discursively positioned as citizens of whom a sacrifice is expected. Like the formulaic Vietnam veteran characters and the ninjas and the samurai of entertainment prime-time television, the actors are being positioned as expendable. In the national print media of our "*Platoon*-meets-*La Bamba*-America," the following analogy is circulating: as the warrior-citizen sacrifices himself for the good of the nation, latino actors are to sacrifice themselves for the good of the film and television industries. Like the blue-burning Hollywood star that haloes Olmos's head on the *Time* mural, these actors are to burn more intensely than their anglo counterparts, to give more and to do more.

In a certain sense, it is an old formula: those whose civil rights have been violated are expected to get the violators to stop . . . the injunction is not on the violators themselves to be part of the collectivity and to change their ways. What is new in this instance is that the success of Chicano and other political and cultural movements has been such that the multicultural, multiracial, multilingual reality of the nation cannot be denied, so it must be in some way displaced. In the late eighties it has been displaced onto the war-story trope of the requisite sacrifice of citizens in times of conflict.

The long-term, ongoing struggle to change the film and television industry so that it is responsive to its multicultural American audience is one in which latino filmmakers have played a significant role over the past twenty-five years. There is no doubt that latino actors will continue to create enduring characters in spite of the trope of latino sacrifice on screen and in the press. But their job has only gotten more difficult in these recent years, because the national collectivity does not hold anglo actors, writers, directors, and producers equally responsible as all other citizens for multicultural representation. One of the consequences of this is, as Eduardo Díaz, former codirector of CineFestival, wrote in 1988, the year in which the trope was extended from characters to actors: "While the picture on the small and large screen looks better for the latino community, the necessary wherewithal is still beyond the regular grasp of our best talent."[8]

From September 9 to December 9, 1990, the UCLA Wight Art Gallery in Los Angeles hosted the exhibition *Chicano Art: Resistance and Affirmation, 1965–1985*, which will tour nationally and internationally for the next three years.[9] In the introduction to the exhibition's informational tabloid, the National Advisory Committee states three overriding principles of the exhibition: that it reflect in all aspects "multi-vocal Chicano sensibility," that it must be truly national (indicating that it should not privilege just one or two regions), and that the "art must maintain in its character a *locura* (fury) and retain the beauty of the *plebe*, or the working class from which it springs." It is to be hoped that in the decade of the nineties the dynamic multiculturalism of the United States, which drew the attention of García Canclini in his studies of the Americas, will override the dynamic of racism that has kept the film and television industries anglocentric and unresponsive to the national populace in its entirety. It is long past time that U.S. citizens who are English-monolingual learn that *locura* means fury—a furious energy and strength—and that no citizen should be asked to sacrifice anything for something as untranslatable as a "mainstream."

Notes

1. "Si en los Estados Unidos existen más de 250 estaciones de radio y televisión en castellano, más de 1500 publicaciones en nuestra lengua y un alto interés por la literatura y música latinoamericanas, no es sólo porque hay un mercado de 20 millones de 'hispanos,' o sea el 8 por ciento de la población estadounidense . . . También se debe a que la llamada cultura latina produce películas como *Zoot Suit* y *La bamba*, las canciones de Rubén Blades y Los Lobos, teatros de avanzada estética y cultural [*sic*] como el de Luis Valdez, artes plásticos cuya calidad y aptitud para hacer interactuar la cultura popular con la simbólica moderna y posmoderna los incorpora al *mainstream* norteamericano" (291; Mexico City: Grijalbo, 1990). The source of these statistics is not cited in the text.

2. For further analysis, see *From Hanoi to Hollywood: The Vietnam War in American Film*, Linda Dittmar and Gene Michaud, eds. (New Brunswick and London: Rutgers University Press, 1990). See also Susan Jeffords, *The Remasculinization of America: Gender and the Vietnam War* (Bloomington: Indiana University Press, 1989).

3. For further analysis of *Lethal Weapon*, see Robyn Wiegman's "Negotiating AMERICA: Gender, Race, and Ideology of the Interracial Male Bond" in *Cultural Critique* 13 (Fall 1989): 89–117.

4. It is important to recall that although Olmos as the director could have determined the blocking of each scene and the shot composition, the meanings generated in the final broadcast version always exceed the production team's control: larger social discourses inform the text's reception.

5. For an analysis of racial allegories in science fiction, see Charles Ramírez Berg, "Immigrants, Aliens, and Extraterrestrials: Science Fiction's Alien 'Other' as (Among Other Things) New Hispanic Imagery," *CineAction!* 18 (Fall 1989): 3–17.

6. The painting can be found on the back wall of the parking lot of El Mercado. I cannot confirm whether other sections have been added since August 1988. At that time, the portrait ended just beyond what is shown framed on the cover. Note that the publisher does not detail Gonzalez's history as an artist, as would have been appropri-

ate given the importance in the issue attributed to both the commissioned work and to latino art in general.

7. Pat Aufderheide, "Reel Life," *Mother Jones* 13, no. 111 (April 1988): 24ff.

8. "Latino Cinema in the U.S.," in the exhibition catalog *Latin American Visions,* Patricia Aufderheide, ed., Neighborhood Film/Video Project of International House of Philadelphia, 47.

9. Olmos was the chair of the National Honorary Committee for the CARA exhibition. A catalog of the exhibition has now been published; see Richard Griswold del Castillo, Teresa McKenna, and Yvonne Yarbro-Bejarano, eds., *Chicano Art: Resistance and Affirmation, 1965–1985* (Los Angeles: Wight Art Gallery/UCLA, 1991).

Who is Maria? What is Juan? Dilemmas of Analyzing the Chicano Image in U.S. Feature Films

Carlos E. Cortés

I'm watching, for the first time, an obscure 1950 movie named *Mystery Street*. A call goes out for Police Lieutenant Pete Morales. Have I discovered another Chicano movie cop? Catch that accent. Probably so. Who's that playing him? Ricardo Montalbán. Of course Morales must be a Chicano. Wait a minute! Morales works in a Portuguese American district on Cape Cod? Well, scratch Mexican American. Make him Portuguese American.

So it goes in the often-frustrating process of recreating and assessing the historical treatment of Chicanos (Mexican Americans) and other ethnic groups in U.S. motion pictures. To reconstruct the longitudinal development of an ethnic group's film image demands time, patience, attentiveness, luck, and a continuous weighing of necessarily incomplete, tauntingly inconclusive, and often contradictory evidence. It also requires a willingness to confront and consider each new piece of filmic evidence, which may reinforce your current generalizations, suggest new interpretive avenues, or even challenge your long-held beliefs.

Ethnic stereotyping in movies certainly does occur.[1] My own analysis of film-based historical evidence, however, has convinced me that much of the literature about how certain ethnic groups have (supposedly) been depicted actually creates and often reinforces its own distortions—stereotypes of movie stereotyping. Therefore, analytical clarity and rigor are critical for creating an accurate historical portrait of movie ethnic image-making. That quest attains even greater significance given the powerful role that feature films play in contributing to public perceptions of ethnic groups.

Movies as an Educational Curriculum

Schools are not synonymous with education. They are only part of education. Alongside schools operates a parallel educational system, the "societal curriculum"—that massive, ongoing, informal curriculum of family, peer groups, neighborhoods, churches, organizations, institutions, and other societal forces that "educate" all of us throughout our lives.[2] Within that societal curriculum, the media serve as pervasive, relentless, lifelong educators. This includes not only the nonfictional media, which purport to present facts and analysis, but also the so-called entertainment media, which have a major impact in shaping beliefs, attitudes, values, perceptions, and "knowledge" and in influencing decisions and action.[3]

In short, movies teach. The celluloid curriculum teaches about myriad topics, including race, ethnicity, culture, and nationality. The degree to which feature films actually *create* intercultural perceptions and stereotypes can be debated. Beyond debate is the fact that, whether intentionally or not, they *contribute* to intercultural, interracial, and interethnic understanding and misunderstanding. However, specifying precisely what that movie curriculum has taught and identifying what different individuals have learned from it pose a considerable scholarly challenge. In addressing this issue, at least four central questions need to be addressed.

1. What analytical factors must be considered in examining the content of this movie curriculum on race and ethnicity?

2. What have movies taught audiences and what messages have they transmitted about race and ethnicity?

3. How have American moviemakers functioned as textbook writers about race and ethnicity?

4. What dilemmas must be faced in attempting to assess the impact of films on public learning about race and ethnicity?

Analyzing the Movie Curriculum on Race and Ethnicity

When I began to study the visual media treatment of ethnic groups some fifteen years ago, I based my early judgments on diffused and fragmentary written evidence, popular generalizations about media stereotyping, decades of extensive but casual viewing, the purposeful analysis of selected motion pictures and television shows, and a blend of logic and intuition. As I decided to make it a subject for serious scholarly investigation, not just a titillating topic for public lectures and teacher workshops, I discovered the enormous conceptual, methodological, and temporal challenges of trying to reconstruct a history of the visual media's message system on race and ethnicity.[4]

Because of the explosive proliferation of television programs, a process hypertrophied by the emergence of cable, I decided to focus on the "smaller" universe of motion pictures. After all, *only* 21,000 feature films were produced in the United States between 1900 and 1951, and *only* 300–500 have been added each year since then. About half of all pre-1950 films have disappeared or been destroyed, however. That fact combined with the temporal impossibility of seeing all existing films makes reading about unviewed films a necessary but limiting supplement.

A systematic examination of this movie curriculum requires combining the rigor of sociological content analysis, such as identifying, categorizing, and evaluating ethnic characters, and the insights of semiological analysis, such as extracting the various meanings of relationships involving ethnic characters.[5] Since I was also concerned with learning (impact), not just teaching (content), two additional issues arose. First, what direct evidence can be found that movie content has actually had a learning impact? Second, when such direct evidence does not exist, how can content analysis be massaged in order to tease out conclusions about the media's *potential* impact on viewers?

For example, precision in content analysis requires categorical rigor in separating Americans of different but closely related ethnic backgrounds (for example, Mexican Americans, Puerto Ricans, and Cuban Americans) and distinguishing between Americans of a particular foreign heritage and citizens of the foreign nation itself (for example, Mexican Americans and Mexicans).[6] In the assessment of potential audience impact, however, such distinctions lose their cogency. Depictions of all Latin American-origin ethnic groups contribute to a generalized image of Latinos, and the myriad movies about Mexican bandits and Mexican Revolution violence have contributed to perceptions of Mexican Americans.[7] Broader ethnic and transnational groupings need to be considered when addressing impact.

To deal with the more than 40,000 U.S. feature films that have been produced, I developed a coding scheme for classifying information about the treatment of ethnicity and foreignness.[8] This coding system includes such categories as traits of individual characters (such as race, ethnicity, age, gender, and occupation), functions of ethnicity within the film, and relations among characters and institutions. Those data are later entered into my Ethnicity and Foreignness in Film Data Bank in the Laboratory for Historical Research, Department of History, University of California, Riverside. This coding and computer entry has proven incredibly time-consuming, and the "coding gap" has rapidly grown, with films actually coded inexorably falling further and further behind those analyzed.

Yet the process of creating and applying the coding system has proved more important than the actual data bank itself, as it has infused, informed, and strengthened my film analysis. It has forced me to question continuously my interpretations and even my perceptions. In turn, this has led to new insights into film content and helped me develop more thoughtful, evidence-based theories about potential impact, including alternative audience readings of films.

For example, the first problem confronting the would-be analyst of Chicano film images is ascertaining just exactly who on screen is a Chicano. Sometimes no problem exists. In movies like *Boulevard Nights* (1979), *Walk Proud* (1979), and *La Bamba* (1987), which focus on Chicano *barrios*, we can assume that most of the Spanish-surnamed characters are Mexican Americans. But in many other films, categorization becomes problematic when attempting to distinguish Chicanos from three other groups: American Indians, Mexicans, and other U.S. Latinos.

What about Chicanos and American Indians? Take Pearl Chávez in the 1946 epic, *Duel in the Sun*. With a father named Chávez (referred to in the film as a Creole) and an Indian mother, Pearl is labeled a "hot tamale" and a "papoose." As a *mestiza* with some element of Hispanic ancestry, she *might* be classifiable both as a Native American and as a Mexican American, although the film does not explicitly state her father's ancestry.

What about the host of Mexican-descent characters who live on the U.S. side of the U.S.-Mexican border, such as businesswoman Helen Ramírez in the 1952 classic, *High Noon*? Are they Mexican Americans (by birth or by naturalization), or are they Mexicans temporarily living in the United States? Because in so many Westerns the distinction between Chicanos and Mexicans has no plot importance, those films often fail to provide sufficient evidence for a definitive categorical separation.

As for U.S. Latinos, specific national origin can sometimes be inferred from a film's overall context. The general filmic rule goes as follows: if it's Los Angeles, they must be Chicano; in New York, color them Puerto Rican; in Miami, clearly Cubano. Although simple and commonsensical, these truisms are often misleading because of growing intra-Hispanic diversity in those cities. *Scarface* (1983) focuses on Cuban Americans, but it also features Colombians and Bolivians (or are some of them Colombian Americans and Bolivian Americans?). Although the second half of *El Norte* (1983) takes place in Los Angeles, the two main Latino characters are Guatemalan undocumented immigrants.

When it comes to movies set in contemporary Chicago, Detroit, or Kansas City, one might as well toss a dart at a map of Latin America. For example, of what Latino national background is Chicago's brutal, sadistic Paco Morales in *Bad Boys* (1983)? Except when films explicitly state a character's ethnicity, the analyst must weigh various types of clues.

Surnames help. However, the national-origin varieties of U.S. Latinos, the extensiveness of interethnic marriage, and the impact of the great American name change (sometimes through the proselytizing of colonial Spanish priests or the mindless acts of immigration officials) mean that surnames become clues rather than certifiers of ethnicity. New Mexico's Mountain Rivera in *Requiem for a Heavyweight* (1962) is probably a Chicano (or a *Hispano* in northern New Mexican parlance), but he might also have New Mexican Indian ancestry.[9]

Physical appearance helps. Although most useful for identifying African Americans and Asian Americans, physical appearance alone fails to reveal the national origin of recent African or West Indian immigrants, and it does not certify the specific national ancestry of every Asian American character. Physical appearance becomes least effective as an identifier among white ethnics, yet some filmmakers try to make characters "look" Jewish, Polish, or Italian. In the middle stand Latinos. Despite the complex racial heritage of Latinos, when moviemakers decide to make characters "look Mexican," they opt for physical stereotypes, choosing actors who fit their Mexican preconceptions or making up actors to fit presumed audience expectations—for example, brown contact lenses to transform Robby Benson into a Chicano in *Walk Proud*.

Language helps. If a character speaks a foreign language, this provides a clue to ethnic heritage, but it certainly does not guarantee ethnicity. In movies as in life, many non-Latinos speak Spanish, Latinos represent various Spanish-speaking national origins, and some Latinos do not speak Spanish.

The list of clues goes on, including dress, film location, religious symbols, and organizational membership. Except when a film provides an explicit statement of ethnicity, identity conclusions must be based on a careful assessment of such clues. Based on my research experience, I have developed the following content analysis guidelines.

1. To the degree possible, ethnic and foreign depictions should be categorically separated, but with an awareness that these two types of depictions may well reinforce each other in fostering viewer images of either the ethnic group (like Mexican Americans) or the related foreign culture (Mexico).

2. Similarly, categorical distinctions should be made between ethnic groups (for example, by national origin or tribe), while recognizing that the movie treatment of related groups may both influence viewer images of individual groups and create a more comprehensive ethnic cohort image (like U.S. Latinos).

3. Distinctions must be made between race and ethnicity. For example, Latinos fall into a variety of racial and racially mixed categories, and Americans of African ancestry may also have Jamaican American or Panamanian American ethnicity.

4. Both semiological and sociological content analysis should be used. That dual approach should address not only how individual characters are depicted, but also how they fit into the social structure of the film and how they are involved in various relationships—within their ethnic group (or groups), with individuals of other backgrounds, between ethnics functioning as groups (for example, in *West Side Story*, 1961), and between ethnic characters and societal institu-

tions (for example, Angel Chávez and the judicial system in *Trial*, 1955).

5. Whenever possible, individual ethnic group depictions should be assessed in the comparative context of other ethnic groups and of Americans in general in films of the same era and in the same genre. This helps in determining if the identified depiction patterns are specific to that ethnic group, represent the treatment of various ethnic groups, or merely exemplify current film or genre treatment of all Americans.

6. Whenever possible, film depictions of an ethnic group should be compared to the group's treatment in other media of the period, in ethnic humor, and in such other sources as school textbooks, in order to assess patterns of representational reinforcement or challenge.[10]

7. Whenever possible, film treatment should be considered in the context of contemporary historical realities, societal conditions, and prevalent values in order to establish in what respects movies reinforce, reflect, challenge, or provide alternative perspectives.

8. The longest possible time dimension and greatest number of films should be used in order to ascertain continuities and changes in patterns of treatment.

9. Analysts should not begin with the assumption of movie stereotyping. That label should be reserved until accumulated evidence has demonstrated a pervasive pattern occurring within a historical period or over time. Until then, less loaded terms should be used such as depiction, portrayal, or treatment.[11]

The Movie Curriculum as Message System

Beyond the issue of group images stands the question of the categories of *messages* that movies transmit concerning race, ethnicity, culture, and foreignness. In concert with other media, movies serve five general idea-disseminating functions.

1. *Movies provide information about race, ethnicity, culture, and foreignness.* People cannot be at all places at all times, nor can they travel into the past. Therefore, they must rely on mediating forms of communication—the mass media and such other sources as books—to engage today's world as well as to explore the past. Because nobody can develop in-depth experience-based knowledge about every ethnic

group or nation, people necessarily acquire much of what they know about these topics through what historian Daniel Boorstin has termed the "pseudoenvironment," principally the mass media.[12]

The information issue goes well beyond the question of factual accuracy. In news, the constant reiteration of certain themes, even if each story is accurate, tends to perpetuate limited, thereby distorting, ethnic group images. Similarly, the repetition of ethnic images by the entertainment media adds to viewers' pools of "knowledge"—both correct and incorrect—particularly if news and entertainment treatments coincide in theme, perspective, and frequency.

Sometimes movies themselves provide begrudging recognition of their power to contribute to intergroup perceptions. For example, Brian De Palma's 1983 remake of the Depression-era Italian American gangster classic, *Scarface*, transformed the head hoodlum into a contemporary Cuban immigrant drug dealer, Antonio Montana. After more than two hours of Latino gangland killings, heroin snorting, and unrelenting sadism, the following postscript appeared on screen:

> *Scarface* is the fictional account of the activities of a small group of ruthless criminals. The characters do not represent the Cuban American community and it would be erroneous and unfair to suggest that they do. The vast majority of Cuban Americans have demonstrated a dedication, vitality, and enterprise that has enriched the American scene.

These platitudes could not mitigate the film's powerful images. In fact, when I viewed the film in a commercial theater, the howls of audience laughter that erupted upon the reading of that ridiculous disclaimer suggested that it might have done more harm than good. Yet the disclaimer did suggest Hollywood's admission that its films do have teaching power.

Scarface added to the Hollywood tradition of trying to have it both ways, first exploiting ethnic violence and then warning audiences not to take the group depiction seriously. An almost identical disclaimer appeared prior to the 1977 network television showing of Francis Ford Coppola's *The Godfather Saga* (a revised and expanded version of the two *Godfather* feature films). It has been used since in movies like *Year of the Dragon* (1985), which did a similar gangland number on Chinese Americans. Where *The Godfather* reinvigorated the long Hollywood tradition of Italian American organized crime movies, *Scarface* gave impetus to a new wave of screen Latino drug dealers, ranging from television's *Miami Vice* to such feature films as *Code of Silence* (1985), *Stick* (1985), *Running Scared* (1986), *8 Million Ways to Die* (1986), *Above the Law* (1988), and *Q & A* (1990).

2. *Movies help organize information and ideas about racial, ethnic, cultural, and national groups.* Beyond providing information, movies (and television) help shape viewer structures for perceiving, receiving, processing, thinking, and organizing new images. Much as folk stories and fairy tales have done for centuries, these media now provide a type of "ritualized glue" that helps audiences make sense out of the increasing information glut that overwhelms readers, viewers, and listeners.[13] Reporting in 1977 that there had been more than 2,300 research papers on television and human behavior, psychologist George Comstock addressed the relationship of the entertainment media to the reification of social structures:

> Several writers have argued that television is a powerful reinforcer of the status quo. The ostensible mechanisms are the effects of its portrayals on public expectations and perceptions. Television portrayals and particularly violent drama are said to assign roles of authority, power, success, failure, dependence, and vulnerability in a manner that matches the real-life social hierarchy, thereby strengthening that hierarchy by increasing its acknowledgement among the public and by failing to provide positive images for members of social categories occupying a subservient position. Content analyses of television drama support the contention that portrayals reflect normative status.[14]

In other words, movies and other entertainment media tend to reiterate and legitimize racial, ethnic, and social hierarchies. By repeatedly depicting ethnic or racial dominance or subservience or consistently portraying members of some ethnic groups in limited spheres of action, media contribute to the shaping and reinforcement of viewer reception schema for absorbing future images into a coherent, if distorted, mental framework. For example, when films present ethnic slurs as normative expression—as in film titles like the "greaser" movies of the 1910s—they legitimize the use of such demeaning language.

3. *Movies influence values and attitudes.* Media critics have argued this for decades. The controversial Payne Fund studies of the 1930s, for example, included Henry James Forman's provocatively titled *Our*

Movie Made Children.[15] As recently as 1975 media historian Robert Sklar selected *Movie-Made America* as the title for his widely read cultural history of U.S. motion pictures, although he avoids the "hypodermic needle effect" propensities that pervade the Payne Fund studies.[16]

Hollywood's Motion Picture Production Code (Hays Code), written in 1930 and adopted by the movie industry in 1934 in the face of the growing threat of federal censorship, provides evidence of Hollywood's recognition of its critics' assertions—that filmmakers need to address the values they are disseminating. Section 2, rule 6, stated one of the code's value positions, its opposition to interracial love: "Miscegenation (sex relationship between the white and black races) is forbidden." The code's miscegenation rule specified "the white and black races," but Hollywood also applied it to other groups (like Latinos), with illuminating and sometimes perplexing variations.[17]

Movies have tended to differentiate Latinos on the basis of "coloredness" and "whiteness." According to the Hollywood canon on race and class, "Spanish" Latinos, particularly Zorro-type upper-class ones, functioned as white. Dark Latinos functioned as colored. When it came to Latino-Anglo screen love, this racial differentiation was further complicated by a movie gender gap.[18]

Dark Latino men often provided interracial sexual threats to Anglo women, with Anglo males (usually Anglo cowboys) asserting their superiority by riding to the rescue of their racially-sexually threatened damsels and whipping the bumbling Mexican villains. Simultaneously, dark Mexican women longed for, surrendered to, and sacrificed for Anglo men. Latino-Anglo screen love occasionally flourished, even leading to marriage, but these cases usually involved aristocratic, light-skinned Latinos, thus defining the relationship as intraracial, not interracial.

Until the code's decline in the 1950s (Hollywood formally buried it in 1968), movies maintained the stand that miscegenation should be avoided. When it occurred or seemed about to occur on screen, death or retribution usually followed. To a degree this element of Hollywood movie textbook values reflected widespread American social mores. When surveys conducted for Gunnar Myrdal's 1944 classic, *An American Dilemma: The Negro Problem and Modern Democracy,* asked southern whites what discriminatory lines must be upheld, their most common answer was "the bar against intermarriage and sexual intercourse involving white women."[19] Moreover, through interviews for his 1930 study of Mexican labor in the United States, economist Paul Taylor documented powerful Anglo opposition to intermarriage with Mexicans. For example, in justifying the barring of Mexican students from the local school, one south Texas Anglo tenant farmer argued:

> Because a damned greaser is not fit to sit side of a white girl. Anybody who wants to get into trouble around here can just try to put them in the same school. A man would rather his daughter was dead than that she should marry a Mexican.[20]

Yet, although the Supreme Court did not ban state antimiscegenation laws until 1967, interracial marriage had long occurred in the United States. But Hollywood elevated value lessons over the presentation of social reality. In adopting this pattern of portrayals, moviemakers functioned simultaneously as learners (reacting to the perceived existence of such social mores among many moviegoers), as teachers of values (adhering to these antimiscegenation "curriculum guidelines"), and as profits-at-all-costs capitalists (fearing that movies with interracial love might not "sell" among Anglos, particularly in the south).[21]

4. *Movies help shape expectations.* The Hays Code also ordained that movie crime could not pay. Screen criminals must ultimately receive their just desserts. But with the death of the Hays Code, Hollywood moved from a crime-cannot-pay to a crime-may-or-may-not-pay position of expectation-shaping.

This more flexible pedagogical stance toward the prospective results of criminality took over precisely during the rise in ethnic-theme films spurred by the civil rights movements of the 1960s. This confluence between societal and movie-industry developments has resulted in a flood of movies with ethnics and ethnic gangs as the principal perpetrators of crime. Hispanic Americans (along with Italian Americans) have now become nearly synonymous with screen crime. Simultaneously, newspaper and television newscasters have developed a fixation on ethnic gangs, and their often-sensationalistic coverage has reinforced and been reinforced by the movie-TV entertainment curriculum.

The impact of this media combination became depressingly apparent to me on the morning of September 18, 1986. Relaxing with a cup of coffee while reading the newspaper, I chanced to turn on the popular American television game show, *The $25,000 Pyramid*. That show's competition involves two pairs of unfamiliar contestants. For each team, a series of words appears on a screen in front of one player, who gives clues to guide the partner into identifying the maximum number of words within the time limit.

Suddenly the word "gangs" popped onto one contestant's screen. Without hesitation, he shouted, "They have lots of these in East L.A." (a heavily Mexican American section of Los Angeles). Responding immediately, his partner answered, "Gangs." Under competitive pressure, two strangers had instantly achieved mental communion through their coinciding visions of a Chicano community as synonymous with gangs. Moreover, they had transmitted this ethnic stereotype to a national television audience.

Unfortunately, East Los Angeles does have Chicano gangs. But it also has a multitude of far more prevalent elements, like families, schools, businesses, churches, and socially contributing organizations. Yet gangs, not any other element of East L.A. life, had rapidly and reflexively linked these total strangers. Why? The answer lies with the media, whose continuous fascination with Latino gangs—from news reports and documentaries to TV series and feature films—has elevated and reinforced them as *the* popular vision of East L.A. (and many other Latino communities).

5. *Movies provide models for action.* Anecdotal evidence provides myriad examples of movies' and television's popularizing clothing styles, verbal expressions ("Make my day"), and other forms of behavior. Fearing such imitation, protesters have railed against the release of such youth gang films as *A Clockwork Orange* (Great Britain, 1971), *The Warriors* (1979), and *Colors* (1988)—with Chicano gangs prominent in the latter—for fear that young people would imitate the screen gang violence. Although a few fights did break out near theaters, extensive imitative gang violence did not occur, which baffled those who proclaimed such deterministic positions about media impact.

But more critical, more subtle, and also more difficult to assess are "disinhibiting" effects. The important issue is not whether movies provoke people into action, but how they may subtly reduce or remove inhibitions to previously repressed actions. Have movies that celebrate vigilantism (like the *Death Wish* series) or flicks that make

teenage sex appear normative or "safe" contributed to societal violence or teenage promiscuity (and pregnancy) by "disinhibiting" such
behavior? Some African American comedians, for example, have
dropped the word "nigger" from their routines because of concern
that they may have unwittingly helped lower public inhibitions
against using it.

The movie curriculum on race and ethnicity, then, involves more
than the creation and dissemination of images. It involves the trans-
mission of information (correct or incorrect, balanced or tilted, contex-
tualized or distorted). It also involves the organization of information
and ideas, the influencing of values and attitudes, the shaping of
expectations, and the providing of models for action. Systematic longitudinal film content analysis should attempt to identify those messages.

Moviemakers as Textbook Writers

Content analysis can be used to reconstruct the history of the U.S.
movie treatment of Chicanos and suggest the potential effect of those
films.[22] This approach also raises collateral issues of control analysis
(why such films were made) and impact analysis (how such films
have actually influenced viewers). *Image* provides a good starting
point for examining these areas, as it refers to three focal points: the
creator of images, the film as captured image, and the viewer as
processor of these films into perceived and retained images.

Image creation occurs at both conglomerate and individual levels.
Conglomerate image-making occurs formally when an entire film
industry agrees on avoiding certain themes or presenting them in
specified ways, as when Hollywood studios accepted Hays Code gov-
ernance. Such image-making occurs informally when filmmakers
develop a "pack mentality," such as in the late 1960s and early 1970s
when the civil rights and ethnic power movements propelled
filmmakers into exploring—more often exploiting—ethnic themes
because they were hot. It also occurs when numbers of ethnic
filmmakers attempt to create alternative group images, as has happened episodically among Chicano filmmakers.

Yet despite these conglomerate tendencies, individual filmmaking
varies. Some filmmakers intentionally try to create celluloid ethnic

images. Others do so incidentally through the exclusion, inclusion, and depiction of ethnic characters, including background figures. Some create either ethnic characters or characters who just happen to have selected ethnic traits (such as surname or physical appearance), without suggesting that they are typical of any ethnic group. Others consciously attempt to create ethnic group portraits.

Filmmakers have used ethnic characters to examine national character and values. During World War II, movies consciously manipulated ethnic diversity to provide models for action, spreading the message that all Americans, including Latinos, have fought for their country and should be happy to continue doing so. In contrast, anti-Vietnam War movies, like *Platoon* (1986) and *Casualties of War* (1989), employed minority-group servicemen, including Latinos, as victims of battlefront dehumanization, societal sacrifice, and a misdirected foreign policy, as well as a backdrop for activist, center-stage white heroes and villains.

Filmmakers have sometimes tried to influence societal attitudes toward ethnic groups. Many post-World War II films consciously challenged antiethnic bigotry, including prejudice and discrimination against Mexican Americans in such films as *A Medal for Benny* (1945), *Trial* (1955), and *Giant* (1956). Other moviemakers have just as consciously disseminated negative images of ethnic groups, as occurred during the early silent era in such anti-Mexican flicks as *Bronco Billy and the Greaser* (1914), *The Greaser's Revenge* (1914), and *Guns and Greasers* (1918).

Some filmmakers have simply taken advantage of existing audience predispositions (often fueled by other movies) in order to provoke conditioned emotional responses. Films have played upon audience fears by manipulating the Latino menace, iconographically generated by groups of gun-toting Mexican horsemen in the Old West or swaggering young Latinos—presumably gangs—in contemporary urban films. Other times films have sought cheap laughs, like repeatedly portraying Mexican men as incompetent and Mexican señoritas as tempestuous—for example, the *Mexican Spitfire* series with Lupe Velez—in both cases stacking the deck by having them speak in heavily accented, garbled English. While trading on and manipulating these audience predispositions, filmmakers simultaneously reinforce images and further condition their audiences for future movies. In addition, this hinders revisionist filmmakers, including Latinos, in their quest to gain critical acceptance of alternative presentations—for example, portrayals of Latino *barrios* that *don't* feature gangs. [Similarly, some white critics attacked African American filmmaker Spike Lee because he did not include drug dealers in *Do the Right Thing* (1989), and what's a ghetto without drug dealers?]

As with textbook writers, once filmmakers have completed their work and their films begin to be shown, the movies (like textbooks) take on lives of their own. Celluloid images may go on for decades as television reruns and on videocassette. With each viewing further removed temporally from the societal context in which the films were made and originally screened, the filmmakers' textbooks become increasingly independent of original intentions.

The Dilemma of Assessing Media Impact

Beyond content and control analysis stands the question of impact analysis—the images that ultimately take root in the minds of viewers as they "read" and absorb the film. Viewers may react consciously by analytically considering the film's treatment of ethnic characters. Far more often they react unconsciously, since people usually go to feature films to be entertained, not to be educated about ethnicity. Only occasionally, such as when some viewers select social problem films, do they go to learn about ethnicity and interethnic relations. Moreover, major variations exist as to what different viewers consciously or unconsciously extract from the same film, how these readings interact with their existent sets of beliefs, and what becomes incorporated into personal images of various groups or cultures.[23]

Scholarly and popular analyses of the societal impact of the media, particularly the entertainment media, have tended to become polarized. Many analysts, including some scholars, have taken a nearly deterministic position, asserting a "hypodermic needle effect" based on the assumption of a direct causal (sometimes unicausal) link between media and the development of individual, group, and national attitudes and behavior. At the opposite extreme stand most feature filmmakers and creators of entertainment television, who generally claim that they make fictional media merely to entertain, reject responsibility for what their films might incidentally or unintentionally teach, and at times even deny their teaching potential. In the middle stand those scholars who agree that media, including movies and fictional television, do teach, but argue that research to date has generally failed to reveal the precise nature of audience learning. For example, in *The Media Monopoly*, Ben Bagdikian argues, "It is a truism among political scientists that while it is not possible for the media to tell the population what to think, they do tell the public what to think about."[24]

Research to date does provide insights, however. Scholarship on the impact of movies and television on intergroup perceptions has been sporadic and temporally limited, focusing overwhelmingly on the measurement of short-range effects of specific shows, often in empirically controlled settings. Research has concluded that films and television shows have sometimes reinforced prejudices, and at other times have modified them.[25]

Although research results vary, they do coalesce around two basic conclusions. First, feature films and fictional television do influence interethnic perceptions; viewers do learn about race and ethnicity from the entertainment media. Second, the nature of that influence varies with the individual viewer, who provides a key variable concerning the extent, content, and tenacity of that conscious and unconscious learning. In short, scholarship confirms that old social-science axiom, "*Some* people are influenced by *some* media, at *some* time."

Unfortunately for those interested in the effect of ethnic-content motion pictures, such studies virtually ended in the late 1940s with the advent of television, as communications-impact scholars turned their attention to television, the new kid on the media block. Moreover, as Garth Jowett and James M. Linton note:

> Most of the research on movie influence deals with individual movies, but it is the cumulative effect of years of viewing movies which so far defies adequate measurement and which is of real interest in any assessment of the movies' impact on society and culture.[26]

In recent years, however, scholars have developed provocative new methods for deriving insights into film impact. After examining the responses of Hispanic and non-Hispanic critics to various Latino-directed or produced films about Chicanos—including *Stand and Deliver* and *Born in East L.A.*—Chon Noriega determined that ethnicity was a primary factor separating reviewer reactions. Latino critics focused on the films' cultural content and social conflict, and Anglo critics complained about the absence of violence and criminality, deriding the films for portraying Latino communities as too wholesome and for not presenting Latinos as social deviants. Burdened by their own media-driven expectations, Anglo critics berated these films because they failed to conform to *their* stereotypes of Latino *barrios*.[27]

Analysts have also proposed theories of intercultural perceptions, in which the entertainment media play a significant role. Sam Keen's *Faces of the Enemy: Reflections of the Hostile Imagination* and Vamik Volkan's *The Need to Have Enemies and Allies: From Clinical Practice to International Relations* argue that people—individuals, groups, and nations—have an innate psychological need to hate some racial, ethnic, cultural, or national "other."[28] In his article "The Convenient Villain: The Early Cinema Views the Mexican-American," Blaine Lamb asserts that Mexican characters served that "other" role for early U.S. movie audiences, who needed an easily identifiable, easily despised foil for Anglo heroes.[29]

Other scholars have examined the process of media learning by applying different theories of audience reception, drawing on such ideas as schema theory, Gestalt psychology, Albert Bandura's concept of the "sleeper effect," and Leon Festinger's theory of cognitive dissonance.[30] Taken as a whole, these psychological and communications reception theories can be synthesized into the following rules of thumb when applied to movie depictions of ethnic groups or foreign nations.

If a depiction coincides with already-held beliefs, it tends to reinforce them. In contrast, if that depiction directly challenges a viewer's beliefs, particularly if these are deep and emotional, the viewer tends to reject, modify, or mute that film's portrayals as a source of generalizable knowledge. But if a depiction falls only marginally outside of the viewer's perceptual framework, without directly challenging it, these new images will more likely penetrate and modify the viewer's belief system, add to the pool of knowledge, and influence personal ideational schema. In particular, if a movie portrays an ethnic group or nation about which the viewer knows little or has no deep feelings, that "information" is most likely to become part of the viewer's personal intercultural "encyclopedia." For viewers who live in places with no Mexican Americans, *Colors* and *Boulevard Nights* might well be basic sources for their knowledge about Chicanos. In contrast, Chicanos who live or spend time in *barrios* can draw on personal experiences to test the validity of those films and either internalize or reject those images.

Conclusion

Movies teach. Although we can never be certain what any individual may learn from movies, evidence clearly demonstrates that feature films have contributed to intergroup stereotyping and understanding, as well as to positive or negative self-concept. They form, in short, a powerful public textbook.

This phenomenon has implications that reach far beyond either scholarship or the movie industry itself. Movie teaching is inextricably linked to school education, simultaneously reinforcing and impeding school efforts to build better interethnic understanding and self-concept. Long after school education has ended, we continue learning through the media. To prepare students for this eventuality, schools need to develop their media analytical literacy, particularly about multicultural representation.[31] By investigating the roots of interethnic perceptions and carefully applying this knowledge, such as in schools, we can make strides toward mitigating interethnic misconceptions and strengthening self-concept as one avenue to societal equity.

Notes

1. See Ellen Seiter, "Stereotypes and the Media: A Re-evaluation," *Jour+nal of Communication* 36, no. 2 (Spring 1986): 14–26.

2. For a discussion of this concept, see Carlos E. Cortés, "The Societal Curriculum: Implications for Multiethnic Education," in *Education in the 80's: Multiethnic Education*, James A. Banks, ed. (Washington: National Education Association, 1981), 24–32.

3. I address this issue in greater detail in my book in progress on the history of the U.S. motion picture treatment of race and ethnicity.

4. For an examination of content analysis dilemmas, see Carlos E. Cortés, "The History of Ethnic Images in Film: The Search for a Methodology," *MELUS: The Journal of the Society for the Study of the Multi-Ethnic Literature of the United States* 11, no. 3 (Fall 1984): 63–77.

5. One classic and oft-cited example of the socio-semiological analysis of film is Will Wright, *Sixguns and Society: A Structural Study of the Western* (Berkeley: University of California Press, 1975). Among the introductions to content analysis are Bernard R. Berelson, *Content Analysis in Communication Research* (Glencoe, Ill.: Free Press, 1952) and Klaus Krippendorff, *Content Analysis: An Introduction to Its Methodology* (Beverly Hills, Calif.: Sage Publications, 1980).

6. In this essay I reluctantly use the term "American" to mean people and things of the United States. I do so not only because it is used that way in the United States, but more importantly because I have not found an appropriate alternative. This usage has become a source of rightful indignation on the part of Latin Americans, who correctly claim that they, too, are Americans (the Western Hemisphere is composed of North and South America). This may be a terminology problem without a happy ending. In Spanish, *norteamericano* serves as a convenient label for persons of the United States, but "North American" and "North America" do not work in English as reasonable substitutes for the United States, as those terms apply to the entire North American continent. Other verbal artifices—for example, "United Statesian" or "United States of American"—are simply too precious and cumbersome. Therefore, after struggling for years with this problem, I have unhappily come to the conclusion that, despite the word's distorting aspects, it is best to use "American" for United States people and things . . . until someone comes up with a better alternative.

7. For the analysis of the U.S. feature film treatment of Mexico, see Carlos E. Cortés, "To View a Neighbor: The Hollywood Textbook on Mexico," in *Images of Mexico in the United States*, John H. Coatsworth and Carlos Rico, eds. (San Diego: Center for U.S.-Mexican Studies, University of California, San Diego, 1989), 91–118.

8. For their help in this quest for categorical rigor, I would like to thank my friends Charles Wetherell, director of the Laboratory for Historical Research, University of California, Riverside, for his appropriately scathing criticisms of my efforts to create a valid and systematic approach to content analysis, and research assistants Thomas Thompson and Richard Turner for their insights and patience in helping me to transform some of my ideas into realities.

9. For an analysis of *Requiem for a Heavyweight*, see Arthur Ramírez, "Anglo View of a Mexican-American Tragedy: Rod Serling's *Requiem for a Heavyweight*," *Journal of Popular Culture* 13 (Spring 1980): 501–4.

10. Gerald Michael Greenfield and I have adopted this approach in our article "Harmony and Conflict of Intercultural Images: The Treatment of Mexico in U.S. Feature Films and Textbooks," *Mexican Studies/Estudios Mexicanos* 7, no. 2 (Summer 1991): 283–301.

11. For a discussion of this issue, see Charles Ramírez Berg, "Stereotyping in Films in General and of the Hispanic in Particular," *Howard Journal of Communications* 2, no. 3 (Summer 1990): 286–300.

12. Daniel J. Boorstin, *The Image, or Whatever Happened to the Importance of Fairy Tales* (New York: Knopf, 1976).

13. Bruno Bettelheim, *The Uses of Enchantment: The Meaning and Importance of Fairy Tales* (New York: Knopf, 1976).

14. George Comstock, *The Impact of Television on American Institutions and the American Public* (Honolulu: East-West Communications Institute, East-West Center, 1977), 20–21.

15. Henry James Forman, *Our Movie Made Children* (New York: Macmillan, 1933).

16. Robert Sklar, *Movie-Made America: A Social History of American Film* (New York: Random House, 1975).

17. "Colored" in this essay refers to individuals or groups that have been categorized as nonwhite in American history or culture (primarily by mainstream white American perceptions or official government labeling).

18. I examine this issue in my forthcoming article, "Gender Gap/Gender Trap: Hispanic-Anglo Love in U.S. Motion Pictures," to be published in the proceedings of the Fourth International Conference of the Hispanic Cultures of the United States.

19. Gunnar Myrdal, *An American Dilemma: The Negro Problem and Modern Democracy* (New York: Harper & Brothers, 1944), 60.

20. Paul S. Taylor, *Mexican Labor in the United States,* vol. 1 (Berkeley: University of California Press, 1930), 389.

21. Thomas Cripps, "The Myth of the Southern Box Office: A Factor in Racial Stereotyping in American Movies, 1920–1940," in *The Black Experience in America: Selected Essays,* James C. Curtis and Louis L. Gould, eds. (Austin: University of Texas Press, 1970), 116–44.

22. For more lengthy discussions of this issue, see Allen L. Woll, *The Latin Image in American Film* (Los Angeles: UCLA Latin American Center Publications, 1977; rpt. 1980), and Arthur G. Pettit, *Images of the Mexican American in Fiction and Film* (College Station: Texas A&M University Press, 1980).

23. I address this issue in "Pride, Prejudice, and Power: The Mass Media as Societal Educator on Diversity," in *Prejudice, Polemic, or Progress?* James Lynch, Celia Modgil, and Sohan Modgil, eds. (Hampshire, U.K.: Falmer Press, forthcoming).

24. Ben Bagdikian, *The Media Monopoly* (Boston: Beacon Press, 1983), xvi.

25. For example, see Ruth C. Peterson and L. L. Thurstone, *Motion Pictures and the Social Attitudes of Children* (New York: Macmillan, 1933), 35–38; Irwin C. Rosen, "The Effect of the Motion Picture 'Gentleman's Agreement' on Attitudes toward Jews," *Journal of Psychology* 26 (1948): 525–36; and Louis E. Raths and Frank N. Trager, "Public Opinion and 'Crossfire,' " *Journal of Educational Sociology* 21, no. 6 (1948): 345–68.

26. Garth Jowett and James M. Linton, *Movies as Mass Communication* (Beverly Hills, Calif.: Sage Publications, 1980), 110.

27. Chon Noriega, "Chicano Cinema and the Horizon of Expectations: A Discursive Analysis of Film Reviews in the Mainstream, Alternative and Hispanic Press, 1987–1988" *Aztlán: A Journal of Chicano Studies* 19, no. 2 (Fall 1990): forthcoming.

28. Sam Keen, *Faces of the Enemy: Reflections of the Hostile Imagination* (New York: Harper & Row, 1986), and Vamik Volkan, *The Need to Have Enemies and Allies: From Clinical Practice to International Relations* (Northvale, N.J.: J. Aronson, 1988).

29. Blaine S. Lamb, "The Convenient Villain: The Early Cinema Views the Mexican-American," *Journal of the West* 14, no. 4 (October 1975): 75–81.

30. For example, see Leon Festinger, *A Theory of Cognitive Dissonance* (Evanston, Ill.: Row, Peterson, 1957), and Albert Bandura, *Social Learning Theory* (Englewood Cliffs, N.J.: Prentice-Hall, 1977).

31. See Carlos E. Cortés, "Empowerment through Media Literacy: A Multicultural Approach," in *Empowerment through Multicultural Education,* Christine E. Sleeter, ed. (Albany: State University of New York Press, 1991), 143–57.

Pochos and Other Extremes in Mexican Cinema; or, El Cine Mexicano se va de Bracero, 1922–1963[1]

David R. Maciel

To the memory of German "Tin Tan" Valdes, creative and authentic "pocho."

Introduction

Mexico's concern for its population in the United States dates as far back as the Texas Rebellion of 1836 and continues to the present. Mexican scholarly and cultural works have shown constant preoccupation with the Mexicano/Chicano community in the United States,[2] with this interest and attention manifesting itself in diplomatic, political, and educational efforts.[3] Within Mexican cultural production, cinema has been particularly instrumental in depicting Mexico's views toward and interpretations of *el México de afuera*. Since 1922, Mexican cinema has produced over one hundred narrative features on this specific theme. Although these films vary in structure, ideological constructs, artistic worth, style, and narration, they nonetheless encompass the following general characteristics: (1) All of these productions have strong didactic messages, the most common being that if you emigrate to the United States only heartache, disappointment, and oppression await you. (2) Related to the previous point is that most of these films end in tragedy. The migratory experience is consistently portrayed negatively. The main characters always return to Mexico; none of the principals ever chooses to stay permanently in the United States; and those Mexicanos/Chicanos who do reside north of the Río Bravo often speak of a return to their native country. (3) Mexican cinematic preoccupation with this theme responds to internal issues, cycles of Mexican emigration to the United States, and to Mexican foreign policy. (4) Many of the most outstanding Mexican filmmakers,[4] such as Miguel Contreras Torres, Alejandro Galindo, Pedro Armendáriz, Lola Beltrán, Eulalio "El Piporro" González, Jorge Negrete, David Silva, and Lucha Villa, participated in such productions. (5) As a filmic cycle, these films include comedies, musicals, melodramas, and action features; it is the only Mexican cycle that has yet to run its course. Even at the present time, there are films in production that deal with the Chicano/Mexicano experience in the United States.

These films, widely viewed on both sides of the border, clearly merit scholarly inquiry and analysis. Up until the 1960s, motion pictures were the most important artistic forms of popular entertainment in Mexico.[5] Mexican cinema has been of equal significance in the United States, where an extensive chain of Spanish-language theaters throughout the Southwest, and in other areas with large Latino populations, has operated on a year-round basis.[6]

As a subject of analysis, Mexican films that focus on the Chicano/Mexicano experience in the United States open a wealth of avenues for study. Aesthetically, these productions serve to display the origins, technical and artistic aspects, and development of filmmaking in Mexico. As historical documents, they are essential primary sources for understanding the evolution of Mexican thought and attitudes about compatriots north of the Río Bravo. As such, then, these films are an important chapter in the complex and dynamic relationship between Mexico and Aztlán.

Aztlán in the Cinema of Mexico: The Early Decades, 1922–1965

El Cine Mexicano se va de Bracero

Whenever a rich, industrialized economy borders on an underdeveloped nation, labor exploitation and worker immigration are bound to occur. This was precisely the situation that faced the American Southwest and the Mexican North over the past century, a century marked by dynamic capital growth north of the border and increased, controversial emigration from the south. The northward migration provided great benefits for the industrializing Southwest, whose mines, factories, and agricultural fields reaped the unearned increment left by an exploitative "Mexican scale." It also engendered a century of bitterness toward immigrants on both sides of the border.[7]

Mexican immigration to the United States has been continuous since the days of the California Gold Rush (1849). It reached its height between 1910 and 1929, due to three main reasons: the overall effects of the Mexican Revolution, the economic growth of the Southwest, and increased labor demands in the United States because of World War I. It has been estimated that during the first three decades of the twentieth century, more than one million Mexicans, nearly ten percent of the entire population of Mexico, crossed the Río Bravo in search of a better life.[8]

In 1910, social and political upheaval erupted throughout Mexico. This transformation, which started as a political movement against the dictatorship of Porfirio Díaz, had significant effects in the shaping of the current modern Mexican state and society. On a more immediate level, it greatly affected the process of immigration. Intense internal warfare rocked an already fragile economy. Agricultural production fell drastically, as did other sectors of the Mexican economy; unemployment and poverty increased; and laborers were forcibly recruited away from the factories and countryside into the armies.[9] As the fighting intensified in Mexico, the movement northward did also. People began leaving their land mainly for economic reasons, but many Mexicans who had been on losing sides of the battles left for fear of political reprisals. It has been estimated that about one-third of a million Mexicans immigrated to the United States between 1910 and 1920.[10]

Throughout the 1920s, the number of Mexican immigrants continued to increase. Approximately 427,000 Mexicans were admitted legally into the United States in the period from 1920 to 1929, as the difficult socioeconomic conditions in Mexico, the unprecedented growth of the U.S. economy, and the wage differential between Mexico and the United States all combined to spur immigration. In 1925, a cost-of-living study revealed that agricultural workers in most parts of Mexico did not earn wages "sufficient to afford a livelihood." The study further showed that a Mexican worker's purchasing power was only one-fourteenth that of an Anglo American worker.[11]

The continuing departure of emigrants became a national Mexican concern. A twofold policy on emigration was undertaken by Mexican authorities: first, to provide for the legal protection of those who had already gone north from Mexico; and, in order to dissuade against further emigration, to disseminate information about the harsh working conditions and related problems that awaited Mexican workers in the United States. A systematic campaign was aimed at informing prospective emigrants of social discrimination and economic exploitation encountered by the Mexican-origin population. Based on former accounts, consular reports, and published testimonies, Mexican federal and state authorities distributed such information on a massive scale.[12]

Meanwhile, the return of U.S. military personnel at the close of World War I and a recession in the early 1920s in the American economy resulted in nativist feelings and policies designed to restrict and regulate Mexican labor more effectively. As would be the case in later periods of economic downturns, Mexican immigrants became the scapegoats. Throughout the southwestern states, Mexicans by the hundreds lost their jobs in massive firings and found themselves facing hardships even worse, at times, than those they had left in Mexico.[13]

Mexican immigration subsided in the decade of the 1930s as a result of massive unemployment and the deep economic crisis in the United States. To diffuse the frustration of the U.S. private sector and public opinion in general, a policy was put into effect to repatriate thousands of workers back to Mexico. It has been estimated that all together over one-half million Mexicans were sent back during the years of the Great Depression.[14]

In the decade of the 1940s, national and international events and notable changes in the bilateral relationship prompted additional interest and concern in resuming Mexican immigration to the United States on a broad scale. The onset of World War II created the need for an extensive labor force. Through mutual accord, the governments of Mexico and the United States began the first large-scale recruitment and contracting of Mexican migrant workers in the United States. The Bracero program was renewed several times during the war years, amended and again renewed throughout the 1950s and the early 1960s; it was finally terminated in December 1964.[15] In this period, many Mexican workers, who either were not contracted as *braceros* or did not want to adhere to *bracero* agreements, began crossing the border illegally.[16]

The Bracero program and emigration issues in general became a national concern in Mexico, and subsequently received extensive attention from the printed media, the scholarly community, and the cinema. Altogether, five Mexican narrative films were produced that directly dealt with aspects of the *bracero* experience: three dramas and two comedies.

The first production that dealt with the Mexican emigrant experience was the 1922 silent *El hombre sin patria*, produced, directed, and starred in by Miguel Contreras Torres. This pioneer motion picture clearly reflected and reinforced Mexican attitudes and concerns toward its emigrants. The film recounts the misadventures of a young, upper-class Mexican who leads a wasteful and frivolous life. After numerous conflicts with his father, he is finally kicked out and disinherited. He opts to follow the example of others and emigrate to the United States. Since initially he has ample funds, his early stay is a continuation of his previous escapades in Mexico. Soon, however, his money runs out, and he begins to experience the cruel realities of Mexicans in the United States. Various discriminatory practices and degrading employment patterns make up the greater portion of the film. The low point is reached when in self-defense he kills an evil and racist foreman. Fearful for his life, a no-longer-young Rodolfo returns to his homeland. He reconciles with his family and begins to make amends for the past. The film ends on a happy note with the main character now a mature, hardworking, patriotic Mexican finding true love and a rightful path to life.[17]

El hombre sin patria was far from the best feature in the long and distinguished career of Miguel Contreras Torres.[18] Yet the film is a seminal one on two accounts: it is the earliest Mexican motion picture on the subject, and the first one shot on location in Los Angeles and San Diego. The film was so well received that Contreras Torres added sound and years later released a second version of the same film, now a "talkie."[19] Its ideological message is direct: if you emigrate to the United States, nothing but racism and oppression await you. As difficult as your situation might be in Mexico, you still will have family warmth, familiar surroundings, and the opportunity to work toward building a postrevolutionary Mexico. The title of the feature, "man without a country," is consistent with Mexican attitudes toward those compatriots who left for the United States and thus have no real homeland or roots.

Not until 1938 would Mexican cinema address a similar theme again, with the film *La China Hilaria*. This inconsequential and minor feature is one of the precursors to the *ranchera* cycle [20] that would establish itself a year later with *Allá en el Rancho Grande* (1939). *La China Hilaria* narrates the story of a rural worker named Isidro who decides to migrate to the United States seeking better employment. His goal is to find work, save his earnings, and return to his home to marry his sweetheart Hilaria. After a long wait without receiving any news from Isidro, Hilaria relocates and begins a successful career singing in local *palenques* (*fiestas*). Two men court Hilaria, and although she likes one, she remains faithful and waits for Isidro. The prodigal son finally returns, now married, however, to another. Predictably, Hilaria ends with her one sincere love, and the film closes with a happy ending. Similar to *El hombre sin patria*, this production highlights the negative changes in the character of a Mexican after a prolonged stay in the United States. The point is made that Isidro's values and moral fiber were diminished by prolonged exposure to North America. The one other memorable aspect of *La China Hilaria* is the appearance of the great future star Pedro Armendáriz in one of his first starring roles.[21]

A much more interesting early production is Alfonso Patiño Gómez's *Pito Pérez se va de bracero* (1947). The film attempted to combine two important elements: the lovable picaresque main character of the celebrated novel, *La vida inútil de Pito Pérez*, and the Bracero program. José Rubén Romero, one of the major novelists of the Mexican Revolution, imaginatively revived the tradition of the Spanish picaresque novel and adapted it with great success to the time and place of postrevolutionary Mexico. His *pícaro* (rogue), Pito Pérez, travels through various regions of Mexico interacting with a wide spectrum of society and institutions. Through acute observations and biting dialogue, the novel satirizes and denounces many of the social ills and governmental shortcomings of the period. Pito Pérez gained great popularity and became an icon of Mexican popular culture.[22] It is therefore not surprising that filmmakers would envision the same character having an equal success on the silver screen. An added aspect of this film was to place Pito Pérez in the context of current national concern: Mexican immigrant workers in the United States.

The story follows the improbable misadventures of Pito Pérez who, after a series of misfortunes in Mexico, joins a group of prospective *braceros* as they make their way to the United States. Upon crossing, Pito Pérez and the group begin work as field workers. Finding this type of employment exhausting and hazardous, Pito Pérez searches for easier and better-paying work. His next escapade is as a dish-washer in a dance hall where he meets the heroine of the story. It is later learned that she, along with the owner of the dance hall and other accomplices, are in the business of illegal trafficking of Mexican workers. Violence later erupts when police attempt to break up and capture the principals involved. The main leaders are wounded and captured, and Pito Pérez is, because of guilt by association, incarcerated. His blonde friend and his benefactor—who remained aloof from the sting—pay the fine, and Pito Pérez is deported. The film closes with Pito Pérez returning to his native Mexico having learned his lesson and vowing never to return to the United States.[23]

All the charm, freshness, and relevant social satire for which the original Pito Pérez was admired, however, was lost in this opportunistic and little-thought-out production. For Pito Pérez to ridicule the "American way of life" was not as relevant and entertaining for Mexican audiences, who preferred that Pito Pérez address domestic national issues. On an aesthetic level, *Pito Pérez se va de bracero* was not creative, well conceptualized, or even properly cast.

In 1954, Mexico premiered an impressive film, *Espaldas mojadas*, directed by the respected filmmaker Alejandro Galindo. *Espaldas mojadas* opens with an aerial shot of Ciudad Juárez, while the narrator informs the viewer that, "On this side of the Río Bravo it is still Mexico, where Spanish is spoken and songs are sung to the Virgin of Guadalupe . . . on the other side of the Río Grande, as the Gringos call it, are skyscrapers and it's where everyone owns a car." It is a country, the narrator wryly concludes, that "forty years of movies have presented as a place where everyone is happy."

Rafael, the main character, has just arrived in Ciudad Juárez from the city of San Luis Potosí. He has been working as a tractor driver in the region of El Manta. When he goes to a *bracero* hiring hall, he tries to get work as a tractor driver, but he is promptly and unceremoniously informed that for Mexicans there is only one kind of work—as a field hand. Rafael has no "working papers" or passport that would enable him to work legally in the United States. Margarita, a bar waitress, befriends him, whereupon he tells her that he must flee Mexico because of some trouble he got himself into over a woman. The incident involved the son of a prominent and influential leader of the community, and Rafael is fearful of reprisals. Margarita directs him to Frank Mendoza, a *coyote* who specializes in getting *espaldas mojadas* across the border for a Mr. Sterling, who hires undocumented workers on a large scale for agricultural work. That same night, Rafael and a group of migrant workers cross the Río Grande, but tragedy strikes. Shot at by the U.S. border patrol, some in the group are killed or wounded, including a new friend of Rafael, Felipe, who—in a last and symbolic gesture—gives Rafael all his money and asks him to cast his body into the river so that it will float back into Mexico.

Upon his arrival in El Paso, Rafael, who does not speak English, requires the help of a *pocha* (Chicana) in order to buy two hot dogs. He also meets up with Luis Villarreal, a happy-go-lucky *pícaro* who knows the emigrant situation well, having "skulked around" the United States as a hobo.

After working as a dishwasher in El Paso, Rafael decides that one dollar a day is not the kind of money he wants, so he decides to go "on the road." After a run-in with Sterling and a reunion with Luis, Rafael enters a roadside cafe, where he encounters a waitress by the name of María de Consuelo, whom he had met briefly after crossing the border. When a policeman comes in, she hides Rafael as the cop utters the classic line, "You seen a Mexican with a brown leather jacket? Looks more like a wop than a Mexican." After she saves Rafael from being apprehended, María vents her frustrations with the oppressive North American system: "I'm not Mexican, I'm a Pocha. The Mexicans don't like us and the Gringos look down on us."

Alejandro Galindo is the Mexican film director who best captures the agonizing and difficult situation of Chicanos vis-à-vis their country of origin and, at the same time, North American institutions and discriminatory practices. Through the actions and messages of María's dialogues, Mexican viewers were exposed to a sensitive, well-informed, and complex Chicana character. The focus of her character was on the rejection and exploitation that Chicanos are subjected to on *both* sides of the border.

Rafael is very attracted to María; he asks her to marry him and she agrees, whereupon they plan to meet in Juárez in order to marry and settle there. The irony of the plot is that as Rafael tries to reenter Mexico, once again through a hail of bullets (from Sterling and the police), he now runs afoul of the *Mexican* border patrol. A dialogue ensues in which Rafael pleads his case by saying that he is a Mexican national and wants to get back into the country. The officer tells him that there are many people with swarthy skin—Pochos, Greeks,

Italians. "When will you people realize," continues the officer, "the trouble that you cause by crossing illegally? Have you no dignity?" "Dignity?" asks Rafael angrily. "We're hungry, that's the reason."

After giving the Mexican official a brief rundown on the things that are wrong with Mexico, Rafael pleads to be allowed to stay. It works; he is released and continues on his way to meet María. At the cabaret where he meets her, he runs into Sterling. Rafael and others proceed to take revenge on Sterling by giving him a severe beating. It is suggested that Sterling not be killed there but that he should be taken to the river and dumped in. Forced to swim across the river, Sterling is shot to death by U.S. border patrolmen as he attempts to reach the shore.

Leaving the scene of the killing of Sterling, a member of the group reassures Rafael with an irony-laden observation: "Neither you nor we killed him. It was he who stupidly tried to swim to the other side." Thus, trying to make a fresh start, Rafael, María, and Luis decide to move on and they depart to the interior of Mexico, having had more than their fill of being *mojados*.[24]

Espaldas mojadas continues to be by far the single best Mexican commercial production on the subject of Mexican emigration. The film's powerful impact is due to its hard-hitting look at the socioeconomic problems of Mexico: the hopelessness of existence for some sectors of the Mexican population, the need for many Mexican workers to emigrate to the United States as a safety valve, and even the condition of the Chicano community. In addition, the acting, directing, and plot are all first-rate.

During this period, comedian Eulalio González, "El Piporro," addressed Bracero/Chicano themes in two well-received popular films, *El bracero del año* and *El Pocho*. "El Piporro" established a unique precedent in Mexican cinema as the first star who also served as director, screenwriter, and producer.[25]

In *El bracero del año* (1963), "El Piporro" stars as a typical would-be migrant worker. Natalio Reyes Colas (El Piporro) crosses illegally with a group of others in search of work in the Texas agriculture fields. After numerous escapades, all in a lighthearted vein, he is selected as *bracero* of the year. As a prize, our hero asks for and is granted his green card. He flies to Los Angeles where he is further rewarded by being honored with a parade and festivities in his honor. Similar encounters ensue with Natalio's return to Mexico and to his girlfriend whom he had left behind, resulting in a very farfetched and silly Mexican success film.[26]

Pochos and Other Extremes

Mexican views and perspectives toward the Chicano community had had an ongoing and dynamic process. The original relationship between the two Mexican communities—the Chicano and the Mexicano—began and developed in the nineteenth century as one of mutual and sincere support, cooperation and struggle against the forces of colonialism and imperialism.[27] This relationship changed, however, with the advent of the new century, as Mexican immigration escalated and millions of Mexicans permanently settled in the United States, fostering resentment from Mexico. In later decades, these feelings were compounded by the fact that when Mexican travelers visited the United States, they encountered first or second generation Chicanos who seemed to be out of step with contemporary Mexican culture and idiom. The Mexican term *pocho*, which denoted such a condition, came into popular usage.[28]

Specifically, the label *pocho* was placed on Chicanos whom Mexicans believed consciously attempted to assimilate into U.S. society at the expense of their Mexican roots. This term signifies a negative view of *lo mexicano*. Many Mexicans alleged that Chicanos also have a condescending attitude toward the homeland. Later, class biases were incorporated into the stereotypes: most Chicanos were thought to be descendants of the lower classes, since it was widely believed in Mexico that only the poor, the unskilled, and the illiterate emigrated to the United States. Between the 1940s and late 1960s, *pocho* was the most-employed Mexican label for Chicanos.[29] It is not surprising, then, that between 1922 and 1970, Chicano characters in Mexican cinema were, with very few exceptions, portrayed as stereotypical *pochos*.

In *Soy mexicano de acá de este lado* (1951) the themes of the *pocho* and the *bracero* are combined by the veteran director Miguel Contreras Torres. The title of the film—"I am a Mexican from this side of the border"—underscores its message. Through two principal characters, a *pocho* born in Texas but now residing in Mexico, and an ex-*bracero*, striking differences between the Chicano and Mexican communities are accentuated. Implied by the title and theme of the film is that citizens on the Mexican side of the border are true *mexicanos*, whereas those on the other side are no longer *mexicanos*, but *pochos*. This theme is clearly conveyed by Freddie, the *pocho* character, in a lengthy sequence in which he outlines the condition and plight of the Chicano community, stressing its loss of *mexicano* identity, cultural values, and traditions. The effectiveness of such moments is lost, however, in the long and erratic melodrama, which involves three characters: a *cabaretera* (dancer in a saloon), a slick playboy who falls in love with the dancer, and his best friend, the *pocho*. After numerous escapades the two *mexicano* characters wind up together, and the film closes with a happy ending. *Soy mexicano de acá de este lado* exhibits Contreras Torres's fervent patriotism and belief in the enduring Mexican traditions and values, but little else. The main problem is the lack of a defined story or character; too many themes were attempted, but left undeveloped.[30]

Acá las tortas (1951) carries the theme and concept of the *pocho* even further than previous films. Here, *pocho* is even applied to the son and daughter of a Mexican couple who owns a small restaurant that specializes in *tortas*. The son and the daughter, upon returning to Mexico after completing studies in the United States, display American influences, traits, and mannerisms. The film makes the statement that *pochos* are not just Chicanos, but also those Mexicans who live in the United States temporarily and behave in an Americanized manner upon returning to Mexico. In *Acá las tortas*, the point is made even with respect to food. The son redeems himself toward the end of the film by promising to join his parents in selling *tortas* and rejecting non-Mexican dishes.

Acá las tortas displays all the variations of Mexican concerns of the dangers of Americanization. The solution, according to the filmmakers, is to inculcate the country's youth with Mexican values and nationalism, since these youth were thought to be the most susceptible to foreign influences. The "American way of life" is portrayed in a static negative vein: *lo mexicano* is the only positive direction for Mexico; *lo gringo* will only corrupt and degrade Mexican society and traditions.[31]

The *pocho* theme took an improbable twist in the 1963 feature *México de mi corazón*. This time the story is not about the typical assimilated Chicanos, but two very nationalistic pro-Mexican Chicanas who win a talent show for the best interpretation of a Mexican song at the

Million-Dollar Theater in Los Angeles. As first prize, they receive an all-expense-paid trip to Mexico City. The two Chicana first cousins, played by leading Mexican singing stars Lola Beltrán and Lucha Villa, thus are able to visit Mexico for the first time ever in search of their roots. A number of highly patriotic Mexican singing numbers make up the bulk of the film, with the plot centered on the courtship of the cousins by two Mexican suitors. The predictable end has them falling in love with their beaus and with Mexico, choosing to stay in the land of their ancestors.[32]

Although the Chicanas are called *pochas*, they are not ridiculed or satirized. In fact, the beginning narration addresses the Mexican population of Los Angeles in a most positive manner. In comparison to other features that stress the assimilationist aspects of Chicanos, *México de mi corazón* emphasizes the *mexicanidad* of this community. The Chicanas are shown as sincere in their love for Mexican traditions and people. This apparent strength, though, is the film's main problem. It is difficult to accept Lola Beltrán and Lucha Villa, two of Mexico's premier *ranchera* singers, as Chicanas; the sparse use of English and "Spanglish" does not make the characters more believable. Yet *México de mi corazón* did at least acknowledge that within the Chicano community diverse sectors and individuals retain their native language and traditional cultural values.

Another important film is *Los Desarraigados* (1958), an early attempt at a sensitive portrayal of the immigrant experience. The story focuses on a typical family that has left Mexico shortly after the Revolution and immigrated to the United States. As the title—the uprooted—indicates, their existence on foreign soil is a tragic one. The two eldest sons are lost fighting for the Allied cause in World War II. Even with hard work and efforts at accommodation in the United States, family harmony is absent in the home. The parents face severe intergenerational conflicts with their two remaining sons and their daughter. The elder son, Joe, is a struggling reformed alcoholic, who is in constant fear of returning to his old habit. Jimmy, the youngest, has come under the influence of bad company, winds up peddling drugs, and is ultimately arrested and jailed. The daughter, Alice, initially rejects her heritage and runs away from home. After various escapades, the parents finally achieve a partial fulfillment of their dreams through their children. Alice returns home repentent and wishing to start again; Joe promises to travel to Mexico to be with his new love, a woman from Mexico; and Jimmy is released from jail under bond with the assurance that he will leave his life of crime. The Pacheco family at last has some hope for the future.

Again, the main theme here is the human cost of leaving Mexico and immigrating to the United States. Overall, however, the film is somewhat disappointing and does not achieve its full potential. In spite of the fine cast, which includes José Elias Moreno, Pedro Armendáriz, Sonia Furio, Lola Tinoco, and Ariadne Walter, and a script based upon a well-written play, the film fails to develop its theme in a convincing manner. The identity questions that are central to the story are never fully addressed. In a fatalistic manner, the sons and daughter of the family have followed negative paths, with the "American way of life" implicitly blamed for this situation.[33]

El Pocho (1964) is "El Piporro" 's most significant contribution to such filmic themes and perhaps best captures Mexican perceptions about the Chicano community in the 1950s and early 1960s. The production addresses certain fundamental issues of the U.S.-Mexican border, such as identity, music, language, and the complex and at times ambivalent situation of Chicanos.

El Pocho was filmed totally in the border twin cities of Ciudad Juárez and El Paso, giving authenticity to the film. The plot revolves around events in the life of José Guadalupe García, played by "El Piporro." García, a clerk in an El Paso drugstore, is an orphan whose parents drowned trying to cross the Río Grande illegally into the United States. He grows up in El Paso, going by the name of Joe Garsha, the name that he received at the orphanage. Despite the fact that he has been strongly influenced by U.S. culture and values, his *mexicanidad* is very much present, although initially his cultural loyalty is in doubt. The movie opens with José Guadalupe García trying to assimilate into U.S. society by speaking only English and acquiring a "gringa" girlfriend. He soon encounters overt discrimination, however, even to the point where his girlfriend's brother and friends beat him up for dating an "American" girl. This naturally tends to put a damper on García's feelings toward his adopted country.

In his disillusionment, he crosses the border into Juárez. Trying to court a young Mexican woman newly arrived from Guadalajara (played by the noted singer and popular film star, Lucha Villa), he is ridiculed and rejected by her. To add insult to injury, he is accosted by a group of locals who proceed to give him the beating of his life, this

time for dating a "Mexican" girl. The movie closes with García jump-
ing into the Río Grande, mourning the fact that the one true home for
the Chicano is right there in the middle of the river, neither here nor
there. His rejection by both American and Mexican society puts José
Guadalupe in the unenviable position of many Chicanos along the
border.[34]

The theme of the *pocho* on the screen hit home for the Chicano in
the border states. *Pochos* as portrayed in the cinema embodied the
conflict and turmoil afflicting Chicanos who felt they did not fit in and
who encountered rejection on both sides of the border. *El Pocho* clearly
points out the unresolved and problematical situation of the Chicano.
The film's plot is still very valid today in view of the fact that attitudes
toward Chicanos have not altogether changed in either Mexico or the
United States. As a feature, though, *El Pocho* is weak. Eulalio
González, in his multifaceted role of producer, screenwriter, director,
and principal actor, is not successful on most levels. *El Pocho* closed
the *pocho* cycle of Mexican cinema, with a different direction or interpretation emerging in the 1970s.

Rebels of the Río Grande

Legally and formally, the Chicano community emerged as a territorial
minority within the United States as a direct result of the acquisition
of half of Mexico's national territory by the United States through the
U.S.-Mexican War of 1846–48. Within the newly acquired lands, the
Mexican population was given the choice to relocate south of the new
border, or remain on the native lands accepting U.S. sovereignty. The
Treaty of Guadalupe Hidalgo, which ended the hostilities between the
two nations, also guaranteed to those Mexicans who chose to stay "all
the rights of citizens of the United States according to the principles of
the Constitution."[35] But although much was promised to the Mexican
occupants, who now became the first "legal" generation of Mexican-
origin citizens of the United States, little was delivered. One by one,
the various stated guarantees of the treaty were dismissed or violated.
Soon after the American annexation, the Mexican community fell victim to overt racial and ethnic prejudices, class conflict, and outright
violence.[36]

As Anglo Americans flooded into the new frontier, they resented
that so much land and wealth belonged to the "greasers," and viewed

the darker-skinned, racially mixed Chicanos as socially and racially inferior, possessing a traditional folk culture that stood in the way of the country's "Manifest Destiny."[37] Through legal and extralegal methods, the subjugation of the Chicano population began, resulting in a colonial relationship, with the Anglo American as the colonizer and the Chicano as the colonized. Chicano response to this adverse situation was expressed through four basic alternatives:

(1) *Assimilation:* The attempt at total integration into the dominant society, giving up Mexican culture, values, language, and traditions, and adopting "American" ones, eventually losing an identity as a separate community.

(2) *Accommodation:* The process of adapting to the dominant society rather than adopting it entirely, still retaining one's essential cultural patterns and identity.

(3) *Migration to Mexico:* Although the number of Chicanos that migrated back to Mexico is difficult to ascertain, there is evidence that numerous Chicanos fled back to Mexico after facing constant oppression and threats to their lives.

(4) *Resistance:* Either legal within the system, or illegal through armed individual or collective resistance movements.[38]

Resistance was the most isolated response, but nonetheless it was an important one. Individual Chicano avengers or social bandits emerged throughout the Southwest. As the classic study of the significance of social banditry explains, they are "social bandits whom the lord and state regard as criminals . . . and are considered by their people as heroes, as champions, avengers, fighters for justice, perhaps even leaders of liberation."[39] Social bandits have been an inspiration and subject matter for the cinema from Robin Hood to Zorro. In the case of the cinema of Mexico and its interest in Chicano issues, three Mexican narrative features were produced that highlight Chicano "avengers and exerters of power."[40]

Camino a Sacramento, a 1945 Jorge Negrete action film, uses early California as the setting for an off-beat feature modeled on the Corsican brothers' theme: twins separated at birth, each unaware of the other's existence. One of the twins, the one in California, becomes a social bandit, El Halcón (The Hawk), fighting against the evil forces led by the man who ordered the assassination of his parents. After discovering the truth, the other twin returns from Spain to be united with his brother. Together they defeat the villains, and El Halcón rides off into the sunset in search of further adventures.[41]

This is a lighthearted action film that displayed nothing more than a routine plot and occasion for the singing and acting talents of its star, Jorge Negrete. The fact that the action had to do with the hero fighting injustice is coincidental. The film did not make significant use of the historical setting.

In 1956, in what would be one of his last films, Miguel Contreras Torres produced, wrote, and directed *El último rebelde*. The feature traces the heroic and tragic life and deeds of Joaquín Murrieta. The plot loosely follows historical and legendary accounts of the rise and ultimate death of one of the most celebrated Chicano social bandits of nineteenth-century California. The film opens with the death of Murrieta's family at the hands of a gang of thieving Anglos led by a former military man named Lang. This ruthless group has been usurping mines either through fraudulent means or outright violence against mostly Mexicano/Chicano miners. California has just become part of the United States and is still in transition, and very much a frontier, with the limited law enforcement favoring the people who were committing the crimes.

Joaquín, in an act of vengeance and with the help of two other compatriots, takes the law into his own hands. The three become social bandits, avengers in defense of their community. Slowly but steadily, they exterminate the evil gang. Their victory is short-lived, however; they are ambushed and killed by federal troops, and so the life and film of Joaquín Murrieta comes to a sad conclusion.[42] Unfortunately, *El último rebelde* was confined to recounting the vengeance of one *bandolero* seemingly isolated from broader political and societal issues, with little insight into the plight and resistance of the Chicano community after the annexation of California.

In 1959, the famed golden-age director, Juan Bustillos Oro, premiered *El último mexicano*. The action takes place in Texas following the American annexation. Several themes of Chicano responses to colonialism are loosely developed in the film. The hero of the story decided to return to Mexico rather than accept his fortune under U.S. sovereignty. Before departing his native Texas, he successfully defeats evil forces that were land-grabbing and oppressing his compatriots. A love story subplot also has a happy resolution, closing with the main character and his love interest leaving the land of the *gringos* and returning to Mexico, never to leave and become *"el último mexicano."*[43]

This is a curious film whose message and theme are not altogether clear. Mexican resistance to Anglo oppression in the annexed Southwest appears to be the central question, but the subplots obscure this aspect. The return to Mexico as a viable option for a better life could have been most interesting since no other Mexican production, up to the late 1970s, included or focused on this little-known historical chapter of the Chicano experience.

By Way of a Conclusion

Since its development, the cinema of Mexico has displayed a constant if somewhat static portrayal of the Chicano/Mexicano community in the United States. From the first production in 1922, *El hombre sin patria,* to the films of the 1960s, three themes stand out. First and foremost is the immigrant experience of those unfortunate souls that crossed the Río Bravo to the land of dollars in search of an illusive and false El Dorado. Whether the film reflected a dramatic plot or introduced a comic element, the ideological construct and didactic message was similar: no good awaits you in the United States. Rather than bring to the screen thoughtful, well-researched, and well-written scripts that would examine the experiences of their compatriots in the United States, these films responded to Mexican internal concerns and popular attitudes. In the end, the viewer learns much more about Mexico's attitudes and policies toward its emigrants, or even the historical condition of the country at the time of the making of the production, than about the emigrants themselves. The one exception to this rule is the excellent *Espaldas mojadas.*

A second theme is the *pocho* characterization. Mexican films in these four decades consistently display Chicano protagonists or immigrants who have spent a considerable period of time in the United States as assimilated, anti-Mexican, pro-American individuals who have lost their identity or *mexicanidad.* In opposition to this stance, certain Mexican characters in films like *Soy mexicano de acá de este lado* accentuated their nationalism and are portrayed as true Mexicans, not second-class citizens (both figuratively and politically) like the *pochos.*

Throughout the twentieth century, Mexican officials and educators were quite distressed with the possible loss of *mexicanidad* by the Mexican-origin population in the United States. It is important to note that the Mexican consuls were officially given the task to promote and foster *mexicanidad* by any means possible. There is considerable historical evidence that documents this ongoing effort. For example, in many U.S. cities, Mexican consuls organized patriotic festivities and other events aimed at retaining the spirit of *mexicanidad*.[44]

A third and final important theme is the filmic defense of the civil rights of Chicanos by legendary individuals. Loosely based on historical accounts, certain of these motion pictures incorporate nationalism with a sense of outrage over the tragedy of the American territorial conquest, with cinematic heroes that rose against Anglo oppression. None of these avenger films, however, was able to capture effectively the historical drama and significance of the events or of their participants.

It becomes apparent that the Chicano or Mexican in the United States was not well served by the narrative cinema of Mexico in the time frame studied. On the whole, these productions followed and hardened Mexican stereotypes and broad generalizations about Chicanos and *braceros* more than contributing to a more sensitive and complex understanding of the "other Mexico." It is indeed unfortunate that in the pioneer and golden-age periods of Mexican cinema, which produced numerous classic films and reflected a wealth of creativity and talent, only *Espaldas mojadas* expresses an element of support or better understanding of the Mexican population in the United States.

Notes

1. I would like to express my sincere appreciation to all those members of the Mexican film community who graciously shared their time, ideas, and materials with me.

2. Various of the essays in *Al norte de la frontera: el pueblo chicano,* David R. Maciel and José Guillermo Saavedra, eds. (México: Consejo Nacional de Población, 1988) discuss these issues in detail.

3. David R. Maciel, *Aztlán and México: A History of Chicano/Mexicano Relations, 1836–1990.* Unpublished manuscript.

4. The term "filmmakers" is used here to include all members of the film community of Mexico.

5. Interview with Gustavo García, Mexico City, August 10, 1987.

6. See the following articles: William D. Allen, "Spanish-Language Films in the

U.S.," *Films in Review* 1 (July-August 1950): 42–45; and "Las películas mexicanas en los EE. UU.," *Tiempo* 27 (April 1945): 36–37.

7. This theme is developed further in David R. Maciel, "Mexican Immigrant Workers in the United States," in *American Labor in the Southwest: The First One Hundred Years,* James C. Foster, ed. (Tucson: University of Arizona Press, 1982).

8. The well-researched monograph by Mark Reisler, *By the Sweat of Their Brow* (Westport, Conn.: Greenwood Press, 1976) offers a detailed analysis of this process.

9. See the recent study by John M. Hart, *Revolutionary México* (Austin: University of Texas Press, 1989) and the two-volume work by Moises Ochoa Campos, *La Revolución Mexicana* (México: Estudios de la Revolución Mexicana, 1966).

10. Lawrence A. Cardoso, *Mexican Emigration to the United States, 1897–1931* (Tucson: University of Arizona Press, 1980).

11. Juan Gómez-Quiñones and David R. Maciel, *Al norte del Río Bravo. Pasado Iyano (1600–1930)* (México: Siglo XXI, 1981), 106–10.

12. María Rosa García and David R. Maciel, "El México de afuera; politicas mexicanas de protección en Estados Unidos," *Revista Mexicana de Política Exterior* 3, no. 12 (July-September 1986): 19–21.

13. Ricardo Romo, "Responses to Mexican Immigration, 1910–1930," *Aztlán: A Journal of Chicano Studies* 6, no. 2 (Summer 1975): 180–81.

14. The two standard works on this subject are Abraham Hoffman, *Unwanted Mexican-Americans in the Great Depression* (Tucson: University of Arizona Press, 1974), and Mercedes Carreras de Velasco, *Los Mexicanos que devolvió la crisis, 1929–1932* (México: Secretaria de Relaciones Exteriores, 1974).

15. Richard B. Craig's *The Bracero Program: Interest Groups and Foreign Policy* (Austin: University of Texas Press, 1971) is one of the most complete studies of diverse aspects of the Bracero program.

16. Arthur F. Corwin, ed., *Immigrants and Immigrants* (Westport, Conn.: Greenwood Press, 1978), 68–69.

17. Federico Davalos Orozco and Esperanza Vazques Bernal, *Filmografía general del cine mexicano* (Puebla: Universidad de Puebla, 1985), 91–92.

18. Aurelio de los Reyes, *Medio siglo de cine mexicano* (México: Editorial Trillas, 1987), 89–94, provides extensive analysis of the career and films of Miguel Contreras Torres.

19. Interview with Medea de Novarro, the widow of Miguel Contreras Torres, Mexico City, July 12, 1987.

20. *Rancheras,* films that are musical comedies usually situated in a rural setting, are among the most entertaining and enduring of the Mexican filmic cycles.

21. Emilio García Riera, *Historia documental del cine mexicano,* 9 vols. (México: Ediciones ERA, 1969–78), 1: 223–24.

22. F. Rand Morton's *Novelistas de la Revolución Mexicana* (México: n.p., 1947) includes an excellent chapter on the writings of José Rubén Romero.

23. García Riera, *Historia* 3: 209–10.

24. Alejandro Galindo, *Espaldas mojadas* (México, 1953), original screenplay provided by author; and Carl J. Mora, *Mexican Cinema: Reflections of a Society, 1896–1980* (Berkeley: University of California Press, 1982), 88–89.

25. Interview with Tomás Pérez Turrent, Mexico City, June 14, 1984.

26. Eulalio González, *El bracero del año* (México, 1962), original screenplay provided by author.

27. Juan Gómez-Quiñones, "Notes of an Interpretation of the Relations between the Mexican Community in the United States and Mexico," in *Mexican-U.S. Relations,*

Carlos Vazquez and Manuel García y Griego, eds. (Los Angeles: Aztlán Publications, 1983), 434–36.

28. Carlos Monsiváis, "De México y los chicanos, de México y su cultura fronteriza," in *La otra cara de México: el pueblo chicano*, David R. Maciel, ed. (México: Ediciones "El Caballito," 1977), 14–17.

29. Interview with Carlos Monsiváis, San Diego, California, February 12, 1987.

30. David R. Maciel, "Cinema and Nationalism in Mexico: The Films of Miguel Contreras Torres." Unpublished essay.

31. García Riera, *Historia* 4: 339–40.

32. Ibid., 8: 372–73.

33. Ibid., 7: 133–34.

34. Eulalio González, *El Pocho* (México, 1963), original screenplay provided by the author.

35. Richard Griswold del Castillo, *The Treaty of Guadalupe Hidalgo* (Norman: University of Oklahoma Press, 1990), 62–66.

36. David R. Maciel and Juan Gómez-Quiñones, *El otro Mexico (1600–1985)* (México: Editorial Alianza, 1989), 31–34.

37. Robert J. Rosenbaum, *Mexican Resistance in the Southwest* (Austin: University of Texas Press, 1981), 5–15.

38. These responses of the Chicano community are discussed in David J. Weber, ed., *Foreigners in Their Native Land* (Albuquerque: University of New Mexico Press, 1976).

39. E. J. Hobsbawn, *Bandits* (New York: Delacorte, 1969), 17–18.

40. Ibid., 58. An important edited work on Chicano resistance is *Furia y muerte: Los bandidos chicanos*, Pedro Castillo and Alberto Camarillo, eds. (Los Angeles: Aztlán Publications, 1973).

41. García Riera, *Historia* 7: 64–66.

42. Miguel Contreras Torres, *El último rebelde* (México, 1953), original screenplay in the personal archive of the estate of the director.

43. García Riera, *Historia* 7: 258–59.

44. David R. Maciel's unpublished manuscript, "The Unwritten Alliance: Mexican Policies toward Immigration," examines this theme in detail.

Cinematic Orphans: Mexican Immigrants in the United States since the 1950s

Alex M. Saragoza

This essay will explore the meaning of film for Mexican immigrants and their sense of identity in the United States since the 1950s. The intent is primarily interpretive, rather than an analysis of several motion pictures. Specifically, this inquiry will focus initially on the development of the cinematic distance between the experience of Mexican immigrants in the United States and Mexican cinema, as films from Mexico have failed increasingly to provide a source of contestation for *mexicanos* north of the border. Furthermore, this essay will address the inability of Chicano filmmakers to capture the immigrant experience. Thus, this work constitutes a response, albeit partial and confined to cinema, to the continuing confusion over the interface between Mexico, *mexicanos*, Mexican Americans, and Chicanos.[1] This essay will concentrate on cinema, but its larger purpose is to illuminate a major flaw in Chicano studies: the neglect of the *mexicano* dimension to the experience of Mexican-origin people in the United States in the post-World War II era.

As I have proposed elsewhere, the intrinsic nationalism of Mexican film in the 1930s through the early 1950s offered a source of contestation for many Mexicans in the United States during that period.[2] Several factors converged in that era to produce a receptive audience in the United States for Mexican nationalist cinema, not the least of which was an inherent anti-northamerican sentiment among most immigrants from Mexico. In this sense, Mexican film afforded *recién llegados* at that time a form of resistance to the hegemonic cultural and ideological currents in the United States.

Nonetheless, diversity marked the Mexican-origin community during that period, and its response therefore to Mexican nationalist film was not monolithic. For the children reared in the United States of Mexico-born immigrants, for instance, the *mexicanismo* of Mexican movies proved alien over time as a growing number of these young people became estranged from their parents' heritage, traditions, and sense of identity. The impacts of americanization programs, of anti-Mexican attitudes, and of acculturation, among other pressures, worked to push the offspring of immigrants away from their identification with Mexico.[3] Young women in particular were often at odds with the patriarchal strictures and conventions usually idealized in Mexican cinema—and consistent with the views of many Mexican parents, especially fathers.[4] In short, the capacity of Mexican film to be a source of resistance to the dominant society waned with time among the offspring of Mexican immigrants, whose link to *México*, to *patria*, was embodied primarily through their parents. Indeed, the 1950s witnessed the culmination of this process by the maturation of a new, distinct segment among the Mexican-origin population in the United States, what Mario García has called the "Mexican American" generation.[5] This Mexican American generation was characterized by its cultural and ideological formation in the United States, leading to a dual sense of identity: "Mexican in culture and American in ideas and ideology."[6] This ideal was, of course, subject to much variation. Nevertheless, this Mexican American generation was much more likely to see American movies, and their parents found it much easier to identify with the Mexican nationalist cinema of the "golden age." Thus, the generalized sense of *Mexican* nationalism among immigrants who came from the early 1900s through the 1920s was not usually shared subsequently by their children, and ultimately this nationalist sentiment declined considerably. By the 1960s, the grandchildren of that original wave of immigrants had lost much of their identification with Mexico, leading to the so-called "Chicano" generation.[7]

Mexican immigration resumed after 1940 from the hiatus of the depression years and increased dramatically in the post-World War II decade, fueled in part by the *bracero* program, as well as the social consequences of Mexico's inequitable economic policies. Between 1900 and 1910, approximately 50,000 immigrants arrived in the United States, and in the next decade nearly 220,000 more entered this coun-

try. This surge climaxed when over 450,000 Mexicans crossed the border from 1920 to 1930. In contrast, during the 1930s immigration from
Mexico essentially came to a halt as a result of the depression in the
United States. Equally important, that decade also witnessed an
upsurge of anti-Mexican sentiment, as nearly half a million Mexicans
were deported forcibly (or repatriated) back to Mexico by U.S. agencies, and state and local governments. But roughly 60,000 arrived in
the decade beginning with 1940; another 300,000 entered in the subsequent decade. The termination of the *bracero* program in 1964 failed to
stem the tide of immigration, as both legal and undocumented immigration has surged since the mid-1960s. Approximately 500,000 immigrants crossed the border from 1960 to 1970. Since 1970 Mexican
immigration has been substantial, and the passage of new restriction-
ist legislation in 1986 has proved to be ineffective in slowing
significantly the entry of the documented and undocumented from
our neighbor to the south.[8]

Important differences, however, mark the immigrants that arrived
before the Great Depression and *mexicanos* who came to the United
States since World War II. One of those key differences is the meaning
of Mexican film to Mexicans both north and south of the border. First,
the Mexican film industry has changed dramatically since the "golden
age" of the 1940s and 1950s. The motion picture industry has fallen on
poor times as production values and the quality of movies have
declined precipitously for a variety of reasons too complex to enumer-
ate here. Suffice to say that Mexican cinema, with some notable exceptions, has deteriorated enormously; much of its content reflects crude
imitations of past genre, or the mediocre copying of foreign film formulas. As a result, most Mexican motion pictures are often vulgar,
violent, and laced with soft-porn images of females. In this context,
foreign movies clearly, and not surprisingly, dominate the Mexican
film market.[9]

Second, the social significance of Mexican cinema has changed
substantially since the World War II era in the United States. Whereas
most large *barrios* were served with theaters showing Mexican films in
the 1940s and 1950s, this is no longer the case in many communities
with large Mexican-origin *colonias.* In this respect, "going to a Mexican
movie" has become largely confined to recently arrived immigrants,
to dilapidated theaters frequently in the "bad part" of town. For the
overwhelming majority of people of Mexican origin, particularly those

born in the United States, the experience of a Mexican moviehouse has become history. This change has been compounded by the unattractive location of these theaters, which adds a pejorative connotation to the idea of even seeing a Mexican movie. Among Mexican Americans, one is apt to be the object of derision, if not incredulity, for attending the showing of a Mexican motion picture.[10]

Third, given the substantial decline in the attendance of Mexican movies the capacity of Mexican cinema to be a form of cultural resistance has been greatly reduced. The availability of Mexican films on video fails to sustain this potential as well. The large moviehouse of the 1940s and 1950s constituted a collectivity, a critical mass of certain commonalities exemplified by the mutual attendance of Mexican-origin people. In this sense, the cinematic experience for the audience possessed an intrinsic common ground, a sharing of cultural space that is not the case with a VCR in an individual home. Part of the social power of Mexican cinema in the past resided in that common experience of group validation that took place every Thursday night (in my hometown), when the Rex Theater had its "Mexican night." In interviews with older, established immigrants and their children, I found that families rarely sit together to watch rented Mexican movies; parents or grandparents were the most likely to see the film videos (often black-and-white motion pictures of the golden age). In an interview with a Mexican movie rental distributor, the primary market for contemporary-produced Mexican film videos is very recently arrived immigrants (largely male).[11]

Fourth, the political consciousness of Mexican audiences has become much more critical, if not cynical, of the Mexican state. The Tlatelolco massacre of 1968 and the oppositional strength evident in the 1988 Mexican presidential elections represent revealing historical bookends to the emergence of a new political era in Mexico. In this regard, a basic notion of Mexican nationalism found in the "golden age" cinema has been irrevocably lost: the link between nation (*patria*) and state has been shredded by the conservative, inequitable policies of the post-1940 regimes. This erosion of political legitimacy has discredited the ability of the state to personify *lo mexicano,* as manifested most powerfully in the immense popularity of President Lázaro Cárdenas (1934–40). Indeed, one of the ironies of the golden age nationalist cinema—particularly expressed in the films of Emilio "El Indio" Fernández—was its production during the two presidential administrations most responsible for the state's turn away from the populism of *cardenismo,* that of Manuel Avila Camacho (1940–46) and of Miguel Alemán Valdés (1946–52). The nationalist aura of the Cárdenas years carried over, but its resilience ebbed as the consequences of post-1940 policies undermined the credibility of the Mexican state.[12] The controversial exhibition of Luis Buñuel's *Los Olvidados* (1950) signaled the growing crisis of legitimacy of the single-party government of Mexico that would climax with the publication of Carlos Fuentes's landmark novel, *La región más transparente* in 1958.

In brief, Mexican cinema has essentially lost its political "voice" since the golden age, paralleling the loss of political legitimacy of the Mexican state. Nevertheless, the ideological views among Mexicans in Mexico, especially notions of nationalism and culture, sustain an anti-U.S. element. A survey conducted in 1986 by the *New York Times* noted the myriad ways that Mexicans (in Mexico) perceived their country negatively in comparison to the United States, except in one key category: cultural values and attitudes. For the majority of *mexicanos,* the United States remained culturally distinct and, more significantly, impoverished compared to the culture of Mexico. Thus, the cultural image of the United States in Mexico continues to fare badly when compared to that of the mother country.[13] In this sense, the inherent anti-U.S. character of Mexican popular culture persists with surprising tenacity. The sudden, unexpected, and potent rise of a nationalistic oppositional movement in Mexico in the presidential elections of 1988 (led by the son of Lázaro Cárdenas) signifies the enduring sense of nationalism among a large proportion of the Mexican population. But this vision differs markedly from that of the 1930s. In fact, the state and the dominant party have betrayed, from this new opposition viewpoint, the nation's patrimony in exchange for foreign investment and economic dependency.[14]

Nonetheless, this political alternative has found no counterpart in the media. Hence, in dealing with the racist, prejudicial views of Mexico and Mexicans in the U.S. media, *mexicanos* have been rendered virtually voiceless in terms of the Mexican mass media generally, and in film specifically. Unlike people of Mexican origin in the 1940s and 1950s, *mexicanos* in the United States since the 1960s and into the 1990s cannot turn easily to imported Mexican films as a source of ideological refuge or cultural contestation. As other scholars have noted, most of the recent films on immigration made in Mexico convey a simplistic message: crossing the border to the United States spells eventual doom. In one of the more crude examples of this "mojado" genre, *Las braceras* (1987) paints the experience of immigration in the most negative terms: murderous INS agents, rapacious employers, sexual abuse of female *ilegales,* and a political system completely oblivious to the sufferings of undocumented workers. In *Las braceras,* a pair of corrupt border patrolmen kill the two heroines and their friends, including the father and boyfriend of one of them (a crusading, pro-immigrant rights Chicano journalist). But the two INS officers ultimately die, too, shot by the vengeful sister of one of the murdered heroines. In *Las braceras* and its counterparts, the consequences of immigration are dark and uncompromising.

This message, however, contradicts the presence of an enormous population of *mexicanos* with many years of residence in the United States and it contradicts the obvious flow of Mexicans to the border in spite of the imagery found in *Las braceras* and related films. Such movies clearly have little meaning for immigrants who have become essentially settlers, rather than sojourners, in this country.

Generally speaking, Chicano scholars have found it difficult to assess the meaning of *lo mexicano* in the United States, especially after the bulge of immigration that ended with the Great Depression. Other than cite the numbers of *braceros* that came during and after World War II, most Chicano scholars have been reluctant, it seems, to tackle the importance of this continuing immigration as a representation of Mexican influence in northamerican *barrios* and its implications, including the persistence of Mexico-based forms of cultural expression such as Mexican film, music, and television. More importantly, there has been scarce research on the extent to which such forms of popular culture represent sources of contestation, resistance, or argument against the dominant society. Only two major publications have addressed Chicano-*mexicano* relations, and both collections of essays concentrate on the political and/or economic aspects of the relationship.[15]

The post-1940s immigrant population apparently held views at odds with the consumer culture and ideology of contemporary America. The *bracero* sojourn as expressed in song, for example, has been shown by María Herrera-Sobek to possess a critical perspective on American society.[16] Furthermore, in Erasmo Gamboa's excellent work on *braceros* in the Northwest, he notes the popularity of Mexican movies shown at the labor camps:

> Simply stated, the films not only aroused nostalgia for the homeland but also appealed to the Mexicans with their conservative and *nationalistic* (my emphasis) message. . . . The popularity of these films was so great that growers would occasionally transport several hundred men by truck to a camp where one of the movies was being featured.[17]

Yet, most students of the Chicano experience have missed the significance of these forms of expression among more recently arrived immigrants.

Alejandro Portes and Robert Bach, for instance, found in a study covering the 1970s that among Mexican immigrants there was a "rapid increase in perceptions of discrimination in the first three years after arrival."[18] In addition, after three years "more than half of the Mexican immigrants believed that Anglos considered themselves superior to Mexicans."[19] More important, this study concluded that as immigrants became more educated, proficient in English, and informed, "the more critical their perceptions of the receiving society and the stronger their perceptions of discrimination."[20] Note should be made here that the study also found that a significant proportion preferred to raise their children in the Mexican way and/or to retain aspects of traditional Mexican child-rearing (35 percent preferred the Mexican way, and nearly 27 percent wanted a combination; three years later, the figures were 27.4 and 33.8 percent, respectively).[21]

In a more recent study, Douglas Massey and his collaborators noted the progressive orientation toward American society of Mexican immigrants settled in the United States. Nonetheless, despite this shift, the residual "pull" of the mother country remained. Massey et al. concluded that living in the United States had an "ambiguous, problematic meaning of settlement for Mexican migrants. Settlement is never an irreversible, irrevocable step in the social process of migration; rather, it involves a *relative* (my emphasis) shift in the focus of orientation between two very different countries."[22] Mexico and *lo mexicano*, therefore, retain a meaning for *mexicanos* in the United States, in spite of the cultural transition away from the mother country. Chicano-produced film has essentially failed to depict this transition and its ideological and cultural importance. Instead, Chicano filmmakers have tended to project a polarized vision of culture, acculturation, and assimilation. In part, this reflects an attempt to refute the negative, stereotypic images that have laced the overwhelming majority of U.S. films where Mexican characters have appeared. More important, Chicano-produced cinema has promoted a dichotomized view of assimilation and acculturation, where the acceptance of northamerican values and attitudes are either demonized or celebrated, usually the former rather than the latter.[23] This nationalistic perspective, as a consequence, idealizes cultural maintenance, romanticizing tradition and condemning the loss of culture: will he/she become an "American" or remain "Mexican"?

This framework has appeared for other groups, notably for Native Americans, but others as well. Spike Lee's recent *Mo' Better Blues* (1990), for example, resonates with this well-worn plot. A similar dilemma is at the heart of the Rubén Blades vehicle, *Crossover Dreams* (1985). In these films, the question of assimilation represents severe costs, as well as certain advantages. Depending on the vision of the director, the dilemma is either to sustain independence, autonomy, "not-give-in"—the resolution in the two films just noted—or to embrace "America" and to sever the bonds of the old country, tradition, and convention. In the past, this latter resolution dominated American cinema, given the pressures of conformity that emanated from American society in the era from the 1930s to the 1950s. To remain "ethnic," e.g., Mexican, was akin to a form of subversion. Although some exceptions were produced in this era, the majority of films on this topic reflected a dichotomous view (to assimilate or not) and a frequent resolution toward idealizing assimilation. There was no middle ground; assimilation appeared usually as an inevitably better decision.[24]

The civil rights era and its aftermath questioned the assimilationist tendencies of the Mexican American generation, as a nationalist ideology took hold in the Chicano movement. Chicano cinema, as a consequence, projected the basic dichotomy of the past, but it favored cultural nationalism rather than assimilation, integration, or acculturation. More recently, Chicano-made films have softened their stance on the costs of cultural change. Nonetheless, the basic dichotomy remains, though the resolution may vary. For instance, in *La Bamba* (1987) by Luis Valdez, there is a celebratory tone to the film that suggests a positive view of integration and, by extension, assimilation. On the other hand, in *Crossover Dreams*, the costs of becoming part of the

mainstream dominate the texture of the film. In a related way, *El Norte*
(1983) holds a similar view, symbolized in the death of the main
female character. Thus, *El Norte*, despite its focus on immigrants from
Central America, sustains the polarities of nationalist cinema, including much of Mexican film.

This view has found exceptions in nonfeature formats. In this
regard, Lourdes Portillo's *Después del Terremoto* (1979) is distinguished
by its portrayal of Central American immigrants and its attention to
questions of gender. *The Unwanted* (1976) by José Luis Ruiz stands out
for its rendering of immigration outside the simplistic them-versus-us
approach. Nancy de los Santos's *Port of Entry* (1981) is distinctive for
its treatment of immigrants in Chicago. Furthermore, Paul Espinosa of
San Diego has produced some fine works on the subject of immigration, particularly at the border. Unfortunately, these efforts remain
largely confined to a limited audience, usually PBS subscribers. These
documentaries, despite their exceptional quality, rarely reach *mexicano*
viewers. Moreover, Spanish-language television (Univision, Gala-
vision, or Telemundo) has generally failed to utilize such noncommercial features. Clearly, one factor in this regard is the implicit if not
explicit criticism of U.S. and Mexican policies that often punctuates
documentaries on Mexican immigration.

Nonetheless, Chicano-produced and Mexican motion pictures con-
verge importantly in their view of immigration and its *cultural* consequences. Yet, very few Chicano or Mexican movies focus on the period beyond the short time span surrounding the crossing of the border.
By reducing the immigrant experience to the tumultuous, jarring, and
painful episode of entry into the United States, both Chicano and
Mexican filmmakers nourish their respective cinematic conventions.
And to press the point further, virtually all films dealing with immigration center on the illegal, the *mojado*, the wetback, the undocumented, the *sin papeles*—despite the large number of immigrants that enter
the United States legally.[25] Chicano *and* Mexican films, regardless of
the resolution of the polarity between assimilation or cultural maintenance, make a fundamental error. To sustain this simplistic framework contradicts history and the present experience of Mexicans in
the United States. Culture is porous, dynamic, and in constant flux.
The "freezing" of this process into static categories (acculturated versus unacculturated) misses reality, distorts the understanding of the
immigrant experience, and eliminates the complexity of the process of

identity formation and change. Worse, this polarized view of culture sustains the centrality of tradition, custom, and convention, minimizing the significance of class, gender, or the context in which identity takes shape.[26]

The changes among Mexican immigrants as they live in the United States are complex and vary over time given their place of residence (urban/rural), legal status, number of children born in the United States, and other factors, including gender. Yet rarely have films depicted this complexity and the nuances of identity that emerge from this process: parent-child relations, sibling relationships, attitudes toward relatives in the mother country, and other aspects of the transition away from Mexico. In this sense, the movie *La jaula de oro* (1986) is exceptional for its treatment of an immigrant (still without proper documentation) after many years in the United States.[27] In this film, the main male character must confront a daughter with a *gringo* boyfriend, an ambitious wife, another daughter seemingly ashamed of her Mexican identity, the loss of proficiency in Spanish among most of his children, and other forms of the ills of acculturation. Laced with several subplots (including the out-of-wedlock pregnancy of one of the daughters), the center of the film revolves around the main character's desire to return to Mexico as a means of resolving the familial (i.e., cultural) dilemmas of living in the United States. Friends, relatives, and family reject the idea, except his youngest son (and presumably the audience).

Unfortunately, the quality of the film—its acting, production values, screenplay, and direction—fail to bring the theme to life. The depiction of the central dilemma of the movie is shallow, simplistic, and cloyingly didactic. Composed of a string of vignettes, the film is populated with characters scarred in various ways by their residence in the United States, including a Vietnam veteran still bearing the wounds of his service to his adopted country. Thus, the cultural complexities faced by immigrants in the United States are lost in the manichean nature of the film. *La jaula de oro*, its title suggestive of its intent, maintains the good-versus-evil dichotomy of formulaic nationalist cinema: stay in Mexico or emigrate to the United States and bear the adverse consequences. In this respect, *La jaula de oro* echoes the message of an old Mexican movie made in 1958, *Los desarraigados*, where the issue of cultural change in a Mexican immigrant family in the United States led inevitably to conflict, chaos, and sadness.

Immigrants from Mexico have become cinematic orphans, minimized by Mexican movies since the "golden age" era and essentially ignored by Chicano filmmakers. In short, the people in between Mexico and Aztlán—to use a metaphor—rarely find a cinematic representation of their experience. Since they fall outside the paradigms of Mexican cinema, they fail to appear in other than the archetypes dictated by nationalist conventions of Mexican motion pictures. Similarly, the underlying antiassimilationist nationalism of Chicano-produced cinema and its paradigmatic polarities miss the flux and nuances of the transition from *mexicano* to *pocho*, to use another metaphor.

Most Chicano observers of Mexican film have tended to note its inability to deal effectively with the Chicano experience. On the other hand, Chicano film has generally failed to address the experience of Mexican immigrants beyond the border and before they become "Mexican Americans," or Chicanos. In historical terms, the "Chicano generation" has tended to understand its experience primarily through the immigrant cohort of the early twentieth century. Mexican intellectuals, on the other hand, have been transfixed by the symbolism of the border and its crossing. And both Chicanos and *mexicanos*, with few exceptions, have had their perspective bounded by a nationalistic vision that limits a filmic understanding of the immigrant from Mexico after the World War II era.

Given the state of the Mexican film industry, one cannot expect much change in the portrayal of immigration in movies made in Mexico. Hampered by the lack of support from major studios, Chicano filmmakers seem unlikely to bridge the current cinematic distance between *recién llegados* and Chicanos. The people in the middle await the opportunity for cinematic voice—a voice still lost in the noisy, nationalist clamor on both sides of the border.

Notes

I am grateful for the help of Lillian Castillo-Speed, Head Librarian of the Chicano Studies Library, and conversations with Loni Ding, Mario Barrera, Jesús Martínez, Rafael Alarcón, and the interviewees mentioned in the notes to this paper. My appreciation for the assistance of Magali M. Zuñiga, Ana Coronado, and Rosa Johnson in the preparation of the manuscript.

1. See Alex M. Saragoza, "The Significance of Recent Chicano Related Historical Writings," *Ethnic Affairs* 1 (Fall 1987): 24–62, especially 44–48; also "Chicanos and

Mexicanos: A Critique of Recent Scholarship," paper presented at the Conference of the National Association for Chicano Studies, Albuquerque, New Mexico, 1990.

2. Alex M. Saragoza, "Mexican Cinema in the United States, 1940–1952," in *History, Culture and Society: Chicano Studies in the 1980s* (Ypsilanti, Mich.: Bilingual Press, 1983), 107–24.

3. See Richard A. García, "The Mexican American Mind: A Product of the 1930s," in *History, Culture and Society: Chicano Studies in the 1980s*, 67–93; Mario T. García, *Mexican Americans: Leadership, Ideology and Identity, 1930–1960* (New Haven: Yale University Press, 1989), especially 1–22.

4. See the various portraits of immigrant women in the classic work of Manuel Gamio, *The Mexican Immigrant: His Life Story* (Chicago: University of Chicago Press, 1931). See also the vignette described in John D'Emilio and Estelle B. Freedman, *Intimate Matters: A History of Sexuality in America* (New York: Harper & Row, 1988), 198.

5. Mario García notes that George I. Sánchez, an important Mexican American leader, came to advocate restrictions on Mexican immigration: "Sánchez warned that the gains Mexican Americans had made in their struggle to integrate into American society and to achieve acculturation were being threatened by uncontrolled mass migration from Mexico" (*Mexican Americans*, 270). In this regard, Sánchez was not alone.

6. Richard García, "The Mexican American Mind," 84.

7. Ironically, despite their cultural nationalism, the Chicano movement's view of Mexico was greatly romanticized and reflected more of an ideological turn rather than a cultural one. On this point, see the insightful comments of Mario García, *Mexican Americans*, 299–301.

8. Alejandro Portes and Robert L. Bach, *Latin Journey: Cuban and Mexican Immigrants in the United States* (Berkeley: University of California Press, 1985), 79. On the continuing flow of Mexican immigrants, particularly the undocumented, see Alejandro Portes and Rubén G. Rumbant, *Immigrant America: A Portrait* (Berkeley: University of California Press, 1990), 234–39.

9. On the decline of the Mexican movie industry, among many works, see Carl J. Mora, *Mexican Cinema: Reflections of a Society, 1896–1980* (Berkeley: University of California Press, 1982), especially chapter 5.

10. Interview with Adriana Olivarez (a daughter of a Mexican immigrant), November 13, 1990, Berkeley, California. Olivarez reported that in doing research on a paper on Mexican film, she attended her local Mexican moviehouse. Her family and friends all were aghast at the idea. Interviews with other Mexican immigrants of long duration in this country made the same point.

11. Interviews, all in Berkeley, California, with Magali M. Zuñiga (November 27, 1990), Alicia Zapiens (November 15, 1990), and Javier Guerrero (November 19, 1990). The movie rental distributor was Ernie Flores, of Madera Cinevideo, Madera, California (November 29, 1990). Little, if any, research has been done on this issue, and the situation in an area like Los Angeles, for instance, may be very different.

12. The literature on the erosion of the legitimacy of the Mexican state is vast. For a recent, wide-ranging, and excellent discussion, see Wayne A. Cornelius, Judith Gentleman, and Peter Smith, eds., *México's Alternative Political Futures* (San Diego: Center for U.S.-Mexican Studies, 1989).

13. Jorge Castañeda and Robert Pastor, *Limits to Friendship: The United States and México* (New York: Alfred A. Knopf, 1988), especially 217–18 and chapter 8.

14. See Jesús Galindo López, "Voices of the Opposition: A Conversation with Cuauhtémoc Cárdenas," *Journal of International Affairs* 43, no. 2 (Winter 1990): 395–406.

15. See Tatcho Mindiola and Max Martínez, eds., *Chicano-Mexicano Relations*

(Houston: Mexican American Studies Program, 1986); Harley L. Browning and Rodolfo O. de la Garza, eds., *Mexican Immigrants and Mexican Americans: An Evolving Relation* (Austin: Center for Mexican American Studies, 1986).

16. María Herrera-Sobek, *The Bracero Experience: Elitelore Versus Folklore* (Los Angeles: UCLA Latin American Center Publications, 1979).

17. Erasmo Gamboa, *Mexican Labor and World War II: Braceros in the Pacific Northwest, 1942–1947* (Austin: University of Texas Press, 1990), 109–10.

18. Portes and Bach, *Latin Journey*, 282.

19. Ibid.

20. Ibid., 288.

21. Ibid., 278.

22. Douglas Massey et al., *Return to Aztlán: The Social Process of International Migration from Western México* (Berkeley: University of California Press, 1987), 276. Note should be made here of the large crowds that came out to hear Cuauhtémoc Cárdenas, the Nationalist opposition candidate in the 1988 Mexican presidential elections, during his trip to California in 1989.

23. See Gary D. Keller, ed., *Chicano Cinema* (Binghamton, N.Y.: Bilingual Review/Press, 1985), especially the essays by Keller and Jesús Salvador Treviño. Space does not allow for a full treatment of this issue, but the question of culture remains a central element in the debate regarding Chicano identity. See special issue of *Cultural Studies* 4, no. 3 (October 1990).

24. For the ideological context of this era, see Stephen Steinberg, *The Ethnic Myth: Race, Ethnicity, and Class in America* (Boston: Beacon Press, 1989), especially chapter 2.

25. David Maciel and Gary Keller, in their essays in *Chicano Cinema*, discuss the image of the Mexican immigrant in both Chicano and Mexican cinema.

26. See Rosa Linda Fregoso and Angie Chabram, "Chicana/o Cultural Representations: Reframing Alternative Critical Discourses," *Cultural Studies* 4, no. 3 (October 1990): 203–11, especially 205–6.

27. Yet *La jaula de oro* parallels earlier films that promote the view that living in the United States means certain trouble if not tragedy: *De sangre chicana*, and the 1977 remake of *Los desarraigados*, reflective of the original movie of the same title produced in Mexico in 1958.

Ni de aquí, ni de allá: Indigenous Female Representation in the Films of María Elena Velasco

Carmen Huaco-Nuzum

As an established filmmaker in popular Mexican cinema, director/actress María Elena Velasco wrestles with themes of alienation and the social displacement of the indigenous female in contemporary society. Velasco portrays the India María[1] as someone caught in a process of social transition between cultural "underdevelopment" and an industrial society that openly discriminates against her. The India María, however, actively resists the racial, class, and gender constraints that pressure her to subordinate and acculturate into white society. The film's dichotomy between industrialization and underdevelopment forewarns the viewer of the danger the indigenous female faces in a foreign culture whenever she becomes identified as "other," opening her as this does to the possibility of being recolonized by patriarchy and dominant culture.

One finds in the work of Velasco a tension between social forces of resistance and acculturation that are played out by the main character, the India María, who struggles to find a space in which to articulate her desires. The films of Velasco have proved to be a box-office success on both sides of the border, not only with the Mexican working-class indigenous and *mestiza(o)* population, but also among numerous Mexican migrants in the United States who frequently travel across geographical borders. The India María as cultural image textualizes the social reality and economic condition of many Mexicans who migrate in search of a better life. The response of Velasco's target audience to this icon has helped to establish her as one of the leading Mexican female popular filmmakers.

An invisible line is drawn between social groups across race, class, and gender that unmistakably separates the identifiable subordinate from the dominant groups. Popular culture emerges out of a desperate need to react against feelings of overwhelming disempowerment, or may emerge as an oppositional voice against hegemonic conditions of relations of power and subordination; it is in this context that it is important to analyze Velasco's work with an emphasis on the representation of the indigenous woman. Of particular interest are the films that Velasco directed: *El coyote emplumado* (1982), *Ni Chana ni Juana* (1985), and *Ni de aquí, ni de allá* (1987). In these films, the India María acts out a narrative of cultural dislocation, as she finds herself caught between rural and urban, *criolla/güera* (European) and *india/mestiza* (indigenous), Mexican and American cultures.

I will focus my analysis on *Ni de aquí, ni de allá* in order to bring to light what makes these films so popular among an indigenous, *mestiza*, and chicana(o) public. What does this type of film offer the Mexican public? These films have been criticized by filmmakers and critics as stereotyping and denigrating the representation of the indigenous female, who—at times—is portrayed as infantile and simpleminded when confronted with an unpredictable social environment. Nonetheless, the infantile female characterization changes in the process of narrative development, with the India María ultimately portrayed as a woman able to take charge over some aspects of her life.

But before I discuss Velasco's work, it is necessary to identify certain interpretations that have traveled across geographical and social borders to end up inscribed in the autochthonous Mexican culture. The problem between language and identity is that language has a capability of distorting the meaning of those groups it is attempting to identify. The contraction of the two names, India/María, denotes a conflation between the indigenous Mexican woman and the European white female. The name María, derived from the European Virgin Mary, was introduced to Mexico by the church and came to represent an "idealized" form of white femininity. Later the Virgin of Guadalupe was introduced to the Mexican indigenous and *mestiza* population as a means of providing them with a more immediate form of identification, but the dark Virgin also became identified as a politicized social symbol of Mexican nationalism. Thus, the Virgin of Guadalupe, like her white counterpart, provided an "idealized" female image for the marginalized groups in order to facilitate their integration into the normative social and gender behavior established for them by a white patriarchal, hegemonic system.

The representation of the India María in Velasco's films, like that of the Virgin of Guadalupe, affords the indigenous and *mestiza* spectator with an opportunity to identify with a familiar cultural image. Although stereotyped, the image of the India María nevertheless provides a more direct form of pleasure-in-identification for its female audience. Moreover, the image of the India María functions as a female cultural symbol that, to some degree, helps to reduce the *social* invisibility of the indigenous female image in Mexican culture.

One cannot speak of the character of the India María without bringing to mind the renowned Mexican film comedian Cantinflas (Mario Moreno), a Chaplinesque character who, as a social outcast, managed to survive in a hostile urban environment. The India María is similar to Cantinflas even though she lacks his "sophistication" and ability to construct florid repartee. Rather, her wit is a native one, based on well-placed puns and double entendre. In this manner, María Elena Velasco proves in her films that she is a gifted comedienne who, like Cantinflas, manipulates or subverts language in order to achieve moral superiority in the battle against social forces that attempt to destroy her.

Because María Elena Velasco is herself a *mestiza* of indigenous heritage, she imbues the character of the India María with a unique representational persona. In Mexican "classic" films such as *María Candelaria* and *Flor silvestre* (both 1943), Dolores del Rio masquerades as an indigenous woman, creating a representational gap that must have impeded a large section of the indigenous and *mestiza* population from directly identifying with her character. Furthermore, this form of masquerade inevitably conjures up colonizing images of the past that are best put to rest. The indigenous roles portrayed by Dolores del Rio were an expression of the neoindigenism of Mexican national culture, which was influenced in part by the agrarian reform of President Lázaro Cárdenas (1934–40), and the treatise on indigenism expounded by José Vasconcelos and others. In *Medio siglo de cine mexicano (1896–1947)*, Aurelio de los Reyes points out that Dolores del Rio's portrayal of an indigenous female was an attempt by the Mexican film industry to "invent a mask" rather than represent an "authentic" Mexican female Indian. De los Reyes suggests that the

Mexican film industry, influenced by the Hollywood "star system," appeared most concerned with portraying an "idealized" indigenous female image that would be socially acceptable and commercially bankable.[2] Moreover, the indigenous image functioned as a shield for the changes taking place in the normative cultural identity of Mexican *criollas(os)* in relation to European and North American white culture. Within this context Velasco's films obtain increased significance for the indigenous female, *mestiza,* and Chicana spectators whose image in Mexican films is often displaced from its historical referent. De los Reyes also notes that during the Cárdenas presidency, the Mexican film industry found itself polarized between two extremes, out of which emerged two different film genres: the "comedia ranchera," which initiated a conservative nostalgia for the "Porfiriato" (Díaz dictatorship), and the liberal folk regionalism of "indígena" films influenced by the work of Sergei Eisenstein and Robert Flaherty, which attempted to recreate an "idealized" Mexican indigenous aesthetic that spoke to the dominant white culture.[3]

The social inscription of cultural images of people of color is also a concern for cultural theorist Homi Bhabha, who in "The Other Question" points out how discursive stereotypical practices of cultural difference have become inscribed in colonial discourse through a process of "fixity," which functions as a containment strategy and connotative cultural sign that determines "otherness."[4] For Homi Bhabha, the process of "fixity" works to seal the representation of color into a fixed position of negative connotations from which there is little possibility to negotiate new terms of placement.[5] Homi Bhabha's notion of "fixity" is one that pervades Velasco's films, for her films suggest that individuals of color such as the India María are assigned to a restrictive "space" within dominant culture from which possibilities of change are often impossible. What critics have missed, however, is the manner in which established positions of race, gender, and class are temporarily interrupted when the India María is able to exercise some degree of agency and control over her desire.

In *Ni de aquí, ni de allá,* the India María leaves her village for the United States in search of higher wages. On arrival in Los Angeles, she is separated from her employers and suddenly finds herself alone in a large city, dodging the clutches of an assassin and the immigration department. The India María wrestles with an unfamiliar, technological culture in which her attempts to succeed at numerous jobs are often interrupted by immigration raids. Unable to acculturate into modern, Anglo society, the India María seeks employment as a private nurse to a white family, a position that eventually dooms her to deportation when she introduces folk remedies to cure a moribund male. In the closing shots of the film, the India María is shown with her head reclined against the window of a bus, her spirit temporarily defeated. An existential dilemma awaits her upon her return to her village: caught between two cultures, she belongs—as the title forewarns—neither here nor there, *"ni de aquí, ni de allá."*

The film opens with a shot of the India María seated in a bus on her way back to Mexico. A flashback shifts the story to the chronological beginning, prior to the India María's departure to North America. The India María is depicted a devout churchgoer, her prayer representative of the religious fervor of the underprivileged class. Dressed in her identifiable costume of *campesina*, she leaves the church to sell baskets in the plaza. This sequence conveys the commercialization and consumerism of folk artifacts that Market Day in Mexico has come to represent, with the quality of goods rapidly declining. As the India María bids farewell to her father, he questions her motives for leaving the country: "Why don't you go to the capital?" "No," she responds, "you saw what happened to Chala, she returned to our village with a basket full of kids."[6] In her word play, the India María reveals the sexual vulnerability that single women face when they leave their homes to work in urban centers, but also—through language and humor— she sets herself apart from that process. Implied is the message that a *campesina* might be sexually safer in the United States where she possibly might experience less sexual harassment. This becomes evident during the opening scene in which the India María repels a Mexican male who, seated next to her, insists on pushing himself on her. In Velasco's films, the India María ignores, evades, and deflects the sexual advances of men.

In a continued effort to dissuade his daughter from leaving the ranch, the India María's father again questions her: "I don't know why you have to go in search of dollars if Mexico is the cornucopia (*el cuerno de la abundancia*)." "The abundance (*la abundancia*) is for others," she counters. "For us, the Indians, they continue to give us nothing but the horn (*el cuerno*)." Again, in a clever play on words, the India María uses humor to convey a social commentary on the socioeconomic conditions and policies that force some segments of the indigenous population in Mexico to leave their *ranchos*. The negative sexual and religious connotations for *cuerno*—in Spanish, one can "give horns" or cuckold, or send one to the "horn" or devil—further extend her critique of the dominant culture. The India María's father, however, continues to voice his concern. "They are going to change you," he warns her, "they are going to humiliate you, and soon you will be neither part of here, nor part of there." Thus, as an underlying theme of the popular comedy, the forces of underdevelopment, as embodied by the India María, will meet head on with industrialized capitalism and produce an irremediable culture clash.

As the narrative unfolds, the India María is seen as culturally impacted by her refusal to climb aboard the plane that is to take her to North America. Her cultural difference and lack of sophistication prompt white people to respond to the India María in a patronizing and paternalistic manner. The India María stands out in bas-relief with her *campesina* costume, "*huaraches*," and *vaquero* hat, which, along with her box of chiles, represent the visible part of her cultural identity. When the flight attendant reminds her to fasten her seat belt the India María misunderstands: "Oh, I thought you wanted me to put on my chastity belt." This exchange shows the semiotic difference that exists between the white and indigenous culture, making manifest (if not the object of laughter) the restrictive sexual moral codes still operative in Latin American culture.

On her arrival to Los Angeles, the India María is separated from the North American couple who have hired her as a servant. Her impending servitude represents that of the numerous undocumented Mexican nationals who are economically seduced by individuals and corporations into working at exploitative wages. When the India María returns to recover her box of chiles she is apprehended by a customs agent who treats her disparagingly. Not only are her chiles confiscated, but now she has become identified as suspicious and undesirable. Unable to read the signs on the door, the India María mistakes the men's bathroom for the customs office and walks into the aftermath of a murder. The murderer drags the India María out like a rag and manhandles her throughout the airport while people ignore her life-threatening danger. The India María manages to outwit her captor and break free of him. In slapstick humor reminiscent of the Hollywood silent era, the India María jumps in back of a moving van, dodging bullets from the criminal who is in hot pursuit of her. In these extreme occurrences, the film makes a humorous yet strong statement about the dehumanization that awaits the Mexican immigrant in a large American metropolis such as Los Angeles.

Having once more outwitted her assailant, the India María, alone, hungry, and lost, wanders through the streets of Los Angeles in a daze. The subjective point of view of the camera allows even the sophisticated spectator to see modern, industrial Los Angeles from the India María's "naive" perspective as cultural outsider. Her stroll leads her to a theater lobby where, among oversized photographic displays of Mexican movie stars, she recognizes a photograph of herself (María Elena Velasco as the India María), and turning to the audience she smiles a message of cultural complicity that helps to collapse the distance between the India *María* and *María* Elena Velasco. This intertextual joke between spectator and representational image is another way in which the cinematic apparatus interpellates the female indigenous, *mestiza*, and Chicana viewer within a particular gender, race, and social identification. Moreover, it is important to note how the process of denotation and connotation functions in relation to this scene. The image of the India María, which is also that of María Elena Velasco, signifies on at least two levels for the indigenous, *mestiza*, and Chicana viewers. Although the image of the India María remains the same, the connotation changes because the iconographic cultural subcode (here, in terms of class) is different.[7] On the one hand, an indigenous female spectator could identify with the image of the India María, who represents a working-class, rural indigenous Mexican female. On the other hand, *mestiza* and Chicana viewers might identify with the image of María Elena Velasco as urbanite, middle-class Mexican *mestiza*. Both identifications, then, are able to find extratextual reinforcement in the "India María-María Elena Velasco" star persona.

On every occasion on which the India María comes into contact with the urban environment, she runs into danger of being abused and exploited by society. Wherever the India María turns, there is an attempt to force her to assimilate and acculturate to North American culture. Toward the latter part of the film, the India María finds employment as a private nurse to a dying elderly white man. Convinced that he is suffering from *mal de ojo* (evil eye), she proceeds to perform a *limpia*.[8] In the process she accidentally incorporates some marijuana plants into her ritual. Although the *limpia* is fraught with unexpected accidents, it nevertheless proves to have miraculous effects on her patient, who revives to dance a jig. Again, the incongruity and clash between cultures in which the India María finds herself produces humor, as it subtly criticizes modern, technological (hence, "American") methods of patient care.

The majordomo of the house, who is also economically marginalized, nevertheless discriminates against the India María and diligently attempts to acculturate her by demanding that she dispose of her costume. She strongly refuses, however, because her costume represents that part of her identity that she is not willing to relinquish at this time. Although she temporarily agrees to wear a nurse's cap, the India María soon discards any semblance of foreign attire. When she is finally deported back to Mexico, however, she returns wearing a pair of tennis shoes and carrying a "ghetto blaster," which indicate that she has assimilated some aspects of capitalist consumerism that she now brings back to her village. This scene is played out to provoke laughter from the viewer, as well as to convey the social and economic reality of the undocumented. As the India María is let out of jail, one of the guards catches a glimpse of her incongruous attire and, perplexed over her tennis shoes, inquires: "Oh, you are a sportswoman (*una deportista*)?" "No, I am a deported woman (*una deportada*)," she answers. The play of words and misunderstood meanings uses humor in order to cover the underlying tragedy of deportation. Moreover, this scene suggests that although the indigenous Mexican migrant makes an effort to retain her or his cultural heritage, once the two cultures meet there is an inevitable cultural change and social displacement that must take place in the process of cultural "modernization." As the India María's humor and manipulation of language suggest, however, this change contains some self-conscious choices or mediations, and may or may not be regarded as progress, depending on which cultural values are compromised in the process of "modernization."

Throughout the film the theme of persecution is paramount. The Immigration and Naturalization Service (INS) is looking for the India María to deport her because they suspect her to be trafficking drugs. The Federal Bureau of Investigation (FBI) has targeted her as a dangerous spy, and the criminal also attempts to silence her for the murder she has witnessed. These male bureaucratic (and criminal) systems are portrayed as blundering, inefficient idiots. In this manner, the India María is placed in opposition to male forces of power who, reminiscent of narratives of film noir, persecute her in the effort to inculpate her for a crime she did not commit. The narrative conveys a much deeper meaning, however, that suggests that it is the India María's racial difference that poses a threat to these segments of the white male population. The film is able to mask with comedy the strong element of racial, sexual, and economic persecution that undocumented migrants face on their arrival to the United States, underscoring how systems of patriarchal power manage to create an invisible labor force, or expel from society those individuals who become identified as socially and racially antithetical to dominant culture.

Some of the problematic aspects of acculturation are best illustrated in the scene where the India María wanders lost through the streets of East Los Angeles, and, thinking that she has recognized a friendly face, stops a dark-looking *mestizo* couple to ask for directions. The *mestiza*, humiliated and shaking her head, refuses to speak Spanish. "No speak Spanish," she tells the India María, and turning indignantly toward her male companion complains in Spanish: "Who does she think I am? Can't she see that I am a *güera?*"[9] Here, the dialogue critiques how internalized racism is prevalent among marginalized groups who, in an attempt to be accepted by the dominant group in power, deny their own cultural heritage. But more important still is the implication of how the process of acculturation functions to fragment *chicana-mestiza* female subjectivity across class and race.

In the films of Velasco, the India María is not represented as a commodity, victim, or sexual object; on the contrary, she is portrayed as a female character who is able to take action in the effort to establish some control over the unsettling events that surround her. In contrast, however, one finds in Velasco's films other female characters who are not as favorably represented. In *El coyote emplumado*, the blonde female lover of a gangster is objectified in a manner reminiscent of female characters in film noir, who are persistently silenced or mistreated by the men they serve. In *Ni de aquí, ni de allá*, a woman in a jazz class is photographed at close range by a camera that closes in tightly on her thighs and buttocks. These female representations are portrayed as sexualized objects to whom any form of articulation has been denied. Even though the subtext of these film narratives attempts to comment on the class and racial stratification that exists among women, a problem emerges when Velasco unfavorably represents *criolla* women because she fails to take into account that white women are also marginalized by patriarchy.

In contrast to the other, sexualized female representations, the India María displays an asexuality that imbues her with an almost mythological aura, while it also insinuates that the character has the capability to go beyond the established gender placement. Velasco appears to have anticipated some feminist concerns in her refusal to assign the character of the India María a conventional "feminine" representation. Moreover, when Velasco ascribes an asexual quality to the character of the India María, she breaks away from traditional forms of female representation.[10] One could argue, however, that the India María's asexual characterization, which maintains her in a two-dimensional plane, may prevent the indigenous female and *mestiza* viewer from experiencing a more in-depth identification. Nevertheless, it is important to stress that this distance created between the female subject and object on the screen may provide the indigenous female and *mestiza* spectator with a respite from imposed patriarchal forms of female representation.

One of the reasons for the popularity of Velasco's films is the pleasure they offer. As Teresa de Lauretis has pointed out, "all films must offer their spectators some kind of pleasure, something of interest, be it technical, artistic, critical interest or the kind of pleasure that goes by the names of entertainment and escape."[11] Terms of cinematic pleasure require a mechanism of identification that can provide the viewer with direct or indirect pleasure. In Velasco's films, pleasure is achieved from an immediate cultural and gender identification with the image of the India María. Velasco's screen and star persona, although stereotyped, provides the female indigenous and (to some degree) *mestiza* spectators the experience of seeing one's cultural likeness represented on the screen. Even more, in many instances, that likeness, the India María, exercises agency over her desire, even if only temporary.

In *Ni de aquí, ni de allá*, cinematic pleasure can also be found in the way in which music is woven into the narrative and directly linked to the action of the main character. In particular, the music switches from English to Spanish as the India María crosses geographical borders. The songs' lyrics further reinforce the theme of social displacement and cultural alienation. In the United States, a female voice sings the blues, "I don't belong here and I don't belong even there"; in Mexico, a *corrido* or ballad asks, "Why did I leave my home?"[12] The India María, as an indigenous female, is socially dislocated whether she travels to the Mexican capital or to the United States, where she remains sexually vulnerable, racially discriminated against, and economically exploited.

María Elena Velasco admits that her main purpose in making films is to entertain and to provide a message of pleasure and laughter to *el pueblo*. She also concedes, however, that there is a need to provide her audience with a social message, which—with the exception of *Ni de aquí, ni de allá*—often remains well hidden in the subtext of the narrative. There are some contradictory aspects to Velasco's ideology in filmmaking. While she claims that paramount to her work is the desire to entertain her public, Velasco also warns that social messages, although important, must remain in context relatively light.[13] Velasco is concerned that her audience might lose interest in her work if asked to become more consciously active. But pleasure, entertainment, and politicized commitment are not exclusive of each other, and this does not necessarily mean that one has to preclude the possibility of active conscious participation on the part of the spectator. Could it be that Velasco underestimates the intellectual capability of her audience? After all, *Ni de aquí, ni de allá*, her most explicitly politicized film, was also the highest grossing Mexican film of 1987.

In conclusion, it is important to continue to examine the films of María Elena Velasco who, although she may stereotype the indigenous female, for the first time provides a voice to this marginalized group, a voice that interrupts the established subaltern position of the indigenous female in popular Mexican film.

Notes

I would like to thank Teresa de Lauretis and Carmen Leon for their insightful comments.

1. Interview with María Elena Velasco, Mexico City, 1988, by Carmen Huaco-Nuzum. Velasco's portrayal of the India María dates back to the early 1970s, when she appeared in the theater and on the Televisa variety show *Siempre en Domingo*. She starred in some half-dozen popular features—beginning with *Tonta tonta pero no tanto* (*Foolish But Not Too Much*, 1971)—before her directorial debut in the early 1980s. Velasco claims that she borrowed the name María from the name commonly used to address indigenous women who leave their rural villages in search of work in an urban environment.

2. Aurelio de los Reyes, *Medio siglo de cine mexicano (1896–1947)* (Mexico City: Editorial Trillas, 1988), 196–97.

3. Ibid., 186–97.

4. Homi K. Bhabha, "The Other Question," *Screen* 24, no. 6 (November/December 1983): 18–24.

5. Ibid.

6. Dialogue from the film *Ni de aquí, ni de allá* (1987), directed by María Elena Velasco. This and subsequent passages of the film are translated by the author.

7. Umberto Eco, "On the Contribution of Film to Semiotics," *Film Theory and Criticism*, ed. Gerald Mast and Marshall Cohen (New York: Oxford University Press, 1979), 219–226. Eco examines how the semiotic process of denotation and connotation works in film when different cultural iconographic subcodes and images are interpreted by a culturally diverse audience.

8. *Limpia*, known in Mexico and some areas of Latin America and the United States, is a cleansing ritual performed on an ailing patient to cleanse the individual of unfriendly spirits or forces trapped inside the body. Selected herbs, prayers, and incense are often used in this ritual.

9. *Güera* is the Mexican term used to identify a person of fair complexion. The use of *güera* in the exchange here reflects the invocation of a false racial distinction in order to mask a class one.

10. Interviews with María Elena Velasco, Mexico City, 1988 and 1990, by Carmen Huaco-Nuzum. Velasco claims that she deliberately chose not to portray the India María in subjective scenes of intimacy because "the character of the India María belongs to all the people and not to any particular gender group."

11. Teresa de Lauretis, *Alice Doesn't: Feminism, Semiotics, Cinema* (Bloomington: Indiana University Press, 1984), 136.

12. Musical lyrics from the film *Ni de aquí, ni de allá* (1987), directed by María Elena Velasco.

13. Interview with María Elena Velasco, Mexico City, 1988, by Carmen Huaco-Nuzum.

Part Two
Critical Issues in Chicano Cinema

Between a Weapon and a Formula
Chicano Cinema and Its Contexts

Chon A. Noriega

This essay will attempt to outline a schema for Chicano cinema that includes historical overview, conceptual framework (production, exhibition, signification, and reception), and selected textual examples that highlight culture-based and hybrid styles, narrative structures, and formal properties. The schema presented is both initial and incomplete, and should be taken as an attempt to open up potential avenues for future Chicano film scholarship. To the extent possible, I have tried to foreground both the social history and cultural elements that inform Chicano cinema. Unfortunately, I have not been able to do more than point to the broader categories of Latino, ethnic, and American cinemas, and the extent to which individual filmmakers negotiate within and between these categories.

Historical Overview, 1965–1990

By 1965, diverse and multilocal social protests in the Southwest had coalesced into a national civil rights movement variously known as the Chicano Movement, El Movimiento, La Causa, and La Lucha. These protests included the farmworkers' struggle, the New Mexico land-grant movement, the Denver Crusade for Justice, high school blowouts (or walkouts), anti-Vietnam War marches in East Los Angeles, and the voters' revolt in Crystal City, Texas, which led to the formation of the national La Raza Unida Party.[1]

Between 1968 and 1970, Chicanos who had been active in the student and farmworkers' protests turned to film and television as a means to spread the message about the Chicano Movement. Mocte-suma Esparza, one of the "L.A. Thirteen" indicted on conspiracy charges in the March 1968 blowouts in East L.A. high schools, orga-nized the UCLA Media Urban Crisis Coalition program, which recruited thirteen ethnic minorities. To the north, in San Juan Bautista, Luis Valdez, who founded El Teatro Campesino amid the Delano grape strike, filmed *I Am Joaquin* (1969), based on Rodolfo "Corky" Gonzales's epic poem of the same name.[2]

In the early 1970s, UCLA served as a training ground for most Chicano filmmakers. Given the imperative to spread the message about the movement, students often turned to television projects while still in school, producing minority public affairs shows and spe-cials created as a result of organized protests. The most crucial lesson learned concerned how to subvert the discursive parameters for mass media so that Chicano filmmakers could work within and yet against the industry and its conventions. One of the more innovative shows was *Reflecciones* (KABC-TV in Los Angeles, 1972–73), in which Luis Garza, Susan Racho, and David Garcia mastered the objective dis-course of reportage in order to pioneer a new form of television, the political documentary series, which protested the Vietnam War, advo-cated a farmworkers' union, and exposed the criminal legal system. *Reflecciones* used no on-air host. Instead, each episode began in medias res and developed its critique through shot composition, fast cutting, and perspective shots, all reinforced or counterpointed through the use of diverse musical styles. Since television shows were shot on 16-mm film, producers could use the film stock for documentary seg-ments. Bobby Páramo's *Carnalitos* (1973), for example, was filmed un-der the aegis of Jesús Salvador Treviño's talk show *Acción Chicano* [*sic*].[3]

In 1974, the efforts initiated within the social protest movement began to acquire an institutional dimension with the creation of the Latino Consortium, based out of PBS-affiliate KCET-TV in Los Angeles. The Consortium, which received modest support from the Corporation for Public Broadcasting (CPB), served as a national syn-dicator of Latino-themed programming to public television. Accord-ing to the first (and current) executive director, José Luis Ruiz, the Latino Consortium owes its survival to its institutional status, which helped it secure the long-term funding and organizational continuity that the other, volunteer, groups lacked. These efforts built upon those

of earlier protest and community groups, in particular *Justicia*, orga-
nized by Ray Andrade, Pete Rodriguez, and Bob Morones at
California State-Los Angeles. In many respects, *Justicia*, which had a
significant impact on the studios and networks, helped bring about
Chicano-produced local television shows such as *Unidos* and
Reflecciones (both KABC-TV), *Impacto* (KNBC-TV), and *Acción Chicano*
(KCET-TV) in the early 1970s.[4]

In 1975, *Realidades*—a local public television program in New York
created when Puerto Rican activists took over the station—became the
first national Latino series.[5] *Realidades* commissioned numerous
Chicano films, including *Cristal* (1975), *Garment Workers* (1975), *De
Colores* (1975), and *Guadalupe* (1976). In addition, producer Humberto
Cintrón organized the National Latino Media Coalition, which lob-
bied public television, government agencies, and Congress. The coalition held the first pan-Latino media conference in San Antonio, Texas,
in 1976, and, with Chicanos José Luis Ruiz, Grace Negata, and
Antonio Parra, continued until about 1980.

Also in 1975, the national Chicano Film Festival was founded in
San Antonio. Adan Medrano, the festival's first director, cited the festival as a response to both the "thirst for films that express the
Chicano lifestyle, and a lack of a showcase for the Chicano artist." At
about this time, Chicano filmmakers began to leave television stations
in order to form independent production companies. The move was at
once a response to the limited opportunities within television stations
(low-budget public affairs shows) and an attempt to acquire greater
control over the development, production, and distribution of
Chicano-themed films. Jesús Salvador Treviño related these efforts to
the Chicano Movement's call for "our own institutions." Independent
production companies included Moctesuma Esparza Productions,
Learning Garden Productions (Severo Perez), Ruiz Productions (José
Luis Ruiz), and New Vista Productions (Treviño). In addition to the
Chicano Film Festival, community- and university-based exhibitions
created an important alternative Chicano circuit for the independent
films made for television.[6]

In 1978, Chicano cinema acquired its own professional organization when the Los Angeles-based Chicano Cinema Coalition met for
the first time to screen and learn from classic Hollywood films in
Treviño's living room. In its brief existence, the coalition would serve
as a resource for filmmakers and as a platform for protests against

exploitation films and industry hiring practices. The coalition also played a significant role in the redirection of the Chicano Film Festival toward a more pan-Latino and Latin American orientation. The coalition's *Chicano Cinema Newsletter* (Fall 1978-Spring 1980) reported on Chicano film production, organized protests and other activities, and shared information on production resources and strategies.

These various local and national efforts represented an initial step in the development of independent dramatic and feature-length projects funded by the CPB, PBS, and National Endowment for the Humanities (NEH), in particular *Seguin* (1981), *The Ballad of Gregorio Cortez* (1983), and *El Norte* (1984). In December 1980, José Luis Ruiz coordinated a Hispanic Southwest Regional Conference on "Media and the Humanities," funded by the NEH Media Program. The four-day conference brought together humanities scholars, filmmakers, and funders in order to exchange and develop strategies for future NEH projects. In addition, papers were presented by Chicano scholars Carlos E. Cortés, Cordelia Candelaria, and Juan Bruce-Novoa, among others. At the heart of the conference, however, was the question of Chicano scholar and filmmaker collaboration on humanities media projects: historical dramas, literary adaptations, and documentaries. The scholar-filmmaker relationship continues to have relevance, especially insofar as foundation grant sources also adhere to the NEH model for humanities media projects.

In this period, the filmmakers also published the initial studies on Hollywood's Chicano stereotypes in popular and academic journals and offered "Chicano cinema" as the alternative in a series of manifestos.[7] In "Towards the Development of a Raza Cinema," Francisco X. Camplis situated the emergent practice within the context of New Latin American Cinema, concluding that "[a] Chicano or Raza Cinema must by necessity be a weapon!" While the rhetoric belongs to the revolutionary manifestos of Solanas and Getino, Sanjines, and Rocha, Camplis's manifesto is rooted in his experience of the Chicano Movement as he traveled throughout the Southwest. In other words, for Camplis and Cine-Aztlán, who wrote within the latter years of the Chicano Movement, the initial frame of reference for the manifestos was the political turmoil of the late 1960s and early 1970s, in particular the police riot in East L.A. that ended the peaceful Chicano Moratorium against the Vietnam War on August 29, 1970. And though Johansen did not publish his manifesto or "notes" until five years later, it came at a time when many filmmakers, under the Chicano Cinema Coalition, were beginning to place their work within the context of New Latin American Cinema.

In considering the manifestos and the relationship between Chicano cinema and New Latin American Cinema, it is important to keep in mind two things. First, both Chicano cinema and New Latin American Cinema have undergone considerable changes that qualify the earlier radical manifestos. And second, both sets of manifestos must be seen as putting forth a relational "stance" rather than a reified "status" or formula with respect to approaches to form and content. In the expression of an oppositional political and aesthetic stance, the Chicano film manifestos, like those of the Chicano Movement itself, provided an alternative geography or conceptual space within which to work. On both accounts, what these Chicano manifestos often provided was a raison d'être and critical perspective that guided students into the university and filmmakers into the American film industry.

In this respect, José Limón's application of Harold Bloom's concept of the "anxiety of influence" to the Chicano Movement offers some insight.[8] But whereas Limón identifies the Mexican Revolution of 1910 as the object of the movement's anxiety of influence, it seems to me that it was anxiety over "Gringo" influences that led Chicanos to seek models in the Mexican and Cuban revolutions. Likewise, the appeal to New Latin American Cinema masked a considerable anxiety over the all-pervasive influence of Hollywood, an anxiety that the manifestos of New Latin American Cinema also reveal. For Chicano filmmakers, most of whom lived and worked in Los Angeles, Hollywood represented an influence not just on film production, but on the adjacent Chicano communities as well. The Chicano Cinema Coalition and community-based groups reiterated that point in organized protests against *Walk Proud* (1979), which was shot on location in Venice and increased tensions within the Chicano community there.[9]

By 1981, when Universal Pictures released *Zoot Suit*, the early period of Chicano cinema had come to an end as the filmmakers became experienced professionals and broader industry connections were established. The Chicano Cinema Coalition had dissolved, in large part a victim of its own success, as members spent more time on film projects. The Chicano Film Festival changed course and became the more encompassing International Hispanic Film Festival and, later, CineFestival, under the new leadership of Eduardo Díaz. Latino film festivals soon emerged in New York and Chicago: respectively, the National Latino Film and Video Festival (1981), directed by Lillian Jiménez, and the Chicago Latino Film Festival (1985), directed by Pepe Vargas. Some bemoaned the loss of a purely Chicano forum, but these changes strengthened connections made earlier between the Puerto Rican and Chicano communities through the *Realidades* series. The nature of that connection, and whether it even exists on some aesthetic, cultural, or ideological level, has been the subject of debate in recent Latino film festivals. These debates—over a "Hispanic cinema" and "cine de mestizaje"—have taken the form of panel discussions among film scholars, filmmakers, and media professionals.

Connections also reached to Latin America. In December 1979, Havana hosted the First New Latin American Cinema Festival. Treviño, one of the festival founders, led a delegation of Chicano filmmakers and media professionals to Cuba. The Chicano films screened received an award as a group, and Treviño's *Raíces de Sangre* (1977), a Chicano feature financed by Mexico, won the award for best script. The experience resulted in an increased international perspective in Chicano films in the 1980s, one the earlier manifestos had theorized. In 1982, *Zoot Suit* won the Premio Ariel as the best *Mexican* film of the year. Five years later, another Chicano feature made in Hollywood, *Born in East L.A.*, would win the best script award in Havana, speaking to such oppositional standards as the Hollywood box office and the "aesthetics of hunger" of New Latin American Cinema.

In the 1980s, the so-called Decade of the Hispanic, public funding sources, which had been (and continue to be) the mainstay of Chicano-produced film and video, were cut back under the Reagan administration. Nonetheless, several efforts further broadened the scope of Chicano cinema. In 1980, a group of San Francisco-based Chicano filmmakers formed Cine Acción, a national media arts group that serves the Latino community. Cine Acción regularly sponsors workshops and exhibitions, including the recent "Women of the Americas Film and Video Festival" in October 1988. National, if not international, in outlook, Cine Acción finds its counterpart in the East Coast group, the Latino Collaborative. Both groups include filmmakers and media artists and provide networking and distribution services, contacts with Latin America, and professional, production-oriented seminars and workshops.

Chicano filmmakers had been able to produce nine feature-length films in the late 1970s and early 1980s, but these efforts would not achieve significant recognition within the "mainstream" press and markets until the box-office success of Luis Valdez's *La Bamba* (1987).[10] Between 1987 and 1988, Hollywood released four Chicano-Latino feature films: *La Bamba, Born in East L.A.* (1987), *The Milagro Beanfield War* (1988), and *Stand and Deliver* (1988). The success of these films, and *La Bamba* in particular, led studio executives and others to predict a "Hispanic Hollywood." The proof of that claim, however, was attributed to "Hispanic" demographics and market studies on "Hispanic" movie attendance, and not to the two-decade Chicano film movement.[11] The inability of *Break of Dawn* (1988), an independent feature, to secure a distributor in the same period, and the subsequent drought of Chicano- or Latino-produced feature films, signals that "Hispanic Hollywood" is by no means guaranteed, let alone defined as a concept. On the one hand, studios have yet to commit themselves to the grass-roots marketing strategies that ethnic and other specialty films require. And, more often than not, traditional saturation campaigns—especially the television trailers—have played into stereotypes that alienate the films' potential viewers. In their trailers, for example, *Zoot Suit* came across as a gang film, and *The Ballad of Gregorio Cortez* appeared to be yet another "macho" western—the very expectations the films sought to critique and change.[12]

Since *La Bamba*, Chicano cinema has undergone a *renacimiento* that includes a renewed round of organizational activities. In June 1990, the Latino Consortium reorganized as the National Latino Communications Center (NLCC) in order to become more independent of the CPB and expand into production and acquisition. Earlier in the year, Mexico hosted Chicano filmmakers for a weeklong series of screenings and talks on potential coproduction.[13] One outcome of the event, called *Chicanos 90,* was a bringing together of the first generation of filmmakers—Luis Valdez, Moctesuma Esparza, José Luis Ruiz, Jesús Salvador Treviño—for the first time in almost a decade, in addition to a postmovement generation of filmmakers: Gregory Nava, Isaac Artenstein, Paul Espinosa. Since then, the *Chicanos 90* group has met on a regular basis in order to organize a reciprocal event in Los Angeles for Mexican independent filmmakers, scheduled for November 1991.

In November 1990, Cine Acción cofounder and filmmaker Lourdes

Portillo organized the first conference of Chicana and Mexican women filmmakers, media professionals, and film scholars. The event— "Cruzando Fronteras: Encuentro de Mujeres Cineastas y Videoastas Latinas/Across the Border: Conference of Latin Women Film and Video Makers"—was hosted by the Colegio de la Frontera Norte in Tijuana and represents an initial organizational effort in the development of a Chicana counter-countercinema, one whose need can be seen in the all-male *Chicanos 90* roster.[14] Although Chicanas such as Susan Racho, Sylvia Morales, Esperanza Vásquez, and Lourdes Portillo were instrumental in the first decade of Chicano cinema, their work has not received the same critical attention as male-produced films. The neglect is amplified because Chicanas have not produced feature films, which tend to be the focus of most film scholarship. And yet it is the Chicana-produced work that has consistently challenged and redirected the cultural paradigms of Chicano cinema.[15]

As Rosa Linda Fregoso points out in the next essay in this book, many Chicanas choose to work in the shorter formats, since these provide a greater measure of artistic freedom. For Chicanas, video offers the same access and immediacy that television did for an earlier, mostly male generation and, as Lourdes Portillo argues, video may lead to an increase in the number of Chicana media artists, if not the development of a Chicana video aesthetic. It is still too early to define such an aesthetic, but its contours can be seen in the recent experimental video work of Frances Salomé España, Sandra P. Hahn, Beverly Sánchez Padilla, Betty Maldonado, and T. Osa Hidalgo de la Riva, as I discuss in the last section of this essay.

Lourdes Portillo's work is itself pivotal in the development of an alternative Chicana/Latina film practice: from the collaborative nature of her productions, to the playful invocation of popular Latino genres, to the subtle attention to the objects that define social space and the mise-en-scène as Latino or bicultural. Portillo's films—*Después del Terremoto/After the Earthquake* (1979) and *Las Madres de Plaza de Mayo* (1985)—confront international political issues from the personal perspective of Latina resistance. In many ways, *La Ofrenda: The Days of the Dead* (1988) is her first "Chicana" film, examining the relationship between cultural ritual in Mexico and its sociopolitical transformation in the United States.

Conceptual Framework

Given its historical development, on what national, political, and cultural plane can we situate Chicano cinema? If we turn to film historiography, Chicano cinema does not exist at all, either as a movement or as a group of individual films. On the other hand, as Jesús Treviño argued as recently as 1984,

> the films that have resulted are at once an expression of the life, concerns and issues of the Chicano people, and at the same time, the northernmost expression of a political and socially conscious international cinema movement known as New Latin American Cinema.[16]

But even while Treviño and others situated Chicano cinema in this manner, the same filmmakers continued to make inroads into the American film and television industry. From the start, then, Chicano cinema has had to mark out a space for itself between a weapon and a formula, between the political weapon of New Latin American Cinema and the economic formula of Hollywood. Too often, however, these two practices are seen as mutually exclusive, rather than as the thesis and antithesis of a cinematic dialectic at work in the Americas.

The sense of dual emplacement, or that social space from which the text "speaks," is one that finds expression in many Chicano films, often through a direct reference to Aztlán, the Aztec homeland, which is thought to have been in the Southwest.[17] In the mythohistorical introduction to the video adaptation of the *teatro acto* or Chicano theater sketch *Los Vendidos* (1972), Luis Valdez, dressed as an Aztec calendar, takes the concept of Aztlán to its brash yet logical extreme when he proclaims El Teatro Campesino: "The Farmworkers' Theater of Aztlán, of the Southwest, of America, of the Earth . . . of the Universe." Although often read as the affirmation of a "pure" cultural nationalism, statements such as these—most recently in *Chicano Park* (1988)—reveal a complex sense of the competing geographies within which the Chicano filmmakers operate. In Valdez's statement, then, one finds a core metaphor for the project of Chicano cinema (and Chicano art, in general) to reach the Chicano community, as well as broader audiences. One does not, after all, stand in Aztlán without also occupying the other spaces.

In order to understand how Chicano cinema operates within the formula-weapon dialectic, one must first examine the Chicano art movement and the vernacular or culture-based concepts by which it theorizes itself. In their overview of the Chicano experience and the arts, *Arte Chicano: A Comprehensive Annotated Bibliography of Chicano Art, 1965–1981,* Shifra Goldman and Tomás Ybarra-Frausto identify three defining elements of Chicano culture: resistance, maintenance, and affirmation.[18] These can be seen as tactics within a larger strategy expressed in the philosophical concept of *Chicanismo,* a word often poorly translated as "Chicano pride." These tactics—cultural responses to political, economic, legal, and social oppression—overlap to a considerable degree. In many Chicano films, for example, the *corrido* (folk ballad), an early form of Chicano resistance, is used to affirm a political stance on both historical and allegorical levels. Since the *corridos* are often sung in Spanish without translation or subtitles, the form uses language in order to maintain a distinct interpretive community. These tactics, then, work in concert in the expression and construction of a minority cultural identity. Francisco X. Camplis, drawing upon vernacular idiom, refers to such a discursive and aesthetic strategy as cinema *al estilo Chicano* (done Chicano style), the selective adaptation of conventional forms in the service of *Chicanismo.*

Goldman and Ybarra-Frausto's schema covers the period between 1965 and 1981. Since then, however, the need has arisen for a fourth category that describes the area of cultural production that incorporates or engages rather than resists or denies the dominant culture. In the 1980s Chicano filmmakers start to enter the international arena of both New Latin American Cinema and the Hollywood "mainstream." Following the lead of the Border Art Workshop/Taller de Arte Fronterizo in San Diego/Tijuana, we can call this category the culture of *mestizaje.*[19] In its earlier manifestations in Mexican and Chicano thought, *mestizaje* located the historical origins of national character in the racial mixture between the Spaniard and Indian. The end result of the concept, however, was a neoindigenism that sought an alternative to European and Anglo American influences. In recent years, border artists such as Guillermo Gómez-Peña have used *mestizaje* not as a retreat into a "pure" origin or alternative but as a way to deconstruct the notion of a dominant culture:

> . . . everywhere we look we find pluralism, crises, nonsynchronicity
> . . . Dominant culture is a meta-reality that only exists in the virtual
> space of the mainstream media and in the ideologically and aestheti-

cally controlled spaces of the more established cultural institutions. Today, if there is a dominant culture, it is border culture. And those who still haven't crossed a border will do it very soon.[20]

In this vein, Chicano feature filmmakers in the 1980s such as Moctesuma Esparza and Luis Valdez—who was a major force behind the neoindigenism of the Chicano Movement—attempted to redefine the key terms of Hollywood discourse: "universal" and "mainstream." In place of the implicit referent for these terms—that is, middle-class WASP culture—Valdez, like Gómez-Peña, pointed to the de facto cultural *mestizaje* in the United States.[21]

These four elements of Chicano thought and artistic expression—resistance, affirmation, maintenance, and *mestizaje*—provide the basis for a culture-specific analysis of the weapon-formula dialectic within Chicano cinema. Such an analysis, however, must attempt to identify if and how these cultural or bicultural elements come into play within and across the four major areas of cinematic practice: production, exhibition, signification, and reception.

Production. As Goldman and Ybarra-Frausto note, "Chicano filmmakers, of all Chicano artists, function under the most difficult economic and ideological conditions."[22] In fact, Chicano cinema has been a cinema of poor means even in relation to the underfunded independent American cinema. But as José Montoya explains, "Being a Chicano artist means doing something creative with whatever is at hand."[23] In this manner, the "make do" style of Chicano art transforms or subverts a medium that prides itself on formal and technical innovation. The things "at hand," of course, include cultural icons, narrative forms, and language. Filmmakers have employed various *movidas* or coping strategies in order to overcome, mitigate, or co-opt film's economic and ideological constraints. In this respect, production history should be central to the criticism or interpretation of Chicano film and video, not as an apologia, but because the fact of production often figures into a text on a self-conscious, cultural level.

Exhibition. The history of Chicano cinema has been one in which filmmakers sought access to the means of distribution as well as production. Documentaries continue to be produced primarily for public television and are later exhibited at Chicano (and other) film festivals, *galerias*, and community- and university-based *centros*. In recent years, Chicano cinema has gained a greater acceptance within the realm of the art museum. This has been due, in part, to the exhibition *Chicano Art: Resistance and Affirmation, 1965–1985* (also called by the acronym CARA), a national and international tour of the Chicano Art Movement that started at the Los Angeles Wight Art Gallery (September-December 1990) and will continue for three years. There has also been a significant evolution in Chicano-Latino film programming, or how an exhibition or series is selected and arranged into programs. Beginning with the established Latino film festivals, under the direction of Lillian Jiménez and Yvette Nieve-Cruz (CineFestival director since 1988), Chicano-Latino film programming has become more conceptual, addressing aesthetic, political, sexual, and cultural issues. The change from a "default" film programming has been made possible because of the wider selection of material brought about by increased Chicano-Latino production, the accumulation over twenty years of a significant body of work, and the pan-*Américas* orientation that continued to develop throughout the 1980s and into the 1990s.

Insofar as most Chicano filmmakers worked toward the feature format, distribution also entailed an attempt to reach and impact the "mainstream." In fact, Chicano filmmakers have identified a dual audience—whether Chicano and American, or Chicano and Latin American—in both radical manifestos and industry-oriented articles since the early 1970s. And, as David Rosen demonstrates, in such features as *The Ballad of Gregorio Cortez, El Norte,* and *Stand and Deliver,* filmmakers were able to innovate a complex financial and distribution arrangement that combined European presales, PBS broadcast on *American Playhouse,* and a Hollywood theatrical release with a significant grass-roots component.

Looked at from the perspective of distribution and exhibition, Chicano cinema represents an effort to "put [the Chicano film narrative] into discourse."[24] In other words, the *where* (distribution) of Chicano cinema becomes as important as the *what* (signification) and the *how* (production) of Chicano cinema. Where do these films circulate? Who gets to see them, and in what sort of social context or environment? These factors are determined by the nature and extent of a film's marketing campaign, whether it be self-distribution at the grassroots level (*Break of Dawn*), a typical Hollywood saturation ad campaign (*Zoot Suit, La Bamba*), or some hybrid (*The Ballad of Gregorio Cortez, El Norte*).

Signification. Most Chicano feature films are based on true stories or historical events. A recurrent issue, therefore, has to do with the relationship between film and history. These films attempt to reclaim a forgotten past, but also choose to do so within the parameters of narrative—as opposed to documentary—cinema. That the filmmakers attempt to construct a counterimage rooted in the history of the Chicano experience marks the texts in two fundamental ways. On the one hand, the historical discourse operates within a bicultural logic that informs, undercuts, or otherwise engages "History." Films may draw upon culture-based, alternative forms of history telling, as in the *corrido* in *The Ballad of Gregorio Cortez*, and *teatro* in *Zoot Suit*, or, instead, be structured around a culture-based stance or sensibility toward history, as in *rasquachismo* in *Born in East L.A.*, and cultural *mestizaje* in *Break of Dawn*.[25]

On the other hand, these films sustain an intertextual dialogue with previous Hollywood representation. Given the filmmakers' research into Chicano-themed films, for example, it is possible to argue that the first two Chicano feature films, *Raíces de sangre* and *Only Once in a Lifetime*, "signify" upon the Hollywood social problem film, thereby inverting its ideological thrust.[26] In a more general way, the historical films "signify" upon the film genres that have denied or repressed the history about to be told. *The Ballad of Gregorio Cortez* deconstructs both the classical western and the silent "greaser" genre of the period depicted. Likewise, *Break of Dawn* and *Zoot Suit*, which depict the 1930s and 1940s, respectively, speak through and against the film genres from the periods depicted: the Latin musical, film noir, B-films, and the courtroom drama.

The central question that these films raise is, How can Chicanos depict history when historians, journalists, and Hollywood have either distorted, censored, or repressed the history of the Chicano experience? The answer, more often than not, has been to deconstruct the objective discourse of history and proffer instead specific stories of conflict, resistance, and *mestizaje*.[27]

Since Chicano cinema engages a bicultural dynamic, close attention must be given to the function of language, discourse, and sensibility. As an initial hypothesis, I propose that Chicano films and videos at times conflate the weapon and formula, so that beneath the conventional, formulaic genres and narrative structures of American cinema, one can find a substructure based upon traditional or popular Chicano and Mexican forms.[28] Often, as in the *teatro, telenovelas,* and *corridos*, the three-act structure parallels that of the dominant Hollywood film narrative. Less common, but used in seminal texts, are *floricanto* (a neoindigenous concept for poetry) and the *testimonio* (a Latin American form of autobiography). I will examine examples of these briefly in the last section of my essay.

I do not want to imply that all Chicano films operate in this fashion. Rather, I hope to outline the bicultural matrix within which these texts have the potential to operate. Further research and careful analysis will be needed in order to identify the processes of signification in particular films or groups of films. As a first step, however, we must reconsider the two oppositions central to such an aesthetic analysis: form and content; mise-en-scène and montage. Because film critics have not been able to read those cinematic codes that operate within a bicultural and bilingual context, there has been an assumption that Chicano cinema, like other ethnic and protest cinema, is a cinema of content and not one of formal innovation. What has been missed is the way in which ethnic content at times (1) operates as a formal element, (2) becomes a style unto itself, or (3) provides the substructure for a counternarrative. I will look briefly at mise-en-scène and montage.

Mise-en-scène. While Chicano cinema makes significant use of montage, its sensibility is that of mise-en-scène, or the "putting in the scene" of the Chicano experience. For the first time, screen space was filled not just with Chicano "images" but with the aural and visual texture of our culture: the music, languages, home altars, food preparation, neighborhoods. As a film reviewer in *La Opinión* described it, these films were attentive to the "type of life that unfolds along the diverse and colorful streets of East Los Angeles, leaving behind (at last) the old stereotypes with which the North American cinema has judged our culture" (my translation).[29]

Also, montage often operates as a temporal extension of mise-en-scène. Many Chicano documentaries begin with a pretitle montage sequence that outlines the history of the Chicano experience, starting at some point between Aztlán and the Mexican Revolution of 1910, and lead up to the particular moment documented. These films acknowledge the de facto horizon of expectations for films about Chicanos and attempt to resituate the text . . . but not without a sense of irony. In *The Unwanted* (1976), José Luis Ruiz uses sepia-toned clips from motion pictures about the Mexican American War in a subtle comment on how that event is now understood.

Montage. Even montage in the Eisensteinian sense depends upon the ability to read the bicultural codes in the mise-en-scène. The establishing shot for *Cristal,* for example, does not present Crystal City, Texas, but rather a dissolve from the symbol for one worldview to that of another. In the first shot, a billboard put up by the Chamber of Commerce announces, "Crystal City, Spinach Capital of the World." The camera pans left to reveal a Popeye statue beside the billboard and dissolves to another billboard that reads, "Cristal, nacimiento del partido raza unida" [Crystal City, birthplace of the Raza Unida Party]. Beneath the words is the Aztec icon for the party and, along the bottom, the sentence, "José Angel Gutiérrez para juez" [for judge].

In outlining dominant and alternative geographies, the film posits a Chicano-Latino viewer able to read the shift in cultural and linguistic codes. (In fact, the film was commissioned for national broadcast on the *Realidades* series.) First is the linguistic shift from English to Spanish and then, on a content level, a shift from Anglo-controlled agribusiness to the first and most successful voters' revolt of the Chicano Movement. More subtle is the shift in cultural icons: from Popeye, a popular culture adjunct to agribusiness, to another soldier, the Aztec warrior, beneath the message itself.

Reception. Given this example, it is important to keep in mind how culture, language, and gender position us to receive a text. When I first taught a course on Chicano cinema in the winter of 1990, the students were all bilingual Chicanos. After we saw *Salt of the Earth,* the one student from New Mexico, near where the film was shot, took umbrage at the characterization of Juan Chacón. No *hispano,* he argued, would ever call himself Mexican American, nor would he ever display a picture of Benito Juárez, Mexico's first Indian president. Several female students, meanwhile, identified a repressed subtext in Deborah Rosenfelt's chapter in the book *Salt of the Earth* that attempted to silence the embittered voice of Virginia Chacón in order to preserve the film's feminist message.[30] Similarly, several *tejanos* have told me they felt betrayed by a scene in *The Ballad of Gregorio Cortez* where Gregorio Cortez cries (and in front of the Anglos!) when he sees his wife and children in jail. The fault is traced to the more emotional *califas* Chicanos, such as actor Edward James Olmos, who do not understand the stoic *tejano* character.

I mention these above anecdotes in order to foreground the need for a more complex conceptualization of the Chicano spectator and of

Chicano culture, and to avoid to a certain extent the essentialism that
pervades scholarship on cultural and sexual difference. In the end, I
feel that the concept of the "self and Other" often perpetuates the
process that it also describes. For example, as I have argued elsewhere, once one defines the Other as a projection of the self, it then
becomes difficult to talk about anything except the "self."[31]

Textual Examples

In the space remaining, I will consider several documentaries and
short dramas in light of the schema presented above. In particular, I
will examine the use of cultural narratives such as *floricanto, testimonio,
teatro, corrido, telenovela,* and experimental variations in the short formats. As I explained at the start of this essay, these brief "readings"
are initial and exploratory, designed to suggest or explicate what I see
as the culture-specific or bicultural aspects of the texts.

Floricanto is a neoindigenous concept for Chicano poetry, which
derives from the combination of prayer and poetry in Aztec culture.
The Nahuatl (or Aztec-language) phrase *in xochitl in cuicatl* translates
as "flower and song" or, in Spanish, *flor y canto.* Luis Valdez and poet
Alurista were the first to reclaim the concept in the late 1960s.[32]
Floricanto exemplifies both the historical and mythopoetic impulse of
the Chicano Movement, which expressed itself in "epic" poetry, literature, and film. In this regard, *I Am Joaquin* (1969) and *Chicana* (1979)
frame the cultural nationalist period and together delineate its historical, political, and aesthetic vision. The films set forth a worker-based
ideology and cultural identity that are rooted in a pre-Columbian
mythopoetics and the 500-year history of *mestizo* resistance. Camera
movements, music, and the narrators' voices activate the still photographs that constitute the visual text.

In *I Am Joaquin,* Luis Valdez gives a dramatic reading of Rodolfo
"Corky" Gonzales's epic poem, set against still photographs and
Daniel Valdez's improvised guitar music. The camera is unsteady in
its pans, tilts, and zooms, nonetheless creating a sense of movement
through fast cutting and montage. Based on the most famous—and
some argue the "first"—Chicano poem, the film displays all the hall-
marks of a *rasquache* cinema, which is to say, one in which poor means
are transformed into an aesthetic style or cultural stance. One sign of

the film's *rasquachismo* or underdog aesthetics is its irreverence toward the copyright, which gives legal protection to property, something Chicanos have rarely been able to take for granted. *I Am Joaquin* challenges the copyright in assigning it to a collective, El Teatro Campesino, rather than an individual. But it is the C/S (short for *Con Safos*) at the film's end that subverts the copyright. When placed at the end of an artistic expression, *Con Safos* signifies "forbidden to touch, or the same will happen to you," a sort of Chicano copyright. In *I Am Joaquin*, *Con Safos* gives the film a discursive framework within and yet in opposition to the legal structure of mass media.

Chicana appears to imitate *I Am Joaquin* in its skillful use of still photographs and in its worker-based ideology, while it also presents the Chicana history that the "seminal" Chicano film overlooks. In a visual pun on the still photographs that both films use, Sylvia Morales inserts brief live action shots of women at work in the home, bringing movement—the Movement—into the domestic sphere. In effect, these brief scenes and the persuasive narration privilege the quotidian, and mark it as an arena for the affirmation and resistance of the other social protests. In documenting the female presence within the nationalist paradigm, *Chicana* is an initial step in the representation of a Chicano identity that affirms rather than "transcends" the gender, class, and political divisions within the community.[33]

These two films open and close the first decade of Chicano cinema, a decade in which Chicano cinema functioned as an extension of the Chicano Movement. In comparing the two films, it is perhaps most important to note the difference in rhetorical and narrational strategies. In *I Am Joaquin*, Valdez's stentorian voice overpowers the poem's occasional irony and ambiguity. For example, the line that summarizes Mexico's independence from Spain—"Mexico was free?"—is read instead as "Mexico was free!" It is a change of degree, however, and not one of kind, since what Valdez does is to anchor Chicano identity in its own crisis. As Valdez wryly notes in "The Tale of La Raza," "It is not enough to say we suffer an identity crisis, because that crisis has been our way of life for the last five centuries."[34] In *Chicana*, narrator Carmen Zapata, founder of the Bilingual Foundation, counters Valdez's emotional and confrontational voice of the Father with the rational and humorous voice of the Mother. The gender dichotomy is further reinforced by Valdez and Zapata's respective roles as founders of rural- and urban-based Chicano *teatro* companies. Within the texts, these differences are also registered in the play between the narrative voice and the sequence of images.[35]

Teatro. The revival of *teatro* in the mid-1960s, and Luis Valdez's movement toward film, together provided Chicano cinema with a ready-made narrative form. In the first instance, *teatro* solved budget and schedule limitations, since a piece could be performed before several cameras in a television studio, and then cut together as a video.[36] The use of *teatro*, however, was more than a mere economic response, but rather one manifestation of *rasquachismo*. It is important to note, also, that the *teatro* adaptations are by no means "filmed plays," but instead make significant use of close-ups, multiple points of view, and other filmic techniques unavailable to theatrical productions.

In *El Corrido: La Carpa de los Rasquachis*, the "tent of the downtrodden" refers, in part, to the canvas-covered truck in which the *corrido* is performed. *La carpa* also refers to the tent theater tradition of the Southwest.[37] In the feature-length video, the stage curtain consists of the farmworkers' burlap sacks, while in the narrative a rope held by el Diablo/Patrón symbolizes the border that Jesús Pelado Rasquachi —the irreverently named Jesus Poor Tramp—must place around his neck. The turning point occurs when Pelado internalizes the border, tying the loose end around his waist. Televised as part of the PBS-Visions series, *El Corrido* also "makes do" with vernacular language, creating an insider's discourse that could not be broadcast in English. When Pelado takes a train to the Mexico-U.S. border, el Diablo and la Calavera (skeleton) act as engine and caboose, chanting a telling onomatopoeia for the sound of the train: "chingate, chingate, chingate. . . . "

In its aesthetic development, El Teatro Campesino started with agitprop *actos* (skits) aimed at specific political issues, then incorporated *mitos* (myths) that explored culture-at-large. In the video adaptation of *Los Vendidos*, the *acto* of "Honest Sancho's Used Mexican Shop" is framed by two *mitos* on the role of Chicano *teatro*. Likewise, in its stage performances, *La Gran Carpa de los Rasquachis* (1973) presented an *acto* on the farmworkers' struggle framed by two *mitos*. The fact that Valdez placed social protests within a mythical and religious context caused Chicano critics to accuse him of mystification. Valdez, however, was able to combine the *acto* and *mito* through the use of another structural frame: the *corrido*. In the video adaptation, now titled *El Corrido: La Carpa de los Rasquachis*, the *acto* becomes a mythical narrative when it is performed as a *corrido* for the benefit of an urban Chicano who must decide whether he will join the United Farm Workers in strike.[38]

Testimonio. The idea of *cine testimonio* (the testimonial film) has sources or precursors in Latin American cinema, literature, journalism, and oral testimony.[39] The *testimonio* has taken several forms in literature since the nineteenth century, from first-person accounts of historical events (by participants and journalists) to transcriptions of oral testimonies to the *novela testimonio* (a pastiche of sources and genres). In Mexico, Eduardo Maldonado founded the Grupo Cine Testimonio (1969) in order "to put cinema at the service of social groups which lack access to the means of mass communication, in order to make their point of view public."[40] What these various forms have in common is a personal or subjective approach to broader historical movements that challenges the notion of an objective history distinct from memory and self-conscious "making."

In Chicano documentaries, the *cine testimonio* is less concerned with *concientización* than with the personal recollection of a communal experience. In these films, the narration is that of an individual who somehow represents or embodies the community and can therefore speak on its behalf in telling his or her own story: *pintos* (prison inmates) in *Carnalitos* (1973), an elder *curandera* (folk healer) in *Agueda Martínez: Our People, Our Country* (1976), and *santeros* (saint makers) in *Santeros* (1986). The *curandera* and *santeros* represent traditional social hierarchies (seniority, rural context, folk or religious belief systems), and the *pinto* represents the urban male youth in conflict with dominant societal institutions.[41] In these films, there is no external narrator, so that the subject's recollections appear to direct or motivate the visual sequence. The films also break from the strident or militant style of the protest films and express resistance in unexpected ways: the gentle understatement of the gang members in *Carnalitos*; the folk lyricism of *Agueda Martínez*; and the numerous voice-overs of exterior shots in *Santeros*, set in northern New Mexico. These films draw upon the Latin American *testimonio* in the manner in which an individual tells his or her story, not within a linear chronology, but in relationship to one's family, community, and the cycles of the day, seasons, and life.

Corrido. The *corrido* or Mexican folk ballad, like the *testimonio*, expresses a communal experience, but from a different perspective: "Not typically a form of personal narrative . . . the *corrido* tends to take a transpersonal, third-person point of view representing the political and existential values of the community as a whole."[42] According to Américo Paredes, the *corrido* emerges in the context of the Border Conflict era, roughly between 1830 and 1930.[43] Although the *corrido* continues to the present, with a significant revival since the Chicano Movement, most scholars cite its decline (or commodification) after the late 1930s. For Ramón Saldívar, however, "the *corrido* exerts symbolic force in the spheres of alternative narrative arts," and thereby establishes itself as the proto-Chicano narrative.[44] The *corrido* has been used as a cultural narrative in both documentaries and dramas: *El Corrido: La Carpa de los Rasquachis, Ballad of an Unsung Hero* (1983), *The Ballad of Gregorio Cortez, Corridos* (1987), *Una Lucha por Mi Pueblo* (1990), and *The Corrido of Juan Chacón* (1990). The use of the *corrido* in the mass media, however, extends its function and sphere of articulation beyond that of the original *corrido*. In order to maintain a sense of "community" within an open or public discourse, filmmakers sometimes withhold or delay subtitles.

Telenovela. The use of the *telenovela* by Chicano filmmakers replaces one "mass culture" (United States) with another (Latin American) in order to address current social issues within the Chicano-Latino community. The *telenovela*, while similar to the soap opera, is distinct in both textual form and cultural context. In form, unlike soap operas,

> *telenovelas* always have clear-cut stories with definite endings that permit narrative closure; they are shown during prime-time viewing hours; and they are designed to attract a wide viewing audience of men, women, and children.[45]

In context, the high rhetoric and melodrama of *telenovelas* are significant forms in Latin American expressions, including "high art." In the United States, where "high art" tends toward the muted or restrained, melodrama is considered a debased form. Although still a popular form that expresses the dominant ideologies, the *telenovela* also carries the potential "to serve a demystifying cultural function" as it addresses social issues.[46] Ana López describes that paradox in the relationship between the *telenovela* and New Latin American Cinema:

> It is ironic that at the moment when the New Latin American Cinema rejected the melodrama as the embodiment of cultural dependency, television used the melodrama in order to establish a solid audience base and as a result, created a nationalistic (or, at least, pan-Latin

American) form with which to begin to challenge that very same cultural and economic dependence.[47]

Between 1968 and 1970, *Canción de la Raza* (KCET, Los Angeles)—perhaps the first Chicano-produced television series—used the *telenovela* format in order to address the social concerns of the Chicano community. Despite the popularity of the series, CPB has not funded subsequent dramatic series for Latinos, and the networks have limited their efforts to several situation comedies (all written by non-Latinos). Chicano filmmakers, however, adapted the *telenovela* to short dramas and docudramas, a move consistent with the "clear-cut stories with definite endings" of the *telenovela*. In *Después del Terremoto/After the Earthquake* (1979), Lourdes Portillo pioneered the use of the *telenovela* in narrative film as a means to confront otherwise taboo social issues. *Después del Terremoto* broadens the discourse on immigration and the *barrio* to include Central Americans as well as the gender politics of *barrio* assimilation. As in the conventional *telenovela*, mise-en-scène becomes synonymous with the traditional Latino home. Portillo, however, frames the narrative with bilingual title cards and an *acordeón* score that together evoke silent cinema. These elements undercut the soap opera cum romantic melodrama, then redirect its exposed fictional status toward feminist political parable.

Today, the *telenovela* is the genre par excellence for Latino films about AIDS and domestic violence in the *barrio*. *Telenovelas* on AIDS include *Ojos que no ven* (1987), *Vida* (1988), *Face to Face with AIDS* (1988), *Mi Hermano* (1989), and *Between Friends* (1990). These films are sponsored by health organizations and are intended for educational use within the community, rather than for broad distribution. Often, the AIDS *telenovelas* use a generic Spanish, with or without subtitles, that postulates a nonspecific, if not stereotypical, "hispanic" culture characteristic of the more conventional *telenovela*.[48] Again, the cultural context for these films is important: the narratives and their "stereotypes" are intended for internal consumption and discussion within a diverse Latino population.[49]

Experimental Film and Video. Although not usually recognized as contributors to Chicano cinema, the experimental media artists have backgrounds (in the Movement) and thematic concerns similar to those of the other, more political filmmakers.[50] In fact, experimental works often parody or transform the cultural narratives discussed above.

Between the mid-1970s and mid-1980s, Harry Gamboa, Jr., and other members of the Chicano art group *Asco* (Nausea)—Gronk, Patssi Valdez, and Willie Herron—produced a series of satirical "No-Movies" that parodied Chicano cinema as well as the mass media. The No-Movies included performance pieces, the Aztlán or No-Movie awards, and fake movie stills distributed to newspapers around the world. As Gamboa explains:

> They were conceptual performances created specifically for the camera . . . In the 1980s, the "No-Movies" gave way to the *"foto-novela,"* which was an expansion of the traditional Latin American medium to one that required the same hardware as a slide/audio presentation, but that incorporated a hybrid form of bizarre *novela* story line and exaggerated visual imagery.[51]

Like the first *Asco* street performance "Walking Mural," in which members walked down Whittier Boulevard dressed as mural icons, the No-Movies and *foto-novelas* produced an intermedia synesthesia, using one "very affordable medium" as another. In the *Asco* aesthetic in which these transformations can occur, as Gronk explains, "It's making a movie without the use of celluloid. It's projecting the real without the reel."[52] That process involved a self-conscious reworking of traditional Latin American narrative forms. Since 1983, Gamboa has written, directed, and produced seven "conceptual dramas" on video: *Imperfecto* (1983), *Insultan* (1983), *Blanx* (1984), *Agent Ex* (1984), *Vaporz* (1984), *Baby Kake* (1984), and *No Supper* (1987). In these videos, Gamboa—with *Asco* members—combines the political influences of the Chicano Movement, an American 1950s retro-camp, and the narrative excess of the *tele-* and *foto-novela*. More recently, Gamboa has produced an experimental *testimonio* on the impact of freeways on Chicano artists in *L.A. Merge* (1991).

In an innovative strategy developed within the Chicana avant-garde, expressionism acquires a social—rather than individual—voice, and becomes the fulcrum for a feminist reorientation of the spiritual rituals and mythical icons of Chicano nationalism. In *Anima* (1989), for example, Frances Salomé España uses expressionism to explore the Day of the Dead and the relationship of death to everyday life. The video extends that core dialectic on several fronts. The soundtrack blends strains of indigenous wind instruments with contemporary jazz guitar, while three Chicana artists made up as *calaveras* (skeletons) sit in a kitchen, gazing into the camera. The Chicanas' *calavera* makeup co-opts the ritual putting on of makeup or cosmetics for public presentation, so that the inside (skeleton) now gazes out, rather than the outside (fetishized flesh) being gazed upon.[53]

In her most recent work, *El Espejo/The Mirror* (1991), España presents herself, fragmented, through cross-cut images of her face and feet, as she relates an absurd *testimonio* on her life in East L.A.:

> The fragmented body paralleled a fragmented narrative, an autobiographical account that mixed memory and desire, reflection and projection, past and present, reality and nightmarish dreams to reveal the psychological trauma of cultural displacement.[54]

This review unwittingly describes the *novela testimonio* and the autobiographical tradition España draws upon. Given the sharp social humor that underlays España's narration, it is perhaps more apt to speak of the *historical* rather than *psychological* "trauma of cultural displacement."

In addition to España, other Chicanas who use experimental video to transform cultural narratives include Betty Maldonado (*Night Vigil,* 1982), Beverly Sánchez Padilla (*The Corrido of Juan Chacón,* 1990), Sandra P. Hahn (*Replies of the Night,* 1989; *Slipping Between,* 1991), S. M. Peña (*Crónica de un ser,* 1990; *Dark Glasses,* 1991; *Dionysius' Ox,* 1991), and T. Osa Hidalgo de la Riva (*Mujeria: The Olmeca Rap,* 1991).

Various members of the Border Art Workshop/Taller de Arte Fronterizo, mentioned earlier with respect to *mestizaje,* have collaborated on experimental film and video projects, including *Mi Otro Yo* (*My Other Self,* 1988) and *Border Brujo* (1990). The latter video recreates the one-man performance piece by Guillermo Gómez-Peña, a self-styled shaman and performance artist, whose critical writings on border culture have contributed to the new, culture-based conceptualization of *mestizaje. Border Brujo* follows in the footsteps of the work of poet-critics Cherríe Moraga and Gloria Anzaldúa in its attempt to explode various "borders" and reconstruct *mestizo* identities from the fragments of social hierarchies. In his performance, Gómez-Peña transforms himself into the various social types who inhabit the border, so that the social drama of *teatro* becomes instead a stylized *testimonio. Mi Otro Yo* explores the Chicano arts and includes interviews with Luis Valdez, Harry Gamboa, Jr., José Montoya, and muralist Judy Baca, among others. In its poetic narration (by Gómez-Peña) and title—which refers to the neo-Mayan concept "tú eres mi otro yo" ("you are my other self")—the documentary draws upon *floricanto* for its structure. But Gómez-Peña's poem, unlike *I Am Joaquin*, is an anti-epic whose emphasis is on an avant-garde demystification of the border, rather than on a nationalism that "transcends . . . boundaries."[55]

Conclusion

To different degrees, Chicano filmmakers have always drawn upon and mixed the cultures and politics of Mexico and the United States. The cultural narratives considered here, for example, were for the most part produced for public-affairs shows that, during the Chicano Movement, provided Chicanos with access to American television. In a self-conscious move, Chicano filmmakers worked between a weapon and a formula: between the political weapon of New Latin American Cinema and the economic formula of Hollywood. Chicano culture, however, often finds itself denied at both ends, or, as the popular phrase goes, *"ni de aquí, ni de allá,"* neither from here (United States), nor from there (Mexico). That is the imposed definition, one that denies the syncretism of Chicano culture and art. Chicano cinema tells another story.

The articles in the remainder of part 2 provide different perspectives on Chicano cinema that challenge and advance the initial thoughts and conceptual framework presented in this essay.

Notes

1. See Carlos Muñoz, Jr., *Youth, Identity, Power: The Chicano Movement* (London: Verso, 1989).

2. Initially published in chapbook form in 1967, *I Am Joaquin* was later annotated and reissued by Bantam Books in 1972. The poem and film appear in both English and Spanish versions.

3. Bobby Páramo, *"Cerco Blanco, The Balloon Man,* and *Fighting City Hall*: On Being a Chicano Filmmaker," *Metamorfosis* 3, no. 2 (1980–81): 77–82.

4. Harry Gamboa, Jr., "Silver Screening the Barrio," *Forum* 6, no. 1 (November 1978): 6–7; and Jesús Salvador Treviño, "Chicano Cinema," *New Scholar* 8 (1982): 167–80.

5. José García Torres, "José García Torres and *Realidades,"* interview by Aurora Flores and Lillian Jiménez, *Centro Bulletin* 2, no. 8 (Spring 1990): 30–43. For a historical

and critical overview of Puerto Rican cinema, see Lillian Jiménez, "From the Margin to the Center: Puerto Rican Cinema in New York," *Centro Bulletin* 2, no. 8 (Spring 1990): 28–43.

6. Quotations in this paragraph are from Antonio José Guernica, "Chicano Production Companies: Projecting Reality, Opening the Doors," *Agenda: A Journal of Hispanic Issues* 8, no. 1 (January-February 1978): 12–15.

7. Three Chicano film manifestos are reprinted in part 3 of this book.

8. José E. Limón, *Mexican Ballads, Chicano Epic: History, Social Dramas and Poetic Persuasions*, SCCR Working Paper Series No. 14 (Stanford, Calif.: Stanford Center for Chicano Research, 1986).

9. For collected press coverage and position statement, see Gang Exploitation Film Committee, *A Reader and Information Packet on the "Gang Exploitation Films"* [Monterey Park, Calif.: East Los Angeles M.E.Ch.A. (Movimiento Estudiantil Chicano de Aztlán), 1979].

10. In addition to *Raíces de sangre, Only Once in a Lifetime* (1978), *Zoot Suit, El Norte, The Ballad of Gregorio Cortez*, and *Heartbreaker* (1984), I include the three feature-length dramas by Efraín Gutiérrez, a renegade filmmaker in South Texas. In the early 1980s, Gutiérrez and his films disappeared. See Gregg Barrios, "A Cinema of Failure, A Cinema of Hunger: The Films of Efraín Gutiérrez," in *Chicano Cinema: Research, Reviews, and Resources*, Gary D. Keller, ed. (Binghamton, N.Y.: Bilingual Review/Press, 1985), 179–80.

11. I deal with the press response in greater detail in "Chicano Cinema and the Horizon of Expectations: A Discursive Analysis of Film Reviews in the Mainstream, Alternative and Hispanic Press, 1987–1988" *Aztlán: A Journal of Chicano Studies* 19, no. 2 (Fall 1990): forthcoming.

12. On *Zoot Suit*, interview by author and Lillian Jiménez with Severo Perez, February 3, 1990. On *The Ballad of Gregorio Cortez*, David Rosen, *Off-Hollywood: The Making and Marketing of Independent Films* (New York: Grove Weidenfeld, 1990), 20.

13. Patricia Vega, "Chicanos 90," *La Jornada* (México, D.F.) (February 9, 1990): 33; Patricia Vega, "El movimiento chicano tiene una meta: poner su cultura en el centro de EU," *La Jornada* (México, D.F.) (February 11, 1990): 29.

14. The Colegio de la Frontera Norte will publish the proceedings of the conference and has agreed to host it as a biannual event. For a review of the conference, see Rosa Linda Fregoso, "Close Encuentro of a Close Kind: The Cruzando Fronteras Conference," *The Independent* 14, no. 4 (May 1991): 13–16.

15. In addition to the article by Rosa Linda Fregoso in this book, see Chon A. Noriega, "In Aztlán: The Films of the Chicano Movement, 1969–1979," *New American Film and Video Series* 56 (New York: Whitney Museum of American Art, 1991).

16. Jesús Salvador Treviño, "Chicano Cinema Overview," *Areito* 37 (1984): 40–43.

17. For scholarship on Aztlán and its role in Chicano thought, see Rudolfo A. Anaya and Francisco Lomelí, eds. *Aztlán: Essays on the Chicano Homeland* (Albuquerque, N. Mex.: Academia/El Norte Publications, 1989).

18. Shifra M. Goldman and Tomás Ybarra-Frausto, *Arte Chicano: A Comprehensive Annotated Bibliography of Chicano Art, 1965–1981* (Berkeley: Chicano Studies Publication Unit/University of California, 1985), 49.

19. See the BAW/TAF publication *La Línea Quebrada/The Broken Line* (San Diego); and Guillermo Gómez-Peña and Jeff Kelley, eds., *The Border Art Workshop: A Documentation of Five Years of Interdisciplinary Art Projects Dealing with U.S.-Mexico Border Issues, 1984–1989* (New York: Arts Space/La Jolla Museum of Contemporary Art, 1989).

20. Guillermo Gómez-Peña, "The Multicultural Paradigm: An Open Letter to the National Arts Community," *High Performance* (September 1989): 18–27.

21. See, for example, Luis Valdez, "An Artist Who Has Blended Art and Politics," interview, *El Tecolote* (San Francisco Mission District) (October 1987): 9+.

22. Goldman and Ybarra-Frausto, *Arte Chicano*, 46.

23. Quoted in the documentary *Mi Otro Yo* (1988), directed by Amy and Phillip Brookman. See also José Montoya, "Thoughts on *la cultural*: The Media, *Con Safos* and Survival," *Caracol* 5, no. 9 (May 1979): 6–8, 19.

24. I refer, of course, to Michel Foucault's use of "discourse" in *The History of Sexuality, Volume 1: An Introduction* (New York: Vintage Books, 1980).

25. *Rasquachismo* can be described as an underdog aesthetic or sensibility. For an overview of *rasquachismo* as an aesthetic concept, see the exhibition catalogue *Chicano Aesthetics: Rasquachismo*, which contains essays by Tomás Ybarra-Frausto, Shifra M. Goldman, and John L. Aguilar [Phoenix: MARS (Movimiento Artístico del Río Salado) Inc., 1989].

26. See my article on the social problem films "about" Mexican Americans, "Citizen Chicano: The Trials and Titillations of Ethnicity in the American Cinema, 1935–1962," *Social Research: An International Quarterly on the Social Sciences* 58, no. 2 (Summer 1991): 413–38. In Henry Louis Gates's use of the concept, to "signify" describes the process by which an ethnic or racial subculture speaks through and yet against the dominant culture's language. As a concept, *signifin'* is more accurate than *co-opt and subvert*, which imply a zero-sum discursive relationship between subculture and dominant culture. See Henry Louis Gates, Jr., *The Signifying Monkey: A Theory of African-American Literary Criticism* (Oxford: Oxford University Press, 1988).

27. For an in-depth analysis of the objective discourse in two Chicano feature films, see Rosa Linda Fregoso, "*Zoot Suit* and *The Ballad of Gregorio Cortez*," *Crítica* 1, no. 2 (Spring 1985): 126–31.

28. Víctor Fuentes makes a similar argument in his essay in this book.

29. Juan Rodríguez Flores, Review of *Stand and Deliver*, *La Opinión* (Los Angeles) (March 2, 1988): section 2, 1+.

30. Michael Wilson and Deborah Silverton Rosenfelt, *Salt of the Earth* (New York: The Feminist Press, 1978), 93–168.

31. Chon Noriega, "Godzilla and the Japanese Nightmare: When *Them!* is U.S.," *Cinema Journal* 27, no. 1 (Fall 1987): 63–77.

32. Cordelia Candelaria, *Chicano Poetry: A Critical Introduction* (Westport, Conn.: Greenwood Press, 1986), 34–35.

33. In 1969, "El Plan Espiritual de Aztlán" posited that "nationalism as the key to organization *transcends* all religious, political, class, and economic factions or boundaries" (my emphasis). Reprinted in Anaya and Lomelí, *Aztlán*, 1–5.

34. Luis Valdez, "The Tale of La Raza," rpt. in Ed Ludwig and James Santibañez, eds., *The Chicanos: Mexican American Voices* (Baltimore: Penguin Books, 1971), 95.

35. See Rosa Linda Fregoso's extended reading of *Chicana* and *I Am Joaquin* in the next essay of this volume.

36. Several *teatro* pieces have been adapted to video or film: *Los Vendidos* (1972), *Somos Uno* (1973), *El Corrido: La Carpa de los Rasquachis* (1976), *Guadalupe* (1976), and *Zoot Suit* (1981).

37. For an overview of Chicano *teatro/carpa* and an account of the *rasquache* aesthetic, see Nicolás Kanellos, "Folklore in Chicano Theater and Chicano Theater as Folklore," in Stanley A. West and June Macklin, eds., *The Chicano Experience* (Boulder, Colo.: Westview Press, 1979), 165–89.

38. For a more detailed account of the *acto, mito,* and *corrido* in El Teatro Campesino, see Yvonne Yarbro-Bejarano, "From *acto* to *mito*: A Critical Appraisal of the Teatro Campesino," in Joseph Sommers and Tomás Ybarra-Frausto, eds., *Modern Chicano Writers: A Collection of Critical Essays* (Englewood Cliffs, N.J.: Prentice-Hall, 1979), 176–85.

39. Michael Chanan, *The Cuban Image: Cinema and Cultural Politics in Cuba* (London: British Film Institute Publishing, 1985), 168–69.

40. Ibid. For Maldonado, collaborative filmmaking should also engage members of the social group in *concientización* or awareness of the process of film.

41. The *pinto* was an important part of the Chicano Movement, with numerous *pinto* newspapers, literature, and visual arts produced.

42. Ramón Saldívar, *Chicano Narrative: The Dialectics of Difference* (Madison: The University of Wisconsin Press, 1990), 32.

43. Américo Paredes, *"With His Pistol in His Hand": A Border Ballad and Its Hero* (Austin: University of Texas Press, 1958).

44. Saldívar, *Chicano Narrative,* 41.

45. Unlike soap operas, *telenovelas* are not open-ended, but designed to run a certain number of episodes (usually several hundred). Ana López, "The Melodrama in Latin America: Films, Telenovelas and the Currency of a Popular Form," *Wide Angle* 7, no. 3 (1985): 8.

46. Ibid., 10.

47. Ibid., 9.

48. This is done in the Latin American *telenovelas,* because the series are shown throughout the continent, including the United States.

49. For an overview of Latino AIDS media, see Catherine Saalfield and Ray Navarro, "Not Just Black and White: AIDS Media and People of Color," *Centro Bulletin* 2, no. 8 (Spring 1990): 70–78.

50. In addition to the artists discussed here, these include Ernie Palomino, Willie Varela, Severo Perez (early works, 1968–72), Juan and Daniel Salazar, and Juan Garza.

51. Harry Gamboa, Jr., "Harry Gamboa, Jr.: No Movie Maker," interview by Marisela Norte, *El Tecolote* (San Francisco Mission District), n.d. (c. 1983): 3+.

52. Anne Geyer, "Artist's Exhibits Are Street Performances," *The News* (Mexico City) (September 11, 1981): 18.

53. The reference to the "gaze"—and who controls it—is intended to build upon Laura Mulvey's influential essay, "Visual Pleasure and Narrative Cinema" (1975), and to identify the Chicana avant-garde as an area of feminist media production that (1) uses, rather than disavows, visual pleasure, and (2) situates its gender critique within cultural difference. Mulvey's essay is reprinted in Bill Nichols, ed., *Movies and Methods, Volume 2* (Berkeley: University of California Press, 1985), 303–15. For Mulvey's own update to her article, see "Afterthoughts on 'Visual Pleasure and Narrative Cinema' Inspired by *Duel in the Sun*," *Framework* nos. 15–17 (Summer 1981): 12–15. I am indebted to Lillian Jiménez for our discussions of *Anima,* and in particular for her observation about the "ritual" of putting on makeup.

54. Connie Fitzsimons, "L.A. Freewaves: Celebrating the Existence of Independent Video," *Artweek* (December 7, 1989): 20. The video Fitzsimons reviews was a work in progress.

55. "El Plan Espiritual de Aztlán," in Anaya and Lomelí, *Aztlán,* 2.

Chicana Film Practices: Confronting the "Many-Headed Demon of Oppression"

Rosa Linda Fregoso

> Your vision is valid, its expression is valid. Don't let your art be judged on their terms.
>
> Salomé España

Introduction

The epigraph is taken from Frances Salomé España's essay, "Artist Testimony and Raza Survival Guide: A Chicana Obstacle Course for the Exile on Her Own Turf." This is point seven of a ten-point lesson she deems "enabled me and empowered me to make art and contend with the world on my own terms" (personal interview, 1990). Written from the perspective of an artist nurtured in part by the Chicano Movement, España's powerful testimony is emblematic for the *rebelde* (rebellious) Chicana artist who, for years, has felt "exiled on her own turf." That "own turf" is the "canon" of Chicano cultural practices, dating to the cultural renaissance of the Chicano Power Movement of the 1960s (Fregoso and Chabram 1990). Through her essay, España draws attention to the imposition of "politically correct" modes of Chicano art, formulas that constrain artistic creativity. She also speaks to surviving or transcending the inner, culturally specific politics of sexism and marginalization.

Like Chicana writers, the cultural practices of Chicana film and video practitioners serve a "metacritical function." Reassessing the import of Chicana authors to the "canon" of literature, Ramón Saldívar correctly points out that their work "is counter-hegemonic to the second-power, serving as a critique of critiques of oppression that fail to take into account the full range of domination" (173). Moreover, Rosaura Sánchez notes that "what distinguishes Chicana writers is their relative invisibility," nonetheless, they have managed to create "aesthetically superior work" to that of their male counterparts (1985: 61–62). In a similar manner, I will argue that Chicana film practices represent the most innovative and resonant development in Chicano cinema, despite attempts to relegate Chicana works to a secondary status.

The exclusion of Chicana filmmakers from events such as the *Chicanos 90* ceremony hosted in Mexico by Mexican President Salinas de Gortari, their marginalization in film criticism like the Gary Keller anthology on Chicano cinema (1985), and their continual marginalization in festivals such as the recent film series in *Chicano Art: Resistance and Affirmation*,[1] is a complex issue related to many factors including, but not limited to, sexism. The CARA film series, for example, included only three Chicana filmmakers in the program's initial draft whereas roughly thirty Chicano male-produced films were to be shown.

More important, the CARA film series exemplifies the way in which women are systematically excluded from participation by the reification of an artificial category, derived from arbitrary definitions about what constitutes "Chicano" cinema. For instance, implicit in the choice of films to be exhibited in the CARA series as "Resistance and Affirmation" is the contention that the historical agents of political struggle are mostly men. This narrow view of Chicano oppositional practices is representative of a particular social formation of critics and practitioners whose cultural politics are, from both a feminist and a theoretical standpoint, highly problematic. Not only do their politics ignore the contributions of women cultural workers, but they also exclude the work of certain men who are outside or peripheral to the "legitimate" Chicano political circuit, but whose films can also be categorized as "political" if measured by a different, less dogmatic, yardstick. Cheech Marin's film, *Born in East L.A.* (1987), which was not included in the CARA series, comes to mind.

An additional reason for the marginalization of women derives from the fact that Chicana production is exclusively concentrated in short films, and Chicanas have therefore not benefited from the recognition that accompanies the production of feature films. In a society where feature-length films signify mastery over cinematic practice and in which 35-mm symbolizes power, the accumulation of "cultural capital" (Bourdieu 1984) becomes a self-generating process. In other words, making a Chicano 35-mm feature film translates into a certain

prestige that virtually guarantees greater critical and scholarly attention as well as film reviews in the mainstream media. In a phallocentric society, power is measured by *big-ness* (as in feature-length films)
and *penetration* (as into the Hollywood industry). These are the crucial
markers or signs of success, of "making it," of *coming* . . . into
fruition, that is. In this respect, there is little evidence among Chicana
filmmakers of big-ness, penetration, or of coming into the mainstream,
on dominant culture's terms.

Another factor for the omission of Chicanas from the "canon" of
Chicano cinema can be attributed to the limited availability of public
funds, but also to Chicana exclusion from the "good-ol'-*niño* network"
that functions as gatekeeper and power broker. It must be stated,
however, that among many Chicanas, the preference for short films
and for the status of "independents" are self-conscious choices.[2] They
derive from the concern among Chicana film and video practitioners
for the artistic properties of cinema, that is to say, their greater commitment to the craft of cinema as an art-form.[3] Obviously, aesthetic
innovations in the art-form are more manageable in the shorter forms
and more possible if one resists the temptation of entering
Hollywood, which usually forces filmmakers to adopt more conventional techniques and dominant values.

Due in large part to the rationing of public funds for the arts, in
order to make a living Chicana film practitioners often work for private and public media on commissioned pieces for advertising or educational programs. Yet, some of these same filmmakers also continue
to experiment stylistically, producing noncommissioned works that
are featured in film festivals or cultural centers. Others like Salomé
España have chosen to remain entirely "independent."

An analysis of formal aesthetic innovation requires serious attention to the limitations inherent in film production for private commercial media as well as in the works made on a commissioned basis for
public television and educational agencies, because all of these institutions tend to impose conventional norms and styles, resulting in films
that cater to predetermined "targeted" audiences. The focus of my article is on those films produced outside the domains of institutional
media and thereby without the constraints inherent in commissioned
pieces. By examining the noncommissioned works by Chicana filmmakers we can truly gauge the outstanding nature of artistic creativity
and innovation realized in Chicano cinema during the past two dec-

ades. In light of the unparalleled import of Chicanas to the corpus of Chicano cinema, I will highlight elements in their films that articulate both thematic and expressive differences, that is to say, the discursive innovations made by Chicana film practitioners in both content and form.

As a political gesture, I have chosen to discuss three films made by Chicanas during the height of Chicano movement cinema, the pre-Hollywood era (1969–80). These films are *Chicana* (1979) by Sylvia Morales, *Después del Terremoto* (1979) by Lourdes Portillo (cowritten and codirected by Nina Serrano), and *Agueda Martínez* (1977) by Esperanza Vásquez—films that warrant a long-deserved attention. Aside from token gestures of inclusion in film festivals, or paternalistic mention in anthologies of Chicano cinema, these three films have never received critical scholarly examination. I will end by pointing to recent trends in Chicana filmmaking evident in the work of a new generation of filmmakers. In this retrospective analysis that spans fifteen years I would like to pay tribute to Chicana counteraesthetics.

I characterize Chicana cinematic discourse as markedly counteraesthetic because Chicana filmmakers have had to counter two kinds of discourses: the dominant culture's, which has distorted the Chicana subject; and the aesthetic discourse of Chicano males, which "renders them nameless and voiceless" (Quintana 262) and, in the case of film, imageless namely as images, functioning cosmetically as backdrops for male history. Thus, Chicana filmmakers have had to counter, challenge, and confront what Moraga and Anzaldúa call "the many-headed demon of oppression" (1983: 195; quoted in Alarcón 1990: 356).

The works I have chosen represent "woman" as the central subject of their narratives. We must, however, distinguish first of all between works that are feminist and those that are woman-centered narratives. Rosaura Sánchez notes that what distinguishes a feminist analysis in scholarly work is that its focus on "the condition and experience of women provide[s] a critical feminist account of gender inequality" (1990: 17). And although we sometimes unfairly burden creative works like a film with such a monumental project, both *Chicana* and *Después del Terremoto* are created in that spirit. Both films are illustrative of a Chicana feminist counteraesthetics.

The Feminist Re-vision

The first historical film on Chicanas, Sylvia Morales's *Chicana*, counters both the dominant culture and Chicano exclusion of the role of
Chicanas in history. We could perhaps read *Chicana* as the female
counterpart to the first Chicano film, *I Am Joaquin*, made in 1969. Both
I Am Joaquin and *Chicana* are epic accounts of Chicano history: *I Am
Joaquin* from a man's perspective, *Chicana* from a woman's. Both
reproduce the tendency to tell all of our history in one filmic statement—five hundred years in roughly twenty minutes of film. Both
films reproduce the various themes of Chicano cultural nationalism,
namely, they challenge racism and provide historical accounts of
domination (conquest) and struggle. Both celebrate the indigenous
legacy of our people. In terms of form, both *I Am Joaquin* and *Chicana*
make extensive use of stills, the murals of Siqueiros, Rivera, and
Orozco, photographs, and music drawn from an oral tradition.

Despite these similarities there are important differences as well,
and not just in terms of theme or related to the fact that *I Am Joaquin*
tells the story of our male heroes and *Chicana* of our female heroines.
There are major formal/aesthetic and ideological differences, for
Chicana critiques all form of domination.

Whereas male-centered cultural nationalism was critical of *"gabacho"* society and the *"gachupín"* colonialists and landowners, it idealized pre-Columbian society. *I Am Joaquin*'s epic account of conquest
and domination was based on an idyllic, and man-centered, depiction
of pre-Columbian society. *Chicana*'s epic account refuses the tendency
to idealize the Aztecs and offers instead a critical revision of our lineage. Unlike the films of male cultural nationalists, *Chicana* depicts the
enslavement of women and men under Aztec domination, and its "re-
vision" of Malintzín Tenepal (La Malinche) is represented in the context of feminist critiques of Chicano movement ideology (Alarcón
1983).

Formally, *Chicana* draws from an intertextual tradition that combines and juxtaposes distinct artistic practices into a new form.
Chicana is a collage of dramatic reenactment, photographic stills,
reportage, and documentary conventions. Given her work as a television producer with KABC-TV in Los Angeles, Sylvia Morales adds
her expertise in television documentary and reportage to the
slideshow of Anna Nieto-Gómez. She also brings to the film a keen

sense of irony and satire, as is evident in the opening sequence, which subverts commonsense assumptions about Chicana passivity and subservience.

In this dramatic reenactment that opens the film, Morales presents viewers with images of domesticity: one Chicana making tortillas, an elderly woman on a rocking chair, a woman washing clothing, and another potty-training her son. Yet each of these images is punctuated with a voice-over that subverts the image in a humorous fashion. For example, in the potty-training image, as the mother wipes her son's rear end, the narrative voice injects, "we free men to work," a commentary that satirically draws viewer attention to the serious issue of the extent of women's unpaid household labor.

Morales's epic account was indeed a counterdiscourse to man-centered versions of Chicano history. Through its focus on the role of "important" women like Sor Juana Inés de la Cruz, Lucy González Parsons, and Emma Tenayuca, *Chicana* reinvents a lineage for Chicanas, but the film also contests accounts that render women nameless, voiceless, and imageless in the historical process. Therefore, aesthetically and ideologically, Sylvia Morales is the first Chicana filmmaker to confront the "many-headed demon of oppression" on such a grand scale.

Lourdes Portillo's *Después del Terremoto* anticipates *Chicana*, yet, in a similar vein, Portillo's film exemplifies a Chicana feminist counteraesthetics. Portillo has been one of our most misunderstood and distorted film practitioners. Male critics simply don't know what to make of her. She has been called a Nicaraguan filmmaker by Gary Keller in his introduction to the first Chicano cinema anthology (1985). Assuming that only a man could conceive of a national activist film association, Keller also forgot to mention that Portillo was one of the founders of Cine Acción.

Perhaps Portillo herself has added to the confusion, for she has made a film about a Nicaraguan immigrant in San Francisco, another film on the Mothers of the Plaza de Mayo in Argentina (*Las Madres*, 1986), and yet another on the Day of the Dead (*La Ofrenda*, 1989), which dares to give a subject-role to gays in their efforts to revive and transform *el día de los muertos* celebration in San Francisco. Of course, these diverse ways of re-presenting reality may confuse and perplex those who assume that there is only *one* way of being a Chicana, that there is only *one* voice that can speak for all Chicanas, or that there is

only *one* concern that interests Chicanas, in sum, to those who assume
that there is an "essential" Chicana identity. Indeed, the ambiguity in
Portillo's work, the refusal to be categorized, the multidimensionality
of her subject matter, her concern for many and varied forms of
oppression (for instance, military repression in Argentina; the oppression based on gender and sexuality) are what in fact make Lourdes
Portillo *very* Chicana. Not to mention that she herself claims that very
identity. As Norma Alarcón reminds us, what characterizes the work
of many Chicana writers is their rejection of singular notions of cultural identity, that is to say, their preference for "multiple-voiced subjectivity" (1990: 366). Portillo's cinematic trajectory similarly draws attention to the fact that Chicanas are "interpellated by a series of ideological discourses" (Sánchez 1990: 5). Her film *Después del Terremoto*
assigns these multiple registers to the subject-protagonist's quest for
her identity as a woman.

Después del Terremoto's theme may be about the life of a
Nicaraguan immigrant woman in San Francisco, but its concerns are
ours as well. A great deal of the film's subtext is also about the experiences (cultural, political, and sexual) that affect Chicanas within a
dominant culture. In fact, by depicting these conflicts from the perspective of a non-Chicana, Portillo achieves an "objective" distance
from the subjectivity of Chicana identity, an objective distance that
provides the film its clarity of vision. In so doing, by stepping outside
of our culture, the film is transformed into one of the most powerful
critiques to date of culture and gender conflict within our own "community." The film's formal properties set in motion an allegory for
Chicanas' internal cultural and gender oppression.

Después del Terremoto's theme concerns a Nicaraguan working as a
maid in San Francisco. The plot is propelled by an impending meeting
between the film's protagonist, Irene, and her boyfriend, who has just
arrived from Nicaragua where he has been a political activist, impris-
oned and tortured in Somoza's jails. Yet apart from this specificity that
localizes the theme as "Nicaraguan," or the film as a story about
Nicaraguans in the United States, the film's various subtexts can be
read allegorically. And it is the manner is which the film is formally
structured that opens up its allegorical dimension.

The film's narrative is orchestrated around two major events,
Irene's purchase of a television set and the event of the *cumpleaños*,
which serves as a pretext for unveiling women's rituals. The film

opens with the purchase of the TV and closes with an ensuing conflict between Irene and the boyfriend over the act. The television purchase is important given that the filmmaker utilizes the TV as a sign with multiple layers of meaning. On the one hand, it is a signifier for cultural imperialism, the dissemination of U.S. programming to the Third World. But the TV is also, in the United States, a signifier of acculturation, for it is designed not only to homogenize different audiences and organize them as markets, but also to acculturate immigrants into U.S. society. The television also marks success, or it can be read as a symbol of the culture of consumption. What TV does is to inculcate the ethic and logic of consumerism within these communities as a route to becoming "American." The ability to purchase a television, for many lower-income people, particularly immigrants, registers their successful incorporation into U.S. culture, as consumers. Given that success is measured through consumption, access to TV discourse marks their participation in a naturalized and commodified world of consumerism offered by television.[4]

Despite these multiple registers embodied in the film, the dominant reading of the television revolves around its function as a signifier for the signified, a woman's independence and autonomy. From the perspective of Irene, the decision to purchase the television symbolizes her autonomy as a wage earner and her independence as a woman. It is from the act of her purchase of this commodity that Irene entertains the question of her role as either a future (dependent) wife or an independent (perhaps single) wage earner, and as a consumer, since the consumer has come to replace the producer in an advanced capitalist economy.

Another significant feature of the film's structure is located in the contrast between two back-to-back sequences: the sequence that depicts Irene and her friend in the bedroom, discussing gender relations and politics while engaged in the ritual of "dressing up," and the sequence with the two *tías* (aunts) involved in a kitchen ritual of making *tamales* while also talking about gender relations and politics. The contrast between these two sequences is rich with generational conflict and differences. The filmmaker imbues its imagery with the multiplicity of women's discourse, namely, repression through religion but also bonding through ritual. As Irene walks toward the kitchen space of the *tías*, she glimpses one of them before a home altar, praying to Saint Anthony for a husband for Irene. The *tía* has just placed Saint Anthony in an upside-down position, a religious practice designed to ensure the fulfillment of the request. After the aunt leaves, Irene returns the Saint to its upright position and then glances at an image of the Virgen de Guadalupe. Unsure of the significance of religious rituals and icons, Irene returns to the bedroom space where she then asks her friend, "¿Qué piensas de la Virgen?" ("What do you think of the Virgin?"), to which her friend responds, "Nada interesante, la verdad" ("Not much").

Whereas Spanish-language use predominates in both sequences, the film also captures the linguistic structure of code-switching within each generation; in both cases the characters code-switch from English to Spanish, and vice versa. Generational difference in linguistic use is punctuated by an additional sequence, taking place in a third space and visualizing two young girls who do not speak any Spanish at all. The film registers the multiplicity of women's discourse in other ways as well.

In this same segment of the film, the complexity and multiplicity of Chicana identity is captured in the following detail. On the one hand, *las tías solteronas* (spinsters) voice the most traditional values about their desire for a husband for Irene by saying "no se vaya a quedar a vestir santos" ("let's hope she doesn't end up dressing saints"). Yet in a second breath one remarks, "más vale vestir santos que borrachos" ("better to dress saints than drunks"). Indeed, this sequence exemplifies the sophisticated deconstructive and reconstructive style rendered throughout the film. The film's spatial rendition of the quotidian, the everyday rituals, succeeds in illuminating the subversiveness of women's private space. Impregnating onto the quotidian those elements of "resistance" inherent in rituals, Portillo offers a Chicana feminist perspective that critiques the values that imprison Chicanas, salvaging those that liberate.

In its depiction of a central subject whose relation to cultural tradition and religion remains at best ambiguous and distant, *Después del Terremoto* reconstructs multiple-voiced subjectivity. In other words, by assigning "multiple registers of existence" to the main character, Portillo captures cinematically the process that acknowledges that "knowledge" of Chicana "subjectivity cannot be arrived at through a single discursive 'theme'" (Alarcón 1990: 365–66).

Finally, while strongly leaning toward cinematic realism, the film's formal refusal to tie up the threads that make up a fictional text, that is, to achieve narrative closure, opting instead for the ending with the subtitle, "y empezó así . . . " ("and so it began . . . "), leaves an opening, a critical space for the viewer to weave his or her own ending to this ongoing struggle of gender politics.

Woman-Centered Re-vision

A woman-centered counteraesthetics is exemplified by Esperanza Vásquez's *Agueda Martínez*. Also predating *Chicana, Agueda Martínez's* significance rests in its role as a counter to most male-produced documentaries, which focus on grandeur, on the important men and sometimes women in Chicano history. *Agueda Martínez* represents the life of the common everyday woman whose life experience and struggle are just as heroic as those of the "exceptional" individuals. Like *Chicana, Agueda Martínez* challenges dominant assumptions about Chicanas as passive and subservient, for the film is an elegant portrait of a self-sufficient woman. She owns her "rancho," makes her living by working her land, which produces various crops, weaves in the winter, has raised eight children, and proudly claims sixty-seven grandchildren and forty-five great-grandchildren. Agueda lucidly instructs viewers on her various crafts, homecooking, child-rearing, as well as on her views about Chicano culture, history, and tradition. Not only is Agueda resourceful, but her crafts are not at all gendered. Just as she practices traditional New Mexican cooking and weaving (woman's work), so too does she plow the field and till the soil (man's work).

The formal properties of the film mark *Agueda Martínez* as one of the most eloquently crafted films of the period. As opposed to the didactic narrative style of documentary films, which use the authoritative convention of the voice-over, *Agueda Martínez* imaginatively uses direct dialogue. Because the protagonist speaks directly, the film avoids "objective" or authoritative mediation. Specifically, the film's discourse is constructed in a subjective mode, patterning a subject's stream of consciousness. Its central subject, Agueda, slips in and out of narratives of work, cultural tradition, history, and interpretive, critical, and self-reflexive commentary.

Vásquez imbues the central subject's monologue with a dialogic quality that patterns the narrative form of oral history, a quality whose style explicitly assumes an interlocutor. The representation of Agueda's mode of address is realized in a nonlinear fashion, thereby reproducing the oral tradition, but also positioning viewers as active coparticipants in its narrative. For *Agueda Martínez*'s theme, the form of the film's imagery articulates the matrilineal heritage of many Chicanos and Chicanas in the United States.[5]

Structurally, the film reproduces the movement of the day, beginning with sunrise and ending with the setting sun. This visual orchestration overlays onto another marker of time, the cycle of the seasons. Indeed, the cinematic representation is designed in a cyclical fashion, opening with springtime (Agueda's craft of harvesting) and closing with the winter (Agueda's craft of weaving).

Its beautiful depiction of an exemplary elderly woman may strike some as idealized and sentimental, but Esperanza Vásquez's portrayal of struggle in a woman's daily-life existence represents instead a counteraesthetics and a counterdiscourse to what Quintana terms "predominantly masculine interpretations of history and culture" (258).

The "Politics of Representation"

The cinematic production of a new generation of Chicana filmmakers initiates a movement beyond the politics of contestation and toward what Stuart Hall calls "the politics of representation." The emphasis among these new filmmakers revolves around experimenting with form, that is, drawing attention to the expressive aspects inherent in the medium. Less concerned with "setting the record straight," in other words, with rendering "positive" images of women, the more recent film practices illustrate an enormous concern with the artistic properties of the visual form. While they remain committed to a cultural politics insofar as their works deal with the Chicano/a experience, many are less interested in telling it *all* in one film, or with the grand narratives of Chicano history. Rather, the themes embodied in the newer films represent small pieces of the larger puzzle that characterizes the Chicano and Chicana social and cultural milieu.

Here, the question of *a* Chicana cultural identity is less central, explicit, or obvious. Yet a detailed reading of these new cinematic practices discloses that the problematics of identity persist. However implicit, identity, in its varied manifestations, permeates each of these films. But unlike the cultural politics of previous films, these newer ones reveal that Chicana identity can mean different things to different women. Indeed, the new film practices subvert the univocal or bifocal character of previous formulations of cultural identity by infusing these with multiplicity and difference (Fregoso and Chabram 1990; Alarcón 1990).

A cursory look at recent productions by Chicanas indicates that many continue to work within conventional formats and styles, particularly the didactic documentary. An examination of videos shows that many are experimenting with the newer technologies as well. T. Osa Hidalgo de la Riva, for instance, mixes animation with rap lyrics in her imaginative rendition, *Mujeria: The Olmeca Rap* (1991). The musical montage exemplifies an innovative way of drawing attention to cultural identity within the specificity of an urban rap-culture setting. Yet, at the same time, the video also makes reference to an indigenous legacy grounded in female Olmec identity.

Sandra P. Hahn's tribute to the Days of the Dead, *Replies of the Night*, visually illustrates a personal voyage of memory rendered with computer-graphics video production. Her work is thus not simply a tribute to *el día de los muertos*, but more important, it represents Hahn's desire to come to terms with the memory of her grandfather. Using computer graphics and digital voice-reproduction, Hahn animates photographic images of her grandfather, thereby paralleling the cognitive process of reviving him in her own mind. Interestingly, Hahn's grandfather died on the Day of the Dead in 1946.

Beverly Sánchez Padilla's documentary, *El Corrido de Juan Chacón*, imaginatively mixes reportage, film footage from *Salt of the Earth*, and a performance of the *corrido* (ballad) *de Juan Chacón*. Her short documentary deals with one of the major figures in the New Mexico salt-mine strikes of the early fifties—an event that later inspired the film based on these strikes, *Salt of the Earth* (1954). *Corrido de Juan Chacón*'s depiction of Chacón, a major protagonist in the strikes and one of the central characters in the film, moves away from the more conventional documentary styles.

Finally, Frances Salomé España, who prefers to characterize herself as a visual artist, is among the newer filmmakers who take full advantage of the artistic potentiality inherent in the art-form. The three-minute film *Anima* (1989), a tribute to *el día de los muertos*, exemplifies a new experimental style in Chicana filmmaking. España's work draws attention to the representational aspect of cinema, for the film subverts both cinematic time and space. In *Anima*, the filmmaker ritualizes the artistic form through the prolongation of cinematic time as is evident in her extensive recourse to unusual angles and shots, as well as her introduction of dissonance into shots and angles. The short film alternates between three sequence spaces: the cemetery, images of women with painted *calavera* faces (characteristic of the Day of the Dead), and a negative shot of the cemetery in freeze-frame. The alternating movement, back and forth between sequences, is rendered through time-distorted cinematic techniques: jagged or abrupt pans of the cemetery, or images of women with painted faces shot through reflection in chrome mylar. The effect of these distortions cannot be dismissed as simple gimmickry, or film tricks, for España effectively captures, aesthetically, the ritual-based practices that in fact define the Day of the Dead.

Her experimental style is a ritual that is self-reflexive. *Anima* is a ritualized rendition of a ritual, and is therefore thoroughly carnivalesque. In a playful artistic style, España re-creates a ritualized representation (form) of a representation of a ritual (content) of women's painted faces for another ritual, *el día de los muertos*. *Anima* stands out for its infinite representational levels, including the rendering of stylized images of women inserted within another ritual, sitting around the kitchen table. The film's complexity rests in the filmmaker's skillful ability to create a film language that resonates and reproduces the very content of the ritual—a quality that opens up a new phase in Chicana cinematic practices, a movement beyond the politics of contestation.

The work of this new generation of Chicana filmmakers, which includes Olivia Chumacero (*Mbamba*, 1989) and Betty Maldonado (*Night Vigil*, 1982), charts a new direction for Chicana/o filmmaking, cinema made in the spirit of a politics of representation.[6] Like their predecessors, Sylvia Morales, Lourdes Portillo, and Esperanza Vásquez, these newer filmmakers must also confront the "many-headed demon of oppression," for the forces that exclude Chicanas from the "Halls of Chicano cinema" (or the Halls of Moctezuma), and those that oppress Chicanas in a racist, sexist, class-based society, are still haunting us today, fifteen years later.

Notes

I would like to thank the Chicano Studies Research Center at UCLA for its generous support of my research. This essay was written during my tenure as a Ford Postdoctoral Fellow at the Chicano Studies Research Center and the Department of Film and Television at UCLA. I also received funds for my research from the Interdisciplinary Humanities Center at UC-Santa Barbara. I would like to thank Herman Gray for providing comments on an earlier version of this essay. I would also like to express my deepest appreciation to Helena María Viramontes for urging me to write about Chicana filmmakers. Gracias querida. A word on terminology: Practitioners of cinema make a distinction between film and video makers. Given that my analysis departs from the subject-position of the viewer as the producer of meaning, I use the more generic term, filmmaker, to refer to both forms of the cinematic practice, because technical advances in the video format often make it difficult for the viewer to distinguish between each form. Moreover, the rationing of public funds may also make the video format a more viable option for nonindustry practitioners. Besides, most 35-mm films are now released in the video format for home viewing.

1. This month-and-a-half event was held at the UCLA Wight Art Gallery in Los Angeles on October 2-November 13, 1990. In a telephone conversation, Lourdes Portillo informed me that she had called the film series organizer and gave him a list of additional Chicana films and videos for inclusion in the event. Frances Salomé España also comments on the event in the following words: "Of course I knew my inclusion in the UCLA CARA Film Series was an afterthought. The number of Chicana participants was minimal. The place relegated to the women *cineastas* and *videoastas* was a marginal one. I chose not to attend" (personal interview, December 1990).

2. Lourdes Portillo, paper presented at the first conference of Latin Women Film and Video Makers, "Cruzando Fronteras," Tijuana, Mexico, November 29-December 2, 1990.

3. My reference here is to Chicana filmmakers like Lourdes Portillo who have made a self-reflexive choice to remain as independents. There are many others who have entered the mainstream industry, producing both commissioned (commercial) pieces, but also more experimental noncommissioned films.

4. I would like to acknowledge Herman Gray's expertise in mass media and popular culture; he brought many of these points to my attention.

5. I am always struck by the responses of audiences who view this film, either in public forums or in my classes. Someone always comments to the effect, "That's the way my grandmother is" or "Agueda reminds me of my grandmother." Hence, the appropriateness of the film's full title: *Agueda Martínez: Our People, Our Country.*

6. I have made a similar argument about Cheech Marin's film *Born in East L.A.* (1987). See my article, "*Born in East L.A.* and the Politics of Representation."

References

Alarcón, Norma. "The Theoretical Subject(s) of *This Bridge Called My Back* and Anglo-American Feminism," in *Making Face, Making Soul*, Gloria Anzaldúa, ed. (San Francisco: Aunt Lute Foundation Books, 1990), 356–69.

————. "Chicana's Feminist Literature: A Re-vision through Malintzín/or Malintzín: Putting Flesh Back on the Object," in *This Bridge Called My Back*, Cherríe Moraga and Gloria Anzaldúa, eds. (New York: Kitchen Table/Women of Color Press, 1983), 182–90.

Bourdieu, Pierre. *Distinction* (Cambridge: Harvard University Press, 1984).

España, Frances Salomé. "Artist Testimony and Raza Survival Guide: A Chicana Obstacle Course for the Exile on Her Own Turf," *Proceedings of the UC Irvine Conference "Chicana Writes: On Words and Film,"* April 25, 1990 (Berkeley: Third Woman Press, forthcoming).

Fregoso, Rosa Linda. *"Born in East L.A.* and the Politics of Representation," *Cultural Studies* 4, no. 3 (October 1990): 264–80.

Fregoso, Rosa Linda, and Angie C. Chabram. "Introduction: Chicana/o Cultural Representations: Reframing Alternative Critical Discourse," *Cultural Studies* 4, no. 3 (October 1990): 203–12.

Hall, Stuart. "New Ethnicities," *ICA Documents* (Institute of Contemporary Arts) 7 (1988): 27–31.

Keller, Gary D. "The Image of the Chicano in Mexican, United States and Chicano Cinema: An Overview," in *Chicano Cinema: Research, Reviews, and Resources,* Gary D. Keller, ed. (Binghamton, N.Y.: Bilingual Review/Press, 1985), 13–58.

Moraga, Cherríe, and Gloria Anzaldúa. *This Bridge Called My Back* (New York: Kitchen Table/Women of Color Press, 1983).

Quintana, Alvina. "Politics, Representation and the Emergence of a Chicana Aesthetic," *Cultural Studies* 4, no. 3 (October 1990): 257–63.

Saldívar, Ramón. *Chicano Narrative: The Dialectics of Difference* (Madison: University of Wisconsin Press, 1990).

Sánchez, Rosaura. "The History of Chicanas: Proposal for a Materialist Perspective," in *Between Borders: Essays of Mexicana/Chicana History,* Adelaida R. Del Castillo, ed. (Encino, Calif.: Floricanto Press, 1990), 1–29.

————. "Chicana Prose Writers: The Case of Gina Valdés and Sylvia Lizárraga," in *Beyond Stereotypes: The Critical Analysis of Chicana Literature,* María Herrera-Sobek, ed. (Binghamton, N.Y.: Bilingual Review/Press, 1985), 61–70.

Self-Directed Stereotyping in the Films of Cheech Marin

Christine List

In the late seventies and early eighties, Richard "Cheech" Marin and his partner Thomas Chong created more than a half dozen comedy films.[1] Yet it was not until 1987, when Marin went solo to write, direct, and star in *Born in East L.A.*, that any serious study was done of his work.[2] There are two probable reasons for this lack of interest. First, Marin was not credited as a codirector in the earlier films. That fact may have discouraged film scholars from looking at Marin's productions because we tend to privilege an auteur analysis. In 1988, however, Marin revealed in an interview that he did indeed codirect the films credited to Chong.[3] When one considers that Cheech and Chong worked by improvisation, the conclusion that Marin exerted considerable influence over these films is a reasonable one, prompting inquiry as to how these movies represent a Chicano perspective.

A second reason why film scholars may have shied away from the Cheech and Chong movies is that the Chicano stereotypes in these films appear to be derogatory and counter to the progressive nationalist goals that Chicano artists and activists had outlined for *El Movimiento*.[4] Chicano film scholarship has tended to ground itself in the strategy of unmasking negative stereotypes while affirming positive counterimages. The position has been a necessary one given the long history of anti-Mexican sentiment in the United States. Nevertheless, this approach, when applied to the feature narrative, favors films with naturalized characters who have complex psychological explanations for their behavior. Marin's slapstick, one-dimensional Chicano character in the Cheech and Chong films contradicts that aesthetic.

To evaluate Marin's contribution to Chicano cinema, it is necessary to look at how ingroup-created stereotypes might combat negative images imposed from the outside. This strategy of self-directed stereotyping has been used previously by the Chicano Theatre Movement to criticize assimilationism. Other ethnic minorities, such as African Americans and Jewish Americans, have also used negative stereotypes as cultural weapons. With an adequate theory of ethnic humor it is possible to assess Marin's Chicano doper films as actually constructing a subtle critique of ethnocentrism.

Self-Derogatory Humor and the Ethnic Stereotype

Marin's films, aimed at a general audience, have been financially successful at the box office. *Up in Smoke* was the highest grossing comedy of 1978. Marin states that his films enjoy such popularity because his style of comedy makes a positive moral statement by bringing up important social issues beneath the mask of humor. "I've always said that my method is to slip the message into your coffee. You don't taste it. It goes down smooth, but later you feel the effect."[5]

The Chicano character Marin plays in the Cheech and Chong films is a doper who has some street smarts. The opening sequence in *Up in Smoke* establishes the character type he will depict in all his early movies. He awakens on his living room couch surrounded by a hoard of children watching cartoons, and, still drowsy, he stumbles to a filthy bathroom. Too late, he notices that he's been urinating in the hamper instead of the toilet. Next we see him saunter out of the house. A couple of other Chicanos hang out in the front yard cutting hair. He crosses the street and admires his ride, a big old Chevy. The interior has a low-rider look to it: fringe balls, stenciled windows, chain fashioned steering wheel, and crushed velvet interior seat covers. Cheech leans back in the driver's seat, a cool *vato* grin pasted across his face, and slinks ever so slowly away.

As he cruises down the California freeway we discover that this lazy, dirty, low-riding Chicano with too many relatives is also an oversexed macho. When he comes upon two blondes sunbathing by the side of the road, he crosses into oncoming traffic, but the blondes refuse his offer of a good time. Undaunted, he soon spies two giant breasts down the road. Cheech calls out with lascivious intent, "Hey bend over, I'll drive you home, baby," and heads recklessly across traffic once again.

In these opening scenes, Marin paints a picture of the Chicano that, at first glance, affirms preconceived negative stereotypes of the Mexican American.[6] This depiction of self-derogatory images by an ethnic group has long been understood as a manifestation of self-hatred.[7] The pessimistic position has been premised on a reductionist interpretation of all ethnic humor (both inwardly and outwardly directed) as social aggression. In most studies of self-derogatory ethnic humor in Jewish and African American communities, the aggression was viewed as evidence of masochistic personality disorders.

Recent studies, however, have argued that self-derogatory ethnic jokes operate within marginalized cultures as sophisticated means of self-affirmation. Ethnographer E. Oring asserts that the masochistic theory of humor does not distinguish between a simple communicative act and artistic expression. He adds that ethnic jokes are primarily structures of ideas to be perceived intellectually, which means they are based on the creation and perception of an appropriate incongruity or irony.[8]

A central question one must consider when evaluating Marin's use of long-standing Mexican stereotypes is whether he establishes the appropriate aesthetic distance in his films, thereby inviting the viewer to look critically at the stereotypes. Freud, in *Jokes and Their Relation to the Unconscious*, maintained that one way a joke teller succeeds in using self-derogatory caricatures without the listener feeling superior is to make sure the listener knows that the joker has only been pretending to ridicule him or herself.[9] If one looks closely at the visual and narrative style of the Cheech and Chong films, it becomes evident that Cheech and Chong delineate the text as a make-believe space.

Narrative structure in Cheech and Chong films is based on a series of ridiculous scenes clustered about an improbable premise. Plots in these films are practically nonexistent. Just as with a Three Stooges or Marx Brothers film, the viewer of a Cheech and Chong film does not go to see the movie expecting a complicated plot, but rather anticipates a string of cleverly done slapstick sketches.

The opening sequence establishes a cartoonish frame of reference for Cheech and Chong films. *Cheech and Chong's Next Movie*, for example, opens with Cheech and his partner Tommy Chong stealing a garbage can full of gasoline. They decide to pour it in their gas tank directly from the can, spilling gasoline and garbage all over. They pretend no one can see them doing this, although they are at a busy intersection. Saturated with petrol, they hop in the car and speed away. Cheech tells Chong, "Oh shit man, I'm going to be late for work again, man. That's the fifth time I've been late this week, and it's only Tuesday, man." Then Chong lights up a joint and the interior of the car explodes. In the next shot, the two are covered with cinders, clothes are shredded, and eyebrows are seared. Their appearance resembles Wily Coyote after an explosive encounter with the Road Runner. The clownish tone serves as a barometer for the rest of the film.

Mise-en-scène in these movies is also magnified as Cheech translates stereotypes into visual hyperbole. In *Cheech and Chong's Next Movie* the two dopers live in a "vintage ghetto" house. Graffiti decorate both exterior and interior. Trash clutters the lawn, and a property condemnation notice covers the front door. In contrast, we are shown the "Anglo" neighbor's garage neatly painted and obsessively organized so that each object has a hook where it must be placed. By bringing together stereotypes associated with the Anglo suburbs and Chicano *barrio*, the two set designs reinforce the cartoonish quality of the film, encouraging the viewer against reading the stereotypes as realistic.

Strategies of Diffusion

Any ethnic identity can fall prey to stereotyping in a Cheech and Chong film. Chong, who is actually of Chinese Canadian descent, usually plays a nonspecific Anglo hippie character. The doper personality he depicts is just as crude, dirty, oversexed, and unemployable as the Cheech character. Even more so than Cheech, Chong is obsessed with smoking and selling drugs. In *Up in Smoke* his parents are cast as rich WASPS who threaten to put Chong to work for the United Fruit Company (a corporation infamous for oppressing Latin American workers) unless he gets a job. Chong, clad in dirty jeans, wire-frame glasses, and with long hair secured by a bandanna, gives his dad the finger and heads out in search of some weed.

In *Up in Smoke*, other Anglo, Black, and Japanese American characters are humorously presented as gross stereotypes. Stacey Keach plays a narcotics detective. His burr haircut, thinly cropped mustache, and tightly fitted polyester suit accent his patronizing, authoritarian personality. Another ethnic character is Curtis, Cheech's jive-talking African American neighbor and a Hollywood-style hustler who dresses like a pimp. There is also a Japanese American reporter in the film, predictably named Toyota Kawasaki. And, in *Things Are Tough All Over*, Chong plays an Arab who loses his temper at the slightest provocation, causing him to swear murderous revenge in every scene.

When one ethnic group shows another in a disparaging light it is usually taken as a sign of hostile aggression.[10] But if all characters in the films are exposed as having some sort of ethnicity that can be subject to equal ridicule, the negative effects of stereotyping are altered. This is especially true when Anglo characters become ethnicized through exaggerated speech, costuming, and behavioral traits as in the case of Chong and the detective. They are shown to be just as vulnerable to becoming the butt of an ethnic slur as the other "ethnic" characters in the films. In this context the Chicano stereotype is revealed to be as overgeneralized as the Anglo type.

Research on ethnic stereotypes shows that all cultures depict outgroups as dirty, vile, and uncivilized. This of course helps justify oppression of struggling minority ethnic groups.[11] If one looks at the various stigmas attributed to minorities in the United States, it is evident that each group has been similarly characterized by the majority as unclean and barbaric.

Scatological joking is a comic strategy found in the Cheech and Chong films that succeeds in diffusing this stigma of depravity and baseness associated through stereotypes. In *Up in Smoke*, Cheech gets the runs after eating Mexican food. He hurriedly searches for a john, holding his buttocks and muttering, "Come on cheeks, stay together." In *Cheech and Chong's Next Movie*, Chong twice tricks Cheech into drinking from a jar of urine. Later, Chong urinates out the bathroom window onto their Anglo neighbor's bald head. In *Still Smokin'*, Chong performs a comic sketch in which he imitates a dog in the act of defecation.

In *Jokes and Their Relation to the Unconscious*, Freud noted that jokes that rely on bodily degradation for their humor succeed because the listeners recognize that all humanity is equally subject to the same bodily functions. He interpreted grotesque humor in the same manner he explained the obscene joke. Such jokes work by unmasking inhibitions imposed upon the listener. In the case of the Cheech and Chong films, the precarious nature of white Protestant civility is belied by the actions of Chong's Anglo characters. Juxtaposing the baseness of the Anglo and Chicano characters universalizes the dirty Mexican stereotype.

Hollywood has traditionally shown Mexican male sexuality as either perverted or exotic and has generally disapproved of romantic liaisons between Mexican male and Anglo female. Cheech cleverly plays with the stereotype of the oversexed Latin. His character obsessively offers himself to women by making crude statements such as his comment to Chong about a girlfriend in *Up in Smoke*, "I hope she hasn't eaten. I got something for her. Tube steak smothered in underwear."

In an ironic twist, most women enthusiastically accept Cheech's sexual overtures rather than being offended by his bravado. Cheech discovers, to his surprise, that these women are sexually freer and more insatiable than he. In *Nice Dreams*, former girlfriend Donna invites Cheech and Chong up to her apartment to have sex with both of them. In *Still Smokin'*, the Dutch chambermaid uses both men and then sends them crawling away begging for mercy. The scene is intercut with stock footage of rhinos, turtles, and monkeys having intercourse. The film insinuates that Cheech can be considered perverted only if all of nature can be rendered unnatural. Any hint at violation of the women is dispelled because the women are eager and aggressive instigators. They are untainted by false conceptions of Chicano sexual stereotypes (rapist, bandido, gangster), forcing us to see these stereotypes in an ironic light.

Disrespect for authority and the law was attributed to the Mexican American personality and regarded as a cultural flaw. Hollywood films again communicated this through the stereotypes of the bandido, greaser, and gangster. Marin turns the stigma into a positive trait that the audience can identify with by molding his character into a type of trickster.[12] In *Cheech and Chong's Next Movie*, Cheech sneaks off a movie set with his boss's van by pretending not to understand English very well. In *Up in Smoke*, Cheech resorts to stereotype in order to evade the narcotics detective when both end up in the men's room. Cheech plays the Mexican buffoon, making some silly references to his own penis. When he leaves we find out that he was actually urinating on the detective's leg. We are gratified at this clever mode of simultaneous masquerade and revenge.

Freud has noted that rebellion against authority embedded in the hostile joke marks a liberation from its pressure: "We laugh at them (rebellious jokes) because we count rebellion as merit."[13] Cheech's rebellion becomes very pointed in *Up in Smoke* when he sabotages a racist movie production by wandering on a Hollywood set of a typical Chicano gang picture. The exploitation movie's antagonist is dressed in a zoot suit and holds a knife to the neck of a terrified white starlet. The zoot suiter is encouraged to exaggerate his villainy by a bigoted director and his crew. The scene is interrupted when Cheech "innocently" advises a confused actor from backstage to make an early entrance by crashing through a wall of the set. The production is forced to close for the rest of the day.

Cultural critic Sandy Cohen in her study of Jewish humor in the United States asserts that by employing the same stereotypes used against the ethnic minority, the comedian can confront the fact that the dominant culture does not see either the real ethnic culture or its resistance. Old-world folklore of Black and Jewish immigrants provides numerous examples: "Thus we have the Jewish *schlemazel* waiter who because he is 'inept' 'accidentally' spills hot soup on the patronizing customer, or the slave, who because he is 'incompetent' burns down massa's barn."[14]

Marin's films use similar tactics. In the Cheech and Chong movies, ethnicity is worn like a glaring emblem of difference. With the underlying self-consciousness of the trickster, Cheech's character conveys the image of the Chicano as someone who knows he is stereotyped and always tries to resist by showing he is aware of the typing. This is strongly illustrated in *Cheech and Chong's Next Movie* when Cheech sings the lyrics he has composed to a Mexican folk melody. He refers to the ballad as a "protest tune":

> Mexican Americans don't like to get into gang fights
> They like flowers and music and white girls named Debbie too.
> Mexican Americans don't like to go to movies where the dude has
>   to wear contacts to make his blue eyes brown,
> And don't it make your brown eyes blue.

The lyrics make a direct reference to Robbie Benson's stereotypical performance of the Latino youth in *Walk Proud* (1979), an urban violence/exploitation film that was met by considerable protests in the Chicano community. The intertextual comment positions Marin as a self-conscious "Chicano" filmmaker/persona, albeit under the guise of doper humor and understatement.

Marin and Raza Cinema

In terms of style, the Cheech and Chong films fit within a comic tradition of slapstick or bawdy humor incorporated by the Chicano *teatros*, most notably El Teatro Campesino founded by Luis Valdez in 1965. The Teatro produced humorous morality plays called *actos* utilizing broadly played stereotypes of Chicanos as well as Anglos to preach solidarity and pride among Chicanos. One common stereotype employed by Valdez was the *pachuco* or streetwise Chicano youth. This persona started out as Johnny Pachuco in the *acto Los Vendidos* but later grew into El Pachuco, a complex mythological tragihero of Valdez's play and film *Zoot Suit* (1981).

When we compare Marin's streetwise doper with Valdez's *pachucos*, the differences in political messages of the two Chicano filmmakers become more apparent. Valdez created a character that was socially embedded in the Chicano community. He showed us that El Pachuco's identity was formed as a result of confrontation with racist social structures existing since the European invasion and conquest of Aztlán. For Valdez, the gang member becomes a symbolic Aztec warrior, an instrument for channeling political awareness to his audience.

Marin's street character, on the other hand, does not identify with the *barrio* or gang. He mainly cruises in the Anglo world with his Anglo cohort. His enemies and detractors, though obviously racist, do not stir up anger and violence in him, nor do they revive any primordial identity or consciousness. His sarcasm, unlike El Pachuco's, is nonthreatening. In the end, he doesn't have to take a stand in these films, nor would he want to.

This is not to say that one image of the *vato* (dude) is more valuable than the other. Many critics have pointed out the dangers of adopting a mythological vision of identity. They argue that myth obscures history and sometimes encourages a utopian vision that can lull political movements into inaction. But there are also advocates of establishing a mythic identity for its ability to inspire a community in the search for its true cultural roots.[15]

In comparing Marin's *vato* to Valdez's *pachuco* I do not imply that Marin is effacing his own ethnicity or sidestepping all issues of Chicano identity. To the contrary, in the Cheech and Chong films Marin marks himself as Chicano in a very self-conscious way. He associates himself with contemporary low-rider culture, speaks *caló* (Chicano slang), and dresses in the traditional uniform of the *cholo* (contemporary term for *pachuco*): khakis, suspenders, a Pendleton plaid shirt, and stocking cap.

The comedy in his films depends on foregrounding ethnicity as Marin forces Chicano and non-Chicano viewers alike to recognize his otherness. In many respects, Marin's humor is similar in function to jokes told by Chicanos about Mexican folk medicine. These jokes center on the character of the *curandero* (folk healer) whose treatments are often portrayed as absurd and lewd. But while the *curandero* figure is ridiculed for an outdated reliance on indigenous beliefs, the jokes also expose the *gringo* health care system as equally inadequate. Américo Paredes remarks on the double nature of these jokes: "In satirizing of folk medicine and *curandero* belief tales, they express a mocking rejection of Mexican folk culture; in their expression of resentment towards American culture, they show a strong sense of identification with Mexican folk traditions."[16]

Marin's humor is likewise double-edged, oscillating between assimilation and separatism. In *Cheech and Chong's Nice Dreams*, Cheech finally gets rich by selling dope. Living the good life, he has a mansion on a beachfront populated by topless blonde sunbathers. He arrogantly jokes about becoming a sun king (an allusion to the Aztec god central to Chicano nationalism) who throws joints to the natives. Although he dresses in the casual attire of a successful California capitalist, Cheech's character still falls back on his ethnic ways. From his mansion he orders four bottles of "fussy pussy" while he cooks tortillas to make some "Mexican pizza." Later, Cheech loses all his wealth after accepting a bad check from an Anglo who agrees to launder the drug money. In the final scene, Cheech and Chong are forced to take jobs as male exotic dancers, ironically calling their act "the sun kings in paradise."

Cheech's naive desire to fit into the capitalist mold as an ethnic results in his downfall and humiliation. The humorous effect of this comic situation is similar to the way Paredes says the *curandero* jests worked. "It releases a complicated set of conflicting emotions ranging from exasperation to affection in respect to the unacculturated Mexican American."[17]

In *Cheech and Chong's Next Movie,* Marin looks inwardly at his community in a dream sequence in which Cheech appears dressed as an Aztec priest. He approaches his girlfriend Donna, who is costumed as a dead Indian maiden sacrificed on a Nahuatl temple monument. Cheech, with salacious desire, feels her breasts and prepares to rape the lifeless body. The scene suggests that the religious ceremonies of the Aztecs were actually occasions for male perversion. By challenging this symbol of Chicano identity, the icon of manhood, Marin calls into question the sexism embedded within the revival of Aztec heritage in the Chicano Art Movement. As William W. Cook notes, "Satire is a double-edged sword. If it is an instrument for attacking the enemy, it is also an instrument for keeping the tribe in line."[18] In this case, self-derogatory ethnic stereotypes serve as an internal monitor for the community as well as an indictment of falsehoods imposed from the outside.[19]

Conclusion

El Teatro Campesino embraced the image of the *pachuco* (coded as gangster by Anglo media) and transformed him into a heroic symbol of Chicano identity. In mainstream Hollywood films, Cheech Marin presented a depoliticized *pachuco* with many of the same negative traits that have been attributed to Native Mexicans in the United States for centuries. Marin's films, however, do not project a masochistic or demeaning image because humor works to contextualize the stereotypes. Since all ethnic groups, including Anglos, are typed in equally absurd ways, Marin's broadly drawn comic technique forces the audience to consider that ethnic stereotypes are overgeneralizations. His trickster antics appeal to the viewer as Cheech subverts authority figures and institutions like the Hollywood movie industry that he himself operates within. Self-derogatory humor also provides the means for looking critically at the Chicano community by comparing traditional values with new problems.

Groups that have been targets of racial stereotyping have always been faced with the need to generate positive counterimages with their art. Sometimes this results in a kind of "image policing" by artists and critics who are quick to condemn any type of negative character depictions by ethnic artists.[20] Cheech Marin's films show that an ethnic director can take a negative stereotype and, through humor, expose the stereotype as racist (among other things), thereby initiating the process of diffusing its significance for a general audience.

Notes

1. *Up in Smoke* (1978), *Cheech and Chong's Next Movie* (1980), *Cheech and Chong's Nice Dreams* (1981), *Cheech and Chong Still Smokin'* (1983). They also starred in and wrote *Things Are Tough All Over* (1982) and *The Corsican Brothers* (1984).

2. Rosa Linda Fregoso, "*Born in East L.A.* and the Politics of Representation," *Cultural Studies* 4, no. 3 (October 1990): 264–80; Eduardo Tafoya, "Cheech Marin as the New Moses," *Journal of Popular Culture* (forthcoming); and Chon Noriega, "Café Órale: Narrative Structure in *Born in East L.A.*," *Tonantzin* 8, no. 1 (February 1991): 17–18.

3. Dennis West and Gary Crowdus, "Cheech Cleans Up His Act," *Cineaste* 16, no. 3 (July 1988): 37.

4. See, for example, "El Plan Espiritual de Aztlán," reprinted in Rudolfo Anaya and Francisco Lomelí, eds., *Aztlán: Essays on the Chicano Homeland* (Albuquerque: Academia/El Norte Publications, 1989), 1–5; and "El Plan de Santa Barbara," reprinted in Carlos Muñoz, Jr., *Youth, Identity, Power: The Chicano Movement* (London: Verso, 1989), 191–202. For an overview of current political thought among Chicano artists see special issue of *Imagine: International Journal of Chicano Poetry Journal* 3, nos. 1 and 2 (Summer-Winter 1986).

5. West and Crowdus, "Cheech Cleans Up His Act," 37.

6. For an overview of stereotypes of the Mexican American in Hollywood films consult: Charles Ramírez Berg, "Stereotyping in Films in General and of the Hispanic in Particular," *The Howard Journal of Communications* 2, no. 3 (Summer 1990): 286–300; Gary Keller, "The Image of the Chicano in Mexico, the United States and Chicano Cinema: An Overview," in Gary Keller, ed., *Chicano Cinema: Research, Reviews, and Resources* (Binghamton, N.Y.: Bilingual Review/Press, 1985): 13–59; and Arthur Pettit, *Images of the Mexican American in Fiction and Film* (College Station: Texas A&M University Press, 1980).

7. For a summary of research based on this approach consult Mahadev Apte, *Humor and Laughter: An Anthropological Approach* (Ithaca: Cornell University Press, 1985).

8. E. Oring, "Everything Is a Shade of Elephant: An Alternative to a Psychoanalysis of Humor," *New York Folklore* 1 (1973): 149–59.

9. Sigmund Freud, *Jokes and Their Relation to the Unconscious* (New York: Penguin, 1960), 148.

10. Apte, 42.

11. Ibid., 108.

12. There is also a link between Marin's Chicano stereotype and the sixties counter-

culture, especially in the way Cheech's character taps into the "Question Authority" attitude of the time.

13. Freud, 111.

14. Sandy Cohen, "Racial and Ethnic Humor in the United States," *Amerika Studien/American Studies* 30 (1985): 204.

15. The coexistence of works by Valdez and Marin establishes a pop culture dialectic between these two essential views of the role of myth. For a deeper understanding of both views consult Rudolfo Anaya and Francisco Lomelí, eds., *Aztlán: Essays on the Chicano Homeland*.

16. Américo Paredes, "Folk Medicine and Intercultural Jest," in *Introduction to Chicano Studies*, L. I. Duran and H. R. Bernard, eds. (New York: Macmillan, 1973), 271.

17. Ibid.

18. William W. Cook, "Change the Joke and Slip the Yoke: Traditions of Afro-American Satire," *Journal of Ethnic Studies* 13, no. 1 (Spring 1985): 113.

19. José Limón has done a study of *agringado* joking—jokes made by Texas Mexicans that poke fun at Mexican Americans who by Tex Mex standards are too "americanized." He states, "Texas-Mexican joking is not an exercise in self-hatred; rather it takes account of societal differences in expressive ways that strengthen group identity and pride." See José E. Limón, "*Agringado* Joking in Texas Mexican Society: Folklore and Differential Identity," in *New Directions in Chicano Scholarship*, Ricardo Romo and Raymund Paredes, eds., Chicano Studies Monograph Series (La Jolla: Chicano Studies Program, University of California, San Diego, 1978).

20. Consult Salim Muwakkil, "Spike Lee and the Image Police," *Cineaste* 17, no. 4 (1990): 35, for an explanation of how this problem has affected African American filmmakers.

Legislating Languages: *The Ballad of Gregorio Cortez* and the English Language Amendment

Carl Gutiérrez-Jones

Two critical episodes frame the struggle of the twentieth-century Chicano to obtain a legitimate voice in American society. At the beginning of the century stand the trials of Gregorio Cortez, seven in all, dating from 1901 to 1911. At the close of the century stands the English Language Amendment. In what follows, I will read these two particular "moments" in the legal history of the United States as nodal points of our society's search for its own definition, a definition established by playing out interpretations of what constitutes "translation." Because the two moments outlined implicitly raise translation, particularly the question of who should bear the responsibility for translation, as a problem, the moments play out various ideological threats, and scapegoating reactions are always in the air when a community attempts to define its borders, to define the Other and what constitutes the Other's debt or responsibility. After discussing the ways in which issues of translation were displaced during the trials, we will turn to the cinematic revision of the Cortez spectacle, *The Ballad of Gregorio Cortez*, in order to analyze the way in which the film's experimental-documentary form critically rethinks translation. Our final step will be to read the English Language Amendment as a repetition of the displacement enacted during the Cortez episode, a displacement informed by scapegoating mechanisms submerged within Western metaphysics.

Before analyzing the Cortez trials, a historical review of the borderlands will help us to understand the creation of the Cortez legend, and the predominant place the legend has taken in the production of a

Chicano cultural heritage. As Américo Paredes points out, the area in which the Cortez incident took place, originally Nuevo Santander, was unique as a Spanish colony.[1] Because of its isolation, many of the more openly violent tactics common to Spanish colonies were replaced by more subtle forms of ideological control. From its beginning in 1749, the colonial politics relied more heavily on dialogue than on force. This relative displacement of physical violence did not last long. It was followed by one hundred years of strife (from roughly 1830 to 1930), strife too detailed and too involved to recount here. This one-hundred-year interval also marked what Paredes terms the *Corrido* (or Ballad) Century. As Paredes notes, the *corridos* of this period were unified in that the great majority interrogated public rights and particularly their denial. Others, building on Paredes's work, have noted the manner in which the oppositional voices expressed in the *corridos* were founded upon masculinist values that projected a heroic continuity with the past "in the face of the advancing Anglo-American hegemony."[2]

From this capsule history, I will highlight certain trends. First, the unique colonial atmosphere of Nuevo Santander, aided by the presence of the Spanish romance, set the stage for the ballad as a cultural form that could engage political issues by modifying a tradition of public dialogue. Second, the ballad was not simply an accidental vessel for the story of Cortez, but rather a counterhegemonic form that became a formal watershed for the development of Chicano literature. (One might want to consider Rolando Hinojosa-Smith's *Estampas* or the prose-poems of Sandra Cisneros in this context.)

By 1901 the *corrido* tradition was firmly established and it is hard to imagine a case more appropriate than that of Gregorio Cortez for a cultural tradition singing the praises of a hero faced with a conflict of rights. A wrongful arrest propelled Cortez into a shoot-out, which claimed the lives of both the sheriff and Cortez's brother, though accounts suggest that the brother died as a result of his treatment in jail. The chase that followed took on many complex facets. At least one member of the posse compared the excitement of the pursuit to the Indian depredations of an earlier era. The chase held more than a nostalgic significance for the Texas Rangers, who were well aware of the discussion of their disbandment because of the desire of the state to step into the cultural mainstream of the United States. For the

Rangers, a way of life seemed to depend on the successful capture of Cortez.

The Rangers needed evidence that Texas still required their services, yet they also required evidence of their efficiency. In an effort to create a foe worthy of purging, the Cortez Gang was fabricated. As it turned out, the gang consisted of one Mexican, who, in the period of days, walked better than one hundred miles, and rode more than three hundred, managing to elude hundreds of lawmen aided by rail and telegraph. Even though the Rangers did finally capture Cortez, no aggrandizing reckoning ever materialized. The "shoot first, ask questions later" scenario made famous by the Rangers was deflated, inasmuch as Cortez was escorted to the jail "with his pistol in his hand." The spectacle then changed contexts and the ritual of the courtroom took over.

Perhaps the first question we must pose when considering the trials is why the case saw so many return engagements. I would suggest that the case presented a problem that the trial structure found itself at a loss to mediate. Specifically, the case posed the legal question of how to assign responsibility to a discursive act (or "error") that steps outside the register of the legitimate discourse of the courtroom. Yet another way of phrasing the problem is how to account for translation between Mexican and Anglo-Texan culture in an Anglo-Texan legal framework.

The film recounts only the first trial, but the film is from beginning to end informed by the same critical question about translation. At the beginning of the film we are told that what follows comprises the multiple stories of the events recounted. Prior to the introduction of the reporter, the plot pursues a disjunct, bifurcating path that suggests both a crime and a chase. During the initial minutes of the film, two statements stand out. The first, which opens the film, is Boone's accusation of Cortez, and his call to action. The second is Cortez's unrecognized response to the killing, "No fue mi culpa." These two utterances ground the two most important problems posed by the early moments of the film: is Cortez guilty? and how will the linguistic barrier be overcome?

With the arrival of the reporter the film takes on a more unified character. In the course of the first interview, however, one of the main problems of the film is resolved, at least for the Spanish-speaking viewer. It becomes clear as Boone recalls the initial event that his mistranslation, and not Cortez's malicious intent, caused the shoot-out. Given this revelation, the film's focus shifts to the problem posed by the language barrier. For the non-Spanish speaker in the crowd, the question of Cortez's guilt must wait until his repetition of the shoot-out is translated in jail; yet I would suggest that certain clues shift the focus of the film away from the issue of culpability even earlier. In particular, the series of recollections told to the reporter take on a lay-ered or sedimented quality that goes beyond simple juxtaposition. Instead, scenes repeat with slight variations, suggesting exclusions or colorings of remembrances. These variations point toward the limits of memory as an objective source. In turn, motivations become increasingly complex. One thinks of the versions of Boone's encounter with Trimmell after Morris and Romaldo have been shot or the accounts of the Roblero shoot-out. In both situations, the camera angle and position, the editing, and the speed and content of the events depicted are altered to reveal the limitations of the readings each testi-mony would produce.

Like *Citizen Kane*, *The Ballad of Gregorio Cortez* sets up a question that functions as a façade for more complex concerns. Robert Carringer has argued that *Citizen Kane* is not completed with "rose-bud," but rather that the experimental-narrative form of the film itself suggests an entirely different project, in which Welles's critical eye is turned toward the production of testimony.[3] Similarly, *The Ballad of Gregorio Cortez* is not completed by the jury's judgment. If one were to choose the most exciting moment after the chase is completed, the attempted lynching would seem to win out. Yet the climax of this scene is not a judgment of Cortez; Sheriff Fly does not argue Cortez's guilt or innocence while defending him. The climax of the scene is Fly's open-ended questioning of the posse's motives, which again sug-gests that what is most important is not solidifying judgment with an act but rather analyzing the process by which judgments are made.

The film's questioning of the process of judgment carries over to even more primary problems, problems like, how do we read? how do we understand? The film's makers have responded to the thematic presence of these issues by incorporating a narrative process of sedi-mentation (including the repetition of scenes) in order to structure a dialogically sensitive plot. The notion of the dialogic assumes a theory of understanding that emphasizes the role of response. Utterances, understood dialogically, are thought to carry internalized voices of

interlocutors. By suggesting that the film's plot is structured dialogically, then, I am attempting to bring to the fore the interaction of the
scenes as responses to one another. The two versions of the shoot-out
are presented as recollections to emphasize the process by which the
testifying character makes sense of particular events. Inasmuch as the
events of the shoot-outs remain fairly consistent, these recollections
point toward a study of the individual readings of events that are
clearly conflictual. By allowing the different stories to be told and not,
for instance, presenting the film solely from Cortez's point of view,
the film's makers were creating a structure explicitly opposed to the
mock-dialogue between Cortez and Sheriff Morris, in which Boone's
ventriloquism eliminated Cortez's voice, metaphorically killing him
long before the sheriff had a chance.

The structure of the mock-dialogue is repeated in the courtroom,
where the prosecution's complete refusal to engage the defense's
argument subverts the supposedly oppositional form of the trial's
final remarks. In the courtroom version of Cortez's silencing (where
Abernathy is acting as Cortez's legal voice), the film again interrogates
legal interaction between Anglo-Texans and Mexicans; however, the
courtroom version engages the legal system in its most public ritual.
The most pressing question raised by the trial episode seems to be,
how can a forum of judgment that is ostensibly structured for dialogic
debate fail so miserably? The film responds by presenting various
clues about the political and economic pressures of the time: the threat
to the Rangers' survival, the hardened prejudices. But in addition to
these pressures, the film criticizes the sentimental style of reading
invoked by the prosecution, a style that concentrates on the long lone-
ly years Sheriff Glover's daughter will face, with no daddy's knee to
rest her weary head upon.

Bakhtin develops at length the limits of sentimentalism as a form
in the essay "Discourse in the Novel." The two most important points
about sentimentalism for our discussion are (1) sentimentalism develops a historically limited purview common to the tradition of pathos-
oriented writing, and (2) the space of sentimentalism is the private
room.[4] As Bakhtin points out, the discourse of pathos is highly insu-
lated, depending on the virtual collapse of critical distance between
speaker and subject to achieve a sense of complete immersion. When
one combines this collapse with the spatial organization of a private
room, it becomes very apparent why the prosecution chose this form

of reading as an evasion of the defense's argument. Sentimentalism isolates, creating a unified vision that blocks out the problem of translation, and blocks out the existence of the Mexican Americans who are not even worthy of being counted among the dead at the trial.

The film ends with Cortez's departure, accompanied by the ballad; thus the ballad frames the film. The final version of the ballad, however, takes on a special significance inasmuch as the ballad is at this point associated with the public appeal for funds to aid Cortez's defense. The *corrido* consequently gains a political, oppositional association. Beyond a simple framing device, the ballad serves as a communicative response to the trial both in terms of its content and its form. One might even draw the formal aspect out by comparing the ballad "testimony" to the African American tradition of "testifying." In both cases, a particular culture has produced an alternative to the often-insensitive forms of judgment or reading of the hegemonic culture.

When we talk of hegemony, we suggest that the ideas of the dominant class in a society have been coded as "legitimate." The concept of hegemony, then, gives us a way of talking about domination in forms more subtle than outright violence. The process of legitimation remains central within the reproduction of hegemonic culture. That the stereotype of the cruel and treacherous Mexican invoked by the prosecution at Cortez's trial is accepted as valid argumentation reinforces the stereotype as legitimate. Within this frame we may also say that the most important issue raised, yet refused status as legitimate at the trial, is the issue of translation. In counterpoint, the *corrido* and testifying traditions become counterhegemonic forces that challenge by creating their own legitimating processes.

Arguments about translation again battle for legitimacy in contemporary statements about the English-First movement. Inevitably, proponents of English-Only evade the issue of translation by falling back on arguments about the danger posed to national unity by a policy supporting biculturalism. For instance, Imhoff and Bikales, in an article published in *USA Today*, open with the following: "The political forces behind bilingual education are those which promote cultural separatism."[5] The article goes on to argue that the promotion of biculturalism will create political chaos in this country, destroying the glue that holds it together. The McCarthyist ring here suggests an appeal to paranoia, which only clouds discussion. Foremost, I think we need to recognize that dominant attitudes about biculturalism in the United States are historically and culturally specific. Were we, for example, to compare these attitudes, at this time, to those of other countries where students participate in bilingual education from day one, this country would come away appearing exceedingly provincial.

What aspects of history have influenced this country's adoption of provincialism? Certainly the seeds were here from the beginning, locked into a Puritan worldview that scorned sophistication and, as Thomas Pynchon has suggested, proved fertile ground for the breeding of paranoia. In addition, the reaction to the European immigration that took place in the 1920s set the stage for the present English-First movement. Not only was bilingual education in existence prior to World War I, it was often looked upon as a national resource. With the 1920s, however, a growing concern over influxes of European immigrants made it possible for conservatives to sway public opinion against bilingualism by emphasizing the need for national unity.

The resurgence of bilingual education in the 1960s was largely a result of gains made by the Civil Rights movement, gains that were translated into law in the 1968 Bilingual Education Act, and the 1974 Supreme Court decision Lau vs Nichols. More recently, the bilingual mandate has been open to erosion, particularly in the courts. Because the Supreme Court consistently refuses to define specific educational policies, its 1974 decision left the legal ground ambiguous. As a response to the revitalized bilingualism of the 1960s and 1970s, and the rapid growth of Hispanic populations in the United States, the 1986 California English Language Amendment is likewise legally ambiguous, although on one point its clarity is unique. Unlike similar laws, the amendment specifies a process of enforcement that allows private individuals to sue the state. By contrast, the law's statement of purpose seems to elicit the "endless deferral of meaning." It reads:

> English is the common language of the people of the United States and the State of California. This section is intended to preserve, protect and strengthen the English Language, and not to supercede any of the rights guaranteed to the people by this Constitution.[6]

Perhaps the most ambiguous question raised by the law is how the delegitimization of a person's language can avoid impinging upon a person's rights. For instance, plans have already been made to terminate bilingual voting ballots, violating the United States Voting Rights

Act. A more subtle indication of an already dangerous language barrier is reflected in the following statistic: 25 percent of the legally forced, life-threatening cesarean sections that take place in this country are given to non-English dominant speakers. Virtually all of these women are nonwhite.[7] The suggestiveness of this correlation is only enhanced by the fact that one of the highest-ranking officials in the U.S. English-Only organization is also a leading proponent of forced sterilization for Third World and ethnic populations.

Proponents of the law counter that forced assimilation will improve the economic status of the groups involved. Both sides usually agree, however, that none of the studies of education have shown a linguistic advantage to the English-Only approach, otherwise known as the immersion technique. At this juncture, it is important to note that the issue is not English-Only vs. Spanish-Only, but rather monolingual vs. bilingual teaching of English.

The bill's detractors argue that standards beyond English proficiency need to be considered. They ask, how does one measure the loss of science and math instruction in an immersion program? How does one measure the student's sense of self-worth or the student's relationship with family and culture? At the very least we need to be aware that short-term gains may have subtle, long-term effects. One study has indeed shown that a bilingual setting substantially increased high school graduation rates. But, as James Baldwin has suggested, haggling over statistics may become a way of avoiding more dangerous issues concerning race and culture.[8]

The "defense of national unity" reading of the situation is in fact a variation of the sentimental reading that attempted to repress issues of translation in the film. Rather than recognizing the rights of various cultures within our national boundaries, a recognition that would in turn raise questions about mutual responsibility, the posture of defense (preservation, protection) creates a simplistic binary Us vs. Them scenario. Like the sentimental reading of the trial, this binary logic sets up strategic walls, walls that would make the hybrid Mexican American invisible, or the enemy, or both.

Ramón Saldívar, in a recent article on Rodriguez's *Hunger of Memory*, has also shown how binary logic is instrumental to Rodriguez's argument against affirmative action and bilingual education.[9] In doing so, Saldívar draws upon contemporary theory, including deconstruction, for its study of logical displacements. By examining such rhetorical tools as mimesis and personification, this style of reading reveals the ways figures of resemblance have been used to disguise differences, differences that ultimately yield superiority to metaphors of absolute intimacy (Rodriguez with his grandmother), to monolithic genetic history (Rodriguez's understanding of education), and to the autonomous power of the self (Rodriguez as Romantic exile, beating his breast after his family's Christmas dinner). Jacques Derrida has described the sort of "strategic" use of displacements drawn out by Saldívar in terms of the "economy" of particular texts, an economy that reinscribes certain dominant ideas like those submerged in Rodriguez's work.[10] Derrida's work is foremost a critique of metaphysics, not of politics. Yet if we recognize that institutions carry ideological assumptions, that they in fact set processes in motion that legitimate these assumptions, we may start to understand how Derrida's work on the "economics" of the binary may be applied to the events of 1901, and of 1986. Assuming that a process legitimating ideas takes place both within the realm of metaphysics and the realm of institutions, we may start to interrelate critiques of both worlds.

I would suggest that we read the gunslinging "philosophy" of the Texas Rangers not as a peripheral element of Western culture, but rather as an element that might even bear comparison to the intellectual big guns. Consider, for instance, how Hegel, one of the most celebrated philosophers of the modern era (and one of its greatest defenders of Totality and Unity) describes the production of "understanding" in his *Preface* to the *Phenomenology*.[11] Hegel aligns analysis, also understood as the "activity of differentiating," with death. But this death is an ultimately positive experience according to Hegel, one that provides a rebirth. Hegel, therefore, belittles "the life that shrinks from death and keeps itself undefiled by devastation," while he praises "the life that endures, and preserves itself through death," a death that gives rise to the "life of the spirit."

Underscoring the sacrificial element of the process, Hegel states that "the spirit gains its truth only by finding itself in absolute dismemberment." The crux of this filmic scenario is the power gained "by looking the negative in the face and abiding with it." This specular relation (part and parcel of speculative dialectics) "converts the negative" (i.e., the elements that would escape Unity), into one hundred percent recyclable material.

Conversion, of course, is analogous to translation. In Hegel's case it is important to remember that this process serves an overriding function, the achievement of Unity. Analysis and differentiation are only steps on a ladder to the continually present goal of Unity. The Derridean economy of Hegel's philosophy thus incorporates analysis and differentiation as one side of a supposedly symmetrical binary, a side that is scapegoated nonetheless, giving the opposing side of the equation, i.e., Unity, hierarchical priority. In his introductory lectures on the philosophy of history, Hegel calls this sleight of hand "the cunning of reason," which "translates" the "universal idea" into existence through the individuals who "are sacrificed and surrendered."[12] The difference in Hegel's presentation of this scenario is that he is forthcoming about the object to be scapegoated.

Ultimately, both scenarios enact a scapegoating mechanism that, as Dominick LaCapra has pointed out, cannot be separated from the binary logic invoked. "Scapegoating on a discursive level is itself essential to the constitution of pure opposites insofar as internal alterity, perceived as guilty or fallen, is purged, and all 'Otherness' is projected onto the discrete Other."[13] This purging process relies on an appearance of rhetorical resemblance between categories: the Self and the Other, the Anglo and the treacherous Mexican. Nowhere is there room for the hybrid Mexican American. If necessary, a Cortez gang will be created to oppose the posse and to maintain the apparent scenario of self-sacrifice. Ultimately, the creation of the gang masks the latent sacrifice of the hybrid. On an institutional level, such an "economic" creation of the Other constitutes a discourse of colonization. The Mexican American, as part of the trial, as part of our "national unity," may be suppressed by turning him or her into a symbol of destruction, a symbol of "the forces behind cultural separatism."

Taking a moment to search out our own complicity in the sacrificial project that in some sense has defined this country, we who are academics may ask if we have isolated ourselves within our own disciplines to the extent that our own perceived limitations halt effective discussion of the provincial mentality I have outlined. If the displacement of rights and the McCarthy-era paranoia I have noted succeed in this country, it will be due in part to a failure by those sympathetic with issues of translation and biculturalism to create their own counterhegemonic voice.

We might begin by questioning the gains and losses of the rhetoric of "efficiency" set forth by the English-Only movement. We might also dismantle the philosophy of provincialism, and its attendant banking concept of understanding (based on the deposit/withdrawal model), a concept of understanding that, like Hegel's enormous intellectual edifice, functions to exclude the hybrid while "defending" the totality.

We will also need to look toward alternative notions of understanding, and in keeping with the film's own dialogic quality, I will offer one possible course by turning to Bakhtin, who argues that "in its naive and realistic interpretation, the word 'understanding' always induces into error. It is not at all a question of an exact and passive reflexion, of a redoubling of the other's experience within me (such a redoubling is, in any case, impossible) . . . [understanding is rather a] matter of translating the experience into an altogether different axiological perspective, into new categories of evaluation and formation."[14] Once again we return to the importance of rethinking translation and its pervasive implications. Perhaps the most significant difference between Bakhtin's notion of translation and Hegel's rests in their widely differing views about totalization. Hegel, as we have noted, attempts to purify translation by arguing that nothing escapes the process he describes. Significantly, Bakhtin suggests that translation may yield results that need not be purged of their difference.

Bakhtin, of course, was no stranger to hegemonic pressures, pressures that, in different ways, Chicanos also confront. As one alternative, then, we might pursue a dialogue between Bakhtin and Chicano artists and seek out the ways in which these artists have sought to raise ideologically forceful issues of translation, especially where those issues are played out in legal contexts that carry the weight of public sanctions. In doing so, we may also take the lead of recent critical works examining the role of the *corrido* in the development of Chicano narrative; we might thus consider the ways in which the *corrido* form has influenced dialogically oriented cinematic texts of *la raza*.[15]

Notes

1. Américo Paredes, *"With His Pistol in His Hand": A Border Ballad and Its Hero* (Austin: University of Texas Press, 1958), 7–9.

2. For readings of the gender ideology of *corridos*, see María Herrera-Sobek's "The Treacherous Woman Archetype: Structuring Agent in the *Corrido*," *Aztlán: International Journal of Chicano Studies Research* 13 (1982): 13–47; Herrera-Sobek's "The Acculturation

Process of the Chicana in the *Corrido*," *De Colores Journal* 6 (1982): 7–16; Renato Rosaldo's "Politics, Patriarchs, and Laughter," *Cultural Critique* 6 (1987): 65–86; and Ramón Saldívar's *Chicano Narrative: The Dialectics of Difference* (Madison: University of Wisconsin Press, 1990), 38–40.

3. Robert L. Carringer, "Rosebud, Dead or Alive: Narrative and Symbolic Structure in *Citizen Kane*," *PMLA* 91, no. 2 (March 1976): 185–93.

4. Mikhail Mikhailovich Bakhtin, "Discourse in the Novel," in *The Dialogic Imagination*, trans. Caryl Emerson and Michael Holquist (Austin: University of Texas Press, 1981), 396–98.

5. Gary Imhoff and Gerda Bikales, "The Battle over Preserving the English Language," *USA Today* (January 1987): 63–65.

6. Constitution of the State of California, Constitutional Amendments, Article 111, Section 6 (1986).

7. Sara Hill, "Reproductive Rights: A Common Ground for Women?" Conference on Afro-American and White American Women (Ithaca, New York, February 20, 1988).

8. James Baldwin, "In Search of a Majority," in *The Price of the Ticket* (New York: St. Martin's/Marek, 1985), 233.

9. Ramón Saldívar, "Ideologies of the Self: Chicano Autobiography," *Diacritics* 15, no. 3 (Fall 1985): 25–33.

10. Jacques Derrida, "From Restricted Economy to General Economy: A Hegelianism without Reverse," in *Writing and Difference*, trans. Alan Bass (Chicago: University of Chicago Press, 1978), 251–77.

11. G. W. F. Hegel, *Preface* to *The Phenomenology of Spirit*, in *Hegel: Texts and Commentary*, trans. Walter Kaufmann (Notre Dame: University of Notre Dame Press, 1977), 50.

12. Ibid., 83.

13. Dominick LaCapra, "Criticism Today," in *The Aims of Representation*, ed. Murray Krieger (New York: Columbia University Press, 1987), 249–50.

14. M. M. Bakhtin, "Author and Character in Aesthetic Activity," in *Mikhail Bakhtin: The Dialogic Principle*, trans. Tzvetan Todorov and Wlad Godzich (Minneapolis: University of Minnesota Press, 1984), 22.

15. For recent critical works examining the role of the *corrido* in the development of Chicano narrative, see Ramón Saldívar's *Chicano Narrative*, and Renato Rosaldo's *Culture and Truth: The Remaking of Social Analysis* (Boston: Beacon Press, 1989).

Chicano Cinema: A Dialectic between Voices and Images of the Autonomous Discourse Versus Those of the Dominant

Víctor Fuentes

As is well known, the cinema of the so-called Hispanic minorities has had, in the 1980s, its fifteen minutes of fame. Several Latino movies have made it into the channels of Hollywood production and distribution and those of national, public television. This, in turn, has opened up a previously closed door for Latino filmmakers. The best example is the popular success of *La Bamba,* one of the biggest box-office hits of 1987.

The sociohistorical and demographic transformations of our times have compelled the cinematographic establishment to change its attitude toward ethnic minorities, which, in states like California, are quickly becoming a majority. Until very recently Hollywood indulged in a degrading representation of the Latino/a.[1] This attitude, although slowly changing, still prevails in representations of Latinos as gang members and drug pushers as they are portrayed in several Hollywood movies. Nevertheless, we also have the unusual case of Chicano filmmakers, like Luis Valdez and Richard "Cheech" Marin, who have written and directed their own movies within the Hollywood studio system.

In the present essay, through the focus expressed in the title, I will deal with *La Bamba* and *Born in East L.A.,* along with *El Norte,* a movie that, even though made as independent filmmaking, still reveals a great deal of the Hollywood model and expectations. The thesis of my essay is that even though these three movies follow Hollywood models, they also contain elements of a cinema of cultural resistance and affirmation opposed to Hollywood canons. My theoretical framework is derived mainly from Gramsci and Bakhtin. Both thinkers insisted on considering art and literature as an inalienable part of culture, and gave great emphasis to the question of the creativity of popular culture. Bakhtin's theories on social dialogue, inscribed in every utterance, and of the Carnival both as expression of comic popular culture and a subversion of official culture, lend themselves perfectly well to an understanding of a large part of Latino literature and art, including cinema.[2]

Applying Bakhtinian bivocality to the field of criticism, we can establish that although for the Latino critic movies such as *La Bamba* and *Born in East L.A.* deserve serious discussion and cinematographic analysis, this is not the case for the Anglo critics of the cultural establishment. These critics perceive little of importance in the two movies and include them in that amorphous mass of Hollywood movies whose primary aim is to produce monetary profit and some type of consumer entertainment.

For example, Caryn James in the *New York Times* (August 24, 1987, III, 14) completely disqualifies *Born in East L.A.* Her review ends with a cutting negative judgment: "But *Born in East L.A.* never does [succeed], as if all that effort simply buried Cheech Marin's antic side." The critic is bothered by the fact that in this movie Cheech Marin abandons his role as a jester and his stereotype of a *barrio* pot smoker/hipster and tries, on the other hand, to be serious, dealing with the theme of the poverty "that pushes so many Mexicans and Central Americans to cross the border." Of course, contrary to Caryn James's presupposition, the main theme of the movie is not the push of poverty, but rather the violent shoves of the *migra*, taken to the extreme of pushing an American citizen of Mexican ancestry out of his own country. This theme is not a fantasy of the Chicano filmmaker; it has happened in real life.

Likewise, Janet Maslin's review of *La Bamba* in the *New York Times* (July 24, 1987, II, 23) is rather neutral. The critic points out the theme's little originality, since the story of Ritchie Valens parallels that of *The Buddy Holly Story*, adding that, in the case of both movies, it is better to admire them for their innocence and simplicity than to fault them for their lack of sophistication. Nevertheless, she does fault *La Bamba*, criticizing the leading role ("The role is blandly written") and adding that "the film moves on awkwardly to depict the fatal plane crash." She also has some lukewarm praise, noting that "Mr. Valdez gives *La*

Bamba enough warmth to make up for its conventionality as well as a strong feeling for Valens' Chicano roots."

On the other hand, Maslin (January 11, 1984) and the leading critic of the *New York Times,* Vincent Canby (January 11, 1984), bestow high praise on *El Norte.* Both critics emphasize the artistic plasticity of the movie and the pathos of the emigration saga of the young brother and sister, Guatemalan Indians. I think that this positive response by two critics of the establishment was already inscribed in the aims of director Gregory Nava and producer Anna Thomas, since one can assume that they made their movie with the expectation of a liberal Anglo public, the public of the art cinema circuits, in mind, and worked within the narrative conventions of Hollywood cinema. In this sense they hit the target, since the movie, in spite of being subtitled, was a big success. The movie's subordination to Hollywood narrative and expectations is emphasized by Richard Allen, writing for *Framework.* After saying that *El Norte* is an independent film, he adds:

> The way the story is told remains firmly based on the model provided by Hollywood cinema. That is, a story that progresses in a linear fashion through a sequence of events which the spectator experiences vicariously through identification with central characters. (*Framework* 26–27: 88)

In a general way, this procedure of the "straight corridor," typical of Hollywood film narrative, is also followed in *La Bamba* and *Born in East L.A.* Nevertheless—and here we begin with the differences—the three movies have manifest oneiric and mythical-symbolical perspectives. Through these perspectives, they subvert their Hollywood codes, and tap into dimensions of the indigenous and Hispanic popular traditions. Naturally, the critics of the Anglo establishment either fail to see this or minimize its importance. In the three films there are a series of intertextualities and referential and thematic traits that make it possible to include them—in spite of the "Made in Hollywood" stamp—within a movement of an emergent Chicano-Latino cinema.

El Norte is presented as an "art film," and the other two are offered as packaged products of popular culture. Nevertheless, the author-directors, Luis Valdez and Cheech Marin, are talented artists and their films admit two "readings": innocent, as that of *La Bamba* by Janet Maslin, or "malicious," that is to say, an interpretative reading that goes beyond the floating level of the story line, and relates the text to its cultural context and to a subtext.

Maslin limits the scope of *La Bamba* to the conventions of that type of Hollywood film that deals with the rise to fame and the tragic irony of the early death of a young star of popular music: movies such as *The Buddy Holly Story* and *Sweet Dreams*, the biography of Patsy Cline. Valdez's touch of originality was to render a Chicano version of these films, which, as she tells us: "At their best, they bring that music to life all over again."

We know since Barthes, Eco, and the reader response criticism that in the plurality of relationships that are established within and around an artistic text, the perspective of the reader (in cinema that of the viewers) is of utmost importance. Each reader brings to the reading her or his own cultural baggage, expectations, and personal and socio-historical circumstances. With this in mind, we could say that the Anglo critics, to whom I have been referring, have a very light cultural baggage, as well as too limited expectations, for an in-depth under-standing of the creative contradictions of these cinematic examples of an emerging Latino-Chicano cinema, in the very backyard of the Hollywood cinema.

In the case of *La Bamba*, Janet Maslin apparently does not realize the fact that the author-director, "Mr. Valdez," before becoming a filmmaker had already produced theatrical works of universally rec-ognized value. Thus she fails to see that in *La Bamba* there is a series of themes, images, and symbols of the Valdezian world vision, which are brought to the screen, enriching the limited perspectives of the com-mercial cinematographic conventions, within which he finds himself working as well as subverting.[3] A critical view of *La Bamba*, which takes as its starting point familiarity with Valdez's theatrical work and its place within Chicano culture, would enable the critic to find in this film the richness of discursive plurality and intertextuality, which in Valdez's case begins with his own texts.[4]

It would be difficult to say to what extent Valdez does this con-sciously, but the fact is that his Hollywoodesque film, *La Bamba*, is inspired by a world vision already present in his independent theatri-cal productions. In the first sequence of the film, that of Bob's first appearance on his motorcycle, we also see, fleetingly, undulating in the middle of the road, a snake. This image transports us to the vision of reality, which Valdez expressed in his "Pensamiento serpentino" (*Chicano Theatre One* 8–19):

> But REALITY es una Gran Serpiente
> a great serpent
> that moves and changes
> and keeps crawling out of its dead skin . . .

Later on in the film, the same emblem of the snake reappears in the sequence, in which "El Tata," a spiritual healer, living on the outskirts of Tijuana, celebrates a ritual around the life and death of Ritchie. "El Tata" says: "The snake is life. A snake that comes out of its own body, like a dream." This sequence involves Hollywood cinema's profane character and linearity, in which *La Bamba* is inscribed, in a ceremonial ritual: in a circular mythical and oneirical dimension. It brings Luis Valdez's movie close to the "hallucinogenic realism" of Latin American fiction, to which Janet Maslin relates *El Norte*, but not *La Bamba*, a movie in which the "straight corridor" gives way to the labyrinth.

It is also very significant that in *La Bamba*, a movie in which English speaking is associated with success in life (a predicament that has led to severe criticism of Valdez by a certain sector of the Latino community), the deeper words, those of "El Tata," are spoken in Spanish: "El vivir es dormir y el morir es despertar." Furthermore, even if Ritchie doesn't speak the language, he does sing in Spanish, "La Bamba," even after his own death. Bilingualism (and in the case of *El Norte*, trilingualism) plays an important role in the polyphony of voices of those three movies. *El Norte* is a U.S. movie, predominantly spoken in Spanish and in Quiché. In *La Bamba* and in *Born in East L.A.*, even though the Spanish spoken is minimal (but deeply rooted in expression of intimacy and family feelings), it appears without English subtitles: as part of that alien word (in the Bakhtinian sense) that each day increasingly reveals the growing bilingualism of American society. Furthermore, the English spoken in the latter two movies carries the intonation and a gesticulation of Chicano English. The "waas sappenin" of *Born in East L.A.* is a defiant emblem of this English that, at a more serious level, is being enriched daily by the U.S. Latino population, its poets and writers.

In *La Bamba*, Hollywood conventionalisms appear subverted not only by the Valdez of the *mitos*, but also by that of his *actos*. According to César Chávez, the *actos* were representations of the reality of farm-workers' lives.[5] Hence in *La Bamba* the representation of the life of a farmworker family, now moved to a urban setting, is accurately repre-sented, as far as customs, gestures, feelings, and language. The sequences of Ritchie's assimilation (where he has to deal with discrim-ination and a forced cultural assimilation) have an ironic twist, how-ever.

These scenes take us back to the subversive irony of the *actos*: they have an ironic sense very similar to the sequences of the assimilation of the Guatemalan brother and sister into the consumer society of Los Angeles, as depicted in the last part of *El Norte*. Likewise, at the begin-ning of *Born in East L.A.*, we find a similar rejection of that consumer society. It is very significant that in *El Norte* as well as in *La Bamba*, the "American dream" ends up in a nightmare of death, although given the mythical dimension of both films, at another level, death has the positive sense of being an initiatory death.

In the three movies, there is a juxtaposition of scenes, dealing with different sociocultural levels. On the one hand, we see scenes of family life and friendships within the Latino culture; on the other, scenes dealing with the Anglo world. In these juxtapositions we find the con-trast between one's own and the alien: the warmth of love, on one side, and the coldness of alienation on the other.

In *La Bamba*, and in tune with its mythical dimension, family and love relationships are associated with the ritual cycles of growth-fecundity-death-life. In the three movies we find that first social com-munication occurs within the mother-son relationship, a relationship that appears throughout *La Bamba* as a kind of protecting shield. Present also in this movie is the archetype of the enemy brothers, which point to Cain and Abel but also to the Aztec gods Quetzalcoatl and Tezcatlipoca. But the rivalry between them appears surpassed by the "In LAKECH" ("You are my other self," an indigenous antecedent of today's recognition of the Other), a principle derived from Quetzalcoatl's unifying strength, which Valdez incorporated in Chicano theater in the late 1960s and early 1970s.

The character of Bob, Ritchie's brother, in spite of his negative aspects as a stereotype of the Latino *macho*, has a strong appeal for the latino/a viewer. On a social plane, his violence and destructive im-pulses could be interpreted as a symbol of the oppressed's wrath: a sort of spontaneous rebellion against alienation and exploitation.

Likewise, Bob's negative attitudes serve as a refreshing counterpoint to the humiliating trials of assimilation that his brother endures. On the mythical level, his destructive drive has a constructive bent, as a symbol of permanence of the native culture. Toward the end of the movie, we see him playing with his baby and with the amulet that "El Tata" gave to his brother and that Ritchie lost before his fateful trip.

In relation to the critical interpretation of this ambivalent character it is interesting to note that a Chicana critic, Rosa Linda Fregoso, sees *La Bamba* as a movie about Bob and not Ritchie. Janet Maslin declares: "But Bob is one-note boorish character—he drinks, picks fights, sells drugs, steals Valens' girl and then mistreats her—and this part of the film is the weakest."

The three leading young women of the movies (two Rosas, one Chicana in *La Bamba* and the other Guatemalan in *El Norte,* and the Salvadoran Dolores of *Born in East L.A.*) are represented as hardworking women of moral strength and integrity. In spite of their physical beauty, there is very little emphasis on their sensuality. It seems as if there was a conscious intention, on the part of the three Chicano directors, to represent the Latino woman in opposition to her Hollywood stereotype: that of a lazy woman, devoid of morality and given only to sensual pleasure. With the Rosas of *La Bamba* and *El Norte,* we find ourselves in the antipode of *Havana Rose,* to mention just one of those Hollywood movies that spread a degrading representation of Latino women.[6]

One central theme of the three movies is that of the border chronotope. Bakhtin singled out the artistic importance of the chronotope: literally, "space-time," coordinated in the work and framing the world vision that informs it. In the three movies the border chronotope has a determinant significance. In both *El Norte* and in *Born in East L.A.,* there is a special emphasis on the ominous character—a sort of Berlin Wall—of the border barrier; a border not recognized as such by many Mexican and Central Americans who consider the United States as "El Norte," although, as we see in *El Norte,* the areas surrounding the border line have all the characteristics of a war zone.

El Norte has given us one of the most terrifying scenes ever depicted of the "illegal" border crossing: that of the awesome plight of the young brother and sister going through the drainage pipe. (By one of those strange coincidences in which life imitates art, when I was first writing this passage, one of the first recorded attempts of the crossing of the Berlin Wall, through a small tunnel dug underneath it, was being broadcast on television. It was difficult to distinguish if the small hole was under the Berlin Wall or under the Tijuana border, or if the documentary was dealing with Berlin or replaying the passage of Enrique and Rosa in *El Norte*.)

That image has such an effect on the whole texture of the film, that by extending the dreamlike quality of *El Norte* to the entire story, we could say that the last part (that of the "rosy" dream of the assimilation of the youngsters into the consumer society of Los Angeles, and including the tragic anticlimax of Rosa's death) is all Rosa's nightmare, inside the drainage pipe, where—in actuality—the young brother and sister could have died devoured by the rats. It is very revealing that both Vincent Canby and Janet Maslin, who praised the color and the photography of the film so much, kept silent with regard to this dreadful sequence, a devastating indictment of the myth of the torch of the Statue of Liberty, lighting the arrival of the newcomers. In *El Norte* and in *Born in East L.A.*, instead of the torch of liberty, the welcome is lighted by the helicopter ("los moscos") floodlight.

As already mentioned, the *Born in East L.A.* story is a true history: the deportation to Mexico of a U.S. citizen of Mexican origin, a flagrant racist tactic to which the immigration officers resort from time to time. But in the film, this forced emigration to Tijuana acquires, in the chronotope of *Born in East L.A.*, a symbolic and carnivalesque meaning. It could be seen as an initiatory trip, a *regressus ad uterum* for Rudy. Through the harsh trials of the descent to hell and the passages through the shadows (jail, the shoddy nightlife of the Night Club, the bushes, physical assaults), Rudy experiences a rebirth. In Los Angeles, he lived in the cold alienation of the "extasis" of the objects (the TV, the phone, the car, the woman object who parades in the streets and whom he chases), but in his trials in Tijuana, Rudy finds himself, through generosity and love. When he returns to his "center" of East Los Angeles, he returns humanly enriched.

It has a special significance that the versatile Chicano artist, Cheech Marin, takes his comic role to Tijuana. His gesture can be seen as an homage to the great comic actors of the Mexican cinema (Cantinflas, Tin Tan, Fernando Soto, "Mantequilla," and Manuel Valdez, "El loco") and to the land of their common ancestors.

The chronotope of Tijuana in *La Bamba*, besides abolishing the given time-space dimensions, leads us into its mythical-poetical

Scenes from Luis Valdez's *Los Vendidos: The Sellouts* (1972), produced by José Luis Ruiz. *Top:* Scene from the *mito* (mythical tale) that introduces and closes *Los Vendidos. Bottom:* Scene from the *acto* (agitprop skit) "Honest Sancho's Used Mexicans." Courtesy of José Luis Ruiz.

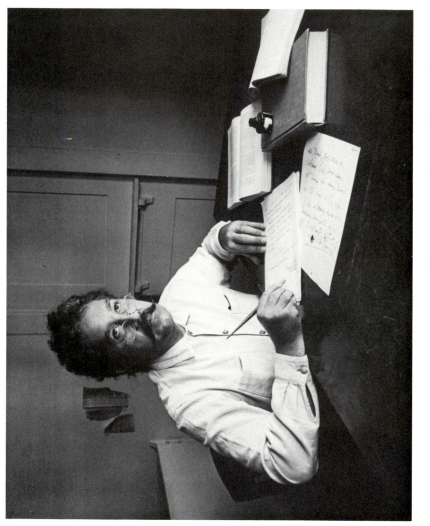

Eduardo Moreno as Ricardo Flores Magón in the documentary *Yo Soy Chicano* (1972), written and produced by Jesús Salvador Treviño. Courtesy of Jesús Salvador Treviño.

Class photo taken in 1930 of one of the Americanization classes at the Lemon Grove Grammar School, composed entirely of children of Mexican descent. From Paul Espinosa's docudrama, *The Lemon Grove Incident* (1985). Courtesy of Paul Espinosa.

Scene from *Esperanza* (1985), a one-hour drama about two
children whose mother is picked up by immigration police.
Courtesy of Sylvia Morales.

Scene from *Después del Terremoto/After the Earthquake* (1979),
written and directed by Lourdes Portillo and Nina Serrano.
Courtesy of Lourdes Portillo.

Scene from *Vida* (1989), an AIDS *telenovela* by Lourdes Portillo and AIDSFILM. Courtesy of Lourdes Portillo.

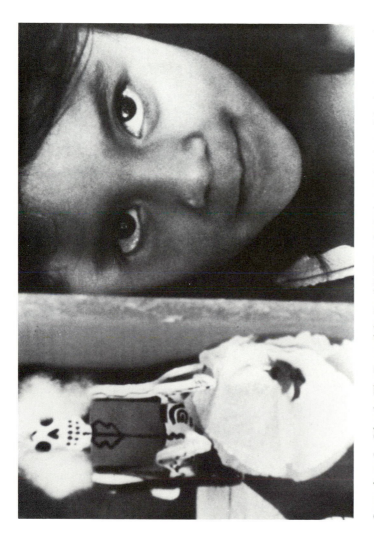

Scene from *La Ofrenda: The Days of the Dead* (1989), a lyrical examination of the history, myth, and politics that surround the celebration of *El Día de los Muertos* in Mexico and the United States. Produced and directed by Lourdes Portillo and Susana Muñoz. Courtesy of Direct Cinema.

Edward James Olmos as the mythical El Pachuco in *Zoot Suit* (1981), written and directed by Luis Valdez. Courtesy of Universal City Studios.

Scenes from Luis Valdez's *La Bamba* (1987). *Top:* Rosana DeSoto and Elizabeth Peña. *Bottom:* Lou Diamond Phillips and Esai Morales. Courtesy of Columbia Pictures.

Cheech Marin gets caught in an immigration raid in the music video "Born in East L.A." From *Cheech and Chong: Get Out of My Room* (1985), directed by Cheech Marin. Courtesy of MCA Home Video.

Scenes from both sides of the border in *Born in East L.A.*
(1987), written and directed by Cheech Marin. Courtesy of
Universal City Studios.

Edward James Olmos as calculus teacher Jaime Escalante in *Stand and Deliver* (1988), written and directed by Ramon Menendez. Courtesy of Warner Brothers.

Scenes from Isaac Artenstein's *Break of Dawn* (1988). *Top:* Oscar Chávez as Pedro J. Gonzalez, Spanish-language radio pioneer. *Bottom:* A "repatriation" or deportation raid in Los Angeles during the 1930s. Courtesy of CineWest Productions (San Diego).

Guillermo Gómez-Peña performs *Border Brujo* (1990), directed by Isaac Artenstein. Courtesy of CineWest Productions (San Diego).

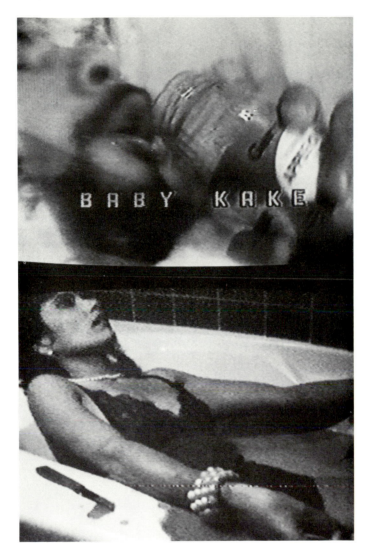

Scenes from two of Harry Gamboa's conceptual dramas on video, performed by other members of the Chicano art group, *Asco. Top: Baby Kake* (1984). *Bottom: Blanx* (1984). Courtesy of Harry Gamboa, Jr.

Scene from Carlos Avila's *Distant Water* (1990), a bittersweet drama about a ten-year-old Chicano who takes a personal stance against the segregated swimming pools of Los Angeles in the 1940s. Courtesy of Carlos Avila.

dimension: to the *ouroboros* circle. In Valdez's movie, more so than in that of Marin, Tijuana is rescued from its stereotype of a "hellhole." Its image of rows of low-life and porno cabarets is shattered in the scene in which "Los Lobos" appear playing "La Bamba." "La Bamba!" exclaims an enraptured Ritchie. This scene is for him an epiphany, because the musical soul of his Mexican cultural roots is revealed to him. Also, Tijuana in its outskirts represents the Mexican Earth, where Ritchie enters into communication with the ancestral wisdom (personified by "El Tata"), which will protect him beyond death.

Another dimension of popular culture appears in these films in connection with the border chronotope: the Carnival. The Carnival is present in the festive side of *La Bamba* and *El Norte,* and plays a main role in *Born in East L.A.* Here, Tijuana becomes the public place of Carnival. Throughout the movie, we hear the music and the laughter and we find the characteristic features of popular and comic culture that Bakhtin outlined in his study of Rabelais: the material and corporeal principle of life, the verbal comic, the attraction of the eccentric, the surprising, the bizarre, profanation, and debasement. . . .

Far from the canned laughter of much of Hollywood productions, the laughter in *Born in East L.A.* points to the tradition of the universal comic popular culture. It is laughter as patrimony of the people: ambivalent, full of joy, but also corrosive and sarcastic, a laughter that, quoting Bakhtin, "denies and affirms, enshrouds and resuscitates."

The moving image that synthesizes the carnivalesque inversion of *Born in East L.A.* appears close to the end of the movie. We see Rudy (Cheech Marin) raising his arms in the manner of an orchestra director or of the universal author. At his signal a whole multitude is set in motion. This uncontainable multitude goes running down the hill, flooding the dividing barrier of the border in their oceanic union, a border that for them doesn't exist in the first place.

To conclude, I could go on analyzing more dimensions of the rich and plural images and voices of an autonomous discourse, rooted in the Indian, Hispanic, and Mestizo cultural and artistic heritage, of these films and other Chicano-Latino movies as well. But I think that the themes and arguments presented in my essay give ample support to my thesis: that of a strong presence in these films of a culture of resistance and affirmation, which subverts the more alienated and repetitive aspect of Hollywood conventions and, at the same time, incorporates some of the elements of popular culture in Hollywood cinema and reinscribes them within the popular and artistic context of Chicano-Latino culture and art.

This dimension is reinforced by the tides that link these movies with Latin American culture and art, especially with its cinemato-graphic expression in the "New Latin American Cinema." The entire first part of *El Norte* relates to themes and images of that cinema, espe-cially to elements of the indigenous cinema of the Bolivian Sanjines. Going beyond cinematic intertextuality, the moving comic and serious image of Marin's film, the one to which I refer above, brings us the strong feeling of oceanic, human solidarity of César Vallejo's poem "Masa" (from his *España, aparta de mí este cáliz*).

Given the prophetic value of art, we don't know to what extent Cheech Marin was aware that with the filming of that image of soli-darity he has already filmed the coming down of the Tijuana Wall, which we may see some day filling the screens of televisions and the pages of the newspapers. And with this hope I end my essay.

Notes

1. Several critics have written on this topic. A comprehensive view is presented in Arthur G. Pettit's book, *Images of the Mexican American in Fiction and Film* (College Station: Texas A&M University Press, 1981), and also in "Presencia del cine chicano," by Jesús Treviño, in *A través de la frontera*, ed. Ida Rodriguez Prampolini (México: UNAM, 1983), 194–201.

2. Robert Stam is the first critic to apply Bakhtin's critical principles to cinema in his *Subversive Pleasures: Bakhtin Cultural Criticism and Film* (Baltimore: Johns Hopkins University Press, 1989).

3. Following Gramsci's idea, we could consider as "organic intellectuals" those intellectuals that every emerging sociohistorical and cultural group segregates from its own body. The early Valdez is, undoubtedly, one of the most representative "organic" intellectuals of the Chicano Movement. In spite of his ideological transformations, his late work preserves the imprint of his early worldview.

4. In an earlier critical review of *La Bamba*, having seen it only once (before its first public showing), I tried to highlight the elements that connected it to the Valdezian worldview, very much influenced by the mythical and symbolical dimension of the ancient Mexicans. See "Luis Valdez. Hollywood y Tezcatlipoca," *Chiricú* 5, no. 2 (1988): 35–39.

I emphasized in that article the destructive elements personified in the figure of Tezcatlipoca, which I related to the entrance of Valdez in the cinematographic industry of Hollywood. Now, following the clamorous reception of the film by Chicano-Latino audiences, I have changed my focus, giving more relevance to the symbol of Quetzalcoatl.

5. "Los actos son muy interesantes, chistosos y representan la realidad de la vida de los campesinos." This quotation from César Chávez heads the book *Actos. El teatro* (San Juan Bautista: Menyah Productions, 1971).

6. Jesús Treviño writes insightful comments about this negative representation in the article mentioned in note 1.

Story Structure in Latino Feature Films

Mario Barrera

Introduction

Story structure is an essential but relatively underemphasized aspect of film analysis. Story structure as used here refers to the various elements that go into a film's plot, and the ways in which these elements are interrelated. Analyzing structure puts the emphasis on film as *drama*. Once we see how the various dramatic elements are related we gain insights into why the story proceeds as it does.

Much too often films are analyzed as if they were simply social or political tracts, intended to reinforce or challenge some aspect of society. Although serious filmmakers do have social themes in mind, the first consideration of a successful screenwriter is whether the story "works" in dramatic terms. If the story does not work dramatically, the film will be a flop, and any social or political themes will not be effectively conveyed.

A great deal of academic film criticism also focuses on the visual aspects of film, understandably so given the nature of the medium. As a result, there is a great deal of discussion of directors, who are responsible for translating the story into visual terms. Within the film industry, however, there is a much greater appreciation of the role of the screenwriter, who initially creates the story. Indeed, it is axiomatic that without a good script there can be no good film.

In recent years a practitioner-oriented literature has developed aimed at teaching how to write good screenplays.[1] The script analysts who have written these works generally proceed by examining successful, "classic" films in order to identify the essential elements that go into making good stories. Different analysts rely on different films, but certain ones come up again and again. Among the most commonly cited American films are *Casablanca, Chinatown, Witness, The Godfather, Butch Cassidy and the Sundance Kid, Kramer vs. Kramer, Midnight Cowboy, Annie Hall, Ordinary People, Rain Man,* and *Tootsie.*[2]

The films chosen for study are not necessarily the biggest box-office blockbusters. Rather, they are films that have been commercially successful and that are also considered successful at evoking strong responses from their audiences. In addition, they are thought of as classics or as likely to become classics, films that will be viewed repeatedly over time.

In identifying a classic story structure, the various analysts have not claimed that all successful films adhere to a single general paradigm. They do claim, however, that the overwhelming majority of successful films do so, and that the exceptions are usually self-conscious deviations by experienced filmmakers.

The advantage of relying on this practitioner-oriented literature in analyzing story structure is that it provides much more of an "insider" perspective than most film theory. The terms and concepts used here are those used by working screenwriters, so that the analytic approach is grounded in the actual creative process.

The procedure I will follow will be to identify key elements that are referred to in the major works. These are elements on which there is a relative consensus, although all writers do not use the exact same terminology. After identifying the key concepts and their interrelationships, I will illustrate their use by referring to seven films about Latinos in the United States. Some of these films are by Latino filmmakers and others are not, but all have been widely discussed in Latino academic circles, and are frequently shown in college classrooms. These seven films have been selected to illustrate variations in the use of classic story structure.

The Elements of Story Structure

The discussion of story structure usually begins with the concept of the *protagonist,* the central character of the story. He or she must have a clearly identified *motivation,* or *desire.* In order to achieve that desire, the protagonist struggles to overcome a series of *obstacles*. The drive by the protagonist to achieve the desire against mounting obstacles provides the *plot* or *spine* of the story.

Generally it is obvious who the protagonist is. In films like *Spartacus* or *Ferris Bueller's Day Off* the protagonist is identified in the title. On the other hand, the protagonist in *Rain Man* is not Raymond, but his brother, Charlie. The protagonist is not necessarily the biggest star or the character who is the most sympathetic—it is the person whose desire drives the plot. Will the protagonist achieve his or her desire? This question, sometimes called the *central* or *seat belt question*, is designed to provide the main dramatic tension in the story. It is supposed to keep the members of the audience glued to their seats until the answer is known. Even if we already know the answer, as in all *Columbo* episodes, we stick around to see *how* the protagonist succeeds, or fails.

A *subplot* is a second story line that unfolds alongside the main plot. It always exists in relation to the plot, and can fulfill a number of functions. It can advance the main story line, or it can add depth to the protagonist or other major characters. The protagonist can be and often is in the subplot, but not necessarily.

Linda Segar refers to the main plot as Plot A. The first subplot she calls Plot B, and notes that it often carries a romantic or other relationship story. Subsequent subplots, if any, are labeled Plot C, Plot D, and so on.[3] In *La Bamba*, discussed below, four distinct subplots can be identified.

One complication with respect to the protagonist and her desire is that motivation can be internal or external. A protagonist's *external desire*, for example, may be to win a race. The *inner motivation* may be to gain a greater sense of self-worth. Outer motivation is always known in a successful film. Inner motivation may or may not be explored. It is also the case that a protagonist's external desire may change during the course of the film.

A further complication is that the protagonist may have an unarticulated *unconscious desire* underlying the conscious motivation. In *Casablanca*, for example, Rick's conscious motivation is to be a tough guy, have power, and make money. But as we learn later, his unconscious desire is to "come back to life" and recapture the love he shared with Ilsa.

Films that explore inner motivation are generally considered "deeper" and more worthy of serious critical consideration. Of the films reviewed in this article, *Zoot Suit* is the one that goes into most depth in exploring the protagonist's psychological dynamics.

Although films do not have the clear demarcations that stage plays achieve by bringing down the curtain, most films are considered to have a *three-act structure*. Roughly speaking, this corresponds to the setup, the development, and the resolution of the story. The transition from one act to the next is provided by events that Syd Field originally called plot points, but are more commonly referred to as *turning points*.

The first act of a feature-length film lasts approximately a half hour. About midway through the first act, what is known as the *inciting incident*, or *catalyst*, occurs. The inciting incident essentially poses the central or seat belt question. It has the effect of upsetting the equilibrium of the protagonist's world, of setting her in motion and getting the story underway. In *Chinatown*, for example, the inciting incident comes when the detective Jake Gittes is hired by a fake Mrs. Mulwray to spy on her husband. In *Kramer vs. Kramer*, it happens when Dustin Hoffman's wife leaves and he must learn how to take care of their son.

The first turning point follows a short time later and marks the transition to act 2. Linda Segar summarizes the nature of a turning point in the following way:

> It turns the action around in a new direction.
>
> It raises the central question again, and makes us wonder about the answer.
>
> It raises the stakes.
>
> It pushes the story into the next act.
>
> It takes us into a new arena and gives us a sense of a different focus for the action.[4]

In *Chinatown*, the first turning point comes when Jake Gittes is confronted by the real Mrs. Mulwray, and finds out that someone has set him up. This turns the story in a new direction.

The second act of the screenplay is almost always the longest, taking up roughly half of the story time. During the second act the story line is developed, and the protagonist is confronted with a series of obstacles to overcome. If it is a good screenplay, the dramatic tension

rises as the obstacles become progressively more difficult and the outcome of the central question is thrown into doubt. Often a *crisis* confronts the protagonist, and a choice that reveals something about his
character must be made. The end of the second act is signaled by the
second turning point, which provides a fresh twist to the story line
and propels us into the final act.

The third act is generally about a half hour long, although it can be
shorter. In this act we have the climax to the story, where the dramatic
tension comes to a head and we find the answer to the question posed
in the inciting incident. Because the inciting incident and the climax
are necessarily tied together, the climax is sometimes referred to as the
obligatory scene. After the climax there is usually a brief *resolution*
(denouement), where loose ends are tied up and the story is brought
to a close.

Within each of the three acts the structure is further broken down
into *scenes*, each one representing an action that takes place at a particular time and location. The scenes often occur in interrelated clusters
that are called *sequences*.

As can be seen from the discussion to this point, the structure of a
film story is integrally related to the nature of the protagonist and his
motivation. In addition, it is tied to a particular *theme* the writer has in
mind. The theme is also referred to as the *premise* or *controlling idea*.
Michael Hauge describes theme in the following passage, differentiating it from message:

> By *theme* in a screenplay, I mean the universal statement the screen-
> play makes about the human condition. This is a level of meaning that
> goes beyond the plot of the film and applies to life in general. The
> theme is an idea that any member of the audience can apply to her
> own life, whether or not she's been in a similar situation. The theme
> gives the audience "words to live by."[5]

Theme is not the same as the "message" of a movie. The *message* is a
more political statement that connects directly to the plot, but it has no
obvious application to the average person's own actions. Themes,
then, are commonly found in films, and are almost always present in
films that are considered classic. Messages are more uncommon
because they do not strike the same sort of universal resonance in
audiences. Still, many classic films embody strong messages, such as
Silkwood, Missing, and *The China Syndrome*. Hauge goes on to note:

There can also be deeper levels of meaning beyond the theme and message of a screenplay: myth, symbol, allegory, and archetype. *Stand by Me* . . . develops a theme of recognizing one's own gifts and pursuing them regardless of others' opinions or approval. But beneath that, it explores the terrifying but necessary death of one's childhood in order to realize one's own gifts. And beneath that allegorical level, the film is a quest story, a Holy Grail myth portraying the journey from childhood to maturity, power, and individuation.[6]

Among U.S. Latino filmmakers, Luis Valdez (*Zoot Suit*) and Gregory Nava (*El Norte*) have sought to combine theme, message, and myth in their films.

Themes are related to story structure through the protagonist and other major characters. Screenwriters will set forth their themes through their choice of protagonists' motivations and choices. The internal dynamics of the characters are generally closely tied in with the central theme, and whether or not the protagonist achieves her goal will generally depend on the particular thematic point that the writer wishes to make. All of this will be illustrated through the films analyzed below.

Latino Films and Story Structure

Straightforward Story Structure: Stand and Deliver

Stand and Deliver (1988; directed by Ramon Menendez; written by Ramon Menendez and Tom Musca) is a drama based on the true story of math teacher Jaime Escalante at Garfield High School in Los Angeles. Escalante, played by Edward James Olmos, quits his job in private industry because he wants to teach Latino kids. Although facing initial resistance in this *barrio* setting, he wins the confidence of the students through his dynamic teaching methods. Despite skepticism from his fellow teachers, he inaugurates a calculus class designed to prepare students for the Advanced Placement test that will give them college credit. Eighteen students survive the rigorous training schedule and successfully pass the test, only to come under suspicion of cheating from the Educational Testing Service examiners who administer the exam. The students agree to retake the test, and all pass again, vindicating Escalante and themselves. They have stood and delivered.

This film is a good one to start with because it is an uncomplicated example of the classic paradigm. There is one clearly identified protagonist, Escalante, and he has a straightforward desire, which drives the story: that of making a difference through teaching *barrio* students. The inciting incident comes early, when he starts to teach and is directed to a math class, although his initial assignment had been to teach computer science. The first turning point comes when he inaugurates the calculus class. During the second act a number of obstacles surface, which need to be overcome: student resistance, unsympathetic parents, and Escalante's heart attack. The second turning point comes when the students pass the initial exam and are accused of cheating. For a while it looks as if the protagonist has failed to attain his desire, but the students themselves restore his drive by expressing their confidence in him. The climax comes when they take the exam again, triumphing against all odds. In the brief resolution, statistics flash on the screen showing the continued success of Garfield students on the Advanced Placement exam in subsequent years.

The protagonist's inner motivation is not explored in the film, and he does not undergo a transformation during the course of the story. He begins idealistic and ends idealistic, having been proved right. There are no subplots. We see little vignettes about various students' lives outside the classroom, but none is sufficiently developed to qualify as a subplot. The turning points, climax, and resolution all come just about where one would expect them. All in all, then, we have here a good example of classic story structure that works well and results in a successful, received film.

This film also illustrates the difference between theme and message. The theme has to do with believing in yourself and succeeding against odds through determination. The message, on the other hand, is that institutionalized racism continues to exist and must be taken into account by non-Whites attempting to improve their lot.

Use of Subplots: **The Milagro Beanfield War**

In *The Milagro Beanfield War* (1987; directed by Robert Redford; written by David Ward and John Nichols; based on John Nichols's 1974 novel) Joe Mondragon is an intermittently employed worker and handyman in a small northern New Mexico town called Milagro. He is turned down for work at the Ladd Devine land development company,

which dominates the economy of the area and has taken over much of
the land and water rights that used to belong to the region's small
farmers. Without meaning to, Joe taps into the Devine company irri-
gation canal that runs by his uncultivated beanfield, and then decides
to go with the flow. Word soon spreads throughout the area. The local
sheriff refuses to act for fear of stirring up the local people, who are
sympathetic to Joe because of resentment toward the encroachments
of the Devine company. Concern reaches all the way to the New
Mexico governor, who dispatches an agent to take care of business.

The second act consists of a long series of moves and countermoves, with Joe and his town supporters on one side and the Ladd
Devine company, the governor's office, and the Forest Service on the
other. The outcome is still in question when Joe shoots the pet pig of
his neighbor Amarante Cordova after finding the pig eating his bean
plants. Amarante comes out with his six-gun blazing and Joe is forced
to shoot him too, and then flees to the mountains. Joe eventually
returns, and he and the townspeople face down the forces of law and
order and gain a victory. In the postclimax resolution, Amarante
Cordova, who has survived Joe's bullet, dies of old age and is led off
by an old man spirit figure who haunts the town and the film.

This film also follows the classic paradigm in its main plot. The
catalyst consists of Joe's starting to water his field, and the first turning point comes when the forces of Ladd Devine and the governor
coalesce and come after Joe. The second turning point is clearly when
Joe shoots Amarante and his pig, and the climax is the final confrontation in the beanfield. The resolution is described above.

In this film, however, we also have two subplots to complicate the
story line. One has to do with the relationship between Ruby
Archuleta, a shop owner, and Charlie Bloom, a lawyer and publisher
of a local newspaper. As she badgers him into writing about Joe
Mondragon's struggle and then representing him legally, a relationship develops between them. By the end of the film they're out irrigat-
ing Joe's field together.

A second subplot deals with the friendship that develops between
Amarante Cordova and an inept graduate student named Herbie. All
true subplots have the same essential structure as the main plot. Here
we see the inciting incident where Herbie comes to town and is disori-
ented. The first turning point finds Herbie interviewing Amarante

Cordova. The subplot develops as Cordova becomes Herbie's guide to the area. The second turning point is when Amarante is shot, and Herbie is thrown into crisis. The climax consists of Amarante recovering from the gunshot and deciding not to prosecute Joe, and the resolution has to do with Amarante's death. As with the main plot, you have setup, development, and resolution.

The Shadow Protagonist: La Bamba

Like *Stand and Deliver*, *La Bamba* (1987; written and directed by Luis Valdez) is based on a true life story. Here the protagonist is Ritchie Valens, whose meteoric rock music career was cut short in 1959 at age seventeen by an airplane accident.

Making a film based on a real historical character presents special problems, particularly if the time is recent. Most people's lives don't fit a neat Hollywood script formula, and there is only so much fictionalization one can get away with if the character's friends and relatives are still kicking around. Making a film based on Ritchie Valens presented an additional problem in that his life was very short. Valdez solved his story problems in part by building a complex subplot structure into the film. I have been able to identify four distinct subplots in *La Bamba*, two involving Ritchie and two that revolve around his older brother Bob.

The story begins with brother Bob on his big motorcycle, riding into a migrant labor camp where Ritchie, their mother Connie, and the other kids are working. Bob offers Connie money to move into the city. She accepts it reluctantly, fearing it is drug money. Bob almost immediately gets it on with Ritchie's virginal girlfriend, Rosie, who becomes Bob's girlfriend when they all move to Pacoima, in the San Fernando Valley. (This whole sequence is fictionalized.)

At Pacoima High School Ritchie develops a crush on a blonde valley girl, Donna, later the subject of one of his hit songs. They begin to date innocently, although her racist father disapproves of Ritchie ("What is he—Eyetalian?"). Already a hot guitarist, Ritchie quickly joins a local garage band and is eventually discovered by a small-time music producer, Bob Keene. Keene supervises Ritchie's first recordings, and persuades him to Anglicize his name, which was originally Richard Valenzuela.

In the meantime, Bob is involved in shady activities and making a mess of his relationship with Rosie. She is pregnant and he is running around and generally acting irresponsible in a colorful, *macho* sort of way. He persuades Ritchie to run off to Tijuana, where Ritchie ostensibly hears a Mexican band (portrayed by Los Lobos) playing the traditional wedding song "La Bamba." Ritchie wakes up the next morning in the shack of a *brujo* (shaman), whom Bob introduces as his Mexican guru. (This is also fictional.) The *brujo* gives Ritchie a talisman necklace to protect him. When they return home Rosie has had a baby girl.

Ritchie's romance with Donna sputters along while his career takes off. Before long he's performing on the East Coast, traveling by airplane although he's had premonitions of dying in a plane crash. On one of his visits back home he and Bob get into a fight, and Bob rips off Ritchie's magic necklace. Shortly after that Ritchie is killed in the crash of a small airplane in the Midwest. In a short denouement we see the reaction of Connie, Donna, and Bob. There is a brief repeat of an early scene, where Ritchie scrambles up a hill with Bob running along behind him.

Luis Valdez is a supreme dramatist, and he apparently realized early on that there wasn't much drama in Ritchie's life, apart from his premature death. Valens's success came early and fairly easily, so there wasn't much there in terms of dramatic tension. His relationship with Donna is detailed in a distinct subplot, but apart from her father's opposition there wasn't much there either. Valdez solved this problem by turning to Bob's story, which is contained in three subplots. In fact, Bob's story is so important to the movie that I would argue that he constitutes a *shadow protagonist*.

As shadow protagonist, Bob has his own story line, which is not as central to the film as Ritchie's but is a complete plot in itself. The inciting incident for his story comes when he is working as a garbageman and finds some discarded animation panels in a movie studio's lot. The discovery stimulates his already-existing interest in drawing. The first turning point comes when he enters an art contest, and the second when he wins it, at about the same time that Ritchie gets his first recording contract. The climax comes when he rips up his artwork in disgust after he fails to get support from Rosie and other family members, and realizes that he will always play second fiddle to Ritchie. Luis Valdez has commented on the Ritchie-Bob contrast:

Ritchie represents the spirit of the fifties, the dream of everyman being able to cry out from his guts and rise to the top. His half-brother Bob was riddled with insecurity and he couldn't free himself to pursue his dreams—he was all caught up in self-doubt.[7]

Bob is a more interesting dramatic character than Ritchie because he is more conflicted. In addition to having his own plot line, he is involved in a major subplot depicting his relationship with Ritchie. Valdez comments:

The problem is that Ritchie had been dead for thirty years, and he was a cherished memory. Nobody wanted to say anything bad about him . . . "Yeah, he was a nice guy, nicest guy who ever lived." I kept asking, C'mon, didn't he ever do anything wrong, he must have been human? . . . I wanted to know, Did he ever get laid, did he do drugs, how was he human? I was getting nowhere. It was all *nada*, until I talked to his half-brother, Bob. He was reluctant, but he did tell me they'd fought, and that it was Bob's own fault. So I thought, well, at least there's a foundation, then, a relationship between brothers. And the real-life conflict between them, and Bob's conflict with realizing that the man who raised him and Ritchie was not Bob's biological father.[8]

This subplot begins with Bob's being reunited with the family and coming into contact with Ritchie again. They hit it off well at first, but then Bob takes Ritchie's sort-of-girlfriend away. In the rest of the film the relationship between the two half-brothers is stormy. Bob both helps and hurts Ritchie's striving. In the climactic physical fight between them, he rips off Ritchie's necklace, symbolically killing him. Right before the end it appears as if there is to be a reconciliation, but it is cut short by Ritchie's death.

The remaining subplot has to do with the relationship between Bob and Rosie. Briefly, it consists of their meeting and moving in together, their fighting, Rosie's pregnancy, and the birth of their daughter. At the very end Bob has given up drinking and has become a good father. Interestingly enough, he is the one who goes through a major character transformation, not Ritchie. His feelings of anger about being the less-favored brother give him much more of a psychological dimension than Ritchie. The reason for considering him a shadow protagonist is that he actually performs many of the dramatic functions that are normally reserved for the protagonist.

Dual Protagonists: **Salt of the Earth**

Of the films reviewed in this essay, *Salt of the Earth* (1954; directed by Herbert Biberman; written by Michael Wilson) is the best example of a message-driven film. That it manages to convey a complex political message and maintain dramatic tension throughout is a tribute to the skill of the writer, Michael Wilson.

This film was made by a group of professional filmmakers who had been blacklisted in Hollywood during the McCarthy era. It is based on a real strike that was carried out in New Mexico from 1950 to 1952 by the International Union of Mine, Mill and Smelter Workers.[9] In the process of writing the script, Michael Wilson consulted extensively with people who had been actively involved in the strike. A number of those participants played important roles in the film.

The point of view that the film reflects is that of Esperanza Quintero, wife of one of the Mexican American millers. The film begins with some background exposition, using her as narrator. The inciting incident is foreshadowed by a near-accident in the mine involving Ramon Quintero and a confrontation between the workers and management over safety rules. When Ramon arrives at home he argues with Esperanza. She is upset that the union is not including issues that the miners' wives consider important in the negotiations then under way with the mine owners. It is clear that their marriage is seriously strained. In this and other conversations we learn that the Anglo miners have certain privileges that the Mexican American miners do not, such as indoor plumbing and hot water in their living quarters.

The main story plot is kicked off with a mine injury caused by an explosion. The miners' union calls a strike over safety issues, and the local sheriff's office cooperates with the mine owners to harass the strikers. The first turning point comes when the company gets an injunction against the picketing, and the miners' wives take over the picket line over the opposition of a number of the miners, including Ramon. Esperanza gradually becomes an activist, despite Ramon. Ramon is left to take over Esperanza's chores, including looking after their new baby. In the process his consciousness about the wives' issues begins to change.

After a series of moves and countermoves by the strikers and the owners, Esperanza and Ramon have a major fight in which she

berates him and the other men for holding the women in a subordinate position: "Have you learned nothing from this strike? Why are
you afraid to have me at your side? Do you still think you can have
dignity only if I have none?" Ramon and some of the other men take
off on a hunting trip, but Esperanza's words finally get through to
Ramon. He brings the men back just in time for a climactic showdown
when the sheriff's deputies try to evict the miners from the company
housing. The company backs down—"for the present." Esperanza
provides the denouement with a short soliloquy about having won a
victory they would pass on to their children.

The theme of this film I would characterize as the idea that the
struggle for equality is indivisible, and extends into our daily lives.
The messages are that the United States is a society characterized by
unequal divisions based on class, gender, and ethnicity. In order to
present these ideas in a dramatic fashion, the writer developed an
intricate structure involving two tightly interlocking plot lines, each
with its own protagonist.

The A plot in this case is that of the workers' struggle with the
mine owners. The events in this plot essentially propel the overall
story forward. The repercussions of those events drive the story line of
the B plot, which is that of the relationship between Esperanza and
Ramon. The protagonist of the A plot is Ramon—he precipitates the
strike and is the strike leader. It is his decision to return from the
hunting trip that leads to the solution presented in the climax.

The protagonist of the B plot is Esperanza. The novelty of this
script is that it makes the point of view of the film that of the B plot's
protagonist, essentially creating two equal protagonists. Each has a
strong motivation: Ramon to win the strike and get greater class/eth-
nic equality; Esperanza to win the strike and in the process gain
greater gender equality. Each goes through a profound personal transformation. Ramon learns that he has been a pigheaded sexist, and
Esperanza learns that she can be a strong leader and activist in her
own right. The use of dual protagonists is unusual and innovative,
although not unique. West Side Story also makes use of this structural
device.

For the sake of clarification, the B plot structure is as follows. The
inciting incident is the initial argument between Ramon and
Esperanza. At the first turning point Esperanza becomes an activist.
She takes over picket duty and Ramon takes over the household

chores. This, of course, happens as a result of what is taking place in the A plot. The second turning point comes when Esperanza confronts Ramon, although it is not immediately clear that it is a turning point. The climax comes when Ramon gets the message and turns back from his hunting trip.

This film has at times been criticized for melodramatic scenes and its use of some nonprofessional actors, but my experience in showing it in the classroom is that it invariably provokes a strong emotional response from its viewers. Its success as a film stems in large part from the writer's successful solution to the structural problems presented by the complex plot. It was never released commercially in the United States because of a well-financed red-baiting campaign organized against it.[10]

The Mythic Level: El Norte

Unlike most of the other films described here, *El Norte* (1984; written and directed by Gregory Nava) is not based on specific historical characters or on a preexisting novel or play. It is an original screenplay that tells the story of a Guatemalan Mayan brother and sister forced to migrate to the United States by circumstances in their native land.

The story begins in a remote mountain village where the Indian people are compelled to labor on plantations owned by large corporations. The two central characters are Enrique and Rosa, young adults still living at home. Their father is killed by government soldiers while meeting clandestinely with other *campesinos* to plot an armed struggle against their oppressors. Their mother is "disappeared" in the ensuing crackdown, and it is clear that a similar fate awaits Rosa and Enrique. Enrique decides to migrate north, and Rosa goes with him.

The two travel through Mexico by bus and arrive in Tijuana to search for a contact who can help them across the border. Before they find him they have a misadventure with a "coyote" who promises to get them across the border illegally but tries to rob them instead. Eventually they make their contact and cross the border through a long abandoned tunnel that their benefactor knows. From there they make their way to Los Angeles.

Once in L.A. they are set up in a dilapidated hut by a Chicano ("Don Mocte") who also doubles as a labor agent. Don Mocte gets Rosa a job in a textile sweatshop. Enrique starts work as a busboy in a fancy restaurant. Both enroll in English classes. Rosa is forced to change jobs after a raid by immigration agents ("la migra") at the sweatshop. With the aid of a savvy undocumented Mexican immigrant woman named Nacha, Rosa is able to avoid the agents. Nacha finds them both jobs as housemaids for a wealthy employer. Enrique is promoted to assistant waiter, so things seem to be going all right for them, until Enrique is turned in to "la migra" by a disgruntled Chicano employee who wants his job. Enrique evades the agents but loses his job.

At the same time Rosa comes down with an infection brought on by rat bites suffered during their tunnel crossing, and she is hospitalized. Enrique is compelled to choose between staying at her side or going to Chicago with an employer who has promised him a foreman job and the possibility of legalization. He remains by her side but Rosa dies. At the end of the film Enrique has gone to work as a laborer on a construction crew, trapped at the bottom of the social order as his father was in Guatemala.

El Norte is an unusually long film, some two hours and twenty minutes in length, as contrasted with the usual feature film's ninety to a hundred minutes. The filmmaker, Gregory Nava, conceives of the structure of the film as divided into four acts.[11] The first section is set off with a title, "Arturo Xuncax," after the name of the father. The second part, labeled "El Coyote," consists of their journey through Mexico. The third titled division of the film corresponds to Enrique and Rosa's experiences in the United States. Nava considers that this last section actually consists of two parts, with the dividing line coming when Enrique is turned in to the INS by his coworker. From that point on everything is downhill.

The author of this screenplay thus sees the structure of the film as consisting of an unorthodox four acts. Some script analysts would disagree with him on that point, arguing that part 2 and the first half of part 3 constitute one dramatic unit, so that there really is a three-act structure. In either case, it is clear that the dramatic act structure of the story does not correspond to the three titled divisions of the film.

El Norte is one of those films that is able to operate at all three levels of theme, message, and myth. The theme of the film has to do with the value of maintaining the integrity of one's communal, family ties in the face of material, individualistic incentives. That is the choice Enrique confronts at the film's climax. The message deals with the exploitative nature of commercial enterprises and their devastating consequences for authentic communities such as those of the Mayan villages. Indeed, Nava was motivated to make this film after witnessing firsthand the deplorable conditions of Mayan immigrants in the Los Angeles area.[12]

What lifts this film above the ordinary and gives it its extraordinary lyrical quality, however, is its connection to myth. The story of Enrique and Rosa, and much of the symbolism in the film, comes from the creation myth of the Maya, the Popol Vuh, and other Mayan texts. As in the Popol Vuh, there are twin heroes who must undergo a series of trials and tests before reaching their goal. The twin heroes represent an inherently dualistic concept of the universe. Throughout the film there are dreams and elements of magical realism that are inspired directly by Mayan symbolism. Even though Nava realized that most of his audience would not be familiar with the Mayan texts, he felt that drawing his imagery from them would give the story a mythic depth that would strike universal chords and create strong emotional reactions in the film's viewers. From my experience in using the film in the classroom, he succeeded.

The Inner Story: Zoot Suit

Of the films reviewed here, *Zoot Suit* (1982; written and directed by Luis Valdez; based on his play) is the one that most develops the inner story of the protagonist. Indeed, the whole film is structured around his internal struggle.

Zoot Suit is based on two historical incidents that took place in the 1940s in Los Angeles. One was the 1942 Sleepy Lagoon murder case, in which seventeen young Chicanos were convicted of the murder of another Chicano. Twelve were sentenced to life in prison, although their convictions were later overturned. The other historical reference is to the 1943 "Zoot Suit Riots," in which American servicemen roamed the *barrios* of L.A., beating up Chicanos who were dressed in the stylized zoot suits then in fashion among young urban *barrio* men.

The film itself is highly stylized. The settings were all filmed inside a theater, and we even see the audience from time to time. There are numerous flashbacks and musical interludes during the course of the film, and there is a central character—El Pachuco—who represents an aspect of the protagonist's personality, and can only be seen by him.

El Pachuco carries on a running dialogue with the protagonist, Henry Reyna, and with the audience. He dictates the pace of the film by snapping his fingers to change scenes.

At the beginning of the film Henry Reyna, leader of the 38th Street Gang, is set to join the navy. He and his girlfriend Della are out celebrating the night before his induction, but Henry is beaten up by a rival gang. Later that evening he and his gang go looking for revenge. Unable to find the other gang, they crash a party in the Sleepy Lagoon area. A fight ensues, and a Chicano youth is killed. Henry and a number of his friends end up in jail charged with murder.

Henry is assigned a sympathetic Anglo lawyer, but the racist and almost hysterically anti-pachuco (zoot-suiter) climate of opinion makes a mockery of the proceedings. (Valdez incorporated sections of the court proceedings verbatim into the script.) During the lengthy appeal process, Henry becomes romantically attracted to Alice Bloomfield, a leftist labor activist assigned to drum up support for his cause. She, however, is married to her work and rejects him.

During this time the Zoot Suit Riots break out, and Henry's brother is among those beaten up. Valdez uses the occasion to point up the cynical, rabble-rousing reporting of the mainstream press, especially the Hearst papers.

Eventually the murder conviction is overturned, and Henry is reunited with his girlfriend. Valdez concludes the story by offering us three possible resolutions: (1) Henry was later sent back to jail for another crime; (2) Henry was killed in the Korea conflict after winning a medal; or (3) Henry married Della and had three kids who went to college and called themselves Chicanos.

Aside from the stylization and multiple resolutions, the most striking aspect of the film is the use of the Pachuco character, who is inextricably linked to the struggle going on inside Henry's mind. We get a good sense of this in Valdez's own words, in a lengthy interview he granted Roberta Orona-Cordova in 1982.

> VALDEZ: I call the Pachuco the internal authority. I know he's been called "conscience," he's been called alter-ego, but he is not so much alter-ego as he is super-ego because super-ego is your conscience that tells you what's right and what's wrong . . .
>
> Henry's story is being observed by the Pachuco most of the time, but occasionally you get Henry's point of view of the Pachuco, and

that's the crux of the story. It's obviously Henry's struggle with himself . . .

. . . as the character in the film, El Pachuco is always getting in
the way of things that Henry's trying to do: his relationship with Della
for one, his relationship with Alice, another, and his relationship with
his family . . . the Pachuco is also goading Henry into a greater level
of self-consciousness . . . At the same time that he represents those
real-life Pachucos, he represents the essence of what Pachuquismo is
all about, which is this struggle for identity. . . .

Henry was in prison and in solitary confinement because of choices that he made, for good or for bad, and that is really the beginning of
his liberation, of his way out. So long as he kept blaming the exterior,
the deeper he was going to be driven into himself. . . . Once you are
left alone and you have to think it through, you are either going to survive or you are not going to survive . . . You have to have a reason
for finding yourself in a tough situation. That's Henry's problem, and
he makes it. He makes it because he comes to terms with himself.

INTERVIEWER: Are you saying the resolution was an internal one, with
himself?

VALDEZ: That's right. Also he is able to get to the point where he hopes
once again . . . I want people to feel that Hank had a greater degree
of self-awareness coming out of prison. The Pachuco is in white and
then we see the three different endings that Henry sees as well . . .
He is much more aware of himself, he is much more aware he has
three choices. All of this, of course, is implied; it's all implicit; it's all
symbolic, but it's there. . . .

The internal authority that is at work is necessary in the psychological process of individuation that we all undergo. Every one of us,
as human beings, undergoes a process whereby we define ourselves as
individuals in life. We do it according to our own personal struggles.
The whole Sleepy Lagoon case is told in *Zoot Suit* in terms of the personal struggle of Henry Reyna. There isn't a single social event that in
some way you cannot define in personal terms, in the personal terms
of the individual involved, because there is always an inside personal
life, and an external social life in any event.[13]

In the same interview, Valdez puts the Pachuco figure in a mythical
context by presenting him as an archetypal rebel with Native
American roots.

I like to use the word myth . . . because myth refers to an underlying structure of a truth that is just below the surface of reality. . . .

Revolutionaries are very frightening, prophets are frightening,
people that have a certain kind of hidden power scare other people.
They are intimidating; there was a lot of that in the Pachuco. But those

in the know cannot fail to recognize him (in the film) as a reincarnation of the ancient god Texcatlipoca. His style, his colors, his powers are all attributes of ancient wisdom . . . El Pachuco is thus a symbol of our identity, our total identity, with ancient roots.[14]

Luis Valdez has thus created in *Zoot Suit* an amazingly complex tapestry that interweaves two historical events, a courtroom drama, two love stories, several musical numbers, political messages, multiple resolutions, and myth. But the core of the story, the element that makes it all hang together, is the inner transformation of the protagonist, his journey toward self-awareness.

Structural Problems: Alambrista

So many factors affect the commercial success or failure of a film that it is impossible to know with any degree of certainty how much influence any one of them has. *Alambrista* (1979; written and directed by Robert Young), the first feature film to deal seriously with the question of undocumented immigration from Mexico, has a number of excellent qualities. It is well acted, and it captures the gritty "feel" of the U.S.-Mexico border as perhaps no other film has. There are a number of memorable scenes, some touching, some funny. Despite this, the film was not commercially viable, and is now all but unavailable. Part of this may have had to do with the fact that the film did not have a "name" actor, or that there is extensive use of Spanish, although this was also true of *El Norte*. It is difficult to escape the conclusion, however, that part of the problem had to do with the structure of the story.

The film begins in Mexico, where a young farmer named Roberto Ramirez has just become a new father. Since his now-expanded family needs the money, he decides to seek work in the north. His mother urges him not to go, and we learn that Roberto's father went north many years ago and never returned.

Roberto makes his way to a border town, and crosses over at night with a group that is caught by the border patrol. He escapes and finds field work in Southern California, but is cheated out of his wages and moves on. At another job he meets "Joe," an undocumented Mexican worker who knows his way around (played beautifully by the late Trinidad Silva, "Don Mocte" in *El Norte*). Joe instructs Roberto in how to act in restaurants, and even how to pick up American waitresses. "But I'm married," protests Roberto. So what, answers Joe—this is the United States. Roberto hooks up with Joe, and they head farther north, riding the rails. Along the way Joe disappears, apparently having fallen off the boards they were riding under the train.

At his next workplace an exhausted Roberto passes out on a sidewalk, and is taken in by a blonde waitress named Karen, who nurses him back to health. In a great scene he attends a fundamentalist Protestant church service with her, looking on wide-eyed. Despite the language barrier between Roberto and Karen, they become romantically involved after she invites herself into his bed. Their developing relationship is cut short when "la migra" raids a dance bar and captures Roberto.

Back on the Mexican side of the border, Roberto and others are recruited to cross over again to break a field strike in Colorado. Exhausted from the arduous journey, Roberto nearly goes berserk upon arriving. His first day at work another worker dies right in the fields, and Roberto discovers that it is his father, Alberto Ramirez. Going through his effects, Roberto finds that his father had another family in the United States. The next day he heads back to Mexico. At the border station he passes a Mexican woman who has just given birth on the U.S. side. "Thank God," she exclaims, "he won't need papers!" Roberto walks on by to Mexico.

From a structural standpoint, *Alambrista* starts off conventionally with a standard setup and inciting incident, and a turning point when Roberto decides to head north. After that, however, there is a long second act in which Roberto's difficulties are shown. There is nothing resembling a second turning point, unless one wants to think about his breakdown as such. This comes close to the end of the film, practically at the same time as the climax, when Roberto's father dies.

The major structural problem, however, is with the subplots. There appear to be two subplots, one being the relationship between Roberto and Joe and the other between Roberto and Karen. In each case interesting characters are introduced and something seems to be developing, and then there is a sharp truncation before there is any resolution. In both cases there is a feeling of incompleteness. It may be that Robert Young was trying by this device to convey a sense of the unpredictability and lack of control that characterize the life of the undocumented worker, but my own subjective feeling was that there was something wrong with the story. I half expected Joe and Karen to reappear somewhere down the line, but they never did.

A third problem has to do with the passivity of the protagonist. It is generally recognized that in successful films the protagonist must act and not just react. Roberto is portrayed as sympathetic and resourceful, but he spends most of his time reacting to his situation. The sense of a passive protagonist is reinforced by the fact that he has very little to say throughout the film.

Conclusion: Protagonists, Themes, and Messages

The purpose of this essay has been to show how the concept of story structure can be used to analyze films about Latinos in the United States. Although there are still relatively few feature films about Latinos, there is a fair amount of structural variation in those films that do exist. In concluding, I want to make a few observations about protagonists, themes, and messages.

One of the more obvious points is that all of the films described here have male protagonists. The only one that has a female protagonist (*Salt of the Earth*) also has a male protagonist. Gregory Nava considers that *El Norte* has dual protagonists in Rosa and Enrique,[15] but my feeling is that Enrique is really the protagonist here. He is the one who makes the decision to go north, which provides the first turning point for the story. At the climax of the film he is the one who makes the key decision again, to stay rather than to leave. Rosa is a central character, but in dramatic terms not a protagonist to the same degree that Esperanza is in *Salt of the Earth*.

The overwhelming preponderance of male protagonists is undoubtedly tied to the sheer numerical dominance of men among writers, directors, and producers. All of the stories looked at here were written and directed by men. The only female producer of any of these films was Anna Thomas for *El Norte*.

One of the key aspects involving protagonists is whether their inner story is developed, and whether they undergo a process of transformation during the course of the film. Of these seven films, the only ones that focus on the inner story of the protagonist are *Zoot Suit* and *Salt of the Earth*. In *La Bamba* there is little development of the inner story of the protagonist, Ritchie, but there is of the "shadow protagonist," Bob.

In terms of themes, most of the films touch on the values of courage and determination in achieving one's goals. A second major theme has to do with affirming family and communal values (especially in *Alambrista*, *La Bamba*, and *The Milagro Beanfield War*). *Zoot Suit* and *El Norte* also have a great deal to say about the value of defending and maintaining one's ethnic identity. These seem to be the three major themes in these films.

As far as political messages are concerned, only *Salt of the Earth* focuses on the unequal role of woman in society. A more common message has to do with the persistence of racist attitudes in American society (*Stand and Deliver*, *La Bamba*, and *Zoot Suit*). A surprisingly large proportion of the films include messages about ethnic exploitation specifically tied to economic interests, an uncommon theme in mainstream American films. This type of message can be clearly seen in *El Norte*, *Alambrista*, *Salt of the Earth*, *The Milagro Beanfield War*, and *Zoot Suit*.

Notes

1. The most influential book of this type in recent years has been Syd Field's *Screenplay* (New York: Dell, 1979). Other important works include Linda Segar, *Making a Good Script Great* (Hollywood: Samuel French, 1987); Michael Hauge, *Writing Screenplays That Sell* (New York: McGraw-Hill, 1988); and Viki King, *How to Write a Movie in 21 Days* (New York: Harper & Row, 1988). A number of other script analysts do not have books out, but popularize their concepts through workshops and videotapes (John Truby, Robert McKee, Tom Schlesinger, Matt Keener and Corey Mandell, Ken Valentine, and others).

This work in turn is part of an older tradition of analyzing drama that includes Lajos Egri, *The Art of Dramatic Writing* (New York: Simon and Schuster, 1946), and extends all the way back to Aristotle's *Poetics*. There is also a parallel in this writing to the classic analysis of folktales in Vladimir Propp's *Morphology of the Folktale* (Austin: University of Texas Press, 1968).

2. Other films often cited in the literature include *Citizen Kane*, *The African Queen*, *Apocalypse Now*, *High Noon*, *The Graduate*, *Body Heat*, *Bonnie and Clyde*, *The Deerhunter*, *Star Wars*, and *Three Days of the Condor*. Interestingly, there is not a single film with a nonwhite protagonist included in this list.

3. Linda Segar, *Making a Good Script Great*, 26ff.

4. Ibid., 16.

5. Michael Hauge, *Writing Screenplays That Sell*, 31.

6. Ibid., 80.

7. Jim Gladstone, "*La Bamba*: Valdez, Valens and the American Dream," *Calendar Magazine*, August 1987.

8. Ken Kelley, "Luis Valdez: The Interview," *San Francisco Focus* (September 1987): 104-5.

9. For a comprehensive discussion of the making of the film, see Michael Wilson and Deborah Rosenfelt, *Salt of the Earth* (Old Westbury, N.Y.: Feminist Press, 1978). See also Deborah Rosenfelt, "Ideology and Structure in *Salt of the Earth*," *Jump Cut* 12/13 (1976): 19-22.

10. This campaign is described in detail in Wilson and Rosenfelt's *Salt of the Earth*.

11. Interview with Gregory Nava, September 29, 1990.

12. Ibid.

13. Roberta Orona-Cordova, "*Zoot Suit* and the Pachuco Phenomenon: An Interview with Luis Valdez," *Revista Chicano-Riquena* 11 (1983): 98, 100, 101, 102, 107, 108.

14. Ibid., 98, 100.

15. Interview with Gregory Nava, cited in note 11.

Crossover: Hispanic Specialty Films in the U.S. Movie Marketplace

David Rosen

Introduction

The 1980s will long be remembered as the "golden age" of American independent filmmaking, particularly for "specialty" or art films. Not only were more independent films produced during the decade than ever before, but many achieved such critical and financial success that they helped launch the careers of many of today's most noted actors, directors, producers, and writers. Such established talents as Edward James Olmos, John Sayles, Moctesuma Esparza, Spike Lee, and Susan Seidelman, to name but a few, built their professional careers during the 1980s.[1]

This chapter examines the performance of three of the most important independent films of the decade: *The Ballad of Gregorio Cortez, El Norte,* and *Stand and Deliver.* All these have been recognized as invaluable Hispanic films, speaking about and to a sizable U.S. "minority" that all too often has gone unrecognized and unappreciated by the dominant Hollywood movie studios. But equally important, and equally unrecognized, each of these films is a labor of love, a testament to the vision and dedication of the filmmakers who made them. Each film is an example of how entrepreneurial creativity and perseverance combined in the filmmaker's marketing efforts to ensure that the film found a committed audience and achieved relative commercial success.

"Specialty" films—and they are "films," not movies, or flicks—are like all motion pictures in that they are by definition feature length (75

minutes or longer) and are intended to have a life in theatrical distribution. Such films are most often produced and distributed outside the
Hollywood system, however, thus permitting the filmmakers to maintain essentially complete control over their projects. This is critical to
ensure that the filmmaker's unique aesthetic vision or point of view is
not lost to the cutting-room floor.

Specialty films are usually characterized as "low-budget" productions, costing between $3 to $5 million as compared to today's standards for studio films, which average $20 million. They can include
both documentary and narrative productions. But perhaps most
important, specialty films can be distinguished from low-budget,
independent genre flicks (e.g., horror, action/adventure, pornograph-
ic) by their common humanism: they are not racist, sexist, or exploitative, and they don't rely on gratuitous violence.

Like all movies and many other works of popular culture, specialty films are first and foremost the personal statements of individual
filmmakers. An equally critical part of this "statement" is the filmmaker's personal dedication to his or her creative endeavor, that commitment required to get the film made and seen by the public. Often how
the film is made and marketed is as illuminating about social relations
as the film itself.

The marketplace mediates human relations, no less for the
Hollywood studios as for independent filmmakers. From an original
vision to its filmic realization to its commercial exhibition, the film
travels a long and tortuous road. Obviously, careers—and fortunes!—
are made annually when this journey is successfully completed.
Unfortunately, the odds of simply getting the film made, let alone
being a success, are staggering. This was especially true during the
1980s, an era in which the movie marketplace was remarkably volatile
and grew increasingly concentrated.

The 1980s was a tumultuous decade, one that witnessed the movie
industry (as well as the larger entertainment and communications
industries) undergo a profound structural transformation. It was a
transformation that took place on a domestic as well as on an international basis. What took a century to accomplish—in making the
United States the global media "mountaintop" disseminating its
vision of modernity to the world—has been fundamentally and forever transformed. The hegemony established by Edison, the Hollywood
studio moguls, and Paley-Sarnoff has turned in on itself: the American

vision remains the source of global mass mythology, but it is no longer the possession of Americans. And the great irony, a true joke of history, is that the ringmaster of this transformation, Ronald Reagan, was none other than Hollywood's most transparent character, the "leading man" least encumbered by a distinct personality like Bogart, Gable, Cagney, or even Wayne.

A set of distinct factors contributed to the decade's tumult. First, extensive federal deregulation of the communications industry, and especially of the Hollywood studios and the cable companies, fueled widespread cross-ownership, spin-offs, and acquisitions. Hollywood studios were freed to acquire distribution arms, most notably movie-theater chains (thus overturning the 1948 Supreme Court *Paramount* ruling) as well as cable services and television stations. Second, monetary policy changes led to the widescale availability of "cheap money" at both the investment-capital and disposable-income levels. Not only did wealthy people and a wide variety of companies have "play money" to invest in film production and distribution, but an ever-increasing number of Americans had the "free money" to go to the movies and pay for the expanded film services of home video and cable, particularly "premium" services like HBO.

These factors contributed to the enormous expansion of demand for filmed entertainment, especially original works. In turn, this led to an increase in film production. Between 1984 and 1988, total feature film releases increased from 410 to 513; by 1990, output had declined to 417. Not surprisingly, the relative proportion of independent films released increased from 58 percent to 69 percent during the four-year period, peaking at nearly three-quarters of the total releases in 1987; by 1990, the proportion of independent releases fell back to 60 percent.[2]

A critical factor contributing to this was the nearly one-third increase in movie-theater screens, from 17,500 to 23,000, during the decade. Movie admissions remained relatively flat at 1.1 billion per year, but theater ticket prices have skyrocketed. Today, in "first-run" theaters in major markets like Los Angeles or New York it is not uncommon to be charged $7.50 for an admission.[3]

Perhaps the most important factor contributing to the rapid expansion of film production during the 1980s was the expansion of what traditionally was called the "ancillary markets": broadcast and cable television, home video, and foreign sales. First, the number of sets in each household nearly doubled to 2.5. Second, the number of TV stations across the country increased by one-third, to now nearly 1,500, with over 250 independent and 350 public stations operating; this increased to over 11 the average number of broadcast stations received per household. Third, cable television penetration increased from less than one-quarter to over half of all households. Fourth, VCR ownership increased from 2 million to about 70 million during the decade. These factors resulted in a fundamental change in the television viewing experience.[4]

These new outlets required more programming, the most appealing often being feature films, be they popular new releases, older "classics," or simply some affordable property to fill an empty scheduling slot. They created all-new revenue streams for movie companies. Consumer expenditures for home video sales and rentals soared from a modest $70 million in 1980 to over $7 billion by 1990 (this is nearly double total box-office "gross" ticket sales); cable subscription fees for basic, pay, and pay-per-view exploded to the point where cable revenues were projected to top $15 billion in 1991. And just when it looked like the movie business was running out of growth, a new and equally lucrative vein was pushed further open with increased foreign sales.

Changes in media regulation, investments and revenue, and consumer viewing habits had profound consequences for the entertainment industry's very character. First, the three major broadcast networks, long the dominant force in mass media, lost considerable ground not only to local independent stations and cable services but to program producers as well. The three major networks lost viewers and advertising revenue, and were taken over: ABC by CapCities, CBS by Tisch, and NBC by GE. Second, the cable industry, long an anarchic collection of small franchises merely retransmitting over-the-air stations, swelled into a powerful original programming source from HBO and Disney, MTV, CNN, and ESPN. Cable systems and programming services are controlled by an ever-shrinking universe of dominant media conglomerates like Telecommunications, Inc., and Time-Warner. Third, the leading programmers, i.e., the Hollywood movie and TV studios, acquired new distribution arms and grew to unprecedented size, yet witnessed fundamental restructuring resulting in either foreign takeovers (e.g., Fox by Murdoch, Columbia/Tri-Star by Sony, Universal by Matsushita, and MGM/UA by Parretti) or integration into more financially secure global media conglomerates (e.g., Disney, Paramount, and Time-Warner). To be a serious contender in the media game today, you have to be a big, global player like Murdoch, Morita, or Mickey Mouse.

These developments occurred as the "baby boom" generation matured into an all-important force driving the nation's consumer culture. Raised on TV, movies, and higher education, they brought not only lots of free time and free money to the media marketplace but, and equally important, an informed and demanding sensibility. They knew about new releases from reviews and discussion with friends, and were knowledgeable about the works of their favorite directors. Thus, they became a countervailing force in the marketplace demanding films with more "quality," with more "creativity," with a "literary" sensibility—or at least with pretensions to such standards.

The filmmakers that emerged during this period were, not surprisingly, near mirror-images of their most supportive audiences. They shared many of the same experiences, spoke the same language, and faced many of the same life choices. And while the Hollywood system was producing teenage formula fare and (ever increasingly) big-budget, high-concept escapist blockbusters, specialty filmmakers were asking different questions of the medium and offering different insights about a very confusing era. Collectively, these filmmakers raised important issues, treated traditional issues with a new seriousness, and contributed to stylistic innovations. One of their least acknowledged but critical contributions to the movie business was helping bring back older, more mature audiences to the movies.

Like studio productions, specialty filmmaking explores a wide variety of filmic genres—from westerns, to mysteries, to family dramas, to love stories, to political and social controversies. But because they are basically undercapitalized business ventures, such filmmaking often displays remarkable ingenuity, spunk, and sheer determination. Limited resources are often the parent of risk-taking originality.

Popular, if limited, support for specialty films comes from two principal sources. First, audiences are drawn from what is euphemistically dubbed "the art-house crowd," those more sophisticated filmgoers sufficiently displeased with most of the Hollywood fare and seeking more original works expressed in either the film's message or execution. Such viewers are often enthusiastic about works that are less professionally (i.e., expensively) produced but express unique or compelling personal visions.

The second important source of support grows directly from the organic group that is the film's subject matter or primary appeal. This group is usually called the "crossover" audience and is often composed of a high proportion of people who would only occasionally or not normally be drawn to an "art" film. Such "crossover" groups are drawn from individual ethnic groups (e.g., Hispanic, African American, Native American, etc.) or other demographic groups (e.g., the elderly, teenagers, gays and lesbians, etc.), regional groups (e.g., New Yorkers, Texans), or people who share particular social or political convictions (e.g., feminists, environmentalists, etc.), among other identifiable characteristics. Securing strong support from these two groups helps ensure a specialty film's viability in the marketplace.

Detailed assessments of specialty-film "crossover" marketing efforts are presented in the subsequent discussions of *The Ballad of Gregorio Cortez*, *El Norte*, and *Stand and Deliver*.

The Making of Three Independent Films

However unique, the three films profiled in this essay share much in common. Beyond the fact that they deal with Hispanic issues, each is, first and foremost, a very personal statement of the filmmakers involved—and the importance of this is no better expressed than in their active involvement in the film's making and marketing efforts. Second, the individual statements expressed in each film are as much of a social or political nature as an aesthetic one; each film employs a dramatic story line focusing on the life struggles of a central character(s) to examine critically a greater social injustice. Third, each film, though highly personal, is an expression of a collective effort, a creative partnership among a handful of key principals working closely to achieve a shared goal; none is the work of an auteur filmmaker. A brief description of each film will clarify these elements.

The Ballad of Gregorio Cortez. This film chronicles the most massive manhunt in Texas history. Gregorio Cortez (Edward James Olmos), a Mexican American farmer in turn-of-the-century Texas, is wrongly accused of a horse theft due, in large measure, to a fateful misunderstanding of the Spanish distinction between "horse" (*caballo*) and "mare" (*yegua*). The sheriff, convinced Cortez is guilty, pulls a pistol and attempts to arrest him. Cortez's brother, trying to intercede, is wantonly shot by the sheriff and Cortez in turn pulls his own gun and kills the sheriff. Led by the Texas Rangers, a posse of 600 men pursues Cortez for eleven days in a chase covering hundreds of miles. Finally captured, Cortez must be protected from a huge lynch mob that threatens to storm the jail. When brought to trial, Cortez is sentenced to fifty years for manslaughter.

The film was produced by Moctesuma Esparza under the aegis of the National Council of La Raza (NCLR), a public advocacy group, based on the historical study *"With His Pistol in His Hand": A Border Ballad and Its Hero* by Américo Paredes. Esparza undertook what became a three-year-long development effort because of his deep personal commitment to the story. Like the film's wrongly accused hero, Esparza had been wrongly indicted by a Los Angeles grand jury during the 1960s because of his political activities. Esparza was committed to making a film that could speak to a broad, multiethnic, multilanguage audience about cultural misunderstanding. He saw the film as "a project of the Chicano community, not *for* it."

With initial financial support from the National Endowment for the Humanities (NEH) in June 1981, Esparza was able to assemble a distinguished production team. Victor Villaseñor wrote the original screenplay and Robert M. Young, the director, worked closely with actors Olmos and Tom Bower, who developed their own dialogue, and prepared the final shooting script. Michael Hauseman served as line producer. *Cortez's* total budget, $1,174,000, came from four sources: the NEH ($600,000), Corporation for Public Broadcasting ($540,000), "American Playhouse" ($100,000), and the German television network ZDF ($65,000).

In addition to cast and crew, two other issues defined the production process and subsequent marketing efforts. First, Young insisted, with Esparza's concurrence, that *Cortez* be conceived as a theatrically released movie, *not* a made-for-TV production. This meant that while being shot in super-16 mm, the film had to be "framed" during photography to allow for a later 35-mm blowup, the format essentially required for theatrical release. Second, the group decided to use a novel dual-language dialogue approach. Intermixing English and Spanish, without subtitles, had both artistic and commercial consequences. Artistically, the filmmakers reasoned that a dual-language

248 Crossover: Hispanic Specialty Films

film would foster among the viewing audience an experience akin to that confronted by the film's characters, thus heightening the emotional tenor. If their artistic approach did not succeed, it would seriously threaten the film's commercial possibilities.

Principal photography commenced in October 1981 and took five weeks; second-unit work took an additional week. For a low-budget production, *Cortez* was a large undertaking, involving 1,500 extras in period costumes, with locations covering three border states. Editing lasted seven weeks and was completed in June 1982; the 35-mm blowup was done by DuArt Labs.

El Norte. This film depicts the flight of two Guatemalan peasants, brother and sister, to the United States, the promised land of "el Norte." Following the brutal murder of their father and fearing for their own lives, the pair flee north filled with fantasies of the American "good life." Undergoing a harrowing journey through Mexico and a terrifying border crossing, these nondocumented aliens finally arrive in Los Angeles only to discover a far harsher reality than they expected.

El Norte was conceived, cowritten, and directed by Gregory Nava, working closely with his wife, Anna Thomas, who cowrote and produced the film. The filmmakers were committed to a highly original and, at initial consideration, a highly noncommercial project. First, although originally conceived as a story about Mexican Indians, the focus shifted to Guatemala following extensive research on its native Indian population. Second, they were committed to creating a highly dramatic epic in line with the innovative Latin American literary style of "magical realism." Third, they insisted on placing the native people at the center of their own story. To be true to the experience of its Mayan peasant lead characters, the story would have to be told in Mayan, Spanish, and English. This posed problems not simply in terms of finding the right actors who could capture the dramatic tenor of the characters, but who could also convey the story's transcendent humanism so that it would appeal to a modern, urban American moviegoer.

The filmmakers spent two daunting years seeking production financing. They were rejected by the NEH, exhausted countless potential private investors, and failed to find support from members of the Los Angeles Latino community. Shelving the project as ill-timed, the couple was working within the Los Angeles independent film community when they met Lindsay Law, executive producer of PBS's "American Playhouse." He asked to read the script, found it compelling, and committed "Playhouse" money—all in a matter of days. With "Playhouse" backing of $425,000, the filmmakers had little trouble raising the initial balance of $155,000 from Britain's Channel Four ($110,000), private investors ($45,000), and deferrals; final production costs would run to $850,000 because of unforeseeable overages that would be covered by the theatrical distribution advance.

Like the story, the production became an epic. Lead actors Zaide Gutiérrez and David Villalpando, experienced Latin American stage actors, were unknown to North American filmgoers. Planned as a twelve-week shoot (with one week for relocations), final production stretched to fourteen weeks spread over a seventeen-week period. The film was shot in 35-mm, involved almost sixty speaking parts, and used over one hundred locations in Mexico and the United States. The filmmakers ran into particular difficulty in Mexico, where they confronted serious logistical problems, terrible weather conditions, Mayan extras who spoke neither Spanish nor English, and—a filmmaker's worst nightmare—gunmen invading the set and, after a reckless car chase, kidnapping the exposed film (and the production manager!) at gunpoint. In what appeared in retrospect as a scene from a "B" movie, the filmmakers met the kidnappers (with submachine guns drawn) at midnight in a deserted Mexico City parking lot and ransomed back the film and production manager for 1.3 million pesos ($17,000). After this, the production was quickly relocated to Los Angeles, adding several weeks to the production and causing considerable financial overages because of added costs of recreated sets, new locations, and flying up some of the cast to complete several scenes.

Stand and Deliver. This film is a dramatic portrait of an exceptional teacher, Jaime Escalante, and his innovative, inspiring methods teaching calculus to students in an East Los Angeles *barrio* high school. His efforts are as much pedagogical as motivational, helping students overcome their low sense of self-esteem to realize their educational and human potential.

Escalante (Edward James Olmos) quits a high-paying job in an electronics firm to teach at Garfield High School. He is a passionate, dedicated man who confronts a shared sense of failure and low expectation in both students and school administrators. The film portrays a representative sample of students, the toughest being Angel (Lou

Diamond Phillips), a sullen *cholo* or bad boy. Escalante disarms the students with a mixture of wit, mockery ("Tough guys don't do math; tough guys fry chicken for a living"), sincere respect, compassion, and, most important, humor.

The administration reacts with hostility to his proposal to teach a course for the calculus Advanced Placement exam. Nevertheless, after months of daunting study, the students pass the exam only to have their grades overturned by the Educational Testing Service (ETS) due to a suspicion of cheating. Distraught, Escalante rallies his kids for a retest that vindicates them and his commitment.

On August 11, 1983, director Ramon Menendez, a recent graduate of the UCLA film school and an American Film Institute fellow, read an article in the *Los Angeles Times* describing Escalante and his confrontation with the ETS. Enthusiastic, Menendez teamed up with a fellow film school graduate, producer Thomas Musca, and they began the long process of getting their film made and marketed. Their first hurdle was to convince Escalante to give them the rights to his story, which took six months. Second, they sought to raise production support on the basis of a twelve-page treatment, only to be rejected by NBC as a made-for-TV movie and by several Los Angeles production companies; they sent out grant applications to 240 foundations and were rejected by 239 of them.

Finally, in October 1984, they received a $12,000 scripting grant from "American Playhouse." During the script revision period, the filmmakers were able to secure the involvement of a number of Los Angeles's most prominent Latino actors. Most importantly, Olmos (then starring in the popular NBC series *Miami Vice*) rallied to the project out of both the acting challenge presented in portraying Escalante as well as the positive social statement inherent to the film. Olmos was joined by then up-and-coming talents Phillips and Andy Garcia; they were about to achieve significant notoriety for their respective roles in *La Bamba* and *The Untouchables*.

These developments helped the filmmakers secure a second, $500,000 commitment from "Playhouse" for the TV rights. This led to additional support from the National Science Foundation ($172,000), Atlantic-Richfield Corporation ($350,000), the Corporation for Public Broadcasting ($175,000), the Ford Foundation ($50,000), and product placement fees from Pepsi and Anheuser-Busch ($49,500). Production costs totaled $1.37 million.

Film production finally commenced in April 1987, three-and-a-half years after the original idea was conceived. Principal photography lasted thirty-two days, with one week for second-unit photography. The production benefited from considerable support within the Los Angeles Latino community, including the principal of Garfield High, Henry Gradillas, the L.A. school board, and use of five schools to provide authenticity.

The Marketing of Three Independent Films

Independent filmmaking can be a harrowing undertaking, involving two marketing efforts: the first to secure a distributor, the second an audience. Not only does the filmmaker have to possess considerable talent and dedication simply to get the film made, but he or she normally makes it without a distribution agreement in place. Thus, the independent courts considerable risk. First, the work may never get seen by reviewers, let alone an audience. Second and intimately tied to the first, there is no guaranteed financial return (however limited), thus placing all who invested in the project at considerable risk.

The three films under discussion did not face this extreme predicament. Each had an "American Playhouse" PBS television distribution commitment as part of its production financing. However, PBS's policies regarding investing in a "theatrical" production underwent a fundamental change that had considerable implications, particularly for *The Ballad of Gregorio Cortez*. Nevertheless, once each film had a distribution deal in place, considerable imagination and effort—by the distributor and filmmaker alike!—were required to bring the film to a supportive audience and achieve the social significance and financial success that each experienced. A brief description of each film's distribution history will help clarify these issues.

The Ballad of Gregorio Cortez. The filmmakers responsible for *Cortez*, most notably Olmos, Esparza, Young, and Bower, were committed to seeing their work achieve a theatrical release. The contracts they negotiated with the production guilds required that the film open theatrically *prior* to its first television airing. According to its "Playhouse" contract, *The Ballad of Gregorio Cortez* was to be broadcast on June 29, 1982, during the series's first season.

Three weeks before the PBS airing, Olmos organized a very

unorthodox theatrical "premiere" in San Antonio, Texas. He "four walled" a local theater (rented a screen and services) with monies contributed by the National Council of La Raza (NCLR) and Esparza. Olmos stood in front of the theater handing out promotional literature and talking to people going to see other movies at the multiplex. At the first screening, on June 4, only two paying customers attended. By week's end, however, favorable word of mouth was drawing 250 people per screening and NCLR recouped its contribution.

Following *The Ballad of Gregorio Cortez*'s successful PBS airings, the filmmakers faced another serious hurdle. With its television broadcast, *The Ballad of Gregorio Cortez* was no longer a "virgin property," no longer suitable for theatrical release. In the movie business, it is an article of faith that a film's "first window" of exposure has to be theatrical exhibition. Therefore, in order to secure a theatrical distributor, the filmmakers were determined to prove that *The Ballad of Gregorio Cortez* was a film people wanted to see.

Seeking to duplicate the San Antonio success in Los Angeles, Olmos and Esparza underwrote the four-walling costs for nine Saturday morning performances at the Los Felix and the Beverly Hills Music theaters. *The Ballad of Gregorio Cortez* quickly became the talk of the town, gaining positive reviews in the *Los Angeles Times* and *L.A. Weekly*. The stir led to an invitation to screen the film for Norman Lear and Jerrold Perenchio, then heads of Embassy Pictures, and a remarkably favorable distribution deal.

Besides a considerable financial investment, Embassy committed to a radically innovative marketing initiative. This involved two elements: first, hiring some of the members of the filmmaking team (including Bower) and five associates (including Robert Hoffman, a publicity specialist, and Daniel Haro, a civil rights activist) to work as part of the company's sales/marketing staff; and second, to initiate an extensive grass-roots outreach effort of audience development. These two elements would at once contribute significantly to the film's very success and undoing at Embassy.

The *"Cortez* group" joined Embassy during a very volatile period. The company had just merged with Avco and the marketing division was being restructured. Lear shifted from the movie to the television division. Significant cost-cutting efforts were under way, leading to extensive job cuts and to the abolition of the special Latino division that Lear had established. Nevertheless, the *"Cortez* group" received remarkably generous support, ultimately reaching an eleven-month service engagement.

The first phase of the marketing effort focused on building up the film's local and national word-of-mouth recognition. The efforts undertaken included: securing favorable film festival screenings (e.g., Telluride and Mill Valley); garnering professional endorsements (e.g., American Historical Association and National Council of Teachers of English); maximizing grass roots support (e.g., speaking engagements at Hispanic community centers, schools, prisons, and juvenile detention centers); and receiving favorable reviews. While these efforts were under way, however, Embassy decided to preempt these efforts and launch the film.

Originally, two incompatible plans had been developed for the film's release. Embassy, reflecting a more conventional studio approach, called for New York City and Los Angeles openings. The "*Cortez* group" sought a slower, more focused, region-by-region release. Embassy decided to market tests in San Francisco and El Paso, two very different urban environments, in August. Only indirectly learning of Embassy's plans, the "*Cortez* group" put their efforts into the San Francisco campaign. They worked extensively with Bay Area independent filmmakers and Hispanic community groups, received very favorable attention at the Mill Valley Film Festival, and generated significant local popular and press attention. The group's ingenuity and risk-taking spirit is typified in a novel publicity scheme.

At one of the final Embassy-sponsored preview screenings at the 300-seat Four Star Theatre, the "*Cortez* group" (unbeknownst to Embassy) printed and distributed 3,000 tickets. Swarms of ticket holders descended on the theater and Embassy management was, to say the least, disturbed. Those who could not get in were entertained by mariachis, jugglers, fire eaters, and local activists, after being calmed by the charismatic Olmos and his consummate crowd-handling skills. The event is still warmly remembered by the filmmakers and Bay Area residents alike.

The El Paso opening occurred one week following San Francisco. Embassy saw it as an opportunity to test a Spanish-language print campaign. Although most of the group's efforts were focused in the Bay Area, extensive community outreach took place in El Paso nonetheless. Despite the city's forty-percent unemployment rate, the film did excellent business.

On the basis of these two experiences, Embassy management decided to push aggressively for a national playoff. As the "*Cortez* group" warned, management mistook the intense marketing efforts for strong audience appeal. Without cultivating solid community interest, few would come out to see the film. These concerns proved all too accurate as later openings, first in New York and followed by Los Angeles, Boston, and other cities, proved.

After rushing the film into release, Embassy was quickly disappointed with what it saw as the film's poor performance. Not getting the level and rate of return on what it saw as a substantial investment (including a $500,000 advance and nearly $1 million in marketing expenses), Embassy pulled the film from national release after three months.

Still strongly believing in the film and their original marketing vision, the "*Cortez* group" optioned a subdistribution agreement from Embassy (and independent of Esparza Productions). The group was made up of Olmos, Bower, Hoffman, Haro, and Greg Friedkin, and their efforts generated an additional $100,000 in film grosses. Their most successful effort occurred in Denver, where Mayor Federico Peña proclaimed August 31, 1984, "*The Ballad of Gregorio Cortez* Day" and joined Olmos and Young at the opening-night ceremonies.

El Norte. Gregory Nava and Anna Thomas had a clear vision of the film's marketing campaign. During postproduction, they showed the roughcut to their investors only, fearing premature exposure would undercut the film's impact. They chose to premiere the film at the Telluride Film Festival in order to maximize interest among distributors. Hand carrying the print in from New York's DuArt Labs, Nava saw his finished film for the first time at the festival and received a standing ovation.

Following the successful festival showing, the filmmakers received numerous distribution offers. They first retained a producers representative ("rep") to help achieve the most favorable contractual terms. Sensing that they had an important film and being committed to highly informed marketing beliefs, they created a kind of "bidding war" among interested distributors. Their criteria included both financial (e.g., size of advance, scale of commitment) and marketing (e.g., film assessment, positioning, and distribution) considerations. Perhaps most important, the filmmakers were looking for a distributor whom they could work with intimately and effectively. They finally chose Cinecom, partnering with Island Alive.

Both companies had strong credentials among a growing number of small, specialized distributors emerging during the early to mid-1980s. Cinecom had achieved relative prominence with its release of *Come Back to the Five and Dime, Jimmy Dean, Jimmy Dean* and *Angelo, My Love,* among others. Island Alive had released *Koyannisqaatsi* and *Android,* among others. Both companies wanted the film and would give it serious attention; neither was handling another major film if *El Norte* took off.

The filmmakers and distributors shared a basic, working assumption in planning the marketing and distribution efforts: because of the film's controversial storyline, it had to be positioned in terms of its humanistic themes, not its political message. For those involved, this did not mean that they did not have strong beliefs about the issues of nondocumented aliens. Rather, they sought to avoid the pigeonholing of the film as simply a message movie or its being misidentified as a documentary.

This approach had a number of critical consequences. First, images, words, and review quotes for the trailer, ad, and publicity packet were selected on the basis of reinforcing the film's magical and dramatic qualities, downplaying its political themes. Second, and in contrast to many social-issue independent films, *El Norte* had very limited exposure in benefit screenings. Third, and in contrast to one of the strongest movie-release conventions, the film was opened in the East as opposed to the West, where, superficially, it should have had its strongest appeal.

Key to the film's overall marketing efforts was reliance on positive reviews within both the English- and Spanish-language press. Extensive prescreenings were held for the press and opinion makers. They led to both reviews and editorial pieces in a wide variety of magazines, newspapers, and television stations. Important positive coverage appeared in such major-market and national newspapers as *The New York Times, USA Today, The Los Angeles Times,* and *Chicago Times.* Among smaller-market press, favorable reviews were in the *Sacramento Bee, San Diego Union,* and *Cleveland Herald.* Not all coverage was favorable, however. For example, New York's *Village Voice* and *New York* gave mixed reviews.

The same techniques were employed promoting the film among

the Spanish-language community. Nava stressed one critical difference: the Hispanic community, and particularly its more educated, influential, middle-class stratum, would take its cue on *El Norte* from the dominant mainstream press. For Spanish-language critics, exhibitors, and filmgoers to accept *El Norte,* an art film, it would require favorable reviews and strong box-office performance within the traditional art-house circuit.

Four audiences were identified and actively pursued through distinct efforts. Art-house patrons were cultivated through positive reviews. Bilingual middle-class Hispanic adults in major markets, though numerically small, were recognized as key opinion leaders and were sought out through special screenings and positive Spanish-language press coverage. English-language and bilingual, Spanish-language-dominant adults in smaller markets were targeted through local press coverage. Finally, monolingual Spanish-speaking people in southern California, the Southwest, and in some northeast and central urban settings required a special version of the film with Spanish subtitles over the English dialogue.

The theatrical release successfully tapped these audience segments. Cinecom, following Nava's non-West Coast approach, planned to open in New York and Chicago before yearend 1983 so as to qualify for an Academy Award. It faced unexpected difficulties, however. In New York, the film's opening was scheduled for the prestigious Plaza Theatre, but was repeatedly postponed—and ultimately moved—because of the unanticipated success of Carlos Saura's *Carmen.* In Chicago, *El Norte* received its premier at the Fine Arts Theatre on December 15, 1983, during one of the most severe cold spells in the city's history. Nevertheless, the film did surprisingly well, running for a total of eighteen weeks in the face of frigid temperatures and traditional low Christmas art-theater attendance.

Picking up on the Chicago success, Cinecom opened the film in New York City on January 11, 1984. It played exclusively at Manhattan's Baronet theater for eleven weeks, then moved to other theaters in the city, New Jersey, and Long Island. In all, it ran eighteen weeks in New York. Building on the accomplishments of Chicago and New York, *El Norte* opened in Los Angeles on March 9. As expected, local critics politicized the film around the immigration issue. But they also praised its artistic and humanistic qualities, thus affirming the overall marketing approach and release strategy.

Stand and Deliver. During production, the filmmakers decided not to screen the film until it was ready for a paying audience. Given the fact that Edward James Olmos, Lou Diamond Phillips, and Andy Garcia were in it, however, the filmmakers received innumerable inquiries and roughcut preview requests from distributors. Ramon Menendez and Tom Musca felt their film might well be a winner and sought to harness the growing excitement so as to maximize their distribution options.

The filmmakers premiered *Stand and Deliver* at the Mill Valley Film Festival, scene of the 1983 screening of *The Ballad of Gregorio Cortez*. Hand carrying the first answer print from Los Angeles, Musca arrived just in time for the screening. The film received a standing ovation and the filmmakers received a number of tentative distribution offers. From Mill Valley, the filmmakers flew to New York to debut their work at the Independent Film Market (IFM), sponsored by the Independent Feature Project. The single IFM screening was a spectacular success, playing to a standing-room-only audience.

Returning to Los Angeles, the filmmakers found themselves being courted by many distributors. They were determined to make the best deal—measured not simply in terms of financial considerations, but equally by the nature of the commitment to ensure the film's success. They finally chose Warner Brothers because of its offer and its proven track record releasing serious movies like *Chariots of Fire, The Killing Fields,* and *Local Hero* as well as such specialty films as *'Round Midnight* and *True Stories.* Not unlike the *Cortez* experience, the filmmakers got Warner to bring on a special team dedicated to the Latino and education markets; this team included former "*Cortez* group" members Robert Hoffman and Danny Haro.

Warner hoped *Stand and Deliver* would duplicate the performance of the recently released *La Bamba.* To try to achieve this, the studio utilized extensive audience testing. These tests, which took place in Sherman Oaks and Seattle, provided helpful information for making a number of necessary editorial cuts and changing the film's name, originally called *Walking on Water.* As part of its overall youth-oriented approach, Warner optioned the song "Stand and Deliver," sung by Mr. Mister, and incorporated it into the film's end.

The key components of the marketing campaign included: (1) creation of a special community outreach team; (2) hosting of nearly 220 prescreenings for highly targeted audiences; (3) organizing numerous promotional tour visits; (4) setting up numerous media interviews by film principals; (5) preparing educational support materials and activities; (6) preparing electronic media support materials; and (7) producing a "Stand and Deliver" music video. These activities proved extremely beneficial in terms of the film's overall success.

Special attention was paid to outreach efforts for the Hispanic community. Warner organized screenings for important Spanish-language print, television, and radio representatives; held screenings for such Hispanic groups as the League of United Latin American Citizens, the National Association of Hispanic Publications, the California Chicano News Media Association, and the California Association of Bi-Lingual Educators; and held benefit screenings for the Garfield High School Alumni Association, Corky Gonzales, and the United Farm Workers. Perhaps the greatest media event occurred when Escalante attended a White House luncheon honoring outstanding educators hosted by President Ronald Reagan. A photo of Escalante and Reagan, with a mention of *Stand and Deliver*, was featured throughout the country. Warner prepared Spanish-language media materials including videotaped interviews with Olmos, Phillips, and others; Spanish-dubbed film clips; and a promotional film of Escalante teaching. These materials were utilized by the Spanish-language television networks Telemundo and Univision and services (e.g., Desde Hollywood) as well as many Spanish-language magazines and newspapers. These activities helped generate strong support for the film in the Hispanic community.[5]

The theatrical release benefited significantly from the combined effect of these efforts. *Stand and Deliver* opened in Los Angeles over the March 11-12, 1988, weekend in thirty theaters and grossed over $400,000. Warner decided in favor of Los Angeles—as opposed to New York, site of most theatrical openings—because it would play to one of the film's strengths. Select "exit polls" showed attendees coming from all age groups, slightly more women than men, and forty percent of the viewers were Hispanic. Los Angeles was the film's home base, however, and thus the favorable response had to be carefully considered.

After thirty sneak-preview screenings in the New York area in mid-March, Warner felt confident about the film's appeal. It performed less than expected, achieving box-office grosses less than those realized by *La Bamba*. Subsequent releases took place throughout the country with mixed results. For example, *Stand and Deliver* exceeded projected expectations (i.e., quotas) in Boston, Chicago, Cleveland, Dallas, Denver, Detroit, Kansas City, Los Angeles, Minneapolis, Philadelphia, San Francisco, Seattle/Portland, and Washington, D.C. In addition to New York, it fell below the quota in Atlanta, Charlotte, Cincinnati, Jacksonville, and New Orleans.

Assessing the Performance of Independent Films

Success is defined differently by different independent filmmakers. For some, it's simply getting one's work completed; for others, it's achieving critical recognition; for others, it's repaying their investors; and, for a small handful, it's achieving the acclaim that leads to a sizable theatrical performance and significant financial return. Whatever the definition, success helps a filmmaker achieve what all filmmakers, independent or studio, most desire: to make another film.

Each film demonstrates the filmmakers' dedication to their work. They each believed wholeheartedly in their film. Their passion for their project was expressed in their dedication to the total making and marketing efforts. It was reflected in the inventiveness by which they raised their financing and pulled off the production process. It was embodied in how they put themselves at the heart of the release efforts, resulting in quite unorthodox marketing activities that resulted in significant accomplishments.

Each of the three films discussed in this essay has been recognized as a success. These films raised issues that were important not only to the Hispanic community, but to the larger American public as well. And they each did this in a manner that was aesthetically appropriate and compelling. Perhaps because of this, they achieved relative commercial success as measured by the box-office performance and the financial return to the filmmakers. They garnered considerable critical acclaim, two of them receiving Academy Award nominations (*El Norte* for best original script and Edward Olmos for best actor in *Stand and Deliver*). These achievements allowed all the filmmakers involved to go on to make other films.

The Ballad of Gregorio Cortez, El Norte, and *Stand and Deliver* are exceptional films. They were critically and commercially successful, true exceptions in an otherwise cluttered movie marketplace dominated by highly questionable productions. They spoke to and about the real life of the Hispanic community, a social group that is all too often excluded from favorable representation by the American movie industry. One can only hope that as the Hispanic community continues to grow in numbers and influence within American society more films will be released that fulfill the promises raised by these films.

Notes

1. David Rosen (with Peter Hamilton), *Off-Hollywood: The Making and Marketing of Independent Films* (New York: Grove Press, 1990), from which most of the material in this piece is drawn.

2. *Off-Hollywood*, 263; "New U.S. Feature Film Releases," *Variety* (December 24, 1990).

3. "Number of U.S. Theater Screens, 1948-1989," *Variety* (October 29, 1990).

4. Data compiled from *Five Year Home Media Outlook*, LINK Resources, 1990; *Broadcasting*, February 25, 1991; National Association of Broadcasters, National Cable Television Association, and Video Software Distributors Association.

5. Nancy Sher and David Rosen, "Independent Features: Foundation Support for Narrative Films," *Benton Foundation Bulletin* 4 (1990).

A Chicano Reporter in "Hispanic Hollywood": Editorial Agendas and the Culture of Professional Journalism

Victor Valle

The message pulsed across the top of my Coyote VDT in cool neon ciphers. "Are we going to have a *La Bamba* story for Friday?" my editor asked. Though I'd conducted interviews in preparation for the story a month earlier, the request still caught me by surprise. I'd just wrapped up a grueling three weeks of covering the much-heralded walkout by the 2,500 members of the Directors Guild of America. A dozen or so articles and newsbriefs later, however, the strike to beat all Hollywood strikes had lasted no more than a dozen minutes. And now I had two days before my next deadline.

My apprehension eased a bit when I remembered the approach I'd planned to take. I was writing a trend story, the kind of dollars-and-screens approach the *Calendar* section loves to repeat. Later I'd write a summary paragraph that posed the story's theme as a question: "With the biggest simultaneous Spanish-English release campaign—64 Spanish-dubbed and 13 Spanish-subtitled prints deployed in about 30 major cities nationwide—Columbia pictures becomes the latest in a growing list of major movie studios to ask the same question." Obviously, Columbia had, at least for this film, answered the question in the affirmative.

It wasn't hard to be impressed with the answer. Historically, the major studios had treated the domestic Spanish-language market as a stepchild to their international distribution schemes. "Typically," I wrote in the July 1987 story, "this has meant that Latinos have had to wait for weeks or months before Spanish-dubbed or subtitled prints produced for European and Latin American markets became available

in the United States." But now Columbia, following the precedent set
by Universal Pictures, had temporarily inverted the process. This time
Spanish-speaking Latinos would see *La Bamba* the same time as
English-language moviegoers.

The experiment paid off with a public relations coup, which made
perfect sense in Hollywood. In an industry that thrives on Cinderella
stories, *La Bamba* reaffirmed Hollywood's favorite narrative clichés.
Ritchie Valens (née Valenzuela) was the minority outcast who ascend-
ed into the rock 'n' roll heavens, which is almost the same as becoming a movie star. Clearly, director Luis Valdez had tapped into those
aspects of Valens's life that reaffirmed one of the bedrock storylines
upon which the Jewish movie moguls built Hollywood into the
world's dream factory. The hardworking ordinary underdog who succeeds through sheer will and natural virtue is just a populist version
of the Jewish immigrant story stripped of its overt ethnicity.

But this was not the film I saw weeks before in a Columbia
Pictures screening room. It became apparent to me that evening that
Valdez, like other Latino bricoleurs adept at juggling several languages and cultures, was capable of telling several stories simultaneously.

This other narrative begins with a close-up of a rattlesnake sliding
across a hot asphalt highway, which is shot pavement level against a
clear blue sky. Seconds later, a Harley's chrome spoke wheels blur by
in a blast of roadhouse blues, nearly creasing the serpent. It was clear
to me, knowing Valdez's previous work, that the snake was an allusion to Quetzalcoatl, the sky serpent, bringer of knowledge, teacher of
the arts, literature, and urban civility. Danger here radiated from the
guy astride the motorcycle, Valenzuela's brother, Bob. The juxtaposition of images prefigured Ritchie's eventual conflicts with his brother,
but also a struggle between terrestrial and celestial forces. Valdez gave
me a few more clues. Bob is prone to violent rage when he drinks. His
alcoholic tendencies identify him with Tezcatlipoca, the moral obfus-
cator, the wizard of the smoking mirror who, according to myth,
envied and eventually corrupts Quetzalcoatl.

Valdez confirmed my observations three months later during an
interview inside La Golodrina Restaurant in La Calle Olvera: "When I
first pitched the idea for the screenplay, I told Taylor [Hackford] about
. . . all the symbolism. He loved it. But [the mythic elements are] not
overemphasized. It's part of the film's structure. That's the reason the

snake is peeled. Here's a curandero skinning a snake, you know, as a symbol of Quetzalcoatl. So when he gives Ritchie the rattles, he is essentially giving him a new skin." The Tezcatlipoca parallel was also intentional. "That's Tezcatlipoca," Valdez said. "He introduced this evil [*pulque*] into the world. When you think about it, it's not so hard to figure out. That was Bob's problem. When I looked at his reality, I realized that this guy's got Tezcatlipoca in him, right?"

But I knew that night in July, when I first saw *La Bamba,* that I'd have a hard time selling a mythic take on this film. To write such a story would risk raising questions that existed outside the experience of my editors, answers my editors were likely to interpret as exotic, esoteric, and pretentiously academic. This wasn't the first or last time I'd face such a quandary. It happened whenever I trusted my deepest instincts to describe the world as I saw it, and not as my editors were accustomed to seeing it. These experiences, however, were not uniquely mine.

Most reporters find it necessary at one time or another to fight for a story. This adversarial tension is built into the news business. But I believe this condition is exaggerated for minority reporters, especially those few who are thoroughly bilingual and biliterate. At least that was my experience. My cultural otherness was a guest who could not overstay his welcome. The stubborn linguistic and cultural parochialism of many of my editors made it hard for them to listen. This tendency is not exclusive to journalism, or Hollywood, for that matter. It represents, as Octavio Paz illustrates by means of a culinary metaphor, a central contradiction of a United States American culture based on democratic dialogue:

> Like the conversation among those at [an American] table, the relation between substances and flavors is direct: sauces that mask tastes, garnishes that entice the eye, condiments that confuse the taste buds are taboo. The separation of one food from another is analogous to the reserve that characterizes the relations between sexes, races, and classes. In our countries food is communion, not only between those at table but between ingredients; Yankee food, impregnated with Puritanism, is based on exclusions. The maniacal preoccupation with the purity and origin of food products has its counterpart in racism and exclusivism. The American contradiction—a democratic universalism based on ethnic, cultural, religious, and sexual exclusions—is reflected in its cuisine.[1]

Because U.S.-styled journalism also perpetuates this parochialism, the minority reporter bears the full burden of translating his or her culture to an often indifferent or hostile editor. In my case, this meant that a whole universe of signs was unavailable to most of my editors because they were monolingual and monocultural. This also meant that I could not assume that any Latino authority—the Cuban novelist Alejo Carpentier or Mexico's journalist/novelist Elena Poniatowska—would be understood or appreciated by these same editors. I found this particularly galling. After all, Spanish is not a foreign language in the Southwest, and the Spanish-speaking world has had a tremendous influence on world literature, art, and music.

Los Angeles Times media writer David Shaw uses the language of power relationships to frame this conflict. News, he argues, is what editors who assign stories and put them in the paper decide is news, and even the most conscientious editors (and reporters) are largely captives of their own experiences, interests, and perceptions. In our still largely segregated society, most whites—and especially most whites old enough to be high-ranking editors—don't have the daily experiences and exposure that would enable them to automatically incorporate a minority sensibility in their own decision-making.[2]

Shaw is essentially correct. The figures he offers on the minority presence in the nation's major newsrooms show how the print news media still is among the most segregated sectors of corporate America. This is especially true in the key decision-making positions. In the city of Los Angeles, which is now majority minority, and the county, which is more than one-third minority, only nine percent of *Los Angeles Times* editors are minority. An even fewer number of editors are Latino; there are no full-time minority art or mass-media critics.

To be fair, the *Los Angeles Times* has made notable efforts to hire and promote minority journalists, particularly in its metro and suburban sections. But it has also had more difficulty discovering ways of making its predominantly white, male, and upper-middle-class professional journalistic culture more inclusive. As with most professional elites that have transformed their special access to knowledge into a form of property, and therefore class power, journalists—like medieval guild members—have always tried to admit peers who share their professional values. The authors of *Power in the Highest Degree* see this gatekeeping function as simple self-preservation: "On their road to class power, knowledge groups of all stripes—whether witch doctors or modern professionals—have to fight battles for the mind. If others lose faith in their knowledge, it ceases to be economically useful."[3]

In a major metropolitan newspaper like the *Times*, the task of molding and enforcing the newsroom's intellectual culture is left to the mid- and lower-level editors as well as the reporters and specialist writers who abide by these rules. This empowerment is no accident, but the result of a covenant in which management concedes certain privileges to the knowledge group in exchange for the group's willingness to suppress the latent class interests that divide it internally—editors against reporters—as well as externally—editors and reporters against upper-level management and the lay public.[4] The job of interpreting the corporation's needs and policies are almost always filtered through this group's efforts to secure or improve its position in the bureaucratic hierarchy. That's why, despite the well-intentioned support of affirmative action policies expressed by management and individual employees, it remains in the class interests of editorial professionals to restrict access to the newsroom. As with doctors and lawyers, the exercise of their gatekeeping power enhances their profession's power and prestige.

The "minority" reporter at the *Times* may therefore face a double exclusion: one culturally defined with features peculiar to the postcolonial Southwest, the other peculiar to the newsroom's professional culture. This does not mean that accommodations can't be reached. At the *Times*, the Metro Program, which recruits and trains minority journalists, has provided a workable model for democratizing the paper's editorial workforce without substantially weakening the profession's gatekeeping powers. But not all *Times* departments are equally permeable to change. This is especially true in the *Times* daily and Sunday *Calendar* sections, where the exclusivist tendencies go beyond a grudging reluctance to hire, retain, and promote minority writers and editors. The nature of the exclusion instead has more to do with the way the *Calendar* editors, reviewers, and reporters define and describe their beat. That these sections fall under the ostensibly lighter rubric of entertainment writing does not trivialize their power to validate and perpetuate the worst aspects of mainstream parochialism. Less apparent to outsiders, however, is the complex interplay of the material conditions of production and the resulting division of intellectual labor, which produces a professional journalistic culture where, in the end, "one truth blooms and an infinity of other possibilities is subordinated or weeded out."[5]

In most mass circulation newspapers, the task of evaluating both the fine and popular arts is left to the reviewer or critic. *Times* management gives these writers greater expressive latitude and authority, as well as higher salaries, in exchange for the prestige and readers they are expected to attract to the paper through their ability to produce articles of consistent quality. In the *Calendar* sections, the greater proportion of reviewers to reporters means that the reviewers tend to set the editorial agenda, if only by the number and prominence of their articles. More important, this lopsided division of labor empowers the reviewer with the critical credentials to function as a full-fledged intellectual. But even here the reviewer's enhanced expressive license is narrowly circumscribed. This fact should become apparent to anyone who compares the *Times* approach to cultural criticism with, let's say, the various Latin American styles. The distinction here is not of talent but of tradition and the far greater degree to which U.S.-style journalism has been molded by its political institutions, its love of value-free scientific rationalism, and the pragmatic demands of the marketplace.[6] Said another way, Charles Champlin, the section's former critic at large, is not equivalent to journalist/critics such as Eduardo Galeano, Salvador Novo, or Carlos Monsiváis. Champlin's role as critic is intimately tied to the conception of the review article as a form of consumer service (which movie to see, which play to attend) and as a critical extension of the art form being observed. This approach is object-oriented, ferociously populist, pragmatic, often enamored of empirical reasoning, and, as Alexis de Toqueville observed, deeply suspicious of intellectuals.[7]

In Latin America, the critic casts a different sort of net. This difference resides in the continent's political history, but also because its publishing industries were only recently yoked to capitalist market-driven rationality. For most of Latin America's history, the authoritarian state and the church played dominant roles in stifling critical journalism. Like the blind man who must refine his remaining senses to compensate for the loss of sight, Latin America produced a highly developed literary culture to compensate for its weak scientific and democratic institutions.[8]

This and other adaptations produced a Latin intellectual style that is more literary, discursive, overtly ideological, and interested in broader conceptions of social and cultural history. Works of art, literature, or ordinary news events become points of departure for philosophical or cultural meditations. Moreover, Monsiváis argues, the functions of the critical review, the factual news report, and the personal narrative were fused together into a literary-journalistic form he calls the *crónica*.[9] The best expressions of the *crónica*, Monsiváis adds, transform the act of bearing witness into substitutes for public opinion and open political criticism, or into attempts to sketch the contours of a nation that does not yet exist. The *cronistas* also held to the belief, whether inspired by nostalgia or unsentimental intuitive genius, that it was possible to express the thoughts of "the people."[10] These distinctions are a matter of degree. Monsiváis hears elements of the New Journalism echoed in the *crónica*. And like the modern magazine feature story, the *crónica* is more concerned with recreating a reality by literary means than simply conveying facts.[11]

These distinctions would be academic if it were not for the profound cultural, social, and political forces reshaping the world's postindustrial societies. The United States is no exception. It too has become the Diaspora of choice for Latin American, Asian, Near Eastern, and African immigrants. Unfortunately, the new ethnic pluralities in the nation's image-making cities, to cite one trend, appear to be overwhelming mainstream journalism's narrow descriptive focus. The *Miami Herald's* rush to accommodate a highly vocal, educated, and politicized Cuban community is one dramatic example of how rapid demographic change can undermine a "knowledge group's" intellectual authority. The unprecedented growth of *La Opinión*, which comes at a time when so many other newspapers are faltering, reveals similar forces at work in Los Angeles. Here, the rapidly expanding Latino and Asian communities represent a growing ozone hole of inner city and suburban media consumers escaping to more specialized, technologically sophisticated, and polyglot media, whether HBO Spanish-language simulcasting or Mandarin-language home videos. The *Times* has belatedly positioned itself to play this game. In 1988, it launched *Nuestro Tiempo*, a bilingual supplement inserted into the paper about fifteen times a year and distributed in neighborhoods with high Latino population densities. In Fall 1989, Times Mirror purchased fifty percent of *La Opinión's* stock, an investment estimated to be worth $40 million.

These recent overtures to the Latino market appeared to signal a

profound change in Times Mirror advertising and marketing strategies. Suddenly discarded was the former corporate dictum that said
no financial advantage could be had from publishing a Spanish-language edition of the *Times*.[12] A closer examination of these events suggests that they were neither as sudden nor as sweeping as they initially appeared, but merely the latest episode in a continuing debate over
the future direction of Times Mirror's editorial and corporate culture.
On one side of the issue are Times Mirror corporate managers who
believe they risk losing their traditional upscale advertisers and mid-
dle- and upper-class white suburban readers if they pursue the growing multiethnic, urban audiences too aggressively.[13] Countering this
cautiousness are a handful of editors and marketing analysts who
have accepted the fact that the Southland's growing Latino and Asian
communities represent the paper's next generation of readers.[14] In this
context, recent Times Mirror investments in *La Opinión* and *Nuestro
Tiempo* take on the features of a short-term compromise designed to
satisfy competing needs. The Latino market will be exploited, but
through a compartmentalized strategy that insulates the paper's
English-language readers and journalists from direct contact with the
region's other public languages and cultures.

But even this grudging recognition is more than the *Calendar* sections have conceded; they instead appear content to describe Southern
California's troubling and liberating cultural ambiguities with an outdated repertoire of story scenarios and clichés. With few exceptions,
Calendar's story agenda seems preoccupied with documenting the dismemberment and decline of once-dominant media and cultural institutions instead of the region's new *mestizaje*. How many more articles,
for example, do we need to read about the steady ratings ruptures of
CBS, ABC, or NBC; about Roseanne Barr's boorish manners,
Hollywood's pornography of money and egos, or art and music
reviews that could be written in New York or Boston? This intellectual
rut, this being at a loss for words, as it were, calls out for a new language of ideas with which to render the emergence of new audiences
and cultural forms, new conceptual tools with which to objectify this
emerging reality. The city as Post-Modern-Latino-Asian cultural com-
binatory represents, to my mind, the biggest story of this decade and
the next, one whose telling could be greatly enriched by an aggressive
Latino cultural perspective. *Calendar*, which has cast itself as the
Pacific Rim's arts and entertainment section, has tried to cover what is

ineptly labeled "multiculturalism," but its initial attempts have been flawed by a patronizing travelogue approach. A few editors and reporters in the *Calendar* section privately point to the section's coverage of the Los Angeles Festival during September 1990 as evidence of this failure. The reason, they claim, is that few full-time reviewers, except for some part-timers and a handful of "minority" staffers, bothered to prepare themselves to review the festival's myriad art forms and artists. Worse, few spoke the languages in which these works were presented. The only solution, one editor said, was to scramble to hire free-lancers and knowledgeable community members who might understand the aesthetics of the various art forms and artists featured in the festival.

But would hiring and promoting minorities to editor or critic be enough to "incorporate a minority sensibility" in *Calendar*'s decision-making? There are no easy answers. The battle—and that's what it is—over how to expand the paper's professional journalistic culture will be decided by larger cultural forces, the marketplace, and, as the following anecdote suggests, the subversions of individual journalists.

> "Who are we exactly? The offspring of the synthesis, or the victims of the fragmentation; the victims of a double colonialism (Europe and the United States), or the bearers of a new vision in gestation?"
>
> Guillermo Gómez-Peña, 1987[15]

More than a month before writing my *La Bamba* story, I started a project that would have to wait more than twenty months, or 130 stories later, to get into print. Its first incarnation took the form of an interpretive essay about Edward James Olmos's performance in a *Miami Vice* episode titled "Duty in Honor," which I completed on June 15, 1987. In the episode, Olmos's Lieutenant Martin Castillo acted opposite Dr. Hang Ngor (*The Killing Fields*), who plays Nguyen Van Tran, an undercover agent for North Vietnamese intelligence who has tracked down and killed a former CIA agent and the human killing machine he had unleashed years before in Vietnam.

The piece was the first close examination of the Asian threads Olmos had deliberately woven into his onscreen character, Castillo, and recognition of the way this episode represented a radical break with most post-*Platoon* depictions of the "enemy." Through Olmos's Castillo we appreciate the suffering the war inflicted on Ngor's character. Except for *The Killing Fields*, none of the new crop of Vietnam war movies had bothered to explore the Southeast Asian perspective of the Holocaust.

The point of the essay, however, was more ambitious. "It seems that Olmos has discovered a link between the extreme sense of formality, the magic and ritual life that permeates Indian Latin America, with distant points of resonance in Asia," I wrote then. My idea was simple: to open a creative door, to show how Latinos also participated in the dialogue of Pacific Rim cultures. But when I turned the piece in at least five days before the episode was scheduled to air, my recently promoted editor in *Daily Calendar* sat on the piece. The editor never really offered an explanation as to why the piece did not run until the publishing opportunity had passed. The editor said something about the essay's "lyrical" qualities and how it required major revisions.

When I asked the *Sunday Calendar* editor to read my story, I got a completely different response. He said he would have run the article without revisions had I given it to him in time. He then promised to run the piece if it were written as a feature profile instead of an interpretive essay. The issue, it appeared, was a question of conceptual packaging. Unfortunately, the same editor with which I'd struck a deal would end his tenure as *Sunday Calendar* editor before I got a fresh news hook to write the story.

My next shot at revising the story came in spring 1989, when David Kishiyama, then an assistant *Sunday Calendar* editor, asked me if I would like to contribute a story for a project he had launched dedicated to the "Arts and Culture on the Pacific Rim." I proposed the Olmos profile, which he enthusiastically accepted.

My first task was to momentarily deconstruct the actor's image as ethnic artist, as *Stand and Deliver* underdog and son of immigrants preaching the bootstrap gospel of hard work and self-responsibility. You see, Olmos had told me in the course of several interviews that he saw himself as a kind of prototypical Pacific Rim man who fuses Pachuco, Asian, and rock 'n' roll strains into a new hybrid of American culture. This isn't a new idea in Latin America. Since the beginning of the Manila trade in the sixteenth century, Mexican poets and intellectuals have envisioned their country as a halfway point and mediator between the European West and Asian East. In Olmos's case, his becoming a "fusion artist" had a lot to do with growing up in Boyle Heights. "In the late '40s and '50s," I'd later write, "his Russian, Jewish, Japanese, Italian, Chinese, and Mexican neighbors . . . were precursors of the ethnic diversity now commonplace throughout Los Angeles."

Valdez, like Kishiyama, could easily grasp what Olmos was intuitively aiming at: the barrio is not an insular cultural prison for all its residents. "In Eddie's case, I guess his uniqueness comes from the fact that he grew up in East L.A.," Valdez said months earlier at La Golondrina. "There's a lot of Asian-Chicano fusion, even though it's not acknowledged. But it should be. I think fusion is it, man. You can fuse Asian and Chicano and Latino qualities and come up with some very interesting abilities."

But the possibility that a Latino might choose to define himself as a member of a global community was not so apparent to the former editor who oversaw both *Calendar* sections. Two days after my story had been cleared by *Sunday Calendar* section editors, and five minutes before it cleared the composing room, Kishiyama walked up to my desk and uttered the words guaranteed to strike terror in a *Calendar* reporter's heart: "He said he doesn't understand your story." A comment such as this from an editor could, on almost any other occasion, mean a story was about to be killed or at least delayed. Anxiously, I awaited the next message to pulse across my VDT.

Holding back such a prominent, theme-setting story (it ran on page 6) would not only punish me, but Kishiyama's project as well. I don't think this editor could have justified meddling with this project so late in the game. Too many people had collaborated in it, too many people in the community and inside the paper were expecting it to run. Doing so would have been too transparent. But that doesn't mean that he could not try to undermine Kishiyama's confidence at a critical moment in his career, or forgo the pleasure of making me squirm.

Kishiyama's answer appeared several minutes later: "Go home. Your story is running Sunday." "The Fusion Man" ran March 19, 1989.

Notes

1. Octavio Paz, "At Table and in Bed," *Convergences: Essays in Art and Literature* (San Diego: Harcourt Brace Jovanovich, 1987), 74.

2. David Shaw, "What Makes the News? White Editors Make the Call," *Los Angeles Times* (December 13, 1990): A36.

3. Charles Derber, William A. Schwartz, and Yale Magrass, *Power in the Highest Degree: Professionals and the Rise of a New Mandarin Order* (New York: Oxford University Press, 1990), 12–14.

4. Ibid., 71–73, 95–97, and 119–21.

5. Ibid., 15.

6. Ibid., 33–35.

7. As quoted in Ibid., 69–70.

8. Octavio Paz, "Introduction" to *Taking to the Street* by Elena Poniatowska (New York: The Viking Press, 1975), xiii.

9. Carlos Monsiváis, *A ustedes le consta: Antología de la crónica de México* (Mexico City: Ediciones Era, 1980), 39–52.

10. Ibid., 48–52.

11. Ibid., 42–46.

12. Felix Gutiérrez and Clint C. Wilson, II, "The Demographic Dilemma," *Columbia Journalism Review* (January-February 1979): 53.

13. "A Latino Newspaper for Southern California, Stage 1: Data Search and Formal Briefing Addendum. Expanded Chapter 3: Summary of Executive Interviews," a study performed by Haug Associates, Inc., for the *Los Angeles Times*.

14. "Hispanics in Los Angeles: An Increasingly Important Market," a confidential study performed by the *Los Angeles Times* Marketing Research Department, March 1988.

15. Guillermo Gómez-Peña, in *La Línea Quebrada/The Broken Line* (a Border Arts Publication, San Diego-Tijuana) 1 (1987): 3.

Part Three
Manifestos and Testimonials

Ya Basta con Yankee Imperialist Documentaries! (1974)

Cine-Aztlán

Today cinema has become a major productive force in the world. Its function is more than economic. It manipulates the human psychology, sociology, religion, and morality of the people, in a word the ideological super-structure of modern capitalist society. Modern cinematic technology has become a powerful weapon in the struggle for social justice used by capitalists and socialists alike.

After seventy years of white-chauvinist cinema, the relationship between this industry and La Raza has changed very little. It has become clear that the reformist attempts undertaken in the sixties, which tried to open the door in Hollywood, New York, and other film centers, was futile. Cinema as a medium continues to close its lenses to the social and the political realities of La Raza. Now we are entering a class struggle against "yankee imperialism" and its puppet ruling oligarchies in America del Sur in which the film medium will play a crucial role.

We conclude this: under rotting inflationary capitalism, all workers, regardless of sex or race, now stand a greater chance of losing the jobs they presently hold. It is absurd to think there will be job opportunities for a struggling American nationality wishing to engage in cinema production. The present inflation has brought massive unemployment to the American cinema proletariat. It is twice as bad for La Raza, which suffers from racism and employment discrimination. We do not see any hopes of bettering the unemployment situation of La Raza in the cinema industry under the Ford-Rockefeller dictatorship or the present system.

If we seem too critical about how cinema works against the social, political, economic, and human wishes of all the American people, it is because after seventy years of bourgeois imperialist cinema, La Raza has had enough of the denigrating lies, slander, and racial characterizations that the bourgeois film barons have tried to embed in the minds of the rest of the world about us. We are now at a point in history where the exploited people of the Americas see how the white-chauvinist cinema industry plays a giant role in the forces aligned against our interest as a working class community. We must learn to control our own cinema, socialize its knowledge and technology, and use it as a weapon for educating the masses in the interest of all workers in the world who are in struggle and in revolution with us.

What Is Cinema? How Can It Help La Raza?

Cinema has become the strongest art form for social struggle in the world. It is the best suited for communication with the world masses and it has become the most popular means of communication in making direct revolutionary or reactionary appeals to the masses. It is no surprise that Lenin and the Bolsheviks after the Russian Revolution of 1917 believed that of all the arts, film was the most important for constructing a socialist society. Fifty-seven years after the October Revolution the Russians and Americans still contend for dominance in this art form. Cinema can help La Raza only if we gain control of its production.

What Is White-Chauvinist Film Imperialism?
How Has It Affected La Raza?

The film industry today encourages the impression that achievement and improvement of society can occur on the basis of the way things are. We challenge white-chauvinist cinema because it is operating against the interest of the masses, encouraging the notion that the middle-class status quo is good and that revolutionary change is bad. Cinema is not getting better under the ruling class, it is getting worse. Nostalgic trips such as *Bonnie and Clyde, The Godfather,* and *The Sting* show man exploiting, robbing, killing other individuals in order to stay in power. Bourgeois film imperialism is cinema produced for America Latina by the film barons in the United States and received gratefully by the puppet ruling class of America Latina. The same process is true for La Raza in the United States.

Imperialism robs the masses of their land and their means of production. In Aztlán we have been robbed of our land, and the right to control our own production. We are left without power to develop and determine our lives. America Latina is now struggling to win its independence from U.S. colonialist rule. If imperialism and colonialism are two faces of one coin keeping America Latina economically underdeveloped in its industries and its arts, then the same forces, here in Aztlán, are the root cause of La Raza's economic condition. In both cases, La Raza in Aztlán and the peoples of America Latina lack a medium of mass communication for 250 million people caught in the yoke of Yankee exploitation.

The puppet ruling class of America Latina sees itself through the eyes of gavacho film productions. In the United States the film industries have tried to integrate members of La Raza into their class-structured productions. They have succeeded to some extent, acquiring a few token brown faces who lack insight into the class and race struggle that *Los Movimientos de Liberación* are now waging.

White-chauvinist film imperialism is an effective weapon in preventing the masses from understanding the root of their problem and in retarding the development of any form of revolutionary consciousness that can overpower the bourgeois modes and centers of production. Their control is exerted through restriction of insurrectionary film production and by overloading the cinematic programming with police shows or middle-class soap operas. The bourgeois class has centralized the production machinery and appropriates the finished products for private gain. By owning the means of production in the cinema industry, the ruling class can reduce production, when conditions are unfavorable, and expand, when conditions are favorable, for greater profit.

Cinema is a creative art, but in the hands of the bourgeois it is a destructive weapon working against the proletariat of the world. It is a means to distort the truth, exploit cultures, and denigrate races and women. Under rotting capitalism, the film industry serves as the most potent machine to master the minds of millions, showing murderers, gangsters, racists, sexists, hypocritical missionaries and politicians as the heroes of "World Peace."

It becomes clear that the underdevelopment of La Raza in cinema is the result of a politically conscious act by those who rule. The capitalist class of America daily involves itself in a class war and race struggle with the world masses in order that we not learn the technology that will help us overthrow their domination.

Documentary Cinema: How Has It Affected the Chicano in Aztlán?

Documentary cinema is an informative and educational form of film production that can show the plight and the existence of the masses as they really are. There is great need for documentary cinema because the people hunger to become informed on the things, ideas, and events that are shaping the present world. But in a class society, only those who control have the power to interpret the situation of the masses. That is why capitalist documentaries will never trace the source of the problem and the injustices that the world masses experience under a system of exploitation and human oppression.

A film industry controlled by a small class of white capitalists will reflect the interest of the sponsors, which means that capital controls what the people see. Documentaries have become a basic propaganda tool for conveying "middle-class" ideas and norms, and the bourgeois automatically biases opinion against a society whose foundation doesn't rest on capitalism. The bourgeois news mediums, such as CBS, ABC, and NBC, are masters at trying to discredit socialist societies such as Cuba and, at one time, Chile.

The documentary monopoly by "private" white chauvinist corporations has not permitted full participation by the Chicano in the cinema industry. Neither have Chicanos acquired enough power to pressure these racist institutions into portraying an accurate image of America. The fact that Chicanos are never in the directing or producing positions, where policy is formulated, demonstrates this reality. There will never be enough Chicanos to protect our interest as a working class and fight for La Raza inside this industry. Instead, the film industry will continue to portray the Chicano and the Latino as stereotypes. The small private and film producing and distributing documentary centers thereby constitute another major source of racism and class oppression.

In four years of pre-viewing documentaries on La Raza, and studying the way documentary production centers operate and affect society, we have encountered the following experience:

(1) In the middle 1960s, the film industry attempted to respond to accusations of racism by a token integration of America's oppressed nationalities onto the screen. Behind this "humanitarian" concern the capitalist commercial motive of selling its products in the barrio was easily recognizable. Today Chicano filmmaking and distribution is still run by gavacho film agencies as just another money-making activity, not as a serious effort to portray the feelings, knowledge, and experiences of the Chicano and Latino in the United States. Although we were given token opportunity to be on the screen and use the cameras, we were left excluded from any control, from any substantial economic gain with which to develop a Chicano and Latino cinematic industry free of white-chauvinist rule. The large sums of money made from films dealing with Chicano subjects have gone to the gavacho film corporations instead of the Chicano and Latino communities to enable them to develop film training and educational media programs.

(2) There has never existed a great number of Raza skilled in documentary cinema and, under capitalism, there will never be enough to fulfill our needs. As the decade of the Sixties ended, the challenge to gavacho films began with the production of a few authentic Chicano documentaries that challenged the lies and distortions of Hollywood and other commercial film centers. Chicano cinema production was born in California with *I Am Joaquin* in 1968, a popular epic poem visualizing the historical development of the Chicano in still photographic montage. Later followed the famous *Requiem 29*, a documentary that dealt with the inhuman treatment of 35,000 Chicanos and the death of *L.A. Times* journalist Rubén Salazar at the Chicano National Moratorium in Los Angeles on August 29, 1970. Afterwards, *Yo Soy Chicano*, filmed by Jesús Treviño, portrayed through an interview format the different leaders of the Chicano Movement.

(3) How did the bourgeois class, which controls all of the institutions of the country, especially education, react to these Chicano films? Many school systems reacted negatively and began to ban them

from schools. This is typical. Chicano film documentaries have not
been able to penetrate public and private institutions.

(4) Chicano and Latino film-workers now are looking critically at
white-chauvinist media enterprises. The gigantic film corporations
always set limitations as to what one may film and see. Historically,
the film media show how the bourgeois controls cultural and ideological consciousness of communities. It is no great surprise that a large
number of our Chicano communities do not know how to speak
Spanish, or that La Raza has gained very few hours of televised programming for fifteen million Chicanos and Latinos in the United
States.

Mexican-Americanism in Filmmaking Is Neither the Answer Nor the Alternative

Mexican-Americanism in filmmaking is the white-supremacist, petty
bourgeois substitute for the Chicano in Aztlán. The ruling class tries to
integrate or buy off those Mexican-Americans with opportunistic tendencies and make them spokesmen for the oppressed. Hollywood,
New York, and other film centers are loaded with such Mexican-
Americans who help to extend stereotypes and class biases against La
Raza. Mexican-Americanism in filmmaking is aimed at combating and
preventing *El Movimiento de Liberación Chicano* from gaining media
control with which to communicate with the masses.

In the cinema industry the participation of La Raza legitimizes that
industry and serves as window dressing. The Mexican-American reinforces through stereotypes the idea that our community lacks initiative to create its own cinema. Mexican-Americanism identifies with
the bourgeois cinema industry contributing to a confusion over who
should control the means of production—the Chicano proletariat or
Hollywood film barons?

Mexican-American filmmaking is a political and social strategy
without effective economic power. It serves to cover up the monopoly
control of the medium by the film oligarchy. Mexican-Americanism
attempts to pacify dissatisfaction with current film productions. It pre-
vents the Chicano community from coming to grips with deciding for
itself how it wants to resolve the contradictions that exist between
Hollywood and La Raza.

Is fighting stereotypes in cinema and trying to acquire more jobs with the capitalist film industry the answer? Settling accounts with the film oligarchy on stereotypes and employment simply legitimizes their rule. The real task is for Chicanos to gain control of their own means of media production.

Cuban Film Documentaries Gave Us an Answer . . .

The relationship between the film barons of Hollywood and La Raza is that of oppressor and oppressed. The history of La Raza is one of white chauvinism, blatant racism, and exploitation. Cine-Aztlán recognizes that it is impossible to have an alternative by participating in an institutional structure in which film production is part of the capitalist mode of production. Mexican-American filmmaking is reform, i.e., getting into the institution to change it, while Chicano cinema is revolution, which sees no fundamental change as possible when the people have no power of control.

Recent Cuban documentaries have begun to have an effect on Chicano and Latino filmmakers. Films recently produced by Cubans are now recognized as critically important in the struggle against capitalist ideology. In Cuba, independent film productions mean independence from bourgeois national and international control and ideology. Documentary films in Cuba are instruments of decolonization, of a nation struggling to free itself.

The significance of Cuban Cinema is that it expresses the people's will to achieve the revolutionary goals of prosperity and the well-being of the community and state.

The objective of Cuban Cinema is to awaken individual consciousness by showing social, political, educational, historical, and economic misery and tracing its roots. Cinema in the hands of the proletariat is.5 REVOLUTION. In Cuba highly skilled technicians now dedicate their lives to construct a new man and woman, based on socialistic and humanistic principles.

Cuban Cinema gives a message to Chicanos and Latinos of the importance of cinema in revolutionary struggle. It asks us to join with the oppressed masses of Aztlán and America Latina in the struggle against Yankee Imperialism.

La Raza Filmmakers Have an International Responsibility

In this analysis we have been able to draw a small sketch of our history in cinema and what cinema has meant to us politically and socially; how cinema, when controlled by one race and one class, will oppress all other American nationalities and classes; how the liberal and the conservative filmmaker are only interested in making money, and use those who are exploited to do so; how Mexican-Americanism is the tendency for members of our Raza to be opportunistic for their own individual interest; and how Cuban Cinema has given us a better understanding of our situation in cinema in relation to liberation and self-determination. We conclude by asking, what should be our role as Chicano and Latino filmmakers?

To the Chicano and Latino filmmaker in the United States, the visual creation of La Raza should attempt to unify Raza interpretations with the total human circumstance in a class-structured society. Since the present film industry only exploits and does not promote the interests of our people, the struggle for Chicano and Latino cinema becomes revolutionary in that we must gain control of our means of production. It is our responsibility to acquire the cinematic tools that can bring the power of film to the service of those millions who are struggling to get out of their social and economic misery.

Chicano self-determination in cinema productions means seeking joint film projects, film presentations, and photographic displays with those who want to see us liberated. The unity of the arts shown by *Frente de Trabajadores de la Cultura de Nuestra América* represents the great hope for the American working class.

Chicano cinema production can become a free union of film workers working together. Chicano and Latino cinema is now developing a conscious productive and revolutionary spirit that will someday incorporate all workers in the world. To do cinema or display cinema works of other workers in struggle elsewhere in the world is an international honor and responsibility. History demands that Raza filmmakers unite with other workers in an international Marxist-Leninist cause.

An international, revolutionary cinema will be a decisive propaganda tool in the fight for socialism. In making common cause with other socialist cinema groups, we can help to bring together oppressed people throughout the world to fight the bourgeois, imperialist film barons and prevent further brainwashing of a new generation with their sexist, racist, and class-biased films. History has shown us that *unidos venceremos!*

Towards the Development of a Raza Cinema (1975)

Francisco X. Camplis

Chicano Films—La Raza Cinema

There is no Chicano film on the market today. There have been numerous Hollywood films and documentaries about Mexicanos and Mexican-Americans and virtually none has escaped stereotypes. This should come as no surprise. Thomas Martínez, in his essay, "Advertising and Racism: The Case of the Mexican-American," states that the symbolic function of advertising is one level of understanding the racist implications of the mass media, especially regarding the Mexicans and Mexican-Americans. Television commercials and magazine advertisements (and films) symbolically reaffirm the inferior social status of Mexicans and Mexican-Americans in the eyes of the audience.[1] However, it is not the purpose of this paper to examine the stereotyping of racial groups, or the extent and effectiveness of such racist practices by the media, especially the film industry, or to investigate the tragic results and irreparable damage done to masses of peoples such as the Asians, Chicanos, Indians, Blacks, and other people of color.

If one accepts the fact that the United States policies are imperialistic and racist in nature, then it can be more clearly understood that United States films are used as a weapon against those groups and peoples considered hostile to those policies or designated as targets by those policies. It can also be understood why the use of this weapon is tightly controlled through distribution, expensive equipment and high film stock costs, censorship, theater chains, racist employment practices, and racist unions.

It is for this reason that Fernando Solanas, Argentino filmmaker, *La Hora de los Hornos*, states that the camera must become a gun and the cinema must be a guerilla cinema. It follows that since Chicanos have been the targets of U.S. racist policies (any casual socio-historical study will affirm this) and since one of the manifestations is to maintain a racial superiority and control through the mass media, Chicanos and other racial groups remain invisible to white America and invisibility means you don't exist, which is another way of saying we don't have to deal with you. Such invisibility reflects powerlessness to fight against white America's formidable array of resources used to oppress; invisibility reflects a neo-colonialist reality. A Chicano or Raza cinema must by necessity be a weapon! It cannot be anything less.

What is the difference between Chicano or Raza? Rodolfo Acuña, in his book *Occupied America*, makes the following distinction: in his book dealing with the twentieth century and the changing situation in the United States, "Chicano" is used to distinguish Mexicanos living north of the border from those residing in Mexico. He elaborates a little further by stating that "some U.S. citizens of Mexican extraction might object to the identification of 'Chicano' for many call themselves simply Mexicanos or Mexicans."[2] Moreover, a minority refer to themselves as Spanish-Americans or Latin Americans. The label Mexican-American, following the hyphenization tradition of other ethnic groups and whose use was promoted by Anglo-Americans, has been questioned recently and is not universally accepted. At first some just dropped the hyphen while others sought to identify themselves with a name of their own choice, "Chicano." Acuña goes on to state that "American" is the identification that Europeans gave to two continents. When the name was later appropriated by the thirteen colonies, the designation "American" was deemed the exclusive province of the new nation, and United States citizens considered themselves the "Americans." Chicanos, as well as other peoples, however, refute this exclusivity and correctly maintain that all inhabitants on both north and south continents are Americans and that the whole hemisphere is indeed America. Thus in referring to people of the United States, I have used the term Anglo-American to underline this distinction. Chicanos like their brothers the Native Americans are native peoples. Hyphenation then is exclusively reserved to reflect the transplanted status of Europeans and other nationalities, e.g., Swiss-American, Italian-American, Irish-American, German-American, et al.

"Chicano" represents the need for people of Mexican descent to come to grips with the elemental fact of their identity; this problem has by no means been resolved. For many Chicanos the term has certain political, philosophical, and ideological implications. Generally speaking, the term "chicanismo" has the connotation of struggling towards liberation and a certain level of consciousness or awareness in Mexicanos. Although "chicanismo" is not limited to Mexicanos because it is synonymous with "Carnalismo" (literally love for your brother), the term is not immediately accepted by others, i.e., Puerto Ricans, Latin Americans and Mexicans (in Mexico), Native Americans. The term "Raza" on the other hand does apply to peoples of the Americas and Caribbean sharing the Indio-Hispano experiences, culture, language, history, and in a more political sense sharing the effects of oppression and colonialism. "Raza" is a more embracing term and suitable to the experiences of Native Americans and people of Mexican and Latin American descent who find themselves in this country. "Raza," in my opinion, has an international connotation as well as the philosophical and ideological implications. Therefore, "Raza Cinema" could conceivably include in addition to Chicanos, Puerto Ricans, Native Americans, and Latinos, Cuban filmmakers residing in the United States who are in agreement with the struggle for liberation of Raza politically, philosophically, and aesthetically. Raza Cinema could also reach out internationally and form linkages with other Mexicanos and Latin Americanos and other Third World oppressed peoples struggling for liberation; Chicano theatre and poetry have an international perspective.

Latin American Militant Cinema

In my opinion, Latin American militant cinema takes on several forms: Latin American cinema is conditioned by circumstances prevailing in each country that are not extensive to other countries. There exists a different set of circumstances reflecting a distinct socio-economic-political reality for Cuba, for example, which is distinctly different from that of Chile. Octavio Getino, Argentino filmmaker, writes about the brutal restriction of democratic liberties, the termination of the so-called university autonomy, the constant threats of intervention in union organizations, the cinematographical repression law, etc., all of which prevent the dissemination of militant cinema not only in conventional places but in the layers centered around the students, union, urban, and other organizations. This impossibility of reaching such layers determines the character that the militant cinema attempts to approach.[3] It is an understatement to say that it is very difficult and dangerous to develop militant cinema in repressive countries such as Brazil, Chile, Bolivia, Mexico, etc. It is also difficult to make militant cinema in Puerto Rico and in the United States. But nevertheless, Latin American militant films are coming out of such countries.

What is Latin American militant cinema? In order to answer this question it is necessary to discuss briefly the development of early filmmaking in Latin America. In the late twenties virtually all of the films made for Latin American consumption were produced in Hollywood. Several films were made in Argentina and Spain and a few in Mexico. Mexican actors and actresses such as Ramon Novarro, Dolores Del Rio, Lupe Tovar, and Spanish actors had gone to Hollywood to work for Fox, Columbia, Universal, and Paramount studios. The more important Hollywood movies bearing important directors or stars were transformed into *películas hispanas* class B and used as fillers or double programs. The birth of sound in 1930 also signaled the beginning of the Cine Sonora Mexicana, Mexican Sound Film Industry. By 1931, Hollywood no longer was in the business of mass producing *hispana* movies (thirty were made that year). For many years, until recently, Mexico provided Latin American audiences with Spanish-speaking films. Argentina and Spain, as well as other countries, continued to develop their film industries. It is interesting to note that the silent films made in Hollywood were not as popular as one might imagine because a great number of the Latin American audience were illiterate. Hence, the significance of the sound films can be appreciated.[4] Many technicians, Hollywood trained, and actors returned to Mexico to become major directors, writers, producers, and actors. Hollywood's influence did not diminish in Latin America, as can readily be seen by the content of the media in many countries. Through joint ventures, intermarriage, loans or credit through corporations and banks, control over international distribution, the Hollywood film industry and other American interests continue to exert a strong influence over the media in Latin America.

In their article "Toward a Third Cinema,"[5] Fernando Solanas and Octavio Getino wrote:

> Just a short time ago it would have seemed like a Quixotic adventure in the colonialized, neo-colonialized, or even the imperialist nations themselves to make any attempt to create *films of decolonization* that turned their back on or actively opposed the System. Until recently, film had been synonymous with show or amusement: in a word, it was one more *consumer good*. At best, films succeeded in bearing witness to the decay of bourgeois values and testifying to social injustice. As a rule, films only dealt with effect, never cause; it was cinema of mystification or anti-historicism. It was *surplus value* cinema. Caught up in these conditions, films, the most valuable tool of communication of our times, were destined to satisfy only the ideological and economic interests of the *owners of the film industry*, the lords of the world film market, the great majority of whom were from the United States.
>
> How could the problems of turning out liberation films be approached when costs came to several thousand dollars and the distribution and exhibition channels were in the hands of the enemy? How could System-imposed repression and censorship be vanquished? These questions, which could be multiplied in all directions, led and still lead many people to skepticism and rationalization: "revolutionary films have been possible only in the liberated countries"; "without the support of revolutionary political power, revolutionary art or film is impossible." The mistake was due to taking the same approach to reality and films as did the bourgeoisie. The models of production, distribution, and exhibition continued to be *those of Hollywood* precisely because, in ideology and politics, films had not become the vehicle for a clearly drawn differentiation between bourgeois ideology and politics. A reformist policy, as manifested in dialogue with the adversary, in coexistence, and in the relegation of national contradictions to these between two supposedly unique blocs—USSR and USA—was and is unable to produce anything but a cinema within the system itself. At best it can be the *"progressive" wing of Establishment cinema*. When all is said and done, such cinema was doomed to wait until the world conflict was resolved peacefully in favor of socialism in order to change qualitatively. The most daring attempts of those filmmakers who strove to conquer the fortress of official cinema ended, as Jean Luc Godard eloquently put it, with the filmmakers themselves "trapped within the fortress."[6]

For Solanas and Getino, the revolution does not begin with the taking of political power from imperialism and the bourgeoisie, but rather begins at the moment when the masses sense the need for change and their intellectual vanguards begin to study and carry out this change through activities on different fronts. "There exist *our* culture and *their* culture, *our* cinema and *their* cinema. Because our culture is an impulse towards emancipation, it will remain in existence until emancipation is a reality: *a culture of subversion* which will carry with it an art, a science and *a cinema of subversion*." (Truth amounts to subversion.)

They further state that "we must develop a culture by and for us. The anti-imperialist struggle of the peoples of the Third World and of their equivalents (Chicanos and others) inside the imperialist countries constitutes today the axis of the world revolution. *Third Cinema* is, in our opinion, the cinema that *recognizes in that struggle the most gigantic cultural, scientific and artistic manifestation of our time*, the great possibility of constructing a liberated personality with each person as the starting point—in a word, the decolonization of culture."[7]

Finally, Solanas and Getino state:

> The man of the *third cinema*, be it *guerilla cinema* or a *film act*, with the infinite categories that they contain (film letter, film poem, film essay, film pamphlet, film report, etc.), above all counters the film industry of a cinema of characters with one of themes, that of individuals with that of masses, that of the author with that of the operative group, one of neocolonial misinformation with one of information, one of escape with one that recaptures the truth, that of passivity with that of aggressions. To an institutionalized cinema, he counterposes a guerilla cinema; to movies as shows, he opposes a film act or action; to a cinema of destruction, one that is both destructive and constructive; to a cinema made for the old kind of human being, for them he opposes a *cinema fit for a new kind of human being, for what each one of us has the possibility of becoming*. . . .
>
> If we choose films as the center of our propositions and debate [and not some other form of artistic communication], it is because that is our work front and because the birth of a *third cinema* means, at least for us, *the most important revolutionary artistic event of our times*.[8]

The urgency and immediacy of revolutionary cinema is sounded by another filmmaker. In his article "Cinema and Revolution," Jorge Sanjines, filmmaker (*El Chacal de Naheltoro*), wrote:

> Never has it been as important to our countries to fight confusion, never has it been so urgent to say things clearly, because never has time for acting or perishing been so short. From this urgent and vital necessity comes forth a new cinema in the third world. Revolutionary cinema which by definition proposes to create a consciousness for liberation. The most important, most vital task, because it is a matter of

surviving not merely as peoples, but as cultural beings, as non-depersonalized human groups. This struggle proposes not just to illustrate misery . . . because that is of no interest to the peoples who know it well and suffer it in their daily lives, but to denounce their structures of exploitations and power which cause this misery. This denunciation which must single out the guilty ones, explain the mechanisms involved, and identify the enemy . . . will find a new audience eager to know the truth. The exposure of truth is the most revolutionary cultural action. Ayme has said: "The most important cultural act is revolution." Obviously, there is identity because revolution is truth.

The danger which threatens those dispossessed of land is not only death by inanition, but death of their identity, and it is preferable to disappear physically than to extinguish culturally, spiritually. Therefore, the struggle for liberation is a struggle not only for liberty, but also one that seeks to find and assert the existence of these oppressed peoples. It proposes to fight the different forms of alienation and to seek the definition of its very cultural values.

Sanjines continues that

to create a consciousness for liberation involves the struggle against enemies of the people; against several aspects of an effort to deform it; aspects that assemble to corrupt the popular mind and to exploit it; nevertheless, all of them as a whole, the national sepoys and the foreign consortia, obey the common enemy; they have the same origin: imperialism. Given the power, experience, shrewdness and covetousness of this enemy, one must conclude that there is no time, neither for idle pursuits of estheticism, nor for personal realization. There remains only the necessary time to be responsible and consistent. We must free ourselves of many intellectual prejudices and face reality and history with more humility because what matters today is not the creator or the work, as isolated results. These are only important in relation to their usefulness, to the cause of liberation.

The revolutionary cinema is therefore a cinema at war against imperialism. This kind of filmmaking excludes profit, star complex, competition. Those who work for profit, feed their star complex, or promote competition are enemies. Communication with the people is the objective of this cinema and this struggle. To attain that communication, it must reject all outlines and formulas of commercial and alienated cinema which because of its structure of concessions encourages escape and deforms the public mentality. Therefore, this cinema which, contrary to the commercial one, proposes to tell the truth, must search for another language capable of recovering the spectator while following in the process his inner rhythms as well as the mental structures and cultural characteristics of each people.

Sanjines concludes that

> the work of revolutionary cinema must not limit itself to denouncing
> or to the appeal for reflection. It must be a summons for *action*. It must
> appeal to our people's capacity for tears and anger, enthusiasm and
> faith. We must participate in the effort to remove them from the slum-
> ber and confusion to which oppression and misery have submitted
> them. We must contribute to shaking away the apathy which pseudo
> revolutions' failure and frustration have sown in popular conscious-
> ness.
>   If we consider the capacity to drive ahead and to promote, which
> this cinema can have, we can say that revolutionary cinema does not
> tell "stories." It is a cinema that *makes history*. It makes history not only
> because it rebuilds it, deepens it, and expresses it, but because it par-
> ticipates in the historical phenomenon, at the same time it influences
> it.[9]

Notes on Raza Cinema

Chicano *teatro*, poetry, and art appear to be more developed forms of
Chicano cultural expression. Chicano literature and film are just getting off the ground. Film perhaps is the least developed of the two,
primarily because it is an expensive medium. This lag presents a serious problem to Raza filmmakers. The difficulty lies in the fact that
there is little in the way of Chicano literature, historical documentation, and written material with which the filmmaker can do creative
research and base his films upon. As we have seen earlier there is only
a handful of novels and not very many published short stories.
Although Chicanos are writing more and writing better, the situation
is not entirely encouraging since, currently, there is less publishing
activity and fewer publications available to Raza. However, a probable result will be that more quality Raza written material will be
selected for publication.

     But Chicanos involved in *teatro* experienced the same problem.
There were virtually no contemporary Chicano plays and literature in
libraries so they began by writing their own plays and *actos* at the
same time they were organizing *teatros*. They also learned the rudi-
ments of stage, direction, acting, and theory: *al estilo Chicano*.

     Earlier, I stated that there are very few, if any, Raza-Chicano full-
length feature films (for those who do not recall the distinction: every
Chicano is Raza but not every Raza is Chicano) that have been made

available for theater distribution. *Salt of the Earth,* which was blacklisted during the McCarthy hearings of "subversives," has been barred from regular theater distribution and has not been shown on television. For all purposes, this early "Chicano" film has not been seen beyond student, youth, and young adult groups. There remains a much larger Chicano audience who frequents local theaters and Spanish-speaking theaters and whose daily fare is television and radio. *Los Desarraigados* with Pedro Armendáriz, actor, was a good Mexican film about Chicanos. Another Mexican film portraying Chicanos featured a comedian, El Piporro; it was not a very good film and included many stereotypes. What this indicates is that for mostly political reasons Mexican and Hollywood films have been unwilling to portray the Chicano experience except through distortion, deception, or stereotype.

Since there is not very much literature and virtually no films of relevance to serve as models, the Raza filmmaker is left to his own experiences or to seek in a more direct way the *barrio* experiences. He must get them firsthand—this may be an advantage. But in another sense, there is less opportunity to interpret the written collection of someone else's experiences. Some may feel disappointment for the lack of opportunity to engage in intellectual exercise. But there is also excitement and intellectual challenge in the raw material of the *barrio.*

In connection with Chicano *teatro,* I think we will see some distinct differences between it and films. In retrospect, Teatro Campesino identified itself very early with the principle of nonviolence as advocated by César Chávez. Of course, this was due to its close relationship with UFWOC. There will be little disagreement that the development of *teatros* would not have been possible without the work, inspiration, and influence of Teatro Campesino. Because Teatro embraced the principle of nonviolence in much of its work, most if not all the *teatros* similarly have not pursued the theme of "violence," no matter how justified, in redressing the oppression of Raza.

Juxtapose the psychological assault upon the public from the "violence" in themes of television and films and the physical assault of violence from the prisons, the *barrio,* the ghetto, from police; this is our daily reality and we understand the theme of "violence" as more than simply "good" triumphing over "evil." Rather, it means the inevitable triumph of the system, the reinforcement of the notion that in terms of "violence," violence means power and that awesome power remains clearly and unmistakably on the side of the establishment, of "law and order"—*eso es el mensaje*, that is the "image reality"; it is reality. I am not questioning whether the strategy of either violence or nonviolence is a viable one, rather, I am in agreement with those that feel that oppressed peoples must have available to them as many options as possible in determining their strategies for defense and struggle. The poets, for example, and the artists have not limited themselves to a specific ideology or approach. I think it is less an example of the individualism and nonconformity of the artists and poets and instead an example of the high level of organization of the *teatros*.

Some of the Latin American artists, notably Glauber Rocha, caution: "We should resist against systematizing of political thinking because we are on one hand colonized by the culture of 'mass cultures' and on the other hand, colonized by the European left."[10] I feel it is important that our expression be unfettered. I find little inconsistency, generally speaking, between the purposes of films of Raza and those of Third World filmmakers who say we must make:

1. a decolonizing cinema; a film of disruption.

    - Our films must decolonize in a different way. We are Raza living in "occupied Aztlán" and suffering all the effects of occupation. Our films must be provocative.

2. a cinema of class: chooses its public and not one of cultural coexistence with a generalized public.

    - Our audience is Raza. I make films for Raza because I am Raza.

3. cinema of liberation, historic cinema of political and ideological themes.

    - A film of argument.
    - Raza films to liberate. Trenchant in its analysis and blunt in its message. A film of arousal, of substantial information; *una espina y un machete*: film as weapon. Film as self-defense.

4. cinema of profound analysis.

5. cinema which is violent, intense, expressive, using research, language and expression, a guerilla film.

    - Raza films must be film action. Raza films should try to develop film praxis. Our films should be experimental, beautiful, and should explore and discover our own sense of aesthetics. Our own language.

6. a film of and for the masses.

- Film for the masses makes sense only in the context of connecting our struggle with oppressed peoples of the total continent.

I think it is appropriate for Latin American Third Filmmakers to speak about making and directing their films to the masses. It is also consistent to speak about using their films to stoke the revolution, to speak about "revolutionary" cinema. I submit, our reality is markedly different than theirs. A revolutionary potential exists in Latin America precisely because of the masses. Only a small percentage of the population represents the total upper and middle classes; the masses are the majority in numbers. In the United States oppressed peoples represent a significant minority population any way you look at it. Therefore, "revolution" and "masses" have to have another meaning for Raza. "Revolution" in the United States means suicide, and for a basic reason. In a racist country, people of color who will be the potential revolutionaries are identifiable and can be easily dealt with. We need go no further than this country's record: Hiroshima, Japanese concentration camps, My Lai, Attica, etc. Raza filmmakers should see the struggle and revolution differently. Our contribution should be to the revolution that most certainly will take place in Latin America. Our films should prepare Raza for that eventuality. For that reason our films should strive to connect our struggle internationally, by educating and informing in an international context. Raza films will reflect and transmit our efforts to build a strategy for struggle, a plan for liberation: "revolutionary action" that is in contact with the revolution of oppressed people everywhere.

I think it is helpful to note some of the problems of the Third Filmmaker:

1. *Ideology:* How can the filmmaker realize radical, revolutionary, and political content in films?

2. *Form:* How can the filmmaker communicate such content to a normally passive audience; to an audience of a different ideology? Is the answer direct didacticism? New, consciousness-expanding forms?

3. *Praxis:* How to transpose communication into action? Can it be done through film?

4. *Aesthetics and Politics:* What of the conflict between filmmaker as artist and political activist? How to redefine art to resolve tension? How to politicize art?

The Raza filmmaker will have to consider and come to some conclusions regarding these problems. This can best be done through dialogue, discussions, and more communication between filmmakers and others having something to contribute. However, I have a few words of comment. In terms of form and content, I believe the Raza audience is capable of handling different forms, our form should not be merely simple, not basic, but also exploratory. We should test different forms, and combinations: didactic, documentary, symbolic, dramatic, *novelas,* serials, etc. The conflict between the artist and political activist is a particularly difficult one. Once the difference becomes ideological the artist finds it increasingly harder to resolve. It is difficult indeed for the artist to reconcile aesthetic sensibilities with political necessities. The Mexican muralists to a large degree were able to do this. For Raza, they continue to be our models.

Because many of us are at a beginning level of the filmmaking experience I feel that it is necessary to study all films in order to arrive at the best approach in composing a Raza film. I must be familiar with the cinematic language of Eisenstein, Griffith, Rosellini, Fellini, Bergman, Truffaut, Godard, Hawks, Coppola, Buñuel, and Alvarez before I can develop and use a language of my own intelligently. However, I am aware that for Raza, Europe and Hollywood represent alien models to our culture. The films of Solas, Alvarez, Sanjines, and other Third filmmakers are more closely in tune with our reality and have more to offer us. While Rocha warns that Hollywood is dangerous for us but so is Sartre, I feel that our search for ideas and models that will help us develop our own Raza cinema does not end with Rocha, Sanjines, et al. But their inspiration and motivation has given us a certain sense of direction.

Teatro is both verbal and nonverbal. Perhaps it is more verbal because of the agit-prop form, its emphasis on music and didacticism. Although less symbolic, visual, nonverbal communication may take place through staging, dance, decor, costumes, lighting, slides, and other visuals. Also, some of the *teatros* are basically communes. A good practice is their attempt to engage the audience in discussion following their performances. This is consistent with their basic purpose to educate La Raza.

Incidentally, perhaps even less developed in terms of a Raza consciousness are our musicians and dancers. For example, many communities have some kind of *baile folklórico* group organized to dance at community *fiestas* and events, but there is virtually no contemporary Raza dance group. An exception is a modern dance group of nonprofessional Raza dancers meeting regularly to explore Raza themes, *música*, and *bailes folklóricos* through the technique of modern dance. The group, Chilam Balam, located in San Francisco, was led by Mrs. Berta Barajas. There is another San Francisco dance group, Las Cucarachas, led by Sonia Ramirez, which, while not necessarily using modern dance, does attempt to use dance form in a Raza context. There may be a handful of other dance groups located on campuses throughout the Southwest. Although *teatros* have encouraged *música* and dance in their *actos*, it is curious that modern dance groups have not been organized through them.

Literature, on the other hand, is more individualistic and nonconformist, much like the artists. For several reasons, a common purpose has not resulted for *literatura* as *los teatros*. Similarly, few painters, for example, have committed themselves collectively to a common purpose or cause although there has been ample discussion by them. Their works were not tied to specific manifestos, for example, but individually painters may or may not see their works as having political content or direction towards *la causa*; they see a universality in their paintings. On the other hand, a loose form of Raza *colectivas* reflecting political purpose and concern can be seen in the many Raza art groups, i.e., mural teams, silkscreen workshops, *galerias, talleres,* graphic art centers, etc. Raza artists are concerned with the experiences and struggles of Raza. Much of their art is objective art but there are several artists who use symbolism and are interested in nonobjective art. There is much that is verbal in our art because of the murals, political messages, silkscreen posters, paintings, and other works; even titles of the works and exhibit space are used creatively by the artists in order to extend the statement by using every possible space. Also, many artists work closely with the poets, utilizing their poetry in their works.

Many artists feel that their work is for and of the *barrio*. Murals almost exclusively painted in the *barrios* receive immediate feedback upon completion in the form of graffiti as embellishment or indicating disapproval. Also, many artists continue to exhibit in the *barrio* and speak to the people about their artwork—yet they know they run the risk that their work may be stolen or damaged because of lack of security. But they continue to take their chances and continue to exhibit in the community.

Raza cinema should also reflect a collective spirit. We are in a good position, since we are starting to develop our own form, to engage the audience by discussing our films with them after showings. We should be self-critical and prepare ourselves for the pain of criticism; welcome candidness by rejecting the superfluous, the irrelevant. Tune out glib, pretentious *gabacho* critics in order to hear more clearly constructive criticism of substance from Raza as well as non-Raza. We must try to use Raza in our camera crews, casting, in all facets of production where possible. We must consider using *gabachos* only where all other possibilities have been exhausted. Raza films with Anglo surnames (non-Raza) must give way to Raza films crediting Raza personnel. We need to be exposed to new equipment, to new ideas and techniques; we must train Raza and share resources with each other. Development of Raza is inherent in the development of our cinema. Therefore, films about Raza by non-Chicanos are not acceptable in our community. For example, a recent hour-length film on Mexican Americans was made by a Black. Similar to earlier examples of efforts by non-Raza, this film was professionally well made, with Anthony Quinn as the narrator. Beyond its professionalism the film offered little more than an exploration of the problem of job discrimination and unemployment. William Greaves, the Black filmmaker, is well qualified to make the definitive film on Blacks, but, in my opinion, he is not amply qualified to make Raza films. It is a fact that Blacks are more involved in television and films and although some may question the quality of that involvement, Black penetration into mass media remains a fact. Exploitation by Anglos and other non-Razas is still exploitation. What makes this a matter of serious concern is the fact that due to the exclusion of Chicanos from the making of films, documentaries, educational films, Hollywood, television, TV commercials, industrial films, college and high school films, etc.—few Raza make films. It is essential that this change. And as more of us make films, it is important that we do so on our own terms. We are not alone regarding this concern. Walter Achugar, filmmaker of Uruguay, states, "we want to create a national cinema, reflecting the country's reality and helping to transform it. We want to make militant Uruguayan films, with Uruguayans on the screen, by Uruguayans behind the camera, for Uruguayans of the third world audience. We want to participate at last in the creation of a culture at the service of Latin American liberation. We have the people, ideas, organizations, and energy—we lack only money."[11]

Joint ventures should be sought very carefully. It is very important that Raza filmmakers do not lose control of their films—we must not be used or become *vendidos*. Joint productions are encouraged where possible and on equal terms with allying groups, for example, our *carnales, los Indios, y los Boricuas*.

Most films by Raza have been documentaries. The documentary form is still a very effective means of educating and reconstructing fact, truth, and history. However, new approaches should be explored, such as drama, musicals, satire, comedies, animation. What is Raza cinema? How is it different from other films we have seen?

I agree that it is not enough to say that our films should be merely for or about Raza. Rather, like our art, like our *teatro*, Raza cinema is a serious attempt to find our own unique idiom, to make films that reflect our own themes and experience, our unique point of view. We have three levels to work with: the visual, musical, and verbal. For example, our music may combine contemporary classic with folkloric; music variations might include jazz, *guajira*, rock, classical, *bolero*, *sones, rancheras, norteños*, Afro-Cubano, Indio, *rituales, guapangos, danzones*, Latin-Rock, country western. Our dialogue would not be limited to Spanish and English but a Chicano audience would understand "caló." Further, Indian languages of our forefathers conceivably could be used, such as Nahuatl. Above all, Raza must speak: we have much to say and it must be heard.

Therefore, Raza films will visually and aurally talk of a lot of things. We must talk of Mexico, of Latin America, of the Third World, of corporations, of the United States, neo-colonialism, imperialism, oppression, liberation, revolution, *guerillistas*, universality, life and death, racism, anger, hatred, the material and the spiritual, of regaining our spiritual roots, we must talk of our Indian roots and our European roots, our Asian roots, our Black roots, colonial experiences, *los mitos,* of boundaries, our ties to the land, *Pochismo, carnalismo, cannibalismo,* pain, *amor, unidad,* ancient religion, Catholic religion, conquests, resistance, civil wars, slavery, Marxism, anarchy, heroin, peyote, democracy, hypocracy, the pyramids, duality, the triangle, *la Raza Cósmica,* Toltecas, Mayas, Olmecas, Aztecas, Tlatelolco, Cuba, Chile, Mexicas, Hopi, Yaquis, Navajos, Apaches. But Hollywood and European films have dealt and continue to deal with many of these themes. In terms of the necessity to reveal a different set of facts, a different perspective that has been lacking for too long, different sensibilities, our experiences and our truths as reflected in our films will be substantially and qualitatively distinct. Ours will be films of conflict. Conflict of struggle, of life. Orozco, like Eisenstein in his montage, urged conflict in art. We can relate the pre-Columbian theme of duality to dialectics—conflict. Hollywood films, for example, are more concerned with image reality than reality itself, whereas for us, the reverse is true. Hollywood transmits a specific international point of view, a specific ideology: U.S. Capitalism. In depicting the image reality of war, political and social struggle, who speaks for the victim? And who best speaks for the victim, if not the victim? At last we are the actors, we can create our own ideology, we can create and assert our own cinema and break away from "their cinema." Yet, our struggles, hopes, and dreams are universal because we are human beings. No longer invisible, our presence will not be denied us. Santiago Alvarez, Cuban filmmaker, stated that the qualifications of a filmmaker must be a passion for your work and a great universal political culture. He says that he will never make a film without political content because the enemy constantly uses politics, aggressive politics. This is a world of constant struggle, combat, war, and to make a film without political content would be alien to this world.[12] If our films are decolonizing films, they will be political. Film act means political. For example, Europe and Hollywood have promoted and exalted the "güera" in Latin America. Our films must emphasize and reestablish the intelligence, beauty, naturalness, of the *Indígeno, la morena, los prietos.*

There is also Godard's view of society. "He [Godard] is speaking in general of the problems of life. He is not giving us a recipe for a better life; this is not his job, but he is enriching our understanding of it. Like many artists, he is a reformer. It is up to us to decide how practical his reforms are."[13] Raza cinema must go beyond Godard. Our films will not merely dust off the cobwebs from moldy relics of our pre-Columbian past but provide a viable connection from the past to the present and beyond into the future. We should ask: How will films help us to relate our political and cultural existence to the science, religion, mythology of our *antepasados*? How do we use the history, the legacy, the mysteries, the beauty, the profundity of the Aztecs, Mexicas, Toltecs, Mayas that form our culture to improve our lives, to plan our struggle, to become better human beings, to reestablish ties with *carnales, los Indios*?

> "The Man Say We Making Noise . . . *hacer ruido*
> *vidrios rotos lumbres calles gasoline. . . . .*"
> —Alurista

Chicano Films

The following are brief comments on a few Chicano films.

Yo Soy Chicano—a film by Jesús Treviño, 1972. The film is important for several reasons. It is a good documentary, it attempts a historical survey of early Chicanos, and it profiles contemporary Chicano leadership. It also attempts to dramatize historical events and personalities. The film profiled such early Chicanos as Ricardo Flores Magón, early architect of the Mexican Revolution held as a prisoner in U.S. federal prison, and Juan Nepomuceno Cortina, who waged war against the Texas Rangers. It humorously described the Pachuco and his zoot suit. It profiled the Vice President of the United Farmworkers Organization, Dolores Huerta; Reies Tijerina, political federal prisoner, land-grants issue, in New Mexico; Corky Gonzales, militant leader in Denver; and José Angel Gutiérrez, founder of La Raza Unida Party. The film, made for television viewing, was professionally well made and gave a polished historical overview of the Chicano. However, it seemed to stay within the margin of what is politically acceptable to television concerning sociopolitical problems; it lacked in urgency and anger.

Untitled—a film by José Camacho, Stanford University. A short color film on the theme of drugs. Although a student film, it was technically above average. Good use of drama. Violence in ending suggested one solution to problem of drugs.

I Am Joaquin—a film by Luis Valdez, 1970. This film's impact over the years has not diminished. It continues to express the Chicano's anger, spirit, and hope. Its use of still color photography for the sake of economy is imaginatively done. The film is important because it is the first Chicano film. Its concern is identity, its theme is struggle, its perspective is historical, its message is *organizense* Raza. I was disappointed that it wasn't a total Raza production.

Other films recommended for viewing (although I have not personally screened all of them) are: a film on Raza and Vietnam by San Francisco filmmaker Ray Rivera; *Requiem 29,* David Garcia, about the East Los Angeles riots of 1969 in which Rubén Salazar was murdered; a film by Ralph Maradiaga (San Francisco), a dramatized documentary about the first woman executed by hanging in California, a Chicana; a film on prisons and Chicanos, by Ricardo Soto, Stanford University.

Summary

This paper does not pretend to be a definitive analysis. Rather, I attempted to highlight for the reader and examine some of the background, ideas, and ingredients necessary for discussion:

1. We have the capacity to invent our own Cinematic expression. Like other Third World Filmmakers we are beginning to develop our Cinema and although we lack financial resources and control over distribution we will continue to make films because of the need for our films.

2. Form and content will be distinctively Raza. We have much in common with Third filmmakers, but also many differences. We also have much in common with Blacks, but our experiences and approach will be different.

3. Raza cinema reflects our *teatro* and *arte*. Development of cinema is taking place at the same time other related forms of expression are developing and contributing resources to each other. The filmmaker can join his talent with those of the poets, artists, writers, dancers, musicians, et al.

4. We are well aware that we are Chicanos and Raza living in an Anglo society; we are constantly reminded of this fact. Some filmmakers have tried to use the didactic approach and the documentary. We are ready to try new approaches, drama, anima-

tion, and experimental films. Our films must say Listen! when we speak.

5. Raza cinema means films of conflict. It must reflect struggle; offer new ideas; contribute to *la raza nueva; la vida nueva.*

6. Raza filmmakers are ready for a new type of film: FILM ACT. A new type of VISION: *VISION COSMICA.* A new language expressing and asserting our humanity. *Somos Vida. Somos Amor. Somos Libre. Somos Raza. SOMOS RAZA.*

Notes

1. Thomas Martínez, "Advertising and Racism: The Case of the Mexican-American," *Voices* (Berkeley: Quinto Sol Publications, 1971), 49.

2. Rodolfo Acuña, *Occupied America: The Chicano's Struggle toward Liberation* (San Francisco: Canfield Press, 1972).

3. Fernando Solanas and Octavio Getino, "Toward a Third Cinema,"*Cineaste* 4, no. 3 (Winter 1970–71).

4. Emilio García Riera, *Historia Documental del Cine Mexicano,* vol. 1 (México, D.F.: Ediciones Era, 1970), 17.

5. Alternatives to cinema as spectacle and consumption cinema—cinema of ruling classes: *First cinema*—"auteur cinema"; *Second cinema*—cinema novo, "expression cinema"; *Third cinema*—cinema of liberation, cinema made outside and against the system.

6. Fernando Solanas and Octavio Getino, "Toward a Third Cinema," 1.

7. Ibid., 2.

8. Ibid., 10.

9. Jorge Sanjines, "Cinema and Revolution," *Cineaste* 4, no. 3 (Winter 1970–71): 13.

10. Glauber Rocha, "The Aesthetics of Hunger," *Cineaste* 4, no. 1 (Summer 1970).

11. Walter Achugar, *Cineaste* 4, no. 3 (Winter 1970–71): 52.

12. Santiago Alvarez, *Cineaste* 4, no. 3 (Winter 1970–71): 50.

13. Richard Roud, *Jean Luc Godard* (Bloomington: Indiana University Press, 1967), 123.

Notes on Chicano Cinema (1979)

Jason C. Johansen

Recent festivals in San Antonio, Texas, and Mexico City reflect the wide spectrum of Chicano film. Given the nonrigorous definition of Chicano film, we have films that generally fall into one or more of the following categories: (1) films BY Chicanos, (2) films FOR Chicanos, (3) films ABOUT Chicanos. In addition to its assets, each category inevitably has its inherent weaknesses and limitations.

For example, the first category opens itself to almost any sort of film, providing it is made by a Chicano. Hollywood has seen a rock musical made by a Chicano; it will see a futuristic science-fiction feature-length film by a Chicano. The second category, films for Chicanos, correctly suggests that there are or should be films that address themselves to Chicanos. However, to what ends? The final category obviously allows for almost any sort of film providing it has a Chicano, regardless of the portrayal.

With all the categories, not one addresses questions of purpose. What is, after all, the function of Chicano film? Possibly, the function and purpose of Chicano film lies in the roots, origins, and determinants of the genre's development.

In his article on *cine* Chicano, Jesús Treviño traces the roots of the genre to the early American silents, which identified the Mexican as a "greaser," through the western and its bandits and loose women, as well as stereotyped portrayals by Dolores del Rio, Carmen Miranda, and Lupe Velez, the "Mexican Spitfire."[1]

The basis of his argument was that the Chicano film developed as a response to the stereotypes, i.e., an attempt to rectify the traditionally distorted images. In passing he locates this notion of *"cine* Chicano as a response" as part of the larger sociopolitical movement, linked to the events of 1968: a Chicano student movement in Los Angeles, March; other student movements, Paris, May; and in Mexico City, October. Chicano consciousness specifically grew out of the Civil Rights Movement of the early 60s, the unionizing efforts of César Chávez, and as a reaction to the war in Indo-China.

The Chicano Movement, like others, found film and media in general to be a useful tool in the communication of ideas. It provided exposure and an outlet for Chicano faces and voices. Films such as *Yo Soy Chicano* and *Cinco Vidas* reflected the same attitudes that characterized the movement in the late 60s and early 70s: nationalism and the fomenting of ethnic pride.

The movement has since fragmented and generally gravitated toward two poles, liberal and radical. At one end, Chicanos have entered the middle class and embraced its liberal politics. They point to the relative increase in Chicano politicians, businessmen, and professionals as indicative of the success of the movement.

At the other end of the spectrum, Chicanos are increasingly looking at the exploited working class (witness the undocumented workers) as a symptom of larger problems: socioeconomic relations between the United States and Mexico and even between the United States and Latin America.

Now Chicano cineastes must decide what will be the function of Chicano film. As the nature of the movement has changed, so must the nature of Chicano film. Furthermore, since we see the problems of Chicanos as inextricably connected to those of Mexico and America Latina where, ultimately, symptoms vary little and causes are the same, Chicano film must see itself as part of the same relationship.

Obviously, Chicanos have limited access to the means of production, particularly capital. Therefore, it is likely that filmmakers will look (as they have been) more to the established industries of Hollywood, Mexico, and, possibly, Cuba. It seems less likely that Chicano film at the feature-length level will develop to any large extent with independent monies. Certainly, the documentaries will remain the major product.

Thus, as Chicanos look more to Hollywood and its imitator, Mexico, they must also consider aesthetic questions.

It is no accident that the portrayal of the Mexican in Hollywood has traditionally been degrading, insulting, and overly racist. Two new feature films, *Walk Proud* and *Boulevard Nights,* carry on the tradition. The rectification of the negative images is not merely a matter of placing Chicanos in creative capacities: writing, producing, directing, etc. Nor is it merely a matter of seeking to balance the negative with the positive. Chicano film must also take an ideological position response by recognizing the form and ideological function of Hollywood film.

Hollywood cinema is one of intellectual colonization. It attempts to pass off its distorted realities and values of a ruling class as natural and desirable to Third World peoples, including Chicanos. It is not a cinema that asks us to pause and reflect on our situation. Instead, Hollywood films attempt "to take our minds off our daily problems" by pretending to be entertainment, creating a feeling of well-being and a false sense of security. It is largely escapist fare.

Once we recognize form and content relationships and "signifier-signification" processes of Hollywood cinema, Chicano film can take the appropriate steps toward an alternative cinema—one that fills the gap created by Hollywood and its refusal and/or inability to impart socially useful information to Chicanos.

Chicano film as an alternative cinema requires at least some semblance of a theoretical foundation. Our *compañeros* in America Latina are way ahead of us in the game, and they provide the basis for the following:

1. *The Demystification of Film.* Hollywood filmmaking surrounds itself with a "larger than life" mystique. Dreams are realized on the screen, stars are made, and Chicanos have been alienated. Bringing the filmmaking process to the community and soliciting its involvement places in its hands a powerful communicative tool, a tool that allows the expression of a people's perspective, concerns, and reality. Chicanos need not be awed by a medium that has traditionally been kept out of their hands but of whose products they remain consumers.

2. *The Decolonization of Minds.* As Hollywood and other "foreign" films continue to offer us the ideology of the dominant culture, Chicano film must combat it. To minimize the acculturation process confronting Chicanos, Chicano film must not only

reaffirm its respective culture, but identify the false values and ideology delivered through the media.

3. *Reflective and Open-Ended.* Closure or that a film has neatly and conveniently resolved its problem often suggests that "all is right with the world." For example, such is the ideology of the "happy ending." As viewers we are left satisfied, share in the film's sense of elation, and feel good about ourselves. We are not asked to make a connection between the film's "enclosed reality" and our own reality. Chicano film must give cause for reflection by being open-ended, thereby directing our thoughts to an analysis of the Chicano experience.

4. *The Altering of Consciousness.* Filmic analyses of the Chicano experience, asking viewers to pause and reflect, ultimately must lead to an altering of consciousness. At no time has this ever been inappropriate to the Chicano movement, but was and is still of primary importance.

5. *Effect Social Change.* However, any altering of consciousness must obviously work to effect social change, which necessarily must be the bottom-line thrust of all Chicano film. Given the ability of the medium to reach a wide audience, Chicano film must remain linked to and be an integral part of the revolutionary process.

6. *A Chicano Film Language.* Lastly, the development of Chicano film requires that it find a "film language" suitable to its needs. Such a language manifests itself through camera technique, editing strategies, cultural codes, and "system of signs," all to accommodate the above considerations.

Obviously, the above can only serve as a general framework. As we acquire an understanding of the "colonizing" process of "First World" (Hollywood) cinema, we can begin to look for methods of "decolonizing." Similarly, vague terms such as "film language" require a sharpening of definition before making in-roads toward a Chicano "film language."

Furthermore, as film continues to gain legitimacy in academic circles, likewise Chicano filmmakers must and will broaden their filmic perspective by questioning form and content and the ideology inherent in the relationship.

Notes

1. The article by Treviño referred to here was later published as "Chicano Cinema," *New Scholar* 8 (1982): 167–80.—ED.

Filming a Chicana Documentary (1979)

Sylvia Morales

Editor's note: This article is based upon an interview by Somos *magazine with filmmaker Sylvia Morales on the just-completed documentary* Chicana. *In the text, the film is referred to by its working title,* Bread and Roses.

Most people who know about Chicano history are usually familiar with Hidalgo, Emiliano Zapata, and Joaquín Murrieta, but few people are aware of Malintzín Tenepal, Sor Juana Inés de la Cruz, or Emma Tenayuca. Chicano history celebrates what men have done but often fails to include the story of women in Mexico and in the Southwest United States.

Thus, five Chicanas united their talents to bring to the public a long-awaited Chicana documentary. Writer Anna Nieto-Gómez weaves feminine images into Chicana history, while Sylvia Morales exerts her cinematographic skills as a filmmaker to direct this historical collage of Mexican-Chicana women. Carmen Zapata narrates "her story" in a dramatic oral tradition, while Carmen Moreno's original music score underlines a concrete sense of identity. Photographer Cyn D. Honesto's study of Chicana talent brought together this cast of artists to create total Chicana experience in the film production *Bread and Roses.*

The title *Bread and Roses* is taken from James Oppenheim's saluting the women in the nineteenth century who were striking against child labor and for better working conditions. He wrote, "Hearts starve as well as bodies. Give us bread, but give us roses." This film is a major effort to nourish the hearts and identity of the Chicana by paying tribute to women in history and by recognizing women who have fought for what they believed.

Bread and Roses goes beyond the stereotype of the Chicana as a nurturing woman. It presents a pantheon of images that stimulate a new vitality in the history of the Chicana. Pre-Columbian feminine deities of creation, death, pain, and abundance are revealed. The daily lives of the Aztec women are explored and their contributions to culture and agriculture are recognized. The story of *La Malinche* and the conquest of Mexico are told objectively. And the roots of *machismo* are seen in the colonial legacy of *El Patrón*.

Women fighting for civil liberties demonstrate a brilliant history. The story of Sor Juana Inés de la Cruz is told as a struggle for women's right to education, and Josefa Ortiz y Dominguez is recognized as a freedom fighter for national independence. Women of the United States are shown fighting the Texas Rangers and organizing the labor movements. Outstanding labor organizers such as Louisa Gonzales Parsons, Emma Tenayuca, and Dolores Huerta are saluted as women fighting for what they believe. Interviews with welfare rights advocate Alicia Escalante and equal employment advocate for women Francisca Flores explore the contemporary issues of the Chicana.

There is no doubt that after seeing this film, people will be asking themselves, "Why didn't I know this before?" and "Tell me more!"

Bread and Roses evolved from the slide presentation "Historic Images of the Chicana," by Anna Nieto-Gómez, teacher of Chicana studies for six years. Anna explains that people have a difficult time believing Mexican women made history because Chicana issues are usually approached in an emotional way. Should women be equal to men? Does the Chicana want to be liberated? Is *machismo* good or bad? All these topics are normally used to stir up discussion and entertainment and not to provide facts. Anna says, "When students first begin seriously studying the ideas and issues of the Chicana, they find the new information difficult to accept. They have never heard of women who were poets, politicians, freedom fighters, theoreticians, or labor organizers. I remember when a student read Sor Juana Inés de la Cruz's timeless masterpiece, 'Redondillas' [a poem criticizing the society's double standard against women], the student could only understand that a nun was 'down on men because she was sexually frustrated.' He decided that all Sor Juana needed was a good man and could not understand why she was an important person in history. He was very surprised to find out that she was the poet laureate for the church and state of Mexico in the seventeenth century. An incomplete history victimizes people to believe that Chicanas exist only to love their men and to have their babies. When I realized that Chicana history was so alien to my students, I developed a visual medium to make 'her story' a concrete experience."

Cyn explains, "I knew a slide show documenting the Chicana would have a powerful and positive effect on all people, and I had faith in Anna's ability to create and produce something that was good and long overdue." In the summer of 1977, Anna presented her slide show at a seminar on "Minority Women in the Media," held at the Inner City Cultural Center in Los Angeles. The Chicanas who attended became the future nucleus of a Chicana film. Each Chicana became more enthusiastic about developing stories, plays, songs, photographic themes, and films about the Chicana.

Sylvia Morales, a filmmaker, was impressed with the information presented in the slide show. "I remember saying to myself, 'My God, there is enough here to make ten films about the Chicana.' " With the full support of the Chicano Studies Center at UCLA, Sylvia was able to develop a Chicana film. She received $5,000 from the INS Institute of American Culture, and $1,000 was provided by the Film Fund to develop a Spanish version of the film. Sylvia explains that most of the film budget paid for the film processing and raw stock. "No one got paid for doing this film. All the women worked out of total labor of love and devotion."

After previewing a rough cut of the film, Carmen Moreno, an established artist in the music industry, was inspired to create. "An exciting honesty unfolded before my eyes as events I had always heard about were put together into a story about us, Chicanas! I wanted to bring a sense of self-respect to those women who are asking themselves, '¿de dónde, cómo, cuándo, y por qué estamos en este estación?' "

Participation in this film project also increased the awareness of the history of the Mexican for film and theater artist Carmen Zapata. But she sadly questions, "Where does this kind of learning come from? This is not really taught in the schools. And unless one specialized in the history of the Chicana, may one ever really become aware of her background and heritage as a woman? This kind of project is necessary to make the Hispanic woman realize her value and worth by becoming aware of her roots."

Carmen Zapata also anticipates that this film will have an educational and positive impact on the Hispanic man. She predicts, "Through the film, he will realize that the heritage of the Hispanic woman is as great as his. I hope this film about the history of the Chicana will stimulate a reevaluation of her so that she will be recognized as a great contributor to society, to her culture, and to the culture of the world."

The general portrayal of the Hispanic people in the media has been unfavorable. And the portrayal of the Hispanic woman is usually reduced to a mammary-baby-sex machine who is usually indulging in masochism and paranoia. Carmen Zapata agrees that "We are usually seen from a demeaning point of view as uneducated and unintelligent. We need to change this image. There are mental giants and artistic geniuses in our Hispanic community, and with more exposure, the Hispanic filmmakers can bring these treasures to the public and change our image."

"Eso me está pasando" (1990)

Ray Navarro

Editor's note: This essay first appeared in Tonantzin *in conjunction with Ray's program, "AIDS Media and People of Color," screened on February 2, 1990, at San Antonio's CineFestival 1990.*

I am an HIV-positive Chicano gay man from Simi Valley, California. By looking at me you may not be able to see any of these things. You will also not be able to tell that I am college-educated, a videomaker, and scared to death of my own culture. For the past several years I have grown comfortable with my gay identity, I have marched on the streets, go-go danced in bars, and wept at the death of people I respected who died from AIDS (Acquired Immune Deficiency Syndrome). So now I am also an AIDS activist. Full-time.

When I was nineteen I remember walking into a Latino drag bar in Los Angeles. There I saw many lesbian and gay people. Each one looked like they could've been my aunt or uncle. It shocked and thrilled me to see so many Latinas and Latinos expressing their sexuality openly, defiantly—but it dissatisfied me that the only safe place to do this was in a dark bar off of Santa Monica Boulevard.

To be "gay" was not a reasonable option for me as a teenager. Gays were supposed to be white men with buzzed hair who lived in West Hollywood, not Chicanos. When I sought out my preferred way of expressing myself sexually it was under conditions of extreme secrecy. I was afraid of rejection by my friends and family, not to mention terrified of having my ass kicked by "the dudes." As a "man-

312

child," being queer did not fit comfortably into what I knew was expected of me: college, wife, kids, the English language . . . in short, assimilation. The only Spanish word I knew that described my sexual feelings was a bitter insult: I was a *puto*.

Being HIV seropositive (I have human imunodeficiency virus antibodies in my blood) has ushered me into a kind of second "coming out." Around two years ago at the Los Angeles Lesbian and Gay Film and Video Festival I encountered a remarkable videotape—*Ojos que no ven* by José Gutiérrez and José Vergelin (shown during CineFestival 1988)—that dealt with AIDS from a Latino perspective. I was so impressed by its telenovela form that I could even picture my great-grandmother watching it in her bedroom, where a Spanish-language soap opera marathon ran constantly. Right then and there I became determined to seek out other media works that spoke directly to the Latino community and to people of color generally.

Independent video and filmmakers have responded with particular passion to the AIDS crisis. Working with low budgets and often collaborating with local social service agencies these artists have proven that entertainment, education, politics, and sexuality can be interwoven into remarkable audiovisual tools. My own collaborative efforts in producing AIDS media have driven home lessons I originally encountered in viewing the grass-roots performances of El Teatro Campesino. Clearly, art and activism are comfortable bedfellows in the Chicano community and have been for years. There are several films and videotapes currently available to Latino communities (though still too few) that address the issues of HIV infection and AIDS. But rather than merely describe them to you here, I would like to provoke you somewhat, and inform you about the menace on the horizon. You may be surprised to know that the menace is not, in my view, AIDS itself, or HIV. I am not going to recite statistics, although I assure you that they are grim where Latinos are concerned. It is true, the virus is lascivious and stupid, and the opportunistic infections that attack the person with AIDS are swift and merciless. But what is more threatening to our community is what Amber Holibaugh so appropriately names "The Second Epidemic" in her videotape of the same title. This is an epidemic of discrimination, fear, bigotry, and homophobia, which will certainly damage the Latino communities in a way that will have deeper effects than HIV ever can.

I can only compare this to the legacy of the Conquest of Aztlán itself. We withstood that, didn't we? Our language survived, our culture thrives, but the scars run deep and the memories are painful. And the psychological, social, and economic effects of this racist violence permeate our very souls.

This is AIDS. It began with a lethal lie: that AIDS only affected Gay White men. Homophobia was wielded as a misguided defense against a virus that would travel only by certain routes, primarily through blood. Addictophobia was also called in—misunderstanding and intolerance for substance abusers and intravenous drug users prevented us from reaching out to people who needed understanding and drug treatment, not moral condemnation. Haitians were blamed for the spread of the disease, a racist conception that distracted us from the growing numbers of Latinos and Blacks affected. Women were told they were not at risk. A tradition of anti-sex propaganda was resurrected, the "safe" means of having good sex were withheld from teenagers, women, lesbians, and gays. A perverse anti-logic reigned as Reagan era anti-drug hysteria pushed the community leaders into adopting shortsighted positions such as: "Instructions on clean needle use should not be offered to addicts, it will promote drug use." How many addicts' lives could have been saved had they learned to shoot safely, had they been educated about treatment and recovery instead of left to die at heaven's gate? More shortsightedness: "Teenagers should not be taught about responsible condom use because it will promote premarital sex." How many adolescents have transmitted HIV who could have been helped? (God knows they had sex anyway!) We learned the hard way that "just say no" doesn't work for sex, drugs, or AIDS. But Latino communities are learning even more lessons. AIDS accentuates the lack of access to health care for poor people in this country. It underscores the economic discrimination enacted by insurance companies and the shocking lack of primary health care in communities of color. Already overcrowded emergency rooms explode under the AIDS caseload. Understaffed social agencies find themselves unable to handle the burden of inquiries from the community. Children are dying—thousands of them.

Finally we are able to conclude that the AIDS crisis is part of the larger social agenda of an insensitive government. That old enemy *la migra* is even in on the act as HIV positive immigrants are refused their residency status or are threatened with deportation due to their HIV seropositivity. Women are forcibly sterilized before being allowed to participate in clinical trials for experimental AIDS treatments. These same clinical trials routinely exclude Latinos from admission. A crude and familiar justification is offered: that we fail to meet the "cultural criterion" necessary for collecting accurate data. This begins to sound more and more like Uncle Sam's traditional line.

CineFestival has demonstrated a firm commitment to fighting this crisis by helping to arrange a series of discussions, workshops, and screenings of Latino AIDS media. The importance of these different venues cannot be overstated—part and parcel of these tapes and films is that they be viewed in many different contexts, not only in dark theaters but in brightly lit *clinica* waiting rooms. I hope that you will be able to attend and participate, to debate the significance of AIDS for Latinas and Latinos both locally and nationwide. The videotapes being offered to you, the Latino communities, at this year's CineFestival provide a wide range of perspectives from which to view AIDS. As a legal, sexual, cultural, and political issue, the menu is diverse because this pandemic is complex. Please check the program guide carefully, and take chances with what you choose to watch. As I said, my intention in presenting these works is to provoke my community into action. Here are political analyses, protest images, sexy scenes, angry young men, defiant feminists, and *gente.* You will be hard-pressed to find an "AIDS victim." Rather, we are Latinas and Latinos living with AIDS.

Selected Bibliography

Allsup, Carl. "Who Done It? The Theft of Mexican-American History." *Journal of Popular Culture* 17, no. 3 (Winter 1983): 150-55.

Arreaza-Camero, Emperatriz. "Movimientos, comunicación y resistencia popular: cine chicano." *Comunicación Estudios venezolanos de comunicación* 73 (Primer trimestre 1991): 70-86.

Ayala Blanco, Jorge. "Artenstein y el mito del cine chicano." *El Financiero* (September 10, 1990): 71.

Barrios, Gregg. "Boulevard Knights in Hollywood Satin." *Caracol* 5, nos. 11-12 (July-August 1979): 8-10, 22.

———. "Efraín Gutiérrez y el nuevo cine chicano." *La Opinión* (August 18, 1985): La Comunidad, 3.

———. "Latinos en Hollywood: Ahora y Antes." *Más* 1, no. 1 (Fall 1989): 54-59.

Berg, Charles Ramírez. "Images and Counterimages of the Hispanic in Hollywood." *Tonantzin* 6, no. 1 (November 1988): 12-13.

———. "Immigrants, Aliens, and Extraterrestrials: Science Fiction's Alien 'Other' as (Among Other Things) New Hispanic Imagery." *CineAction!* 18 (Fall 1989): 3-17.

———. "Stereotyping in Films in General and of Hispanics in Particular." *The Howard Journal of Communications* 2, no. 3 (Summer 1990): 286-300.

Broyles-González, Yolanda. "What Price 'Mainstream'? Luis Valdez' *Corridos* on Stage and Film." *Cultural Studies* 4, no. 3 (October 1990): 281-93.

Bruce-Novoa, Juan. "The Hollywood Americano in Mexico." *Mexico and the United States: Intercultural Relations in the Humanities.* Ed. Juanita Luna Lawhn et al. San Antonio: San Antonio College, 1984. 19-34.

Candelaria, Cordelia. "Film Portrayals of La Mujer Hispana." *Agenda: A Journal of Hispanic Issues* 11, no. 3 (May-June 1981): 32-36.

Cardenas, Don, and Suzanne Schneider, eds. *Chicano Images in Film.* Denver: Denver International Film Festival, 1981.

Cine-Aztlán. *La Raza Film Bibliography.* Santa Barbara, Calif.: Cine-Aztlán, 1974.

Cortés, Carlos E. "*The Greaser's Revenge* to *Boulevard Nights:* The Mass Media Curriculum on Chicanos." *History, Culture, and Society: Chicano Studies in the 1980s.* National Association for Chicano Studies. Ypsilanti, Mich.: Bilingual Press/Editorial Bilingüe, 1983. 125-40.

———. "The History of Ethnic Images: The Search for a Methodology." *MELUS (Journal of Multi-Ethnic Literature of the United States)* 11, no. 3 (1984): 63-77.

———. "To View a Neighbor: The Hollywood Textbook on Mexico." *Images of Mexico in the United States.* Ed. John H. Coatsworth and Carlos Rico. San Diego: Center for U.S.-Mexican Studies, University of California, San Diego, 1989. 91-118.

Delpar, Helen. "Mexico, the MPPDA, and Derogatory Films, 1922-1926." *Journal of Popular Film & Television* 12, no. 1 (Spring 1984): 34-41.

Díaz, Eduardo. "Latino Cinema in the U.S." *Latin American Visions: Catalogue.* Ed. Pat Aufderheide. Philadelphia: The Neighborhood Film/Video Project of International House of Philadelphia, 1989. 46-47.

España, Frances Salomé. "Artist Testimony and Raza Survival Guide for the Exile on Her Own Turf." *Proceedings of the UC Irvine Conference "Chicana Writes: On Words and Film."* April 25, 1990. Berkeley: Third Woman Press, forthcoming.

Fregoso, Rosa Linda. "*Zoot Suit* and *The Ballad of Gregorio Cortez.*" *Crítica* 1, no. 2 (Spring 1985): 126-31.

———. "*Born in East L.A.* and the Politics of Representation." *Cultural Studies* 4, no. 3 (October 1990): 264-80.

———. "The Mother-motif in *La Bamba* and *Boulevard Nights.*" *Building with Our Hands: New Directions in Chicana Scholarship.* Ed. Beatriz M. Pesquena and Adela Ala Torre. Los Angeles: University of California Press, forthcoming.

Fuentes, Víctor. "Luis Valdez: De Delano a Hollywood." *Xalmán* 2 (1979): 7-8.

———. "Luis Valdez, Hollywood y Tezcatlipoca." *Chiricú* 5, no. 2 (1988): 35-39.

Fusco, Coco. "The 'Latino' Boom in Hollywood." *Centro Bulletin* 2, no. 8 (Spring 1990): 48-56.

———."Ethnicity, Politics and Poetics: Latinos and Media Art." *Illuminating Video: An Essential Guide to Video Art.* Ed. Doug Hall and Sally Jo Fifer. New York: Aperture/BAVC, 1990. 304-16.

Gamboa, Harry, Jr. "Silver Screening the Barrio." *Forum* 6, no. 1 (November 1978): 6-7.

Gang Exploitation Film Committee. *A Reader and Information Packet on the "Gang Exploitation Films."* Monterey Park, Calif.: East Los Angeles College M.E.Ch.A. (Movimiento Estudiantil Chicano de Aztlán), 1979.

García, Christina Louisa. *Struggles to Act: Six Chicano Careers.* Master's thesis. University of California, Los Angeles, 1975.

García, Margaret. "A Review of the 4th Annual Chicano Film Festival." *De Colores* 5, nos. 1-2 (1980): 133-35.

García Riera, Emilio. "En la frontera mexicana fue . . . " *Dicine* 1, no. 4 (January 1984): 6-9.

———. *México visto por el cine extranjero.* Vols. 1-4. México, D.F.: Ediciones Era, 1987-90.

Guernica, Antonio José. "Chicano Production Companies: Projecting Reality, Opening the Doors." *Agenda: A Journal of Hispanic Issues* 8, no. 1 (January-February 1978): 12-15.

Gutiérrez-Jones, Carl. "Legal Rhetoric and Cultural Critique: Notes toward Guerrilla Writing." *Diacritics* 20, no. 4 (Winter 1990): 57-73.

Hernández, Guillermo. "*Ballad of Gregorio Cortez.*" *Crítica* 1, no. 2 (Spring 1985): 122-26.

Iglesias Prieto, Norma V. *La visión de la frontera a través del cine mexicano.* Tijuana, Baja California: Centro de Estudios Fronterizos del Norte de México, 1985.

———. "El desarrollo del cine fronterizo: análisis de los últimos tres sexenios." *Frontera norte: chicanos, pachucos y cholos.* Ed. Luis Hernández Palacíos and Juan Manuel Sandoval. México, D.F.: Ancien régime, 1989. 501-24.

———. *Entre yerba, polvo y plomo: Lo fronterizo visto por el cine Mexicano.* Vol. 1. Tijuana, Baja California: El Colegio de la Frontera Norte, 1991.

Jiménez, Luis. "Cambia la imagen del latino en Hollywood." *La Opinión* (June 9, 1985): La Comunidad, 14-15.

Johansen, Jason C. "El cine chicano: una breve reseña." *Hojas de cine: testimonios y documentos del nuevo cine latinoamericano. Vol. 1: Centro y Sudamérica.* México, D.F.: Fundación Mexicana de Cineastas/Universidad Autónoma Metropolitana, 1988. 285-300.

Keller, Gary D., ed. *Chicano Cinema: Research, Reviews, and Resources.* Binghamton, N.Y.: Bilingual Review/Press, 1985.

Kotz, Liz. "Unofficial Stories: Documentaries by Latinas and Latin American Women." *Centro Bulletin* 2, no. 8 (Spring 1990): 58-69.

Lamb, Blaine P. "The Convenient Villain: The Early Cinema Views the Mexican-American." *Journal of the West* 14, no. 4 (October 1975): 75-81.

List, Christine. "*El Norte*: Ideology and Immigration." *Jump Cut* 34 (March 1989): 27-31.

———. *Chicano Images: Strategies for Ethnic Self-Representation in Mainstream Cinema.* Dissertation. Northwestern University, 1992.

López, Oliva M. "Proyección Chicana en *Raíces de Sangre.*" *Cine Cubano* 100 (1981): 75-80.

Maciel, David R. "Braceros, Mojados, and Alambristas: Mexican Immigration to the United States in Contemporary Cinema." *Hispanic Journal of Behavioral Sciences* 8, no. 4 (1986): 369-85.

———. "The Celluloid Frontier: The U.S.-Mexico Border in Contemporary Cinema, 1970-1988." *Renato Rosaldo Lecture Series Monograph* 5 (1989): 1-34.

———. *El Norte: The U.S.-Mexican Border in Contemporary Cinema.* San Diego: Institute for Regional Studies of the Californias (San Diego State University), 1990.

Martin, Laura. "Language Form and Language Function in *Zoot Suit* and *The Border*: A Contribution to the Analysis of the Role of Foreign Language in Film." *Studies in Latin American Popular Culture* 3 (1984): 57-69.

Martínez, Eliud. "*I Am Joaquin* as Poem and Film: Two Modes of Chicano Expression." *Journal of Popular Culture* 13, no. 3 (Spring 1980): 505-15.

Martínez Carril, Manuel. "*Raíces de sangre*, Jesús Treviño." *Antología del cine latinoamericano.* Valladolid, Spain: Semana Internacional de Cine de Valladolid, 1991. 160-65.

Mindiola, Tatcho, Jr. "Film Critique: *The Ballad of Gregorio Cortez.*" *La Red/The Net* 80 (May 1984): 11-17. Rpt. in *Southwest Media Review* 3 (1985): 52-56, and *Tonantzin* 4, no. 1 (November 1986): 14-15.

Monroy, Douglas. " 'Our Children Get So Different Here': Film, Fashion, Popular Culture and the Process of Cultural Syncretization in Mexican Los Angeles, 1900-1935." *Aztlán: A Journal of Chicano Studies* 19, no. 1 (Spring 1988-90): 79-108.

Monsiváis, Carlos. "De México y los chicanos, de México y su cultura fronteriza." *La otra cara de México: el pueblo chicano.* Ed. David R. Maciel. México, D.F.: Ediciones "El Caballito," 1977. 1-19.

———. "The Culture of the Frontier: The Mexican Side." *Views across the Border: The United States and Mexico.* Ed. Stanley R. Ross. Albuquerque, N. Mex.: University of New Mexico Press, 1978. 50-67.

———. "Ya veo salir a Speedy González: México, ¿nación de chicanos?" *El Financiero* (June 22, 1990): 74.

Montoya, José. "Thoughts on la cultural: The Media, Con Safos and Survival." *Caracol* 5, no. 9 (May 1979): 6-8, 19.

Muñoz, Sergio, ed. "Cine chicano primer acercamiento." *La Opinión* (November 16, 1980): Suplemento Cultural, 1-15.

Newman, Kathleen. " 'Based on a True Story': Reaffirming Chicano History." *Tonantzin* 7, no. 1 (January-February 1990): 16, 19.

Noriega, Chon A. "What Is Hispanic Cinema?" *Tonantzin* 7, no. 1 (January-February 1990): 18.

———. "The Aesthetic Discourse: Reading Chicano Cinema since *La Bamba.*" *Centro Bulletin* 3, no.1 (Winter 1990-91): 55-71.

———. *Road to Aztlán: Chicanos and Narrative Cinema.* Dissertation. Stanford University, 1991.

———. "Café Órale: Narrative Structure in *Born in East L.A.*" *Tonantzin* 8, no. 1 (February 1991): 17-18.

————. "Citizen Chicano: The Trials and Titillations of Ethnicity in the American Cinema, 1935-1962." *Social Research: An International Quarterly of the Social Sciences* 58, no. 2 (Summer 1991): 413-38.

————. " 'Above all Raza must speak': Chicano Cinema, 1969-1981." *National Latino Film and Video Festival Catalogue.* New York: Museo del Barrio, 1991.

————. "In Aztlán: The Films of the Chicano Movement, 1969-1979." *New American Film and Video Series 56.* New York: Whitney Museum of American Art, 1991.

————, and Lillian Jiménez. "La Indirecta Directa: Two Decades of Chicano and Puerto Rican Film and Video." *New American Film and Video Series 61.* New York: Whitney Museum of American Art, 1992.

Ordoñez, Elizabeth J. "La imagen de la mujer en el nuevo cine chicano." *Caracol* 5, no. 2 (October 1978): 12-13.

Oseas Pérez, Joel. "*El Norte:* imágenes peyorativas de México y los chicanos." *Chiricú* 5, no. 1 (1987): 13-21.

Páramo, Bobby. "*Cerco Blanco, The Balloon Man* and *Fighting City Hall:* On Being a Chicano Filmmaker." *Metamorfosis* 3, no. 2 (1980-81): 77-82.

Pérez-Torres, Rafael. "Chicanos in Film: A New Portrayal?" *Estos Tiempos* 4, no. 2 (Fall 1988): 28, 30.

Pettit, Arthur G. *Images of the Mexican American in Fiction and Film.* College Station, Tex.: Texas A&M University Press, 1980.

Ramírez, Arthur. "Anglo View of a Mexican-American Tragedy: Rod Serling's *Requiem for a Heavyweight.*" *Journal of Popular Culture* 13, no. 3 (Spring 1980): 501-4.

Rosen, David. *Off-Hollywood: The Making and Marketing of Independent Films.* New York: Grove Weidenfeld, 1990. Commissioned by the Sundance Institute and Independent Feature Project.

Rosenfelt, Debby. "Ideology and Structure in *Salt of the Earth.*" *Jump Cut* 12/13 (1976): 19-22.

Ruiz, José Luis, ed. *Media and the Humanities.* Hispanic Southwest Regional Conference, December 4-7, 1980, San Diego, California. Los Angeles: n.p., 1980.

Saalfield, Catherine, and Ray Navarro. "Not Just Black and White: AIDS Media and People of Color." *Centro Bulletin* 2, no. 8 (Spring 1990): 70-78.

Saragoza, Alex M. "Mexican Cinema in the United States, 1940-1952." *History, Culture, and Society: Chicano Studies in the 1980s.* National Association of Chicano Studies. Ypsilanti, Mich.: Bilingual Press/Editorial Bilingüe, 1983. 107-24.

Torres, Luis R. "Hollywood and the Homeboys: The Studios Discover Barrio Gangs." *Nuestro* 3, no. 3 (April 1979): 27-30.

————. "Distortions in Celluloid: Hispanics and Film." *Agenda: A Journal of Hispanic Issues* 11, no. 3 (May-June 1981): 37-40.

————. "The Chicano Image in Film." *Caminos* 3, no. 10 (November 1982): 8-11+.

Treviño, Jesús Salvador. "Jesús S. Treviño habla para *Cine Cubano:* entrevista." *Cine Cubano* 83 (1977-78): 11-16.

————. "Mirando hacia América Latina: entrevista." *Cine Cubano* 94 (1979): 5-10.

————. "The New Mexican Cinema." *Film Quarterly* 32, no. 3 (Spring 1979): 26-37.

————. "Cinéma Chicano aux Etats-Unis." *Les Cinémas de l'Amérique Latine.* Ed. Guy Hennebelle and Alfonso Gumucio-Dagron. Paris: Nouvelles Editions Pierre Lherminier, 1981. 493-99.

————. "Chicano Cinema." *New Scholar* 8 (1982): 167-80.

————, ed. "Feature Section on Chicano Films." *Caminos* 3, no. 10 (November 1982): 6-20.

————. "Presencia del cine chicano." *A través de la frontera.* México, D.F.: Centro de

Estudios Económicos y Sociales del Tercer Mundo, A.C., and Instituto de Investigaciones Estéticas de la U.N.A.M., August 1983. 194-201.

———. "Latinos and Public Broadcasting: The 2% Factor." *Jump Cut* 28 (1983): 65.

———. "Chicano Cinema Overview." *Areíto* 10, no. 37 (1984): 40-43.

———. "Latino Portrayals in Film and Television." *Jump Cut* 30 (March 1985): 14-16.

———. "El desarrollo del cine chicano." *Hojas de cine: testimonios y documentos del nuevo cine latinoamericano. Vol. 1: Centro y Sudamérica*. México, D.F.: Fundación Mexicana de Cineastas/Universidad Autónoma Metropolitana, 1988. 277-84.

Valdez, Armando, ed. *Telecommunications and Latinos: An Assessment of Issues and Opportunities*. Proceedings of the Conference on Telecommunications and Latinos, May 18-19, 1984. Stanford, Calif.: Stanford Center for Chicano Research, 1985.

Vargas, Lucila. "*El Norte*." *The Americas Review* 14, no. 1 (Spring 1986): 89-91.

Whitney, John. "Image Making in the Land of Fantasy." *Agenda: A Journal of Hispanic Issues* 8, no. 1 (January-February 1978): 7-11.

Williams, Linda. "Type and Stereotype: Chicano Images in Film." *Frontiers* 5, no. 2 (Summer 1980): 14-17. Rpt. in *Chicano Images in Film*. Ed. Don Cardenas and Suzanne Schneider. Denver: Denver International Film Festival, 1981; and *Chicano Cinema: Research, Reviews, and Resources*. Ed. Gary D. Keller. Binghamton, N.Y.: Bilingual Review/Press, 1985.

Wilson, Michael, and Deborah Silverton Rosenfelt. *Salt of the Earth*. Old Westbury, N.Y.: The Feminist Press, 1978.

Woll, Allen L. "Bandits and Lovers: Hispanic Images in American Film." *The Kaleidoscopic Lens: How Hollywood Views Ethnic Groups*. Ed. Randall M. Miller. Englewood, N.J.: Jerome S. Ozer, 1980. 54-72.

———. *The Latin Image in American Film*. Los Angeles: UCLA Latin American Center Publications, 1980 [1977].

———, and Randall M. Miller. "Hispanic Americans." *Ethnic and Racial Images in American Film and Television: Historical Essays and Bibliography*. New York: Garland Publishing, 1987. 243-59.

Ybarra-Frausto, Tomás. "The Chicano Alternative Film Movement: Interview." *Centro Bulletin* 2, no. 8 (Spring 1990): 44-47.

Zheutlin, Barbara, and David Talbot. "The Whole World Is Watching: Jesús Salvador Treviño." *Creative Differences: Profiles of Hollywood Dissidents*. Boston: South End Press, 1978. 345-52.

Contributors

Mario Barrera is a professor in the Department of Ethnic Studies at the University of California, Berkeley. He is author of *Race and Class in the Southwest: A Theory of Racial Inequality* (1979) and *Beyond Aztlán: Ethnic Autonomy in Comparative Perspective* (1988). He is also coproducer, with Marilyn Mulford, of the award-winning documentary *Chicano Park* (1988).

Charles Ramírez Berg is an assistant professor in the Department of Radio-TV-Film at the University of Texas at Austin. He is author of the forthcoming book *Cinema of Solitude: A Critical Study of Mexican Films, 1967-1983*.

Francisco X. Camplis has long been involved in the Chicano arts. In the 1970s, he directed several short films, including *Los Desarraigados* (1974). He was one of the founding members of the Latino media arts group Cine Acción.

Carlos E. Cortés is professor of history at the University of California, Riverside. In addition to his numerous publications, he has served as a consultant to school systems and universities on multicultural education and media literacy. He is currently working on a three-volume study of the history of the U.S. motion picture treatment of ethnic groups, foreign nations, and world cultures.

Rosa Linda Fregoso is an assistant professor in the Women's Studies Program and Chicano Studies Program at the University of California, Davis. She is author of the forthcoming book *The Bronze Screen: Chicana and Chicano Film Practices* (Minnesota). She is guest editor, with Angie C. Chabram, of a special issue of *Cultural Studies* (October 1990), "Chicana/o Cultural Representations: Reframing Alternative Critical Discourses."

Víctor Fuentes is a professor of Spanish and Latin American literature at the University of California, Santa Barbara. His book *Buñuel: Cine y literatura* (1988) won the Letras de oro award. He is author of the forthcoming book *Buñuel en México: Iluminaciones sobre una pantalla pobre.*

Carl Gutiérrez-Jones is an assistant professor in the Department of English at the University of California, Santa Barbara. He is author of the forthcoming book *Rethinking the Borderlands: Between Literary and Legal Discourse.*

Carmen Huaco-Nuzum is a Ph.D. candidate in the History of Consciousness Program at the University of California, Santa Cruz. She has written on Mexican female filmmakers and issues in *mestiza* representation.

Jason C. Johansen has taught and written widely on Chicano cinema. He was a founding member of the Chicano Cinema Coalition in the late 1970s.

José E. Limón is professor of English and anthropology at the University of Texas at Austin. He is author of *Mexican Ballads, Chicano Poems: History and Influence in Mexican American Social Poetry* (1992) and *Dancing with the Devil: Society and Cultural Poetics in Mexican-American South Texas* (in progress).

Christine List is an assistant professor of film and video in the Department of English at Chicago State University. She completed her dissertation, *Chicano Images: Ethnic Self-Representation in Mainstream Cinema* (1992), at Northwestern University.

David R. Maciel is a professor in the Department of History at the University of New Mexico. He is author of numerous publications, including the monograph *El Norte: The U.S.-Mexico Border in Contemporary Cinema* (1990).

Sylvia Morales has been a leading figure in Chicano cinema since 1972. Her documentaries include *Chicana* (1979), *Vayan con Dios* (1985), *Sida Is AIDS* (1988), and *Faith Even to the Fire* (1991). In 1985, she wrote, produced, and directed *Esperanza*, a one-hour drama about a twelve-year-old girl's response to her mother's deportation.

Ray Navarro worked as a media activist on AIDS issues in the gay and Latino communities. He was a member of ACT UP and the video collective DIVA-TV, and produced a number of videos, including *Lyric of the Fallen Giant* (1985) and *Jesus Christ Condom PSA* (1988). He died of AIDS in November 1990.

William Anthony Nericcio is an assistant professor in the Department of English at San Diego State University. He is coeditor, with Emily Hicks and Harry Polkinhorn, of the forthcoming anthology *Border Culture: Art and Theory* (Minnesota).

Kathleen Newman teaches Latin American and Chicano cinema at the University of Iowa. She is one of the coauthors of *Women, Culture and Politics in Latin America* (1990) and is working on a book on state theory and cultural studies.

Chon A. Noriega is an assistant professor in the Department of Film and Television at the University of California, Los Angeles. He completed his dissertation, *Road to Aztlán: Chicanos and Narrative Cinema* (1991), at Stanford University. He is guest editor of special issues of *Jump Cut* and *Spectator* (both Fall 1992) and has been the curator of film series for the Whitney Museum of American Art and the American Museum of the Moving Image, among others.

Antonio Ríos-Bustamante is research coordinator of the Mexican American Studies and Research Center at the University of Arizona, Tucson. He is coauthor, with Pedro Castillo, of *An Illustrated History of Mexican Los Angeles, 1781-1985* (1986). In 1991, he produced and directed the documentary *Images of Mexican Los Angeles, 1781-1990s.*

David Rosen is the author of *Off-Hollywood: The Making and Marketing of Independent Films* (1990). His television production credits include the Emmy Award-winning series *The American City* (WNET), *Imagination All Compact* (WNET), and *The Trial of Lee Harvey Oswald* (ABC). He is now an international marketing executive for Commodore.

Alex M. Saragoza is an associate professor in the Department of Ethnic Studies and chair of the Center for Latin American Studies at the University of California, Berkeley. He is author of *The Monterrey Elite and the Mexican State, 1880-1940* (1988) and of several studies on Mexican cinema in the United States.

Victor Valle teaches journalism at California State University, Long Beach. In the 1980s, he worked as a reporter for the *Los Angeles Times*, where he shared a Pulitzer Prize for the series "Southern California's Latino Community." He is author of a book of poetry, *Calendar of Souls, Wheel of Fire* (1991).

Index